Turbulent Streams

Brill's Japanese Studies Library

Edited by

Joshua Mostow (Managing Editor)
Caroline Rose
Kate Wildman Nakai
Sven Saaler

VOLUME 68

The titles published in this series are listed at *brill.com/bjsl*

Turbulent Streams

*An Environmental History
of Japan's Rivers, 1600–1930*

By

Roderick I. Wilson

Dear Ron,

Thank you for all of the
mentoring and camradery
over these past years.

ROD

BRILL

LEIDEN | BOSTON

Cover illustration: Fisher with a *yotsude* net on the Tone River (top). Katsushika Hokusai, "Sōshū Tonegawa," *Chie no umi* (Publisher unknown, 1834–36). Courtesy of the Bibliothèque nationale de France. Steamboat on the Yodo River approaching Osaka's Yoshiya Bridge (bottom). Nomura Yoshikuni, "Ōsaka Ashiya-bashi jōki shuppan," in *Keihan meisho zue* (Kyoto: Ikeda Fusajirō, 1885). Courtesy of the National Diet Library, Tokyo.

Library of Congress Cataloging-in-Publication Data

Names: Wilson, Roderick I. (Roderick Ike), author.
Title: Turbulent streams : an environmental history of Japan's rivers,
    1600–1930 / by Roderick I. Wilson.
Description: Leiden ; Boston : Brill, [2021] | Series: Brill's Japanese
    studies library, 0925-6512 ; 68 | Includes bibliographical references
    and index.
Identifiers: LCCN 2021011062 (print) | LCCN 2021011063 (ebook) | ISBN
    9789004433014 (hardback) | ISBN 9789004438231 (ebook)
Subjects: LCSH: River engineering—Japan—History. | River
    engineering—Government policy—Japan. | Riparian areas—Japan—History.
    | Riparian areas—Management—Government policy—Japan. | Tone River
    (Japan) | Yodo River (Japan) | Japan—Environmental conditions.
Classification: LCC TC505 .W55 2021 (print) | LCC TC505 (ebook) | DDC
    627/.1209520903—dc23
LC record available at https://lccn.loc.gov/2021011062
LC ebook record available at https://lccn.loc.gov/2021011063

Typeface for the Latin, Greek, and Cyrillic scripts: "Brill". See and download: brill.com/brill-typeface.

ISSN 0925-6512
ISBN 978-90-04-43301-4 (hardback)
ISBN 978-90-04-43823-1 (e-book)

Contents

PART 1
Regional River Regimes in the Tokugawa Period

PART 2
Techno-politics of River Engineering in Imperial Japan

Acknowledgments

Like a long river, many a meander have contributed to the writing of this book. The first of those meanders and likely one of several later inspirations was the creek, a fork of the South Umpqua River, that ran through my grandparent's farm in southern Oregon where, during our seasonal visits to help move irrigation pipe, bale hay, and cut wood, I spent hours and days with my sister and cousins tromping along its wooded banks, swimming in its deeper parts, and catching crawdads. That creek taught me a lot without my realizing how much I was learning. It was not until I arrived at Portland State University, however, that I realized creeks and rivers and the places through which they flow also have histories. At PSU, I also began to study Japanese (with my friends Thomas James and David Burgess) under the wonderful instruction of Larry Kominz, Suwako Watanabe, and Patricia Wetzel. It was thanks to Linda Walton that I discovered my passion for history (and changed my major from engineering!) and to Noriko Aso that I learned the rudiments of Japanese history and the meaning of historiography.

It was another meander through the JET Program that took me to teach English for the Board of Education in the mountainous town of Haruno (now part of Hamamatsu City) in Shizuoka Prefecture. There, the Keta River, a fork of the Tenryū River, and numerous friends (too many to list here) taught me about a very different riparian culture of broad rocky floodplains, a history of running logs to downstream lumbermills, fishing for *ayu*, kayaking, *hanami* on the levees under the cherry trees, an annual festival commemorating the two dragons that had in the distant past prevented the breaching of a local levee, and hot and humid summers punctuated by late afternoon downpours and the heavy rains of an occasional typhoon. Having studied Japanese and about Japan both in the classroom and by living in a small community for three years, I felt prepared for graduate school. Fortunately, Jeffrey Hanes and the late Peggy Pascoe at the University of Oregon felt the same way. As the Director of Graduate Studies in the Department of History, Peggy led us new graduate students through a rigorous first-year program where I first learned much of the historian's craft that I continue to rely on to this day and try to share with my own graduate students. For his part, Jeff proved to be equal parts mentor and mensch and whose ability to tell a story on paper and in the classroom are a continuing inspiration.

After earning a master's degree in modern Japanese history at Oregon, I was accepted into the PhD program at Stanford University. It was in the relatively dry California climate of the Stanford campus that this book about rivers in

Japan began to take shape as a dissertation. During my time at Stanford, I was truly fortunate to have benefited from the generosity of so many including from the late Jeffrey Mass who provided me with a grasp of the longue durée of ancient and medieval Japanese history, from the late Mark Peattie who imparted an understanding of the multiple dimensions of the Japanese empire and imperialism, and from the late John Wirth who introduced me to the multiple environmental histories of the Americas. I also began to translate my concerns about recent ecological changes into environmental history through a graduate seminar taught by Richard White and a reading group that grew out of that seminar with my friends Matthew Booker, John Broich, Erika Monahan, and Lise Sedrez. Gi-wook Shin instructed me in the complexities and contradictions within modern Korean history and society. In courses on Japanese history taught by Peter Duus and Kären Wigen, I gained a wealth of knowledge and appreciation for good arguments and compelling histories within my chosen field of study. Both in and outside those courses, I also benefited from the advice, shared meals and parties, and overall camaraderie of Catherine Bae, Alex Bay, Kenji Hasegawa, Michael Foster, Michiko Suzuki, Reiko Shinno, Ethan Segal, and Bob Tierney. Above all, I would like to give special thanks Peter, Kären, and Richard who all served on my dissertation committee, read multiple drafts of each chapter, wrote countless letters of recommendation on my behalf, and displayed an uncommon understanding as I extended my time in Japan to the point that they likely thought I may never return.

Often a short and straight-forward period spent in the archives, my dissertation research in Japan became another meander from which this book and my broader knowledge about Japan have benefited immensely. Thanks to his characteristic kindness and generosity, Jinnai Hidenobu at Hōsei University ensured that I had both a place to work and a community with which to share my research. While a visiting researcher in the Laboratory of Regional Design with Ecology (Eco-ken) that Professor Jinnai founded, I had the unique opportunity to participate in the organization's many research and outreach activities including helping to curate museum exhibits about Tokyo's water history for the International Architectural Biennale in Rotterdam, Netherlands and the Edo-Tokyo Museum in Tokyo. I also owe much to Takamura Masahiko at Hōsei University who turned out be both a trusted mentor and good friend. I learned a great deal from my fellow Jinnai-ken graduate students and good friends Iwaki Yasunobu and Onda Shigenao with whom I spent countless hours talking about our various separate and joint research projects. I also owe a deep debt of gratitude to Yoshida Nobuyuki at Tokyo University who first invited me to participate in his *kuzushiji* course and thereafter in research activities with Itō Takeshi at Tokyo University and the Center for Urban History

(Toshi-shi Kenkyū Sentā) that they established and administered together. Special thanks also to Matsuyama Megumi and Takenouchi Masato who have always been generous in sharing their knowledge about Edo-Tokyo history and their friendship continues beyond our many conversations and meals together at Tokyo University's Hongō campus. Finally, I also want to thank Miyamura Tadashi and Nanba Kyōsuke for letting me participate in meetings of the Kasen-gaku (River School) as well as Patricia G. Sippel and her husband Bill Steele for their encouragement and kindness during my years in Tokyo and on visits after I returned to the United States. I was fortunate to be able to stay in Japan for as long as did thanks to the generous support of a Fulbright Graduate Research Fellowship, a Mellon Foundation Dissertation Fellowship, and the Hōsei University International Fellowship.

I have taught at two universities where this book and my career have benefited greatly in different ways. At the University of Wisconsin-Whitewater, I learned much of what I know about university-level teaching due to a heavy class-load and wonderful colleagues who each brought their own strengths and personalities to our small department. Thank you to Mark Bolton, Bert Kreitlow, Emma Kuby, James Levy, Molly Patterson, Tony Gulig, Jennifer Thibodeaux, and Jeff Zalar. While living in Madison and teaching an hour away in Whitewater as a single parent of two energetic boys, I am also forever grateful to my friends Jim Feldman, Kimberly and David Wasserman, Mila Yasko and John Wedge whose help with childcare and carpools to soccer practice constantly reminded me of how it often takes a community to raise a family.

At the University of Illinois at Urbana-Champaign, I have also been lucky to be part of a thriving and caring academic community where most of this book was written. With my appointment in both the Department of History and the Department of East Asian Languages and Cultures as well as my affiliation with the Center for East Asian and Pacific Studies, I cannot possibly mention everyone at Illinois whose collegiality and encouragement have played a role in this book's publication, but I would like give special thanks to Ronald Toby for his careful reading of chapters and continuous support and to Craig Koslofsky, who as my faculty mentor, has guided me through the publication process. My deepest gratitude also goes to Clare Crowston, Dana Rabin, and Bob Tierney, who as the leaders of my respective departments at different points in time, for their compassion and understanding when I needed to pause my tenure clock in order to take care of first my mom and then my dad before they passed away. I also appreciate the assistance of Bailey Albrecht at an early stage in the writing and to Wataru Morioka for making the maps used throughout the book. Steven Witt, a Japanese Studies specialist and Head of the International and Area Studies Library, ensured that I had access to many of the books and other sources that are cited in following pages. Finally, I cannot say thank you enough for the friendship and healthy distraction offered by Tariq Ali, Ikuko Asaka, Marc Hertzman, Jeff Martin, Mauro Nobili, Gian Piero Persiani, and John Randolph as we shared meals, drinks, gardening tips, and the ever-unpredictable performance of the Portland Timbers. At Illinois, I also benefited immensely from a semester release from teaching duties thanks to a Faculty Fellowship from the Illinois Program for Research in the Humanities and a NEAC Japan Studies Travel Grant from the Association of Asian Studies.

At various workshops and conferences where I presented portions of the research that appears in this book, I learned much and benefited from comments, feedback, and encouragement from Raja Adal, Phillip Brown, Eric Dinmore, David Howell, Ian Miller, Hiromi Mizuno, Jordan Sand, Matt Sterenberg, Brett Walker, Mike Wert, Paul Waley, and Michael Wood. At Brill, I have been fortunate to work with both Inge Klompmakers and Patricia Radder who were always quick and supportive in response to my questions and concerns while revising the manuscript. Special thanks also to those who reviewed and commented anonymously on the manuscript for Brill and especially to Amy Reigle Newland for patiently and carefully copy editing the entire manuscript. Their collective advice has much improved both the arguments and prose herein and whatever weaknesses remain owe entirely to me.

I am also indebted to my friends and family who have over the years encouraged, cajoled, and always supported me in pursuit of my career as an educator and historian and the completion of "the book." First, I would like to thank my wonderful aunt Nancy Webb who worked for most of her career as a writer and editor at the children's magazine *Weekly Reader* and encouraged me from a young age to observe the world around me and have confidence in my writing. Many thanks also to David Stone and his wife Rebecca, my sister Amy Hay and hear husband Gary, cousins Ken Thomas and his wife Pati, Bob Thomas, and Laura Smith and her late husband Casey, and Joe Russo and his wife Maria. Sadly, the recent passing of my parents Susan and Iven Wilson and mother-in-law Joan Bergmark mean that they never had the opportunity to share in the sense of accomplishment that comes with finishing one's first book. For that, I am lucky and grateful for the humor and encouragement of my father-in-law Gary Bergmark and his partner Brian Daggett. Thank you also to my sons Joe and Tye as well as Martin and Declan whose patience and understanding has in the recent years shifted to urging me on with regular cheers of "ganba!" and "good luck!" And, finally, there are not words enough to express my appreciation and affection to my wife Jennifer Bergmark, who despite the turbulent stream of the world around us, has brought so much love and light into our lives. It is to Jen that I dedicate this book.

Figures and Tables

Figures

Tables

Note to Readers

Japanese names are written in conventional order with surname first, except in English-language publications by Japanese authors where this order has been reversed. The names of individuals known by multiple names and titles appear here under the name most commonly encountered in the scholarly literature. All Japanese terms are in italics, aside from those that have entered the English lexicon like tsunami or shogun. Macrons are employed for Japanese names and terms to indicate long vowels except when that name or term has become anglicized, such as Tokyo, not Tōkyō, or Kyushu, not Kyūshū. In some instances, descriptions are provided for Japanese terms and book titles in lieu cumbersome English-language translations.

A lunisolar calendar was used in Japan until the formal adoption of the Gregorian calendar on 1 January 1873. For consistency and ease of reading, all dates have been converted to the Common Era (CE) calendar. Dates in the original calendar are included in footnotes when further clarity may be of help. The following periodization serves as a general reference throughout the text: ancient (710–1185), medieval (1185–1467), Sengoku or Warring States (1467–1603), Tokugawa (1603–1868), and modern (1868–present). Premodern refers broadly to before 1868 and preindustrial to before Japan's rapid industrialization from the early twentieth century.

Until the widespread adoption of the metric system in Japan from the early twentieth century, most measures and weights were recorded in the older system of measurements. All measurements have been converted to their metric equivalent, but the original values and units are occasionally included to emphasize how they appeared in the original documents. The conversions employed for the most common measures mentioned in this book are as follows:

> Linear: *shaku* = 30.3 cm with 6 *shaku* equaling 1 *ken* (unit for measuring distances) and 10 *shaku* equaling 1 *jō* (unit generally used for measuring the length of things); for measuring longer distances, the primary unit was *ri* = 3.9 km

> Area: 1 *chō* = roughly 1 ha (10,000 sq m)

> Volume: 1 *koku* = 180 l (slightly more than five US bushels)

> Weight: 1 *hyō* (sack) varied depending on its contents, but 1 *hyō* of rice generally weighs about 64 kg

Introduction

> The current of the river does not cease, and yet the water is not as it was before. The foam that floats on eddies, now vanishing, now forming, does not stay for long. This is exactly the same with the people and dwellings of the world.
>
> KAMO NO CHŌMEI, *Hōjōki*, 1212[1]

∴

> ゆく河の流れは絶えずして、しかも、もとの水にあらず。淀みに
> 浮ぶうたかたは、かつ消えかつ結びて、久しくとゞまりたる例な
> し。世中にある人と栖と、またかくのごとし。
>
> 鴨長明 『方丈記』 （建暦 2 年）

∴

This epigram, arguably the best-known reference to rivers in Japanese literature, begins the celebrated essay by the poet-turned-recluse Kamo no Chōmei (1155–1216) about recent calamities in Kyoto and the difficulty of overcoming one's attachments to this life. Chōmei wrote *Hōjōki* after several years of living along the banks of Kyoto's Kamo River, and his text refers to floods, droughts, and the movement of people along the region's rivers.[2] In using the river as a metaphor to express the tension between permanence and transience, Chōmei voices a prescient awareness of the difference between what we would call the geological and the biological timescales at which these waters and living beings exist. The paradox he speaks of in the distant past is equally true of Japan's waterways and wetlands and of people's efforts to control and manage them today. Although the country's rivers have been dammed, diverted,

---

1   Translation by author. Kamo no Chōmei, *Hōjōki*, in *Nihon koten bungaku taikei*, ed. Nishio Minoru (Tokyo: Iwanami Shoten, 1957), 30:23–45. For a recent and accessible translation of this entire essay, see "An Account of a Ten-Foot Hut (*Hōjōki*, 1212)," in *Traditional Japanese Literature: An Anthology, Beginnings to 1600*, ed. Haruo Shirane, trans. Anthony H. Chambers (New York: Columbia University Press, 2007), 624–35.

2   For an exploration of Kamo no Chōmei's life and thought through his late writings, see Thomas Blenman Hare, "Reading Kamo no Chōmei," *Harvard Journal of Asiatic Studies* 49, no. 1 (1989): 173–228.

© KONINKLIJKE BRILL NV, LEIDEN, 2021 | DOI:10.1163/9789004438231_002

drained, and buried beneath roads and residential neighborhoods, they continue to fill annually with water from summer monsoons and typhoons. They seek out historic channels and floodplains in their downward rush, supporting Chōmei's claim that the "current of the river does not cease." It is only constant maintenance and vigilance that prevent these waters from bursting through levees to flood the "people and dwellings of the world." Just as the water of the river is "not as it was before," however, the broader environmental relations that once supported past lives and livelihoods cannot be fully restored in the present. Instead, what can be gleaned from this turbulent history are lessons that may serve to deepen our understanding of the complex and interconnected roles people and rivers together play in making the places we inhabit.

Where the Kamo River flowed through Kyoto during Chōmei's lifetime, rivers of many sizes streamed past villages, towns, and cities throughout preindustrial Japan. Today these rivers are often hidden from view beneath urban expressways or behind massive earthen and concrete levees, but Japan nonetheless continues to be a country of rivers. In 2019, the official tally recorded a total of 21,147 rivers.[3] These waterways ranged from the diminutive 13.5 m Butsubutsu River (Butsubutsugawa) in Wakayama Prefecture to the country's longest river, the 367 km Shinano River (Shinanogawa) that descends from high in the Japan Alps to pour into the distant sea. Amidst this rich riparian history, the Yodo River (Yodogawa) and the Tone River (Tonegawa) have been particularly important for their regions and the country as a whole. This book focuses on these two rivers to address the contradictions and changes to the relations between these rivers, the communities living near them, and the successive governments that sought to control and relied upon their waters from the seventeenth to early twentieth centuries.

Rather than compile a "biography" of either of these two important rivers, examine how different kinds of governments have modified them, or highlight how they have struck back with floods and other natural disasters, this study instead inquires into the multiple and mercurial interactions that inextricably

---

3   The Ministry of Land, Infrastructure, Transport, and Tourism (MLIT) classifies all rivers in Japan according to size and importance. In 2019, MLIT counted a total of 14,066 rivers that belonged to 109 Class A (*ikkyū*) river systems and another 7,081 rivers that belonged to 2,711 Class B (*nikyū*) river systems. Broadly defined, Class A rivers are all large waterways deemed as having an important economic role and potential for large-scale flood disaster. Most other rivers fall under the Class B category and are administered by prefectural governments. Since the promulgation of the 1964 River Law (Kasenhō), the tributaries and distributaries of Class A and Class B rivers do not overlap. In addition, there are many other smaller streams that are classified as rivers (*junyō kasen*) and administered by local municipalities. Mizukanri Kokudo Hozenkyoku, "2019 Kasen dētabukku," https://www.mlit.go.jp/river/toukei_chousa/kasen_db/pdf/2019/0-1allv3.pdf, accessed 3 September 2019.

bound these waters, people, and polities together. It traces what I call the "riparian relations" between various river-centered assemblages of rural and urban communities, irrigation and shipping associations, and government engineers and the floodworks they designed. In following these relations through time, it asks how did people interact with these rivers before the advent of industrial science and technology? How did the ruling Tokugawa government modify and manage these rivers before the emergence of the modern state? How did the introduction of modern concepts like nature, society, and state transform the ways people looked upon and interacted with these rivers? How did the country's rivers become part of the formation of the modern Japanese state? An instructive introduction to these relations is represented by the history of Ogura Lake (Ogura-ike), one of Japan's most renowned but now largely forgotten lakes, and the Yodo and other rivers with which it was an integral part until its demise in the 1930s. The history of Ogura Lake encapsulates many of the key questions dealt with in this study.

1   A Riparian History of Ogura Lake

Downstream from Kyoto and more than eight centuries after Chōmei wrote his *Hōjōki*, a man launched his riverboat from a wharf in Fushimi and sailed briefly down the Uji River before slipping into a narrow canal that led through rows of houses to Ogura Lake. One of the three passengers aboard the small boat recalled the Ogura as appearing boundless in the warm predawn darkness of August. He also remembered how the pilot poled the boat forward into this ancient body of water, navigating around shadowy islands of floating lotuses with blossoms of various shades of white, pink, and crimson. These three passengers, like many visitors during the height of summer, had hired the local boatman to take them on this penumbral journey of the region's waters to experience the Ogura and its famous blossoms (fig. 1).

Positioned between the cities of Kyoto and Osaka, the roughly 800 ha Ogura lay at the confluence to four of the Kinai region's most vital rivers—the Kamo, Katsura, Kizu, and Uji—where they came together to form the Yodo River. Over the centuries, these rivers regularly flooded their banks during the summer months, and along with other smaller streams, replenished the Ogura and surrounding marshes with nutrient-rich sediments and cooler, oxygen-rich upstream waters. This frequent recharging of the 1 to 2 m deep, and often mist-enshrouded lake, with river water sustained a healthy habitat for diverse flora and fauna as well as the thousands of people who lived on or near its shores. This ecological variety prompted zoologists and botanists from nearby Kyoto

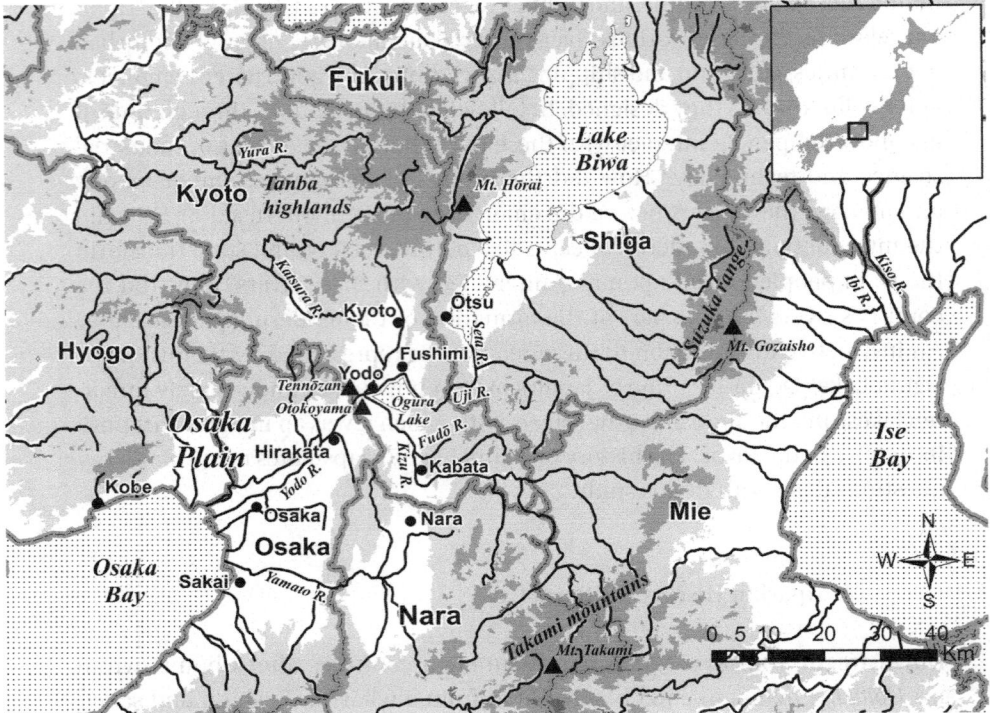

FIGURE 1   Map of the Kinai region and its rivers, c. 1900

University to visit the Ogura in the 1920s to conduct several field studies.[4] In their early studies, they recorded how the Ogura's verdant reeds attracted moorhens, ducks, geese, cranes, and other waterfowl, which in turn drew foxes, racoon dogs (*tanuki*), and other predators to the lake. Below the water's surface, these scientists explained, the Ogura equally provided habitat for different kinds of fish and shellfish, such as the large, edible freshwater snails, *ikechō* mussels, small *medaka* ("rice fish"), and numerous kinds of bottom fish,

---

4   While stressing that Ogura Lake was a fantastic hunting spot, the influential zoologist Kawamura Tamiji (1883–1964) counted over sixty species of birds during his many visits there. See "Chōrui," in *Ogura-ike kantaku shi*, ed. Ogura-ike Tochi Kairyō-ku (Uji: Ogura-ike Tochi Kairyō-ku, 1962), 286–95. For his part, the renowned botanist Miki Shigeru (1901–74) listed at least 167 other kinds of indigenous plants. Miki Shigeru, "Ogura-ike no dōshokubutsu," in *Ogura-ike kantakushi*, 261–65. See also Bandō Tadashi, Tanigawa Yukie, and Sakurai Mayumi, "Ogura-ike kantakuchi (Kyōto) no shokubotsu-sō," *Kyōto Kyōiku Daigaku kankyō kyōiku kenkyū nenpō* 9 (2001): 85–99.

including carp, catfish, and loach.[5] And at the bottom of the lake, all manner of organisms from bacteria to insect larvae contributed to the lake's food webs by consuming its decaying vegetation and the waste dropped from other animals.

People also played an integral role in the webs of life that sustained, shaped, and ultimately led to the demise of the Ogura. In adapting to frequent changes in the lake's water level, locals developed a two-tiered approach to farming. They lifted nutrient-rich silt deposited into rice paddies by floods to build up adjacent fields for dry cash crops like mulberries, figs, pears, and vegetables that could be farmed even during times of drought.[6] Farmers maintained irrigation systems that channeled water from upstream rivers and streams through the area's extensive paddy fields and inevitably into the Ogura. Locals like the aforementioned boatman often earned a living by working directly with the waters of the lake and nearby marshes and rivers. In addition to lotus, they gathered water chestnuts, which were particularly prized as a local snack and could be sold to merchants as a reliable source of seasonal income. In the summer when the water chestnuts were in season, boats covered the lake, with one village sending out as many as one hundred boats to gather the starchy nuts.[7] Later in the year, they harvested the lake's different kinds of reeds for thatching roofs and fashioning a variety of mats, baskets, and blinds to be used in the local tea fields.[8] In the summer, fishers sought out the larger, prized fish, including eel, carp, and catfish, that they sold to merchants who in turn marketed them in the neighboring towns and cities of Yodo, Fushimi, and Kyoto.[9] More predictable and more productive than fishing the lake, in 1886 the local

5   Known in North America as the "Japanese mystery snail," the *ōnanishi* (*Cipangopaludina japonica*) could grow as large as 6.5 cm in length; they are found throughout Japan and were prevalent in the Ogura. See essays by the freshwater ichthyologist Miyachi Denzaburō (1901–88) and the conchologist Kuroda Tokubei (1886–1987), "Kairui" and "Gyorui," respectively, in *Ogura-ike kantakushi*, 266–75, 275–85.

6   *Uji-shi shi*, ed. Hayashi Tatsusaburō and Fujioka Kenjirō, vol. 6, *Ujigawa no seikatsu to kankyō* (Uji: Uji Shiyakusho, 1981), 406.

7   *Uji-shi shi*, ed. Hayashi Tatsusaburō and Fujioka Kenjirō, vol. 4, *Kinsei no rekishi to keikan* (Uji: Uji Shiyakusho, 1978), 655.

8   A corollary to this intensive, yet managed, use of the Ogura's wetlands can be seen in nearby Lake Biwa. The historian Shizuyo Sano shows how local communities since the medieval period have carefully managed the grasses in the ancient lake's littoral area as a commons to preserve the lake's "water quality and biodiversity." Shizuyo Sano, "Traditional Use of Resources and Management of Littoral Environments of Lake Biwa," in *Environment and Society in the Japanese Islands: From Pre-History to the Present*, ed. Bruce L. Batten and Philip C. Brown (Corvallis: Oregon State University Press, 2015), 75–95.

9   Until the reengineering of the Yodo River in the late 1890s, people also reported catching grey mullets (*bora*) and the catadromous sea bass (*suzuki*), which both managed to swim upstream from the bay to the Ogura. *Uji-shi shi*, 4:424.

fishing association (Ōike Gyogyō Kumiai) began operating fish ponds in which they raised eel and tens of thousands of carp fry to be released into the lake.[10] Depending on the season, some fishers also hunted ducks, geese, terns, moorhens, and other kinds of waterfowl.[11] With the growth in tourism and rail travel in the early twentieth century, these locals benefited from their knowledge of the Ogura to guide tourists on scenic boat rides and hunters and sports fishermen to favorite spots around the lake.[12]

While people eked out a living on the Ogura until the late 1920s, by that time most locals had also come to support proposals to drain and replace the lake with rice paddies. The timing of these proposals and the gaining of this cooperation paralleled the declining health of the lake and the people who depended upon it for their existence. Beginning in the 1890s, the Home Ministry (Naimushō) undertook the massive Yodo River Improvement Works (Yodogawa Kairyō Kōji) to reengineer the Yodo River in order to prevent a repeat of the disastrous flooding that occurred in 1885 and 1889. Completed in 1910, this project became a hallmark of modern engineering and governance, and a template for subsequent river projects in Japan. For the Ogura and the people living around it, however, the touted "improvement" (*kairyō*) of the Yodo had dramatic and long-term consequences. The straightening of the channels of the Yodo, Katsura, Kizu, and Uji Rivers, the heightening of their levees, and the dispensing with the Ogura as a place to retain floodwaters further cut off the lake from the waters that fed and sustained it. The result was a decrease in water level and a concentration of farm and residential waste in the Ogura and local irrigation networks that led to a plunge in fish catches and farm produce.[13]

---

10   This fishing association was established in 1886 by consolidating the older five village-based fishing groups.

11   *Uji-shi shi*, 6:409–10.

12   In 1928, the artist Yoshida Hatsusaburō (1884–1955) published a pamphlet with a colorful bird's-eye-view map and short travel guide of renowned places along the Nara Electric Train Company's line running between Kyoto and Nara. The pamphlet included a black-and-white photograph of the Ogura as well as a brief description of how the "lake is loved by citified people" (*tojinshi ni ai serare iru*) as a place for fishing, hunting, and viewing lotus blossoms. Yoshida Hatsusaburō, *Nara denki ensen meisho zue* (Nara: Nara Denki Tetsudō Kabushiki Kaisha, 1928). For an analysis of a similar map by Yoshida, see Roderick Wilson, "Modern Routes through Old Japan," in *Cartographic Japan: A History in Maps*, ed. Sugimoto Fumiko, Kären Wigen, and Cary Karacas (Chicago: University of Chicago Press, 2016), 120–23.

13   In 1923, the municipal government in Osaka decided not to use the Ogura as a source for the city's drinking water after testing revealed high levels of pollution at the lake's only drainage outlet. "Suigen kōhochi no chōsa," *Ōsaka jiji shinpō*, 12 October 1923.

Even more worrisome than the declining quality and quantity of water was the spread of malaria at the lake. A 1919 government report explained that with completion of the Yodo River Improvement Works the mosquito-borne disease had become endemic to the four counties surrounding the Ogura, with infections occurring as early as February and local clinics and hospitals treating hundreds of patients annually for the deadly disease.[14] These problems were further compounded by another problem for those living nearest to the lake—the slow violence of poverty.[15] With the deterioration of the lake and their primary means of livelihood in jeopardy, fishers and those reliant on them increasingly turned to farming and other forms of by-employments, moving away from the area to find work in nearby towns and cities, and to demanding monetary compensation from the government for their losses. By 1928 it was the promise of compensation and a first bid on newly reclaimed land that compelled local fishers to join with local landowners in petitioning the prefectural and national governments to solve the deepening crises surrounding the Ogura by replacing the lake with fields of rice.[16] During the costly invasion of China and on the eve of the disastrous Asia-Pacific War (1931–45), in November 1941 local boosters, together with prefectural and national officials, gathered at a local school to celebrate the completion of the Ogura Reclamation Project, the country's first nationally administered development project (*kokuei kaikon jigyō*). They also lauded the fact that they had turned a fallow, disease-ridden lake and the surrounding marshy shore into 2,294 ha of "beautiful rice paddies" (*biden*).[17]

This description of the Ogura shows how deeply entangled rivers and humans were in the life and death of the lake during the first half of the twentieth century. That entanglement has a much deeper history. Formed about ten thousand years ago, the Ogura has been the site of human habitation throughout the entirety of its existence.[18] For earlier societies living in the

---

14   Naimushō Eiseikyoku Hozen Eisei Chōsashitsu, ed., *Kakuchi ni okeru "mararia" ni kansuru gaikyō* (Tokyo: Naimushō Eiseikyoku, 1919): 27–30.

15   Rob Nixon, *Slow Violence and the Environmentalism of the Poor* (Cambridge: Harvard University Press, 2011).

16   *Uji-shi shi*, 4:345–48.

17   This number includes the 1,660 ha of shoreline land that was also replotted and organized along with a grid of 634 ha directly reclaimed from the lake. "Biden ni kawaru ike," *Yomiuri shinbun*, 9 November 1941, 3.

18   The core samples of the alluvial fan atop which the Ogura sat suggest that the lake was formed about 10,000 years ago. This date is well after the arrival of *Homo sapiens*, who left traces of their arrival in the archipelago as far back as 30,000 BP. See, for example, Yuichiro Kudo, "Absolute Chronology of Archaeological and Paleoenvironmental Records from the Japanese Islands, 40–15 ka BP," in *Environmental Changes and Human*

region, the importance of the lake and surrounding rivers for transport, fishing, and farming is suggested by remnants of pottery, tools, and the area's more
than one hundred tumuli (*kofun*), which mostly date to the fifth century.[19] It
is also noted that the lake and surrounding rivers and marshes resemble the
very name attributed to the country ruled over by the ancient Yamato polity
and succeeding Ritsuryō government in its origin myths—that is, the "middle country of verdant reed beds" (*toyoashihara nakatsukuni*).[20] The eighth-
century *Man'yōshū* and *Nihon shoki* make specific mention of the Ogura and
connecting rivers as conduits for water transport, the digging of a large canal
in the area as well as the survey and division of land with paths and irrigation
ditches into arable fields.[21] These literary examples are not accidental. Owing
to its location at the confluence of well-traveled rivers and highways that ran
between the ancient capitals of Heijō-kyō (Nara), Nagaoka-kyō, and Heian-kyō
(Kyoto), the Ogura and its environs were an important part of the experiential
and literary landscapes of these aristocratic writers. As evinced in Kamo no
Chōmei's *Hōjōki*, throughout the subsequent medieval period the Ogura and
surrounding rivers appear repeatedly in legal, literary, and other writings. It
reminds us of how deeply these waters flowed through the experiences and
imagination of people at the time.

While the population and land under cultivation around the Ogura grew
during these earlier centuries, it was from the late sixteenth century that this
entanglement with the Ogura and the region's rivers intensified. In many ways,

Occupation in East Asia during OIS3 and OIS2, ed. Ono Akira and Masami Izuho (Oxford:
Archaeopress, 2012), 13–32. See also Koji Mizoguchi, *The Archaeology of Japan: From the
Earliest Rice Farming Villages to the Rise of the State* (Cambridge: Cambridge University
Press, 2013); Hiroya Kawanabe, Machiko Nishino, and Masayoshi Maehata, eds., *Lake
Biwa: Interactions between Nature and People* (Dordrecht: Springer, 2014).

19   Kumiyama-chō Shi Hensan Iinkai, ed., *Kumiyama-chō shi* (Kumiyama: Kumiyama-chō,
       1986), 1:91–103.

20   For an example of the use of "Toyoashihara nakatsukuni," see Ienaga Saburō, Inoue
       Mitsutada, Ōno Susumu, and Sakamoto Tarō, eds., *Nihon shoki*, in *Nihon koten bungaku
       taikei* (Tokyo: Iwanami Shoten, 1967), 67:112–13, 142–43.

21   Both the *Man'yōshū* and *Nihon shoki* mention a large canal identified as the Kurikuma
       no ōunade. Its exact location is unknown, but it is believed to have been dug near Ogura
       Lake and was used for both irrigation and water transport. Later chapters in this book
       emphasize the flow of ideas, objects, and people in the modern period. This example
       of a *karabito* in an eighth-century text, however, is a reminder that, although the scale
       was different, even in prehistoric and ancient periods there was an ongoing movement
       of ideas, goods, people, and other organisms between the Japanese archipelago and the
       nearby continent. See also *Uji-shi shi*, ed. Hayashi Tatsusaburō and Fujioka Kenjirō, vol. 1,
       Kodai no rekishi to keikan (Uji: Uji Shiyakusho, 1973), 255–67, 336–38; *Kumiyama-chō shi*,
       1:103–14.

people's activities came to resemble those described above for the early twentieth century. One of the most important changes occurred in 1594 when the warlord Toyotomi Hideyoshi (1537–98) ordered the rerouting of the Uji River, which until that time had flowed directly into the lake, to allow for the use of rafts and riverboats in the construction of the castle town at Fushimi. To limit flooding along the new river channel, engineers also oversaw the building of levees between the Uji and the Ogura and within the lake itself. The result was improved flood control and water transport for Fushimi. A decrease in the amount of river water flowing into the lake, however, lowered its level and encouraged farmers to reclaim more land on its southern shore. The polder-like system of levees provided additional protection from seasonal flooding, but the Ogura still regularly received water when the Uji and Yodo Rivers overflowed their banks. Moreover, it only required a few successive days of rain for these rivers and smaller streams to swell and pour into the Ogura. With less area to spread out, the level of the Ogura could rise by more than a meter to inundate the surrounding lowlands. To avoid being flooded on a regular basis, local villages were mostly located atop natural levees and other available high ground, with houses often built on large mounds of impacted soil. Accompanying these infrastructural changes was a growth in market relations, intensifying people's interaction with the Ogura and the rivers and streams feeding into it. As the tendrils of commerce thickened the bonds between the Ogura's villages and the region's cities, people around the lake began supplying fish and waterfowl, as well as cotton and other commodities, for the urban marketplace.[22] Depended upon the Ogura for their livelihoods, these villages also negotiated and fought over rights and regulations concerning fishing and hunting grounds, access to irrigation water, grasses for fertilizer, and the surrounding woods.[23]

---

22 *Uji-shi shi*, ed. Hayashi Tatsusaburō and Fujioka Kenjirō, vol. 3, *Kinsei no rekishi to keikan* (Uji: Uji Shiyakusho, 1976), 204–12. For a discussion of similar commercial growth and expansion of environmental relations in the Kantō region around city of Edo, see Roderick Wilson, "Placing Edomae: The Changing Environmental Relations of Tokyo's Early Modern Fishery," in "Grassroots History: Global Environmental Histories from Below," ed. Robert Michael Morrissey and Roderick I. Wilson, special issue, *Resilience: A Journal of the Environmental Humanities* 3 (2016): 242–89.

23 Although the Ogura was a commons, the lake was also a highly regulated place and not a free-for-all in the sense that the biologist Garret Hardin (1915–2003) infamously assumed of most commons. See Garrett Harden, "The Tragedy of the Commons," *Science* 162, no. 3859 (1968): 1243–48. For a detailed discussion of the various ways in which commons were managed in rural society under the Tokugawa government, see Philip C. Brown, *Cultivating Commons: Joint Ownership of Arable Land in Early Modern Japan* (Honolulu: University of Hawai'i Press, 2011).

These multiple examples remind us that this turbulent history of engage-ment, modification, and conflict over the Ogura and other riparian systems did not begin in the modern period. In fact, these histories date back to earliest human settlement in the region. While some may see in the twentieth-century reclamation of the Ogura a sign of modern progress and others an instance of modern ignorance and arrogance, it is perhaps more accurate to think of the lake's demise as the coeval result of the activities of rivers, people, and other organisms and the increasing concentration of power in the hands of the few who ultimately played a pivotal role in the design, funding, and building of Japan's modern river regime.

2   Crossing the River between Nature and Society

This overview of the long history of Ogura Lake and the rivers of which it was inseparably a part suggests there are many ways to frame a history of rivers in Japan. Indeed, one of the characteristics of the existing research on these riv-ers is its dispersal across diverse chronologies, geographies, topics, and fields. For the Tone and Yodo Rivers, geographers and historians have researched in rich detail the riparian relations related to fishing, water transport, irrigation, and flood control. Rarely, however, do they discuss these topics together.[24]

---

24   The scholarship on Japan's rivers in English is decidedly thin, but growing. While most of this research is cited throughout this study, the following authors and publications are rep-resentative: Philip C. Brown, "Floods, Drainage, and River Projects in Early Modern Japan: Civil Engineering and the Foundations of Resilience," in *Environment and Society in the Japanese Islands: From Pre-History to the Present*, ed. Bruce L. Batten and Philip C. Brown (Corvallis: Oregon State University Press, 2015), 96–113; Eric Dinmore, "Concrete Results? The TVA and the Appeal of Large Dams in Occupation-Era Japan," *Journal of Japanese Studies* 39, no. 1 (2013): 1–38; William W. Kelly, *Water Control in Tokugawa Japan: Irrigation Organization in a Japanese River Basin, 1600–1870* (Ithaca: Cornell University, 1982); Michael Lewis, "Rivers, Policies, and River Politicians," in *Becoming Apart: National Power and Local Politics in Toyama, 1868–1945* (Cambridge: Harvard University Asia Center, 2000), 73–117; Aaron Moore, "'The Yalu River Era of Developing Asia': Japanese Expertise, Colonial Power, and the Construction of the Sup'ung Dam," *Journal of Asian Studies* 72, no. 1 (2013): 115–39; Patricia G. Sippel, "*Chisui*: Creating a Sacred Domain in Early Modern and Modern Japan," in *Public Spheres, Private Lives in Modern Japan, 1600–1950: Essays in Honor of Albert M. Craig*, ed. Andrew Gordon, Gail Lee Bernstein, and Kate Wildman Nakai (Cambridge: Harvard University Asia Center, 2005), 154–84; M. William Steele, "Across the Tama: Bridges and Roads, Rivers, and Rocks," in *Local Realities and Environmental Changes in the History of East Asia*, ed. Ts'ui-jung Liu (London: Routledge, 2016), 181–204; Conrad D. Totman, "Preindustrial River Conservancy: Causes and Consequences," *Monumenta Nipponica* 47, no. 1 (1992): 59–76.

Historians of river transport, for example, seldom dwell on or cite the work of those researching irrigation and the closely connected topic of flood control. Moreover, histories of water transport and flood control uniformly overlook research on the important inland fisheries for carp, salmon, and other fish.[25] While histories tracing changes in irrigation and flood-control technology have frequently crossed the political and archival divide created by the 1868 Meiji Restoration, those examining local practices and governmental policies regulating fishing, irrigation, water transport, and flood control tend to end or begin on either side of this date.[26] The approach adopted in this book has benefited immensely from this disparate scholarship. It also seeks, however, to cross these topical, disciplinary, and temporal boundaries by tracing and describing the riparian relations that once existed between fish, riverboats, local communities, and government officials. And, in doing so, it addresses larger questions about nature, society, and the state as well as what historians tend to assume about these modern categories and how we might write and think in new ways about past people's roles in their environments.[27]

---

25   This dearth of research on the once thriving and vital freshwater fisheries pales in comparison to the voluminous research on the indisputably important marine fisheries in the Japanese archipelago. One exception to this observation is a growing body of research on Japan's largest body of fresh water, Lake Biwa.

26   The engineering historians Ōkuma Takashi and Matsuura Shigeki have produced valuable histories of flood-control policies and technologies used along rivers in the Kantō region that cross both the 1868 and 1945 divides. Given their temporal scope, it is perhaps understandable that neither of these studies discuss in depth the equally long histories of river fishing or river transport. There are no studies of comparable temporal scope for the Yodo or other rivers of the Kinai region. For river transport, the research by Hino Shōshō on the Kinai region and Kawana Noboru and Tanji Kenzō on the Kantō region are impressive in their detail and analysis of primary sources. Only Tanji in some of his more recent publications has seriously extended his research beyond the Tokugawa period. The following are representative studies by these historians: Ōkuma Takashi, *Tonegawa chisui no hensen to suigai* (Tokyo: Tōkyō Daigaku Shuppankai, 1981); Matsuura Shigeki, *Kokudo no kaihatsu to kasen: jōri-sei kara damu kaihatsu made* (Tokyo: Kashima Shuppankai, 1989); Hino Shōshō, *Kinai Kasen kōtsū shi kenkyū* (Tokyo: Yoshikawa Kōbunkan, 1986); Kawana Noboru, *Kinsei Nihon no kawabune kenkyū* (Tokyo: Nihon Keizai Hyōronsha, 2005), vols. 1–2; Tanji Kenzō, *Kantō kasen suiun shi no kenkyū* (Tokyo: Hōsei Daigaku Shuppankai, 1984).

27   As suggested by the title of this section, an early inspiration for this this book and the deeper questions motivating it is Richard White's history of the Columbia River and the long and complex relations that emerged between Native Americans, White settlers, salmon, steamboats, hydroelectric dams and the United States Army Corps of Engineers. "The boundaries between the human and the natural," White explains, "have existed only to be crossed on the river." Richard White, *The Organic Machine: The Remaking of the Columbia River* (New York: Hill and Wang, 1995), xi.

Two Japanese scholars who recognized early on the problems surrounding the modern notion of nature and the coeval relationship of humans and their environments were the Kyoto-based philosopher Watsuji Tetsurō (1889–1960) and the ecologist Imanishi Kinji (1902–92). Watsuji was one of the three passengers on that lotus-viewing journey down the Yodo River to Ogura Lake in August 1926. In a much later essay from 1950 about his trip, Watsuji concludes that while he had heard about reclamation work at Ogura, he assumed that some of the lake must remain due to its size and so too some of its famous lotus blossoms. Imanishi was one of the students and later a colleague of the aforementioned Kyoto University scientists who wrote about the wildlife in the Ogura before its reclamation in the late 1930s. Whereas his senior colleagues had traveled downstream from Kyoto to study and write about the Ogura, Imanishi had repeatedly trekked upstream to the headwaters of the Kamo River north of Kyoto where he closely observed the behavior and distribution of several species of mayfly nymphs.[28] Both the philosopher and the ecologist wrote about their experiences along these waters and developed influential critiques of the modern worldview that has persisted in Japan and elsewhere—that is, the dualism that separates society and nature into two ontologically distinct realms.

Watsuji's essay recalling his earlier 1926 journey on the Ogura is little read today and Imanishi's 1935 field notes on the Kamo River were only discovered in 2001. Yet the two scholars are best known for two very different and still widely read short books: Watsuji for his 1935 *Fūdo: ningengakuteki kōsatsu* (translated as *A Climate: A Philosophical Study*)[29] and Imanishi for his 1941 *Seibutsu no*

---

28   In 1935, Imanishi recorded his detailed observations and other thoughts of these treks along the Kamo River north of Kyoto in four field notebooks. In these notebooks, it is possible to see the "discovery" (*hakken*) of what he later developed into his influential theory of "habitat segregation" (*sumiwake*). These notebooks have been edited and published together in Ishida Hidemi, ed., *Saishū nikki: Kamogawa, 1935* (Kyoto: Kyōto Daigaku Gakujutsu Shuppankai, 2002).

29   Watsuji Tetsurō, *Fūdo*, republished in *Watsuji Tetsurō zenshū*, ed. Abe Yoshishige (Tokyo: Iwanami Shoten, 1962), 8:5–256. English translation in Watsuji Tetsurō, *A Climate: A Philosophical Study*, trans. Geoffrey Bownas (Tokyo: Government Publishing Bureau, 1961). The most recent edition of *Fūdo* explains that the book has been reprinted thirty-seven times. The book's popularity surely owes in part to its having been taught in high schools and having questions asked about it on university entrance exams. Watsuji further developed some of the ideas introduced in *Fūdo*, especially "relationality" (*aidagara*), in works, such as his 1937 *Ethics (Rinrigaku)*. Republished as Watsuji Tetsurō, "Rinrigaku," in *Watsuji Tetsurō zenshū*, ed. Abe Yoshishige (Tokyo: Iwanami Shoten, 1962), vols. 10–11; in English translation, Yamamoto Seisaku and Robert E. Carter, trans., *Watsuji Tetsurō's Rinrigaku: Ethics in Japan* (Albany: State University of New York, 1996).

sekai (translated as *A Japanese View of Nature: The World of Living Things*).[30] Watsuji explains that the inspiration for *Fūdo* came to him a year after his visit to the Ogura while he was in Berlin and reading the then recently published *Being and Time (Sein und Zeit)* by Martin Heidegger (1889–1976).[31] Committed to developing a particularly Japanese contribution to contemporary philosophy, Watsuji agreed with Heidegger's critique of Enlightenment thought for its universalism, abstraction, and progressive impulse to overcome and discard the beliefs and practices of the past.[32] Although he followed Heidegger in pondering "the question of the meaning of being," Watsuji took issue with what he saw as the German philosopher's prioritization of temporality and the individual over spatiality and the role of society and environment in shaping human experience.[33] He called the all-encompassing world within which individuals come into being and exist *fūdo*, a concept that has since been variously translated as "climate," "landscape," "environment," and *"milieu."* Each region's *fūdo*, he contended, contained an "independent corporal principle" (*shutaiteki na nikutaisei*) that was manifested in time and space and that the "finite and infinitely dual character of humanity appears most in the historical and environmental structure (*rekishiteki na, fūdoteki na kōzō*) of humanity."[34] With this weight on the spatial and social dimensions of being, he organized *Fūdo* in a manner akin to Hegel's world history that moved from east to west to culminate in the freedom of the Germanic nations.[35] In Watsuji's telling, this world history flowed over the centuries from west to east to accumulate as layers of culture that have molded Japan's unique spiritual history (*seishin shi*).[36] He asserted that the successful retention and melding of these foreign

---

30 A prolific writer and avid mountain climber, Imanishi wrote broadly about science and mountaineering. *Seibutsu no sekai* was his most influential text and is the first item in the fourteen-volume anthology of his collected works. Imanishi Kinji, *Seibutsu no sekai*, in *Imanishi Kinji zenshū*, ed. Itani Junichirō and Saitō Kiyoaki (Tokyo: Kōdansha, 1993–94), 1:1–164. See also the English translation, Pamela J. Asquith, Heita Kawakatsu, Shusuke Yagi, and Hiroyuki Takasaki, trans., *A Japanese View of Nature: The World of Living Things* (New York: RoutledgeCurzon, 2002).

31 Watsuji, *Fūdo*, in *Watsuji Tetsurō zenshū*, 8:1.

32 Watsuji Tetsurō, "Zoku Nihon seishinshi," in *Watsuji Tetsurō zenshū*, 4:303–21.

33 Martin Heidegger, *Being and Time* (Oxford: Basil Blackwell, 1962), 1; Watsuji, *Fūdo*, in *Watsuji Tetsurō zenshū*, 8:1–2. For a comparative analysis of Heidegger's and Watsuji's philosophies, see Graham Mayeda, *Time, Space, and Ethics in the Thought of Watsuji Tetsurō, Kuki Shūzō, and Martin Heidegger* (New York: Routledge, 2006), esp. 37–82.

34 Watsuji, *Fūdo*, in *Watsuji Tetsurō zenshū*, 8:16.

35 For Watsuji's discussion of Hegel and history, see esp. Watsuji, *Fūdo*, in *Watsuji Tetsurō zenshū*, 8:227–32.

36 Watsuji, "Zoku Nihon seishinshi," in *Watsuji Tetsurō zenshū*, 4:320. For a discussion of Watsuji's views of history as harmonized strata or foreign and native cultural elements,

and native influences—not a progressive overcoming of the past by the new—
had resulted in the uniqueness of Japan (*Nihon no mezurashisa*).[37] Many of
Watsuji's ideas about Japanese and world history are problematic. He clearly
essentialized Japan and was often ignorant about the places and people about
which he wrote in *Fūdo*. Despite his problematic ideas and approaches to
history, he was ahead of his time in critiquing Heidegger's undue focus on
temporality and the individual, and in offering his own relational approach
to explaining human existence.[38] Yet, Watsuji's influence on later writings in
Japan about the environment has had less to do with his phenomenological
insights than with the layered and exceptionalist views of Japanese history
that infuse *Fūdo* and much of his writing.

  Less problematic, but similarly prescient and influential, were the ecological ideas of Imanishi Kinji. Having already developed novel and important
theories based on his studies of mayfly nymphs along the Kamo River during the 1930s, Imanishi is best known for the aforementioned *Seibutsu no sekai*
(1941). Facing the existential threat of being sent to the front lines in Japan's
expanding war in Asia, Imanishi wrote the book quickly with the justification
that he desired "to leave in my very best capacity some record of one biologist
in Japan."[39] Unlike the cultural particularism of Watsuji's *Fūdo*, the "record"
Imanishi left is foremost that of a scientist offering his own universalizing the-
sis about the nature of life on earth. In five brief chapters, he offers arguments
for why organisms are similar and dissimilar, how structure and function are
fundamental to all organisms, how organisms adapt to their environments *and*
adapt their environments to themselves, how organisms form species-specific

---

see William R. Lafleur, "A Turning in Taishō: Asia and Europe in the Early Writings of
Watsuji Tetsurō," in *Culture and Identity: Japanese Intellectuals During the Interwar Years*,
ed. J. Thomas Rimer (Durham: Duke University Press, 1990), 254–55; Harry D. Harootunian,
Overcome by Modernity: History, Culture, and Community in Interwar Japan (Princeton:
Princeton University Press, 2000), 250–61.

37   See, for example, the section entitled "Nihon no mezurashisa," in Watsuji, *Fūdo*, in *Watsuji
Tetsurō zenshū*, 8:156–69.

38   Harootunian, *Overcome by Modernity*, 268–69. Echoing Harootunian's view, Thomas
Kasulis notes that Watsuji's initial 1928 draft of *Fūdo* "was possibly the earliest book-
length response to Heidegger's *Being in Time* written in any language." Thomas Kasulis,
Engaging Japanese Philosophy: A Short History (Honolulu: University of Hawai'i Press,
2018), 486. See also Mayeda, *Time, Space, and Ethics*, 76.

39   Imanishi, *A Japanese View of Nature*, liii. Due to hastily written nature of the text,
Imanishi's *Seibutsu no sekai* contains few citations to other writings; it nonetheless presented arguments that shaped not only his own subsequent work in primatology and
anthropology, but also the thinking of many others in Japan, such as his colleague and
fellow primatologist Itani Junichirō (1926–2001), the ethnographer Umesao Tadao (1920–
2010), and the economist Kawakatsu Heita.

synusia or "same rank societies" (*dōishakai*) that combine to create complex "life form communities" (*seikatsukei kyōdōtai*), and how species evolve within "evolutionary communities" (*shinka kyōdōtai*) through their adaptive interaction with their changing environments. Undergirding these assorted arguments was Imanishi's holistic view of the world wherein all organic and inorganic aspects of life developed from a single essence and are therefore fundamentally integrative and interactive. "The world of living things was always one whole entity," he wrote, "but it was also an integrated body of the world whose center was each living thing." Through this holistic view of nature, Imanishi criticized prewar ecological and evolutionary theory for its overemphasis on a mono-climax theory (Frederic Clements) and especially its focus on competition and random selection to the neglect of other means by which species evolve, such as habitat segregation and resource partitioning.[40] Imanishi and Watsuji both underscored the co-constitutional role of people and environments as well as a desire to explain the spatial and social dimensions of life in order to augment what both saw as a Western overemphasis on the temporal and individual aspects of life.[41] The two scholars fundamentally differed, however, in their objects of concern. Whereas Watsuji argued that Japan's cultural uniqueness derived from Japanese society's ongoing interaction with its particular history and environment, Imanishi only mentioned Japan in passing and instead presented arguments for the historical or evolutionary development and distribution of all life on earth. Watsuji's and Imanishi's experiences along the Yodo River system played disparate roles in their lives and thought,

---

40   Imanishi, *A Japanese View of Nature*, 71. From the 1970s, Imanishi began pushing more fanciful criticisms of evolutionary theory by arguing, for instance, that the guiding principle by which species evolve is not competition but rather "harmony." Picking up on these later arguments by Imanishi, some American and British scientists denounced Imanishi for his anti-Darwinian views and his undue influence within the Japanese academy. As the entomologist Yoshiaki Itō explains, those criticisms neglected Imanishi's earlier contributions, were based on hearsay and a few of the octogenarian's English-language publications, and cannot be removed from the "Japan bashing" context of the 1980s. Yoshiaki Itō, "Development of Ecology in Japan, with Special Reference to the Role of Kinji Imanishi," *Ecological Research* 6, no. 2 (1991): 139–55. See also Pamela J. Asquith, "Sources for Imanishi Kinji's Views of Sociality and Evolutionary Outcomes," *Journal of Biosciences* 32, no. 4 (2007): 635–41.

41   This commonality between Watsuji and Imanishi is not coincidental since both scholars were influenced the philosopher Nishida Kitarō (1870–1945). The Kyoto-based philosopher Nishida developed Zen Buddhist notions about nothingness (*mu*) and place or topos (*ba*) to argue for a nondualistic worldview wherein individuality emerges historically within a unified wholistic reality. James Heisig, *Philosophers of Nothingness: An Essay on the Kyoto School* (Honolulu: University of Hawai'i Press, 2001), 75–83; Robert E. Carter, *The Kyoto School: An Introduction* (Albany: State University of New York Press, 2013), 13–59.

but each in their own way provided perceptive and provocative critiques of contemporary Western thought and its dualistic worldview. Although their critiques of the modern dualism between nature and society continue to resonate in Japan, it is much easier to identify the cultural essentialism of Watsuji's *Fūdo* and the scientific universalism of Imanishi's *Seibutsu no sekai* in later popular and scholarly writings about people's interactions with their environments.

Watsuji's and Imanishi's writings are useful in representing and framing other Japanese authors' engagement with modernity and the modern transformation of people's experience and understanding of the world around them. Whether in Japan or elsewhere around the globe, for more than a century many authors have written these histories through the modernist dualism that abstracts nature and society into autonomous ontological domains. In Japan, historians have frequently written in the vein of Watsuji's layered view of history, adopting and melding Western ideas and technology with Japanese approaches to the control and improvement of water bodies like the Ogura and its interconnected rivers. For example, the engineering historian Takahashi Yutaka quotes a lengthy passage from Watsuji's *Fūdo* in the introduction to his textbook on Japan's civil engineering history to support his grand historical narrative. He then comments that, "just as in the past when Japan assimilated continental culture after it was introduced and used it to succeed in its own particular development (*dokuji no hatten*)," it met the challenges of the late nineteenth century in an "exceedingly Japanese manner (*kiwamete Nihonteki*) that can be said to have produced on its own an unparalleled experience in world history."[42] Takahashi's historical narratives and those like it often treat the nation-state as the foremost subject of history and essentialize particular national characteristics while simultaneously embracing the universalism of science with its teleology of progress.[43] Despite its essentializing tendencies, this kind of historical narrative is not unique to Japan. It belongs to a broader embrace of progressivism wherein writers credit successful changes to the environment like reclamation or flood control to human ingenuity and hard work. At the same time, they describe subsequent flooding, pollution, or malaria, as was seen along the Ogura and the rivers of which it was a part, as so-called natural disasters or the unintended consequences of good intentions. In this way, historians have credited engineers and political leaders with

---

42   Takahashi Yutaka, *Gendai Nihon doboku shi* (Tokyo: Shōkokusha, 1990), 25, 71.

43   Prasenjit Duara, *Rescuing History from the Nation: Questioning Narratives of Modern China* (Chicago: University of Chicago Press, 1995).

"improvements" and overlook or underplay their role when plans go awry.[44] Yet, these narratives frequently dismiss or ignore the destruction of creatures and their habitats or the harm to people who suffered because of "improvements" ranging from new forms of transport and flood prevention to increased food and energy production.[45]

Another kind of historical narrative sees in this modern transformation of the Ogura and the other waters of Japan a falling away from the bounty and benefits of nature. Many adherents of this "declensionist" perspective follow in the well-trodden footsteps of Watsuji's exceptionalism to romanticize the "premodern" and "preindustrial" past as a time when the Japanese people lived in greater harmony with one another and with nature.[46] "In the course of this long agricultural history," Tokugawa Tsunenari rhapsodizes, "the Japanese learned how to coexist with nature. Rather than working against nature, they learned how to make skillful use of its amazing systems and came to understand that this was a far better approach than fighting nature or attempting to overcome it."[47] As with Watsuji's view of Japanese history, this scion to the Tokugawa family erroneously sees society under his ancestors as largely devoid of internal conflict, living modestly within its means, and "coexisting" with nature. The change, Tokugawa and others contend, came with the introduction of Western ideas, industry, and avarice.[48] Critical of the modern state and industrial capitalism, other writers operating within what Gavan McCormack has aptly called the "dissenting Japanese scholarship" express little patience

---

44   A history of the city of Uji provides an example of this progressive modernization narrative by arguing that the prevention of flooding by transforming the Ogura from a lake to rice paddies and residential neighborhoods began with the Toyotomi's late sixteenth-century levees and continues to this day with the building of upstream dams. *Uji-shi shi*, 6:422.

45   In a rare effort, Ogura fishers allied themselves with "waterwheel" (*mujina*) plants (*Aldrovanda vesiculosa*), which are similar to the venus flytraps in consuming invertebrates, by arguing that the loss of the lake would mark the destruction of both the fishers and these rare plants. *Kyōto hinode shinbun*, 14 June 1925; cited in *Uji-shi shi*, 4:348. See also Miki, "Ogura-ike no dōshokubutsu," 259.

46   Examples include Kitō Hiroshi, *Bunmei to shite no Edo shisutemu* (Tokyo: Kōdansha, 2002); Ishikawa Eisuke, *Ōedo ekorojī jijō* (Tokyo: Kōdansha, 2000).

47   Tokugawa Tsunenari, *The Edo Inheritance* (Tokyo: International House of Japan, 2009), 142. As the current head of the primary lineage of the Tokugawa family, Tokugawa Tsunenari describes elsewhere how his ancestors had helped bring prosperity to the country in part by "taming" the rivers: "A major link between peace and population increase was the 'taming' of the numerous rivers running through the Japanese archipelago. Dikes were built to redirect their flow, converting the river basins into fertile farmland" (72).

48   Tokugawa, *The Edo Inheritance*, 137–43.

for the national essentialism of Watsuji and his latter-day adherents.[49] The
engineer and activist scholar Ui Jun, for instance, claims that the environmental problems of the postwar era were not a "recent phenomenon" and were in
fact "a very prominent feature of the social landscape from the very beginning
of the country's modernization and industrialization period."[50] In a separate
essay on Japan's rivers, McCormack argues that this trend only intensified
following the Asia-Pacific War: "Modern Japan became supremely, perhaps
even uniquely, careless of its environment, obsessed with the achievement of
economic growth at all costs, and in the second half of the twentieth century
turned its back on its own history, resolute almost to the point of obsession in
the concreting of its coast and rivers."[51] Ui and McCormack are but two voices
that closely identify environmental decline with the sacrifices and suffering
of the people and places marginalized in the process of Japan's modernization. While Ui and McCormack clearly differ from Tokugawa Tsunenari in their
ideological stance, they share in his critique of modernity and an assumption
that the people of preindustrial Japan were wiser stewards of the country's
environment.

Historians whose research focuses on the Tokugawa and earlier periods are
neither as pessimistic nor as sanguine about people's relations with the nonhuman world as those adopting these progressive and declensionist narratives.
The historian Mizumoto Kunihiko has rightly dismissed the above declensionist histories as "ahistorical" (*hirekishiteki*) for their partial and selective presentation of the past.[52] Using the example of erosion-related disasters and erosion
controls along the Yamato and Yodo Rivers, Mizumoto examined "nature"
(*shizen*) and "society" (*shakai*) in the Tokugawa era to argue that intensified
efforts to "transform nature" (*shizen kaizō*) led to increased problems and

49   Gavin McCormack, *Japan at Century's End: Emptiness of Affluence* (Armonk: M. E. Sharpe,
     1996), 5–6.
50   Ui Jun, "Overview," in *Industrial Pollution in Japan* (Tokyo: United Nations University,
     1992), 1. Elsewhere, Ui writes that, "At the end of the Tokugawa era, certain new concepts
     arose in an attempt to change the old political system and to develop a modernization
     policy that would encourage enlightened thinking. However, in the process of Japan's
     modernization the means became the ends, producing an intensified level of environ-
     mental destruction and—the other side of the same coin—the extensive repression of
     human rights" (12).
51   Gavin McCormack, "Modernity, Water, and the Environment in Japan," in *Companion to
     Japanese History*, ed. William M. Tsutsui (Malden: Wiley-Blackwell, 2007), 445.
52   Mizumoto Kunihiko, "Kinsei no shizen to shakai," in *Nihon rekishi kōza: kinsei shakai ron*,
     ed. Rekishigaku Kenkyūkai and Nihonshi Kenkyūkai (Tokyo: Tōkyō Daigaku Shuppankai,
     2005), 6:162.

contradictions that were directly linked to broader changes within society.[53] In a like manner, the historian Negishi Shigeo criticizes those who romanticize the widespread and seemingly early reuse and recycling of discarded items within this preindustrial society.[54] Those who highlight the commonplace practices of "recycling" and "reusing" of a community's "waste" also typically fail to contextualize, for instance, the collection of dead animal carcasses for leather manufacture or of human waste for fertilizer within the class and status-based inequality that structured Tokugawa society.[55] Similarly, in his pioneering environmental history of forestry management practices in preindustrial Japan, the historian Conrad Totman cautioned that the successful, if not draconian, forestry policies of the Tokugawa period did not emerge from a "precocious ecological conscious" grounded in an abstract reading of Shinto, Shugendō, and Buddhist thought. Instead, they reflect what could be termed a "practical peasant common sense" in promoting "human-oriented forest production" that had the "corollary effect of nurturing rather than ruining the forests of eighteenth- and nineteenth-century Japan."[56] Elsewhere, Totman emphasizes the practical concerns motivating river work during the Tokugawa period by arguing that it was not undertaken "as an exercise in aesthetics or philosophy" but "reluctantly and only from necessity."[57] These examples suggest that most of the environmental histories written in and about Japan in the past few decades have focused on the archipelago's previous history. As such, these contextualists provide detailed analyses of a variety of sources that elucidate people's activities within their environments and frequently contradict less informed assumptions about the past as a time of impotence before the whims of nature or of harmony with a bountiful nature.

As different as these progressive, declensionist, and contextual approaches are, they nonetheless share a worldview that has been shaped by the nature-society dualism of the European Enlightenment that Watsuji, Imanishi, and others had sought to overcome in their mid-twentieth-century writings. In fact, the sheer weight of the modern world—dams that hold water and generate

---

53   Mizumoto, "Kinsei no shizen to shakai," 6:190–91.

54   For an example of this decontextualized and uncritical adulation of Tokugawa-period Japan as a reuse and recycle society, see Ishikawa Eisuke, Ōedo risaikuru jijō (Tokyo: Kōdansha, 1997); Negishi Shigeo, Ōtomo Kazuo, and Satō Takayuki, eds., Kinsei no kankyō to kaihatsu (Tokyo: Shibunkaku, 2010), 7.

55   Michael Abele, "Peasants, Skinners, and Dead Cattle: The Transformation of Rural Society in Western Japan, 1600–1890," PhD diss., University of Illinois at Urbana-Champaign, 2018.

56   Conrad D. Totman, The Green Archipelago: Forestry in Preindustrial Japan (Berkeley: University of California Press, 1989), 181.

57   Totman, "Preindustrial River Conservancy," 64.

electricity, skyscrapers that shelter and structure social life, roads that smooth surfaces and expedite the movement of people and goods—contributes to the "naturalization" of this distinction between the natural and built environment, between nature and society. Recent studies have shown that this dualism is not universal and is a product of a particular history: a shift in seventeenth-century Europe wherein an ontologically distinct notion of "nature" emerged and was later, in the nineteenth century, coupled with the modern concept of "society."[58] It should be stressed, however, that it was not a revolution in science that progressively revealed a hitherto hidden or mysterious nature but the development of this new notion of nature that led to that novel and scientific worldview. The philosopher Maurice Merleau-Ponty (1908–61), a contemporary of Watsuji and Imanishi, observed in his lectures at the Collège de France in 1956–57 that: "Scientific discoveries did not provoke changes in the idea of Nature; rather, the change in the idea of Nature allowed for these discoveries."[59] As commonly assumed today, this modern sense of "nature" positions animals, plants, cells, soil, and rivers within their own ontological domain and divides them from humans, who are said to possess their own unique ontological status. On the one hand, those entities categorized as belonging to nature are said to lack the will, intent, consciousness, or in short, the agency of humans. They follow scientifically verifiable rules and mechanisms; they are incapable of speaking for themselves or others in the way humans do.[60] "Society" or "culture," on the other hand, is the ontological domain of humans, their interactions, their thoughts. This fundamental dualism of the modernist worldview finds expression in a number of binary concepts, such as mind and matter, symbolic and material, subjective and objective, plural and singular, active human agents examining and acting upon a passive nature, and even the division of labor

---

58   Philippe Descola, *Beyond Nature and Culture* (Chicago: University of Chicago Press, 2013); Patrick Joyce, ed., *The Social in the Question: New Bearings in History and the Social Sciences* (London: Routledge, 2002); Bruno Latour, *We Have Never Been Modern* (Cambridge: Harvard University Press, 1993); Mary Poovey, *Making a Social Body: British Cultural Formation, 1830–1864* (Chicago: University of Chicago Press, 1995).

59   Maurice Merleau-Ponty, *Nature: Course Notes from the Collège de France*, trans. Robert Vallier (Evanston: Northwestern University, 2003), 8.

60   The historian of science Jessica Riskin argues that the European origins of the concept of nature as devoid of agency and acting according to a pre-determined design lies in a post-Reformation effort to distinguish the realm of religion from the mechanical, clock-like explanations then being postulated about other aspects of life. This "contradiction" between a natural world following the design of a "divine Engineer" and devoid of its own forms of "agency and will," she explains, "sits at the origin of modern science." Jessica Riskin, *The Restless Clock: A History of the Centuries-Long Argument over What Makes Living Things Tick* (Chicago: University of Chicago Press, 2016), 4–5.

between scholars in the humanities and sciences. The historian Catherine Knight, for instance, argues that "social" and "political" factors have hampered nature conservation in postwar Japan because of the "historical tendency to see humans rather than the environment as the primary victim of environmental degradation." Knight abstracts the social and political from the natural and sees the suffering of humans as distinct from the degradation of the environments within which they live.[61] Elsewhere, Pamela J. Asquith and Arne Kalland provide a nuanced, yet common, argument for "multiple concepts of nature" that coexist within Japan. From tame to wild, cooked to uncooked, or impure to pure, they argue that within Japanese culture "nature *is seen* as oscillating between two extremes."[62] In these examples, the authors tend to treat society and culture as synonyms wherein societies express a variety of cultural views about an ontologically separate, stable, and universal nature.[63] Be it a discussion of modern or earlier periods, scholars of different disciplines have reflexively adopted this modernist nature-society dualism in their work. The modern worldview may appear hegemonic, with its patina of apparent ancient origin and commonsense, but as the sociologist Bruno Latour asserts, there have always been signs that "we have never been modern."[64]

The ahistorical and uncritical use of this modernist worldview within these progressive, declensionist, and contextual approaches is problematic for a number of reasons. First, in analyzing and describing the past, these approaches generally ignore the very wrought history of the words "nature" and "society" as they emerged in Europe and through a fraught "translingual" process have entered the vocabularies of people around the world.[65] Just as the concepts

---

61   Catherine Knight, "Conservation Movement in Post-War Japan," *Environment and History* 16, no. 3 (2010): 363.

62   Emphasis added. Pamela J. Asquith and Arne Kalland, "Japanese Perceptions of Nature: Ideals and Illusions," in *Japanese Images of Nature: Cultural Perspectives*, ed. Pamela J. Asquith and Arne Kalland (Richmond: Curzon Press, 1997), 13.

63   In his influential essay, the sociologist Richard Biernacki argues that, despite the critique by cultural historians of social history's emphasis on economic explanations and its use of essentialized categories like "class" or "community," they share with social historians a reliance on pregiven categories, such as "culture," "signs," and "patterns." Richard Biernacki, "Method and Metaphor after the New Cultural History," in *Beyond the Cultural Turn: New Directions in the Study of Society and Culture*, ed. Victoria Bonnell and Lynn Hunt (Berkeley: University of California Press, 1999), 65–68.

64   Latour, *We Have Never Been Modern*, 10.

65   Lydia Liu characterizes "translingual practice" as follows: "Broadly defined, the study of translingual practice examines the process by which new words, meanings, discourses, and modes of representations arise, circulate, and acquire legitimacy within the host language due to, or in spite of, the latter's contact/collision with the guest language. Meanings, therefore, are not so much "transformed" when concepts pass from the

of nature and society reflected a new worldview that developed in early modern and modern Europe, these two terms were also intimately entwined in
imperialist and capitalist enterprises of Europe and the United States from the
nineteenth century onward. In response, people in Japan, China, India, and
elsewhere felt compelled to create and adapt words to interpret, translate, and
ultimately construct their own understanding of this novel and different perspective on the world.[66] By the 1870s in Japan, writers and translators were
using *kōsai, nakama, renshū, seken, shakai*, and other terms to translate and
explain the idea of "society" (Fr. *société*, Dut. *Geenootschap*, Ger. *Gesellschaft*)
to people who had never viewed themselves as belonging to an entity called
"society."[67] Similarly, the word "nature" (Fr. *nature*, Dut. *natuur*, Ger. *Natur*) had
a number of translations ranging from *onozukara* and *banbutsu* to *tennen* and
shizen (which was also read as *ji'nen*), all of which suggested parts, but not the
whole, of the totalizing worldview expressed by the notion of "nature."[68] Over
the next few decades of translingual transformation, this variety of vocabulary narrowed to *shakai* (society) and *shizen* (nature), perhaps the two most
abstract and rarely used terms in play during the late nineteenth century.[69]

---

guest language to the host language as invented within the local environment of the
latter." Lydia H. Liu, *Translingual Practice: Literature, National Culture, and Translated
Modernity—China, 1900–1937* (Stanford: Stanford University Press, 1995), 26. For a concise
summary of the changing and multiple meanings of "nature" and "society" in English,
see Raymond Williams, "Nature" and "Society," in *Keywords: A Vocabulary of Culture and
Society* (New York: Oxford University Press, 1983), 219–24, 291–95.

66   For the multiple meanings and nuances of the word "nature" in China and India, see
Chen Shao-Ming, "China: Zi ran (Nature): A Word that (Re)structures Thought and Life,"
and Vinay Kumar Srivastava, "India: On the Concept of Nature," in *Keywords: Nature*, ed.
Nadia Tazi, *Keywords: For a Different Kind of Globalization* (New York: Other Press, 2005),
5:93–111, 141–85. On the capacity of words to move and change worlds, see Carol Gluck,
"Words in Motion" and Anna L. Tsing, "Worlds in Motion," in *Words in Motion: Toward a
Global Lexicon*, ed. Carol Gluck and Anna L. Tsing (Durham: Duke University Press, 2009),
3–17.

67   Yanabu Akira, "Shakai: Society o motanai hitobito no honyakuhō," in *Honyakugo seiritsu
jijō* (Tokyo: Iwanami Shinsho, 1982), 1–22; Kimura Naoe, "'Shakai' ga umare, 'sosaechii'
ga kieru: Meiji-ki ni okeru 'shakai' gainen hensei to kōkyōken no kōzō," *Gakushūin joshi
daigaku kiyō* 19 (2017): 53–78.

68   Yanabu Akira, *Honyaku no shisō: shizen to Nature* (Tokyo: Chikuma Shobō, 1995); Terao
Gorō, *"Shizen" gainen no keisei shi: Chūgoku, Nihon, Yoroppa* (Tokyo: Nōsan Gyoson Bunka
Kyōkai, 2002); Federico Marcon, *The Knowledge of Nature and the Nature of Knowledge in
Early Modern Japan* (Chicago: University of Chicago Press, 2015), 19–23.

69   It is telling that the *Genkai* (literally "Sea of Words"), the first dictionary of modern
Japanese, initially published in four volumes between 1889 and 1891 and edited by Ōtsuki
Fumihiko (1847–1928), has no entry for *shakai*, and that its entry for *shizen* does not con-
vey the breadth of meaning of nature or the use of *shizen* in Japanese today. The entry for

In fact, the translation studies scholar Yanabu Akira believes that words like *shakai* and *shizen* were readily available to assume new roles for a new era because of their former abstractness and limited use. For this reason, he argues that *shakai* and *shizen* should be seen less as "translations" (*honyakugo*) of European words and more as "neologisms" (*shinzōgo*) expressing these emerging concepts and the dualistic worldview they represented.[70]

Clearly integral to understanding and writing about people's past relations with their environments, this translingual history of these keywords is seldom, if ever, mentioned in progressive, declensionist, and contextual narratives about "nature" and the "environment" in Japan. Writers of progressive narratives have often overlooked the particularity of this modern dualism. Or, they uncritically have assumed that the people of earlier periods also held this dualistic worldview and, through innate human rationality and "advancements" in scientific knowledge, came to know and were thereby better able to control "nature." Similarly, those who tend toward a declensionist narrative that romanticizes preindustrial environments and demonizes modernization, quite ironically, embrace this modernist dualism in order to critique the very modernization that helped produce that dualistic worldview. The contextualist perspective offers a more complex and compelling explanation, but nonetheless frames its historical problematique in terms of this modern dualism to advance arguments for how "society" acted upon "nature" or less frequently how "nature" turned the table on "society." The first and second perspectives rely less on historical sources and more on present-day presumptions about the past. In doing so, they mar our understanding of that time with its twofold simplification and romanticization of the past—first by ignoring the inequity and diversity of earlier human experience and second by mistaking poverty for modesty and an inability to radically transform the surrounding world for an older environmental ethic. Even when attentive to the historical record, as encountered in Mizumoto's and Totman's scholarship, three interrelated problems with these contextualist approaches remain. They uncritically use

<hr>

shizen simply reads, "*Onozukara. Ten'nen.*" While *ten'nen* has come to mean "natural" as in natural gas (*ten'nen gasu*) or natural monument (*ten'nen ki'nenbutsu*), the *Genkai* defines *ten'nen* circularly as "*Onozukara. Shizen.*" Much has been written about the meaning of *onozukara*, but its primary meaning generally conveyed "something as it is or has been," which is similar to the meaning in the *Genkai*: "*Monogoto no aru jō no mama ni te. Ko yori kono gotoku. Shizen ni. Ten'nen ni.*" For these definitions, see Ōtsuki Fumihiko, ed. *Genkai: Nihon jisho* (Tokyo: Self-published, 1889–91), 148, 444, 700.

70 Both *shakai* and *shizen* had been adopted into Japanese from Chinese centuries earlier, but the two terms had been little used until the modern period. Yanabu Akira, "Shakai: Society o motanai hitobito no honyakuhō," in *Honyakugo seiritsu jijō*, 22.

"nature" and "society" as ahistorical analytical categories, unwittingly minimiz-
ing the dynamism of the world beyond the human, and as a result tend to sim-
plify people's interactions with that broader arena of phenomena.

   In highlighting the limitations of these narratives, some historians have
recently returned to Watsuji's and Imanishi's critiques of dualism to adopt an
avowedly integrative or "hybrid" approach to their historical subjects. They
have identified what the historian Ian Miller aptly describes as modernity's
"Manichean logic" of "over-powered dualisms," especially that between society and nature. Moreover, they have sought to *historicize* the relatively recent
introduction and consequences of abstracting humans from the environments
of which they are a part.[71] They point out the modernist tendency to assume
that societies are able to know, control, and conquer nature while simultaneously lamenting the resulting alienation and disenchantment from that
"authentic" nature. In this way, these historians have effectively bracketed off
this worldview as one that is itself a particular product of modern Europe that
has over the past two centuries changed as it has circulated around the globe.
Drawing on recent research into the modern and European origins of the concept of nature, Miller calls the nature-society dualism "ecological modernity."
He argues that this very modern worldview, particularly as it has been mate-
rialized through the institution of the Ueno Zoo in central Tokyo, has shaped
Japanese people's understanding, experience, and longing for "real nature."[72]
Focusing on the intellectual and political uses of the idea of nature, the historian Julia Thomas demonstrates how the "intellectual and political leadership
of Japan repeatedly and consciously reconfigured the concept of nature" for
the "radical" creation and transformation of a new national polity and identity after the 1868 Meiji Restoration.[73] The historian Brett Walker also critiques
this nature-society dualism: "My principal argument is that, at a certain level,
Earth has become a gargantuan hybrid environment in which we are deeply
embedded, one interlaced with complex, historically constructed ecological
pathways that, in inauspicious instances, eventually lead from industrial facilities to human consumers."[74] Walker follows the sociologist Bruno Latour in
embracing explanations of hybrid causation to show how the categories of
nature and society are deeply interconnected and thereby predicated upon

71   Ian Jared Miller, *The Nature of the Beasts: Empire and Exhibition at the Tokyo Imperial Zoo*
      (Berkeley: University of California Press, 2013), 3.
72   Miller, *The Nature of the Beasts*, 237.
73   Julia Adeney Thomas, *Reconfiguring Modernity: Concepts of Nature in Japanese Political
      Ideology* (Berkeley: University of California Press, 2001), 3.
74   Brett L. Walker, *Toxic Archipelago: A History of Industrial Disease in Japan* (Seattle:
      University of Washington Press, 2010), 16.

one another.[75] It is in light of these multiple avenues of causality that Walker examines the pain felt by victims of industrial pollution in Japan to highlight people's "embeddedness in nature" and their visceral experience of the nation's drive to modernize.[76] Another historian, Robert Stolz, continues along the path laid out by these histories in his intellectual history of the activists protesting against the catastrophic pollution released by the Ashio Copper Mine and the ongoing development of industrial capitalism in twentieth-century Japan. His interpretation differs in that it eschews the term "hybridity" in favor of the more focused concept of "subsumption," wherein nature is subsumed "in the need to accumulate units of surplus value ... without regard to any other possible valuations or temporalities, whether biological, ecological, political, or even ethical."[77] What these scholars share in their approaches is a singling out of the historical particularity of this nature-society dualism. Through each of their studies, they show how people can only be removed from their lived environments in the abstract and that the consequences of treating humans as separate from their environments in modern Japan can be traced though the formation of national identity and ideology, polluted and poisoned bodies and landscapes, and the hyper-controlled environments of zoos.

3   Riparian Relations: An Expanded Understanding of Rivers

This reemerging critique of the modern notions of "nature" and "society" and the histories that have been written within this dualistic worldview provides the theoretical bases of my exploration into the changing relations communities and governments have had with each other and Japan's rivers from the seventeenth through the early twentieth centuries. In the mid-twentieth century, Watsuji, Imanishi, Heidegger, and Merleau-Ponty developed phenomenological critiques of both idealist philosophy and positivist realism, but the historians discussed in the previous section are responding to a host of new

---

75   Latour, *We Have Never Been Modern*, 10, 41–43.
76   Explaining how the nation physically manifests itself in people's bodies, Walker writes, "Nations are not entirely culturally determined, invented entities, as is so often asserted: the effects of ecological transformation and pollution demonstrate that people really do physiologically experience nations' policies and priorities. Just as bodies can become industrialized, so too can they become nationalized: cadmium concentrations in femoral bones and mercury damage in brains are physical inscriptions of the nation's policies on the body." Walker, *Toxic Archipelago*, 11.
77   Robert Stolz, *Bad Water: Nature, Pollution, & Politics in Japan, 1870–1950* (Durham: Duke University Press, 2014), 17.

and old questions regarding people's perception of, knowledge about, and relations with their local and global environments. Fundamental to these questions are our own ontological assumptions about history. Whether explicitly stated or not, all histories express an ontological stance through the way they discuss time and space, causality and contingency, agency and action, events and experience, subjects and objects and the relations therein.

My own approach begins with an expanded view of the river to include the broader wetlands and riparian relations that these rivers were central in making. These riparian relations are a subset of what I call environmental relations, which are defined here as the salient interactions between heterogenous entities—objects, artifacts, humans, and other organisms—as they constitute and reconstitute their environments. It follows, then, that riparian relations are the interactions between various heterogenous entities *and* rivers. Collectively these interactions are what form and maintain riparian assemblages or ensembles, such as a riverboat or a local irrigation network. These assemblages are in themselves unique entities, being neither the sum of their parts nor simply reducible to those parts, exhibiting their own emergent properties and potential to interact with other assemblages.[78] This is a fundamentally relational approach based on an ontology that embraces both human and nonhuman entities within the same fields of activity. Instead of attempting to reduce downward the necessarily interrelated character of life by identifying the enduring essences of individual entities like a river, a boat, a fish, or an engineer, or to generalize upward to rarefied categories like nature, society, the state, or the market, this approach traces the history of specific durable relations that formed, changed, and dissolved within and between these riparian assemblages. A focus on the histories and geographies created by these riparian relations facilitates an alternative and arguably more accurate description of the different speeds and scales at which life along these rivers changed.

Three illustrations by the Osaka-based artist Takehara Shunchōsai (d. 1801) serve to elucidate elements of this relational approach for the

---

78   Gilles Deleuze and Felix Guattari developed the concept of assemblage (*agencement* in the original French) over time to fit with different parts of their philosophy. Since then, the concept has been adopted and adapted by a variety of scholars in diverse disciplines. My use of the concept of assemblage draws primarily from the following: Gilles Deleuze and Felix Guattari, *A Thousand Plateaus: Capitalism and Schizophrenia* (Minneapolis: University of Minnesota Press, 1987); Gilles Deleuze and Claire Parnet, *Dialogues II*, trans. Hugh Tomlinson and Barbara Habberjam (New York: Columbia University Press, 2002); Jane Bennett, *Vibrant Matter: A Political Ecology of Things* (Durham: Duke University Press, 2010); Manuel Delanda, *Assemblage Theory* (Edinburgh: Edinburgh University Press, 2016).

eighteenth-century Yodo River system.[79] The first from the influential 1780 *Miyako meisho zue* (*Illustrated Guide to the Capital*) is a landscape of the Uji River and the Ogura Lake that assists in explaining the temporality and assembled character of a place or region, a topic developed further in chapter 1. Adopting a bird's-eye-view vantage point above the storied Shigetsu Hills on the north bank of the Uji River (bottom center), Shunchōsai includes "renowned places" (*meisho*) likely familiar to his readers from poetry, warrior tales, and other writings (fig. 2).[80] The Bungo Bridge in the center of the composition draws the viewer's attention to the historic Yamato Highway (Yamato-kaidō) from Mukōjima Village on the distant south bank to the bustling riverport of Fushimi on the near north bank (bottom right). Shunchōsai uses the image of Ogura's famed mist as a compositional element together with the rooftops of the lake's shoreline shrines to express the expanse of the lake and to fill the space between the Uji River and distant mountains surrounding the ancient capital of Nara.[81] With its river and lake, trees and mountains, boats and shrines, and people moving about, this illustration could lend itself to a common modernist reading as an empty "space" filled with these and other discrete objects. Another modernist reading may see in the bridge, buildings, and ancient sites an artificial "second nature" overlaying and starting to replace a primal "first nature."[82] The reality of this and most landscapes is, however,

---

79   Originally published as six volumes in 1780 and republished many times thereafter including a multivolume sequel, the *Miyako meisho zue*, which the historian Mary Elizabeth Berry translates as *Illustrated Guide to the Capital*, pioneered the popular genre of *meisho zue* (illustrated guides to renowned places). The poet and essayist Akisato Ritō (fl. 1772–1830) wrote the descriptions of the places mentioned in the volumes; the painter Takehara Shunchōsai created the designs for the woodblock-printed illustrations. All six volumes have been transcribed and republished together in Harada Kan, ed., *Miyako meisho zue* (Tokyo: Jinbutsu Ōraisha, 1967). See also Mary Elizabeth Berry, *Japan in Print: Information and Nation in the Early Modern Period* (Berkeley: University of California Press, 2006), 164–65.

80   Above the image of Shigetsu Hills are cartouches that name the Shigetsu garden and temples where a learned reader would have known is the location of the graves of the fourteenth-century emperors Kōmyō and Sukō.

81   In the upper half of the right page, three cartouches indicate the names of the Ogura, Iseda, and Okubo shrines. Most readers would also have known that the Yamato Highway (Yamato-kaidō) connected the ancient capital of Nara with Kyoto. *Kumiyama-chō shi*, 1:172–73, 845–49.

82   The Japanese literature scholar Hauro Shirane uses the terms "primary nature," which he describes as being "remote" and "rarely seen" by the aristocrats of ancient Kyoto, and "secondary nature (*nijiteki shizen*)," which he defines as the "re-created or represented nature" found in gardens, paintings, and poetry. Haruo Shirane, *Japan and the Culture of the Four Seasons: Nature, Literature, and the Arts* (New York: Columbia University Press, 2012), 3–4. For another application of this dichotomy in understanding Japanese

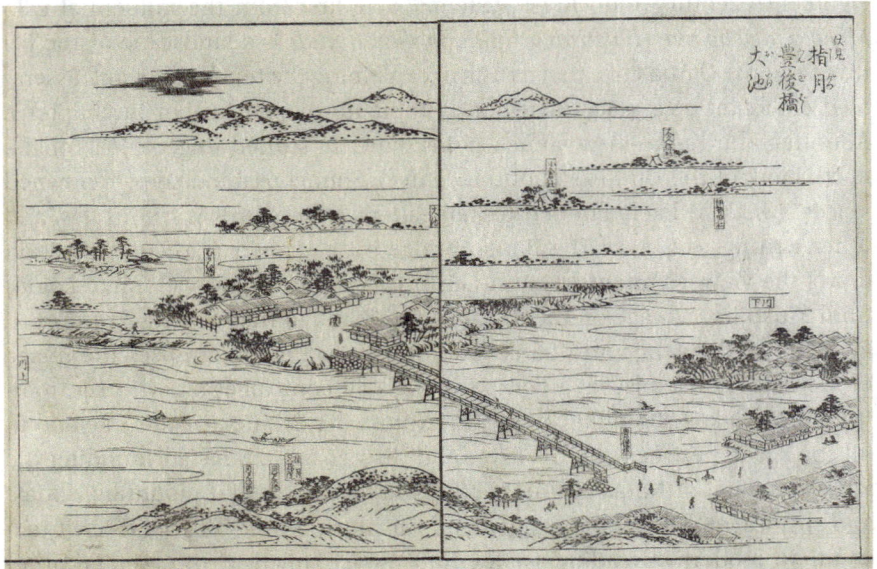

FIGURE 2   Bird's-eye-view from above the Shigetsu Hills looking over the Uji River and
            Bungo Bridge with Ogura Lake in the distance. "Fushimi," in *Miyako meisho zue*
            (Osaka: Kawachiya Tasuke, 1786), vol. 5, unpaginated
            COURTESY OF THE NATIONAL DIET LIBRARY, TOKYO

more complex. The seemingly inexorable flow of the Uji River and quiet presence of the Ogura behind it occupy much of the illustration. As noted above,
human habitation of the region predates the existence of the Ogura and has
long been an integral part of the landscape. More specifically, the Uji River

---

history, see Tsukamoto Manabu, *Ikiru koto no kinseishi: Jinmei kankyō no rekishi kara*
(Tokyo: Heibonsha, 2001). This dichotomy has also been widely employed elsewhere. The
historian William Cronon earlier expressed a version of this "pristine" nature versus a
"built" nature of human design when using the dichotomy between a "first nature" and
a "second nature" in his impressive history about the making of Chicago and the Great
West: "A kind of 'second nature,' designed by people and 'improved' toward human ends,
gradually emerged atop the original landscape that nature—'first nature'—had created
as such an inconvenient jumble." William Cronon, *Nature's Metropolis: Chicago and the
Great West* (New York: W. W. Norton, 1991), 56, see also 266–67, 402. While Cronon traces
the roots of this first-second nature dichotomy back to Hegel, this explanation of historical change has also been frequently employed in more recent histories. For two compelling histories that nonetheless follow the contours of this first-second nature dichotomy,
see Richard W. Judd, *Second Nature: An Environmental History of New England* (Amherst:
University of Massachusetts Press, 2014); Sara B. Pritchard, *Confluence: The Nature of
Technology and the Remaking of the Rhône* (Cambridge: Harvard University Press, 2011), 22.

flowed directly into the lake until 1594, two centuries before the making of this print, when it was routed around the lake to provide the castle town of Fushimi with a viable riverport. At that time, the quality and level of water in the lake drastically changed. And although the three shrines along the shore of the Ogura trace their origins back several centuries, it was only after the rerouting of the Uji and the building of levees (Makishima Levee is shown center left with a person walking atop it) that the fishing village of Mukōjima was founded.[83] Rather than reduce the places depicted in Shunchōsai's illustration to objects occupying an empty field of space or a dichotomy of pristine "first" or built "second" nature, this representation and the actual places it depicts suggest how a relational perspective can be a more practical way to understand the dynamic temporality and dense historical interworking of environmental relations in the formation of place and community.[84]

From a relational perspective, it is possible to follow the various lines laid out by these riparian relations in this and in a second image by Shunchōsai illustrated here from his sequel to the *Miyako meisho zue*, the 1787 *Shūi miyako meisho zue*. This image portrays two fishermen seated in a boat and catching fish just upstream from the Ogura on the Uji River. It offers an example of a basic assemblage and the riparian relations that momentarily brought it into being and into relations with other assemblages (fig. 3).[85] Operating as separate entities—fisher, boat, tackle—it would have been difficult to catch carp but as a whole they possess that *capacity*. And fishermen had to have additional capacities like poling the boat out into the river. The boat, too, had to have the *capacity* to be poled without capsizing. Fish would have also belonged to what ecologists today call assemblages that, among their many capacities like feeding on other organisms and swimming in the river, had in the moment of taking the bait the *capacity* to be caught by the fishing assemblage—that

83   For documents related to the 1594 rerouting of the Uji River to the newly completed Fushimi Castle and the building and later repair of the levee at Mukōjima, see *Shiryō Kyōto no rekishi*, ed. Kyōto-shi, vol. 16, *Fushimi-ku* (Tokyo: Heibonsha, 1991), 457–62. See also Murata Michibito, *Kinsei no Yodogawa chisui* (Tokyo: Yamakawa Shuppan, 2009), 5–15.
84   The following authors offer cogent arguments for seeing places and landscapes as the result of complex interactions between biological, material, and cultural processes: Edward S. Casey, *Getting Back into Place: Toward a Renewed Understanding of the Place World* (Bloomington: Indiana University Press, 2009); Tim Ingold, *Being Alive: Essays on Movement, Knowledge and Description* (New York: Routledge, 2011); Jeff Malpas, *Heidegger's Topology: Being, Place, and World* (Cambridge: MIT Press, 2006); Doreen B. Massey, *For Space* (London: Sage Publications, 2005).
85   This fishing assemblage is an obvious corollary to Gilles Deleuze's and Felix Guattari's nomad warrior as "man-horse-bow assemblage." Deleuze and Guattari, *A Thousand Plateaus*, 404.

FIGURE 3   Just upstream from Ogura Lake and the riverport
            of Fushimi, fishers are shown on the Uji River
            with a view of Mount Kisen in the background.
            "Kisen-dake," in *Shūi miyako meisho zue* (Osaka:
            Kawachiya Tasuke, 1787), vol. 4, unpaginated
            COURTESY OF THE NATIONAL DIET LIBRARY,
            TOKYO

is, a fisher with a boat and tackle.[86] These active and passive meanings of
capacity, necessary for any action to occur, express the asymmetrical relationship within what Gilles Deleuze and Felix Guattari describe as an "affective

---

86   In ecological terms, the meaning of an assemblage typically does not include humans as
      can be seen in the following standard definition of the term: "A collection of plants and/
      or animals characteristically associated with a particular environment that can be used as
      an indicator of that environment." Michael Allaby, ed., *A Dictionary of Ecology* (New York:
      Oxford University Press, 1998), 33.

assemblage."[87] It should be stressed that this interaction between the fishing and fish assemblages in Shunchōsai's illustration were equally dependent on the Uji River, without which no poling, swimming, or fishing could take place.[88] In fact, the archaeologists Andrew Bauer and Steve Kosiba apply the fluvial concept of "entrainment" in their research to emphasize how social action necessarily happens within and contributes to flows of material action that open the way to rethinking social and political problems.[89] In addition, this relational perspective with its attention to capacities allows for a broader and more nuanced explanation of historical agency. As the historian Jessica Riskin demonstrates, the history of the modern concept of agency is a long and restless one that originates in seventeenth-century Europe and continues to shape scientific and popular views of "nature" as intrinsically passive and lacking in agency.[90] Walter Johnson also reminds us that the notion of agency within the discipline of history has left historians with a contradictory "mess." On the one hand, historians use the concept to "recover" the voices of past marginalized groups of people, and on the other the concept is "saturated with the categories of nineteenth-century liberalism" wherein the optimal "agent" of history was seen as the free-willed "individual" abstracted from their historical and social circumstances.[91] The problematic history of agency should be acknowledged, but the concept nonetheless remains helpful as a heuristic for explaining different kinds of historical action and analyzing asymmetrical power relations. Here, I broadly define agency as the capacity of an entity to affect another entity. As such, agency always operates within relations,

---

87   Deleuze and Guattari, *A Thousand Plateaus*, 256–60. My description of capacities is indebted to Deleuze and Guattari and also draws on Manuel DeLanda's development of their many ideas about assemblages. DeLanda, *Assemblage Theory*, 73.

88   Tim Ingold, "Landscape or Weather-World?," in "Making Knowledge," supplement, *Journal of the Royal Anthropological Institute* 16, No. S1 (2010): S126–35.

89   Bauer and Kosiba explain the political dimensions of entrained action as follows: "In these entrained actions, things become particular kinds of actors that can affect historical processes precisely because of how their material properties articulate with cultural values. These material actions can become political when people emphasize how particular materials, things, or other people in a broader assemblage are the causes of social problems." Andrew M. Bauer and Steve Kosiba, "How Things Act: An Archaeology of Materials in Political Life," *Journal of Social Archaeology* 16, no. 2 (2016): 122.

90   Riskin shows how for the past three centuries in Europe the dominant scientific view of natural phenomena is that they act in accord to an "external" design (first attributed to an omniscient god and later to nature itself). This view has constantly contended with another subordinate or "subterranean" view of natural or material phenomena as possessing their own "internal" capacities to change and create. Riskin, *The Restless Clock*, 337–74.

91   Walter Johnson, "On Agency," *Journal of Social History* 37, no. 1 (2003): 115.

such as a fisher casting a line or a fish biting on it or a government ministry reclaiming the Ogura and the lake's residents and waters responding to the new landscape. Agency can be attributed to both small and large, human and nonhuman assemblages.[92] Shunchōsai's illustrations encapsulate a history of these interactions between entities *within* each of these fishing and fish assemblages as well as *between* these two assemblages. These interactions exemplify the riparian relations that are the focus of this book.

Shunchōsai's illustrations are also suggestive of the different temporal and spatial scales at which environmental relations work. The terms "assemblage" and "relation" may express a certain fixedness, but they are no less static than Kamo no Chōmei's river whose current "does not cease" or Imanishi's short-lived mayfly nymphs. In other words, riparian assemblages were not objects coming together to form larger objects like the many boards in a boat or drops of water in a lake. Rather, they were unique and irreducible moments in flows of activity undergoing various rates of growth and decay.[93] Assemblages and their relations were constantly changing—either acting or being acted upon—and part of other processes. The scales of change differed markedly, however, from the gradual erosion of the Shigetsu Hills into the Uji River to the fisherman suddenly snagging a fish on his line.[94] Moreover, they were fundamentally relational in the way that the unseen stones of the riverbed in Shunchōsai's illustration actively shaped the rapid and undulating flow of the Uji River, themselves being slowly molded and shifted by the flow of the river over, under, and all around them. Instead of perpetuating the idea of a fishing boat or river being an inert, fixed object to be acted on by a knowing, acting

---

92   It should be emphasized that having intention is itself an action; therefore, intent should not be seen as necessarily occurring before or being the *cause* of a separate physical action or material event. Nonetheless, a distinction should be made between those assemblages that exhibit what the philosopher Sean Bowden calls "expressive agency" and those who are unable to reflect on the meaning of their actions. Sean Bowden, "Human and Nonhuman Agency in Deleuze," in *Deleuze and the Non/Human*, ed. Jon Roffe and Hannah Stark (New York: Palgrave Macmillan, 2015), 74–78.

93   John Dupré, *Processes of Life: Essays in the Philosophy of Biology* (Oxford: Oxford University Press, 2012); Jenny Helin, Tor Hernes, and Daniel Hjorth, eds., *The Oxford Handbook of Process Philosophy and Organizational Studies* (Oxford: Oxford University Press, 2014).

94   The anthropologist Anna L. Tsing argues that it is important to pay attention to divergences in scale and the "nonscalability" of many relations: "Because relationships are encounters across difference, they have a quality of indeterminacy. Relationships are transformative, and one is not sure of the outcome. Thus, diversity in the making is always part of the mix." Anna L. Tsing, "On Nonscalability: The Living World Is Not Amenable to Precision-Nested Scales," *Common Knowledge* 18, no. 3 (2012): 510. See also Anna L. Tsing, *The Mushroom at the End of the World: On the Possibility of Life in Capitalist Ruins* (Princeton: Princeton University Press, 2015).

subject like a fisherman or an engineer, this approach asks that we see them both as part of the broader flows of life or what the anthropologist Tim Ingold calls the "processes of formation."[95] These assemblages and their relations were therefore not objects; they are better understood as having been activities or events.[96] But history is not like the oft-cited river of time with its flow representing the succession of such events in a single direction from the present to the ever-distant past.[97] History is the manifold and highly contingent unfolding of existing and new processes. This temporality of environmental relations was equally manifest in numerous other ways.[98] In Shunchōsai's illustration of fishing on the Uji River, different temporal cycles, rhythms, and pulses can be

95   Tim Ingold, "The Textility of Making," in *Being Alive*, 210. In a similar vein, Andrew Bauer and Mona Bhan describe how climate change is the result of past and ongoing action between humans and nonhumans, "the materialities of environments are historical products constantly (re)produced through human-nonhuman relationships. This is not simply a process of humans acting and then Nature 'acting back.'" Andrew M. Bauer and Mona Bhan, *Climate without Nature: A Critical Anthropology of the Anthropocene* (New York: Cambridge University Press, 2018), 127.

96   While there is a degree of consensus about seeing assemblages or arrangements as events, those following phenomenological or poststructuralist lines of thought differ in their understandings of what constitutes an event. In his explanation of "timespace," for example, the neo-Heideggerian philosopher Theodore Schatzki explains how social practices, which necessarily involve material arrangements, are "activity events"—the sum cumulation of which he defines as "history." Interpreting Deleuze's ideas about space, the geographer Arun Saldanha writes: "In the most basic terms, events are *transformations of* bodies and things insofar as these come together with others.... Events are absolutely unique and immanent to this coming-together, over here." Theodore R. Schatzki, *The Timespace of Human Activity* (Plymouth: Lexington Books, 2010), 209; Arun Saldanha, *Space after Deleuze* (New York: Bloomsbury, 2017), 165.

97   This popular linear view of time is also a peculiar product of European Enlightenment thought that ultimately replicates the modern dualistic worldview between an active, subjective present and an inert, objective past. While this linear view of time is easy to imagine, it does not accord with how people experience the past in the present as history and memory (i.e., historical interpretations of the past occur in the present just as memories of last week and those of many years earlier are retrieved in the present). Matt Hodges, "Rethinking Time's Arrow: Bergson, Deleuze and the Anthropology of Time," *Anthropological Theory* 8, no. 4 (2008): 399–429; David Couzens Hoy, *The Time of Our Lives: A Critical History of Temporality* (Cambridge: MIT Press, 2009).

98   The following works examine different views and meanings of time and temporality in Japan and elsewhere: Okada Yoshirō, *Kyūreki tokuhon: Nihon no kurashi o tanoshimu 'koyomi' no chie* (Osaka: Sōgensha, 2015); Yulia Frumer, *Making Time: Astronomical Time Measurement in Tokugawa Japan* (Chicago: University of Chicago Press, 2018); Mattias B. Rasmussen, "Seasons, Timings, and the Rhythms of Life," in *Living with Environmental Change: Waterworlds*, ed. Kirsten Hastrup and Cecilie Rubow (New York: Routledge, 2014), 232–36; Michael Dunlop Young, *The Metronomic Society: Natural Rhythms and Human Timetables* (Cambridge: Harvard University Press, 1988).

seen from the regular rolling of the river to the reeling motion of a fisherman pulling in his catch. In the rivers of the Kinai region during the late nineteenth and early twentieth centuries, the fishers exemplified the diurnal and seasonal rhythms of riparian life. Operating on Ogura Lake and its surrounding rivers, they typically launched their boats before dawn to catch carp and other fish when they were most active. They then sold their catch to fishmongers in local morning markets that opened at set times in Yodo, Fushimi, Mukōjima, and Kyoto.[99] Carp would have had their own daily routines of foraging and resting as well as seasonal routines of migration and reproduction.[100] The fullness of the river in Shunchōsai's illustration suggests that this scene takes place at the start of summer when annual monsoonal rains or a possible typhoon would have filled the river to its banks. The semblance of sameness and solidity along the Uji, therefore, owes to this repetition and maintenance of relations that makes them appear as habitual and durable—in reality, its riparian relations fluctuated from moment to moment (fig. 4).[101]

All of these temporal processes—from erosion and reproduction to production and consumption—inevitably have spatial dimensions because in unfolding and materializing they also produce space. The gist of Watsuji's critique of Heidegger's *Being and Time* was that the German philosopher subordinated space to time as the locus of existence. The spatial extent of these kinds of riparian relations can be traced through another Shunchōsai illustration in the *Miyako meisho zue* of passengers eating on riverboats commonly known as *sanjikkokubune* as they floated past the famous waterwheel of Yodo Castle (fig. 4). Measuring about 5 *jō* (18 m) in length and 6–8 *shaku* (about 2 m) in width, *sanjikkokubune* were built with lumber floated downstream from the Tanba, Takami, and Suzuka Mountains or further away.[102] The moniker "*sanjikkokubune*" referred to the boat's large capacity, capable of carrying thirty *koku* (*sanjikkoku*) of rice or a crew of four and about thirty passengers. It was propelled upstream by a combination of poles and towropes and had a normal service life of several decades. With its lumber frame, poles, ropes, crew, and the river, this riverboat assemblage would have belonged to an even greater

---

99   In the winter, these markets opened in the afternoon, so presumably the fishers launched their boats later in the morning. Uji-shi Rekishi Shiryōkan, ed., *Ogura-ike: soshite, kantaku wa okonawareta* (Uji: Uji-shi Rekishi Shiryōkan, 2011), 10.

100   Miyachi, "Gyōrui," 275–83.

101   Gilles Deleuze, *Difference and Repetition* (New York: Columbia University Press, 1995), 72–74; Hoy, *The Time of Our Lives*, 160–61.

102   Officially called *kashobune* (literally "licensed boat"), these *sanjikkokubune* riverboats varied in size and changed over time. Hino Shōshō, *Kinsei Yodogawa suiun shiryō shū* (Kyoto: Dōhōsha Shuppan, 1982), 858, 871; Kawana, *Kinsei Nihon no kawabune kenkyū*, 2:612–21.

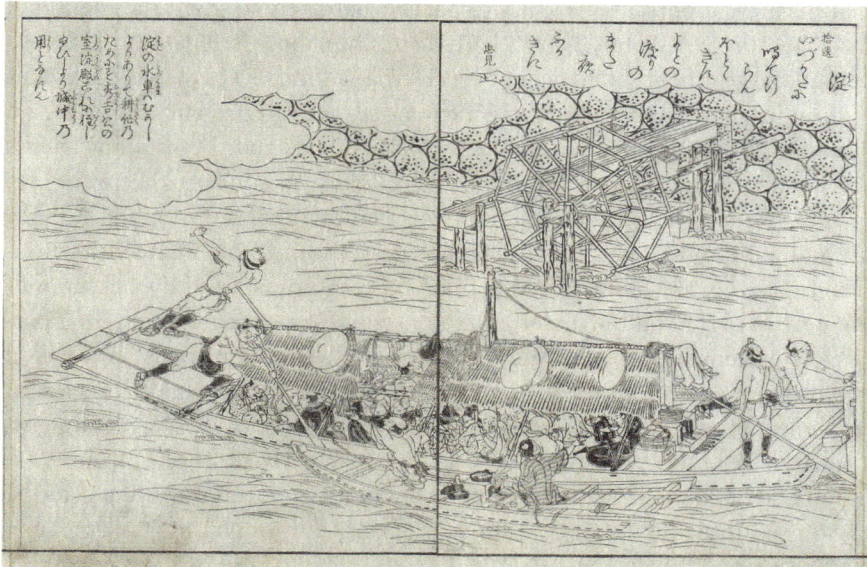

FIGURE 4   *Sanjikkokubune* riverboat with passengers on the Yodo River in front of the
            waterwheel of Yodo Castle. "Yodo," in *Miyako meisho zue* (Osaka: Kawachiya
            Tasuke, 1786), vol. 5, unpaginated
            COURTESY OF THE NATIONAL DIET LIBRARY, TOKYO

assemblage—a licensed shipping agent (*funayado*)—that every day transported passengers between the coastal city of Osaka and the inland city of
Fushimi that was the main riverport for Kyoto.[103] During his extensive travels
in 1851, for example, the wealthy merchant Kinokuniya Chōsaburō traveled
mostly by foot, but when journeying between Osaka and Fushimi to visit business contacts he bought a seat on a *sanjikkokubune* run by the shipping agent
Yamamotoya Kanpei.[104] In addition to their principal business of conveying
goods and passengers such agents also ran their own waterside inns (*yado*)

---

103   In Osaka, shipping agents generally dispatched two boats per day from one of four des-
       ignated wharves (i.e., Hachikenya, Dōtonbori, Higashiyokohori, and Yodoyabashi); these
       vessels employed poles and towropes to make their way up the Yodo on the daylong
       journey to Fushimi where passengers disembarked at one of the city's four wharves (i.e.,
       Kyōbashi, Hōraihashi, Awahashi, Hiradobashi). The reverse trip from Fushimi used the
       current of the Yodo River to arrive in Osaka in just six hours. Hino, *Kinai Kasen kōtsū shi
       kenkyū*, 229–44.
104   Yamamotoya Kanpei contracted to bring passengers to the shipping agent Yamashiroya
       Matauemon in Fushimi. Takiguchi Masaya, "Edo no gōshō no tabi: Kaei yon-nen no dōchū
       nikki," in *Kōtsūshi kenkyū* 61 (2006): 29. For a list of fifty of these shipping agents and their
       contracting partners in each riverport, see Hino, *Kinai Kasen kōtsū shi kenkyū*, 240. On

that became important semipublic spaces where people spent the night and held meetings.[105] Waterwheels like that in Shunchōsai's illustration (visible behind the riverboat) lifted water over riverbanks and levees to feed the canals of local irrigation networks, in effect extending these rivers and their riparian relations far beyond their banks.[106] These riverboats and the shipping agents that managed them can be examined as riparian assemblages that were intimately bound to local and regional river relations shaping so much of daily life along the Yodo River from the seventeenth through the nineteenth centuries. Thus, from the lumber used to build these riverboats and the activities of their crews to the routine undertakings of these shipping agents and their passengers' itineraries, the geographical scope of these assemblages linked rural and urban areas and functioned on a number of local and regional scales. In fact, one of the greatest transformations set in motion by the Tokugawa government's opening of additional ports like nearby Hyōgo (Kobe) to international trade and the 1868 establishment of a new national government was the expansion of the potential geographic scales within which these assemblages could operate.[107] Instead of assuming or naturalizing these various geographic scales, it is important to use scale as an analytical tool that also accounts for how some environmental relations are, as the anthropologist Anna L. Tsing argues, "nonscalable."[108]

travel during this time, see Laura Nenzi, *Excursions in Identity: Travel and the Intersection of Place, Gender, and Status in Edo Japan* (Honolulu: University of Hawai'i Press, 2008).

105   In 1862 and again in 1866, the inn run by the shipping agent Teradaya Isuke became a site for two well-known incidents: the first involving the killing of nine restorationist radicals (*shishi*) from Satsuma domain and the second being a botched attack on Sakamoto Ryōma. Mōri Toshihiko, *Meiji ishin seiji shi josetsu* (Tokyo: Miraisha, 1967), 129–33.

106   Two waterwheels at Yodo Castle were well known for supplying water for use in the gardens and other purposes inside the castle, but many less familiar waterwheels could also be found along the banks of Yodo and its tributaries. For various documents mentioning these and other waterwheels, see *Shiryō Kyōto no rekishi*, 16:666. Now a symbol of Yodo Town, a replica of the castle's waterwheel has been placed in front of the local train station.

107   The historical geographer Kären Wigen shows how in the late nineteenth and early twentieth centuries the opening of the domestic silk market to international trade quickly transformed the Shimoina region along the Tenryū River in southern Nagano Prefecture from a center of production to a peripheral region. Kären Wigen, *The Making of a Japanese Periphery, 1750–1920* (Berkeley: University of California Press, 1995).

108   Anna L. Tsing cautions against ignoring the seepage that necessarily occurs when assuming a seamless nesting of different scales. Tsing, "On Nonscalability," 505–24. Although Deleuze and Guattari did not theorize the term scale, the geographer Arun Saldanha argues that scale certainly factored in their thinking about assemblages via such concepts of molar and molecular as well as territorialization and deterritorialization. Saldanha, *Space after Deleuze*, 96–104.

4   Chapter Organization

A number of considerations shaped the organization of this book. The primary
concern has been to identify and follow key riparian relations along the Tone
and Yodo Rivers as they shifted over time and space between the seventeenth
and early twentieth centuries. Geographical factors were also weighed. The
two chapters in Part 1 concentrate on the Tone River system because it was
central to the development of the Kantō region and the Tokugawa's regional
approach to riparian governance. The three chapters in Part 2 focus on the critical role played by the Yodo River system in the formation of a national framework to administer and reengineer the country's main rivers. Finally, in order
to establish the relevance of this environmental approach to the broader field
of history, this study's five chapters explicitly address the connections between
this rich riparian history and different areas of scholarship on Tokugawa and
modern Japan.

Chapters 1 and 2 in Part 1 examine the role of the Tone River in the formation
of the Kantō region from the seventeenth to the mid-nineteenth centuries. In
addressing the existing scholarship on village studies and the Tokugawa political order, these two chapters highlight key riparian relations that emerged
along the Tone to demonstrate the importance of these rivers in the livelihood
and governance of villages and the region as a whole. Chapter 1 starts by showing how the seemingly "natural" landscape of the Kantō Plain during this time
was the coeval result of extensive fluvial work carried out by the Tokugawa
government, local communities, and the region's waterways. With the transfer
of military and political power from the Kinai region around the ancient capital of Kyoto to the Kantō region surrounding the small castle town of Edo in
the early seventeenth century, the population and numbers of villages in the
Kantō rapidly grew. In turn, this growth led to an expansion and intensifica-
tion in riparian relations throughout the entire region through the increase
in arable land, the building of irrigation systems, and the rerouting of major
rivers, including the Tone. Drawing on source material ranging from a riverboat pilot's logbook to documents from legal disputes over water and fishing
rights, the remainder of the chapter confirms how these new and old villages
were less simple, rustic, and autonomous than they are often characterized.
This chapter reveals how the livelihoods of most peasants along the Tone River
depended on and contributed to a complex web of local and regional riparian
relations formed through irrigation, transport, and commerce. Nonetheless,
many of the riparian assemblages of the Kantō region in the eighteenth and
nineteenth centuries were deeply entangled in local ways of life, thereby lacking the scalability of some of their modern progeny.

Having explored how people's daily lives were deeply intertwined with the waters of the Kantō region, chapter 2 continues with a discussion of the regional riverscape to demonstrate the asymmetrical and what the historian Yoshida Nobuyuki calls "segmented" (*bunsetsu*) power relations between the Tokugawa government that often resulted in a piecemeal approach to riparian governance.[109] This chapter also contends that political histories should look beyond a focus on state-society relations and acknowledge the fact that rivers and other nonhuman elements, together with commoners and governing officials, constituted the environments within which these entities and the relations between them emerged. The Tokugawa government, itself a hugely complex assemblage, exercised its power to extract taxes from rural as well as urban areas and to shape the larger polity that it played a central role in defining. This polity was comprised of members with vastly different capacities, including those from separate social status groups, households from warrior elites to tenant farmers, and the frequently overlooked nonhuman entities, such as fish, forests, and rivers. Unlike the modern state that came into being in Japan in the late nineteenth century, the Tokugawa acted without the expanded organizational and technological capacities of industrial capitalism. Its capacity to change and create riparian relations was rooted in an earlier era of stone, wood, rope, and human and animal labor.

Chapters 3, 4, and 5 in Part 2 trace these riparian relations into the modern period. After the collapse of the Tokugawa government in 1868, the country's young leaders replaced the old segmented approach to governance with a newly centralized national government, promoted industry and trade, and simultaneously solidified the country's boundaries and further opened the country to unprecedented interaction with the outside world. The effect of these swift changes in governance was the shift toward an industrial economy and the formation of a modern state and empire. These three chapters analyze different dimensions of the construction of what I call a "modern river regime," an approach to river management and engineering that resulted from the confluence of more intense and frequent flooding by regional rivers due to widespread deforestation, the introduction of novel engineering technologies and sciences, integration of local and national political interests, and the

---

109   While his research focuses on the social groups and institutions that comprised the city of Edo, Yoshida has also written about the more rural parts of the Kantō region and beyond. Based on this broad research, he argues that these "segmented structures" describe communities and organizations in both urban and rural areas. Yoshida Nobuyuki, "Soshiabirite to bunsetsu kōzō," in *Dentō toshi: bunsetsu kōzō*, ed. Yoshida Nobuyuki and Itō Takeshi (Tokyo: Tōkyō Daigaku Shuppankai, 2010), v–x. See also Yoshida Nobuyuki, *Kyodai jōkamachi Edo no bunsetsu kōzō* (Tokyo: Yamakawa Shuppansha, 1999).

indemnity gained from the First Sino-Japanese War (1894–95) with the Qing Empire. Concentrating on the Yodo River, and to a lesser extent the Tone, during the 1870s and 1880s, chapter 3 discusses the efforts by Japan's nascent national government to create a new administrative system for the country's rivers and to develop regional river systems and their downstream coastal ports into an interconnected countrywide infrastructure for water transport. This chapter asserts that, although an archipelago, Japan had never truly been sealed off and separated from the rest of the world and in the late nineteenth century was fully part of the global flow of engineers, their equipment, and their knowledge and techniques. By examining the plans and activities of Dutch and later Japanese engineers, this chapter argues that, rather than assume a Eurocentric model of "technology transfer" from the West to the rest of the world, it is more useful to understand the work of these engineers and the technologies they employed as belonging to a broader phenomenon that was beginning to transform rivers in increasingly similar ways around the globe at that time. In this way, the once overwhelmingly regional character of riparian assemblages centered on large rivers like the Yodo and Tone began to change as the new government sought to centralize and standardize its administration of the country's rivers. In doing so, it also introduced new techniques and technologies to river management and engineering that were then circulating around the globe.

While the Home Ministry channeled its resources toward maintaining river works along the Tone, Kiso, Shinano, and a handful of other rivers during the 1870s, it was the relatively short Yodo River that commanded its attention in the 1880s and 1890s. The approximately 50 km long Yodo made up for its lack of length by receiving the waters from most of the Kinai region's other major rivers, which together comprised the country's sixth largest river basin, and by flowing through the agriculturally and commercially important area between Kyoto and Osaka. Continued upstream deforestation and extraordinary rain events in 1885 and again in 1889 culminated in the Yodo flooding the surrounding countryside and inundating several wards in Osaka. These floods are a reminder that the Yodo and other rivers of Japan were not passive objects. Chapter 4 discusses these floods with an emphasis on showing how the agency of human and nonhuman entities like rivers acted through their encompassing riparian assemblages. This chapter also establishes how the region's rural landowning class and the Home Ministry's Regional Engineering District in Osaka succeeded in constructing flooding and flood control as an existential problem for themselves and the region as a whole.

Whereas chapter 4 highlights the confluence of historical actors in reframing the complex riparian assemblage centered on the Yodo River in terms of a flood-control problem, chapter 5 underscores how solving this regional problem became a part of a wider national movement. Along the Yodo in the mid-1890s, influential technocrats (*gijutsu kanryō*) in the Home Ministry and members of the new Imperial Diet together developed a techno-political framework described as a "high-water" (*kōsui*) approach to river management that through the 1896 River Law (Kasenhō) and the authority it invested in the Home Ministry formed a template for building of what became Japan's modern river regime. On the one hand, this framework included some riparian relations that were deemed of value by politicians and government officials, such as improved irrigation, stronger flood controls, and eventually hydroelectric power generation. On the other, it externalized and thereby served to disassemble other politically and economically marginal relations like fishing and hunting, gathering material for fertilizer, and river transport. Moreover, the Home Ministry as a crucial part of the national government was in effect helping to construct the modern state itself by exercising the powers invested to it through this techno-political framework. While many histories of the "state" in modern Japan have assumed that most relevant historical activity lay within the nexus of "state-society" relations, this chapter confirms the important role played by rivers and other nonhuman entities in constituting both state and society. Instead of looking upon the modern state as a precursor to the reengineering of these rivers and their riparian relations, this chapter argues that the "state" in modern Japan was, along with the categories of "society" and "nature," an *effect* of these kinds of discourses, practices, and politics.[110] Through a comparison of the devastating flooding of the capital cities of Tokyo and Paris in 1910, this chapter also maintains that this river regime was not unique to Japan. Rather, it was an assemblage that articulated with the transnational movement of engineers, equipment, and ideas that were shaping local riparian assemblages and relations around the world by the early twentieth century. By being a part of this process, Japan's river regime belonged to a broader phenomenon that the historian Zvi Ben-Dor Benite has called "global modernity."[111]

---

110   Timothy Mitchell, "Society, Economy, and the State Effect," in *State/Culture: State-Formation after the Cultural Turn*, ed. George Steinmetz (Ithaca: Cornell University Press, 1999), 76–97; Aradhana Sharma and Akhil Gupta, "Introduction: Rethinking Theories of the State in an Age of Globalization," in *The Anthropology of the State: A Reader*, ed. Aradhana Sharma and Akhil Gupta (Malden: Blackwell, 2006), 1–41.

111   Zvi Ben-Dor Benite, "Modernity: The Sphinx and the Historian," *American Historical Review* 116, no. 3 (2011): 650–51.

PART 1

Regional River Regimes in the Tokugawa Period

∵

CHAPTER 1

Riparian Relations in the Kantō Region

6th month, 17th day: Before dawn, we went downstream. Later, south winds began blowing. Bone-breaking effort. [At] Ninoe, the timing of the tide was poor. Waited for evening. Entered the mouth of the river [Onagi Canal] and worked [the boat forward]. Made our way around the Naka River Checkpoint and entered Edo. Moored at Honjo Yotsume. Many boats ahead of us. Waited and stopped at the same place.

六月十七日：未明ゟ下り、後南風吹立骨折、二ノ江、汐時悪夕方待、川口入相働、中川番所相廻り江戸入、本所四ッめとまり。先々舟込合候ニ付、同所見合泊り。

HONDA KANOSUKE, *Kawajō fūu tomari nikki*[1]
誉田嘉之助、川條風雨泊り日記

∴

On 21 August 1853, the boat pilot Honda Kanosuke (dates unknown) and a pair of boatmen woke before dawn and quickly poled their large *takasebune* (*takase* riverboat) down the Edo River until a headwind began blowing in from the bay to the south. With the wind in their faces, Kanosuke recorded in his logbook that it was a "bone-breaking" (*honeori*) effort to work the boat down to the mouth of the Onagi Canal leading to Edo. When they finally arrived, many boats were already there. After waiting for the tide to ebb so their poles could touch bottom, Honda and the other boats slowly pushed their way past

---

1 This is the entry from the 6th year of Kaei, 6th month, 17th day (21 August 1853) in the logbook kept by the boat pilot Honda Kanosuke. Entitled *Daily Record of River Conditions, Wind and Rain Stops* (*Kawajō fūu tomari nikki*), this logbook is a rarity. Watanabe Hideo, the historian who found the logbook among the Honda family documents, believes it to be the only known record by a riverboat pilot in all of Japan. Watanabe has transcribed Kanosuke's logbook and published it along with detailed commentary. See Honda Kanosuke, "Kawajō fūu tomari nikki," in Watanabe Hideo, "Bakumatsu kawabune sendō no kōko nikki kara," in *Kinsei kōtsū no shiteki kenkyū*, ed. Maruyama Yasunari (Tokyo: Bunken Shuppan, 1998), 339–414.

fields and farmhouses and into the eastern suburbs of the sprawling metropolis of Edo (fig. 5).

Kanosuke's first stop in Edo was a lumberyard in Honjo near the Fourth Bridge (Yotsumebashi) over the Tate Canal. There he and his crew unloaded their portage of boards and moored their boat for the evening. Waking to a veil of mist the next morning, he and his crew made their way to the Mito-domain storehouses in Ko'ume where they unloaded their main cargo of 450 bales of rice. Having lightened their load, they proceeded to the domain's stone yard along the Sumida River, which locals often referred to as the Ōkawa, or "Big River." They spent much of the next two weeks there completing paperwork and loading goods for their return trip to the distant riverport of Kushibiki at the northern tip of what is today called Lake Kitaura in the former Mito domain in Hitachi Province (present-day Ibaraki Prefecture) (fig. 6). This roundtrip journey between Edo and Kushibiki took fifty-five days and was the longest of four such trips Kanosuke made between March and August in 1853.

Kanosuke's logbook is a rare document, but Kanosuke was not by any means a rare figure for his time. He records meetings with other riverboat pilots, lists dozens of riverside ports and wharves, and notes occasional floating bathhouses (*yubune*) that were notorious for their gambling and prostitution. In a country with almost no wheeled transport, it was boats that supplied cities like Edo with everything from soybeans and soy sauce to rice and, of course, sake. But where a river's water tends to flow in just one direction, these boat pilots used sail and "bone-breaking" labor to return upstream to the countryside with sacks of salt, sugar, seaweed, textiles, dried fish, and with all those empty barrels of soy sauce and sake. In the mid-nineteenth century, these boat pilots were not alone in their work with these rivers. Farmers in riverside villages throughout the eastern region of Kantō and beyond similarly built sturdy stone and timber sluices that they constantly maintained along with dense networks of irrigation canals in order to seasonally flood the region's paddy fields with their life-sustaining waters. When not tending these fields, many of these same farmers likewise fished and hunted in the region's plentiful rivers, river-fed lakes, and marshes. In other words, throughout the preindustrial Kantō region, and indeed the rest of Japan, rivers were central not only to the livelihoods of individual families and villages but also entire regional economies. And, because these rivers carried the bulk of the goods and tax-rice that passed into and out of the country's cities, this riparian infrastructure was equally critical to the ruling Tokugawa shogunate (1603–1868) and domain governments.

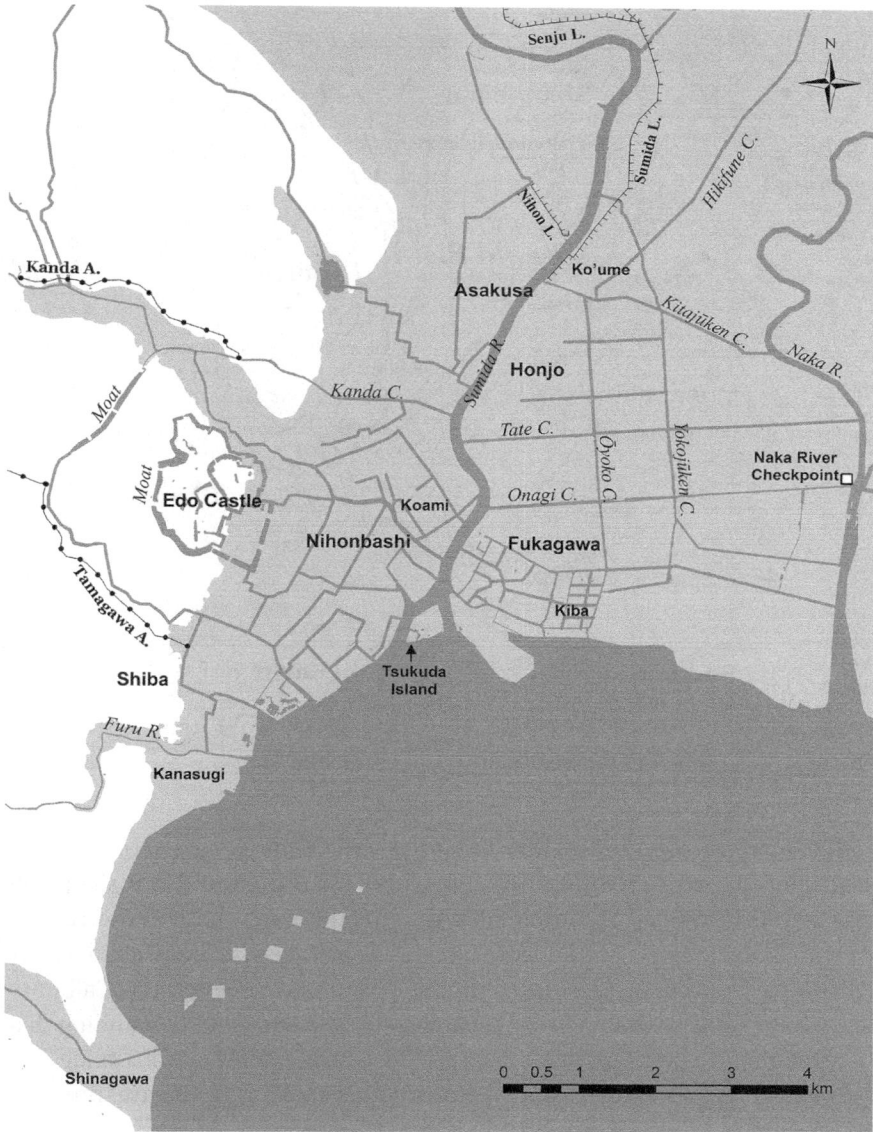

FIGURE 5   Map of Edo and its environs, c. 1855

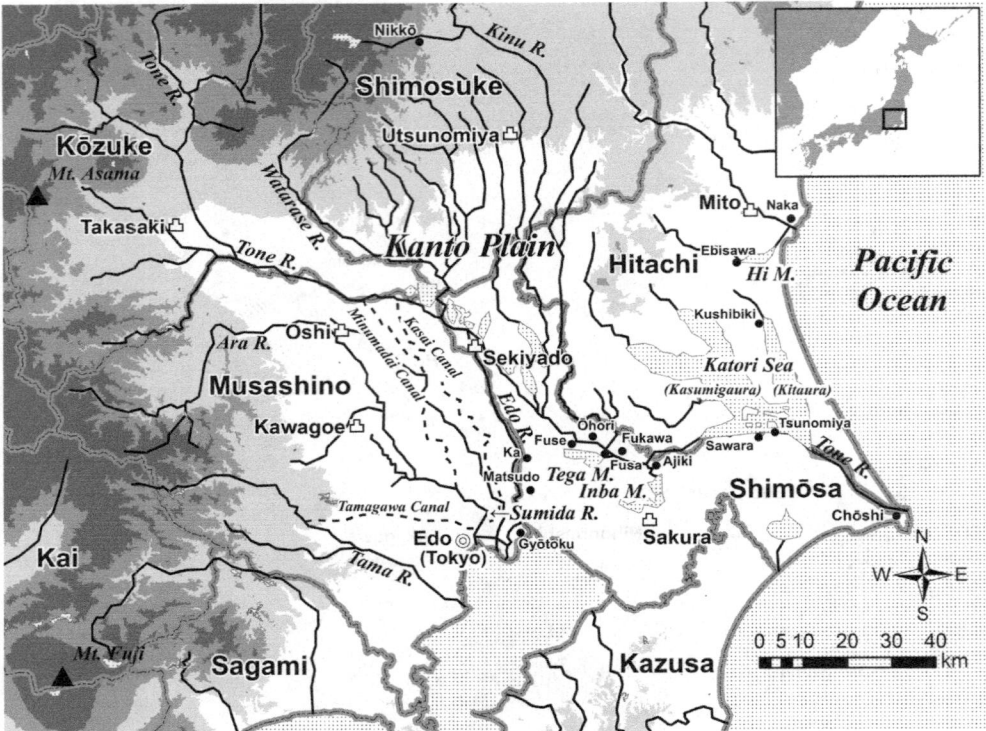

FIGURE 6   Map of the Kantō region and its rivers, c. 1750

Although receiving no mention in Kanosuke's logbook, just weeks earlier
that same summer on 8 July, two side-wheel steamships and two sloops-of-
war had also traveled a considerable distance to reach the waters near the
shogunal headquarters of Edo.[2] These vessels belonged to the United States'
East India Squadron, under the command of Commodore Matthew Calbraith
Perry (1794–1858), and had been dispatched to deliver a letter demanding that
the leaders of Japan sign a commercial treaty and open ports for trade and
supplies.[3] In reaction to the United States' request and show of naval prowess,

---

2   While Kanosuke's logbook is determinedly terse, it does note a few events aside from water
    and weather conditions, such as the departure of the coffin from Edo of the recently deceased
    shogun, Tokugawa Ieyoshi (1793–1853; r. 1837–53), and that all businesses, including boat and
    lighter services, were closed for the day. Entry for 6th month, 4th day on the intercalary cal-
    endar (6 September 1853).

3   Francis L. Hawks, *Narrative of the Expedition of an American Squadron to the China Seas and
    Japan: Performed in the Years 1852, 1853, and 1854, under the Command of Commodore M. C. Perry,
    United States Navy, By Order of the Government of the United States* (Washington, DC:

the Tokugawa leadership ordered the building of eleven stadium-sized battery islands (*daiba*) across the shallow bay that spread out before Edo and revived an earlier plan to dig an inland canal to connect the city to the Pacific Ocean via the Inba Marsh (Inbanuma).[4] By the time Perry and his flotilla returned to Japan in February of the following year, six-and-half of these emplacements had been completed, but the canal existed only on paper. Despite the enormous effort and cost invested in these batteries, they never fired upon a foreign ship. Instead, the shogun, Tokugawa Iesada (1824–58; r. 1853–58), and his advisors grudgingly agreed to the signing of the March 1854 Treaty of Kanagawa, the first of the treaties that began to entangle Japan in European modes of diplomatic relations.

For the captains and crews of both Kanosuke's riverboat and Perry's flotilla, the mid-nineteenth century was still an era of wood, wind, and water. The visit of the East India Squadron to the waters near Edo joined a cascade of other events that led in 1867 to the complete collapse of the Tokugawa government and ushered in the 1868 Meiji Restoration. These political changes had little immediate impact on riparian relations along the country's rivers. It was only at the end of the century that the new national government in Japan adopted a fundamentally different approach to the nation's waterways that no longer sought to balance the needs of small-time, but essential, users like boat pilots and fishers with the more propertied concerns of irrigation and flood control. Until the widespread mining of coal and large-scale international trade of the twentieth century, there were few resources as plentiful and valuable as water in Japan.

River water powered the textile and grain mills of highland villages and towns, where rivers spilled out of the surrounding mountains to meander across broad alluvial and coastal plains. Rivers supplied water to extensive irrigation systems that had been built over several centuries, helping to increase the production and harvest surpluses that had spurred commercial development in different regions.[5] These same rivers replenished downstream lakes, marshes,

A. O. P. Nicholson, 1856). For another perspective on the arrival of the US flotilla in Japan, see M. William Steele, "Goemon's New World View," in *Alternative Narratives in Modern Japanese History* (New York: Routledge Curzon, 2003), 4–18.

4 Tōkyō-to Minato-ku Kyōiku Iinkai, ed., *Daiba: naikai odaiba no kōzō to chikuzō* (Tokyo: Minato-ku Kyōdo Shiryōkan, 2000).

5 William W. Kelly, *Water Control in Tokugawa Japan: Irrigation Organization in a Japanese River Basin, 1600–1870* (Ithaca: Cornell University, 1982); Thomas C. Smith, *Agrarian Origins of Modern Japan* (Stanford: Stanford University Press, 1959); Ishizaki Masakazu, "Nōgyō no hatten to yōhai suiro no kaisaku," in *Kawa o seishita kindai gijutsu*, ed. Ōkuma Takashi (Tokyo: Heibonsha, 1994), 71–86.

and ponds, thereby sustaining the habitats of diverse species of waterfowl and
fish stocks upon which the region's hunters and fishers relied. And, it was boat
pilots like Honda Kanosuke who fed cities throughout the archipelago by delivering sacks of grain, tubs of miso paste, and other soy products from their surrounding countryside as well as fish, fishmeal, and various kinds of kelp and
laver from villages and towns along the sea.[6] In short, from mountain villages
and seaside towns to the large cities of Osaka, Kyoto, and Edo, all counted on
the flow of fresh water that supported their livelihoods. This intensive use and
dependence on rivers also meant these waterways required regular and costly
maintenance, without which irrigation canals silted up, floodworks crumbled,
and rivers, lakes, and bays grew shallow and impossible to navigate.

This focus on the flow of water through villages and the countryside encour-
ages the historian to cross a number of historiographical and epistemological
boundaries. Perhaps the most obvious boundary crossing is that into and out
of the village. In mid-nineteenth-century Japan, the vast majority of people—
at least 80 percent—lived in villages, which were administrative units and
totaled well over sixty thousand.[7] The concentration on villages and the
quotidian reality of rural commoners in this chapter avoids the tendency of
overstating the views and experiences of the better documented political and
cultural elites of the time and the problem of drawing conclusions about rural
life based on the writings of people who spent most of their lives in one of
the country's numerous cities. This emphasis on rural commoners shows that,
even while being labeled agricultural peasants (*hyakushō*), many like Honda
Kanosuke were also engaged in sailing, hunting, fishing, and other work.
Moreover, by following the flow of water through the countryside, it is clear
that villages were not as enclosed and "autonomous" as scholars participat-
ing in the long and vociferous "village community debate" (*sonraku kyōdōtai
ron*) once presumed.[8] Even within the same region, these villages exhibited

6 Tanji Kenzō, *Kinsei kōtsū unyu shi no kenkyū* (Tokyo: Yamakawa Kōbunkan, 1996); Gotō
   Masatoshi, *Kinsei gyogyō shakai kōzō no kenkyū* (Tokyo: Yamakawa Shuppansha, 2001), 21–67.
7 Mizumoto Kunihiko, *Mura: hyakushō tachi no kinsei* (Tokyo: Iwanami Shoten, 2015), iii.
8 The anthropologist Harumi Befu gave the definitive English-language articulation of this
   view of the autonomous village in his article "Village Autonomy and Articulation with the
   State," *The Journal of Asian Studies* 25, no. 1 (1965): 19–32. Overlooking the multiple ways in
   which commoners tapped into regional flows of water to produce and reproduce their livelihoods during the Tokugawa and Meiji periods, the activist and scholar Ui Jun offers another
   ahistorical view of village autonomy resulting in the persistence of a particularly feudalistic
   "village mentality." "In a historical perspective," he explains, "from the period of development of wetland rice farming in the seventeenth century, the single chronic condition facing
   society was a basic lack of water for this mode of production. In order to provide for their
   protection and to maintain control over water resources, people enclosed themselves within

considerable complexity, variety, and interaction with one another, with nearby towns, and with more distant cities. Observing this assumption in the scholarly literature about irrigation during this period of Japanese history, the anthropologist William W. Kelly argued four decades ago that, "a village perspective can prove limiting because most cultivators and most paddy lands in Tokugawa Japan were actually part of multivillage, multilevel networks of irrigation and drainage. The structures of water roles and rules represented an important supra-village, regional level of organization."[9] Similarly, the historian Kimura Motoi more broadly noted, "It is easy to take village life as being closed, but actually village life would not have developed without interactions beyond the village."[10] In this way, many scholars have long seen how villages during the Tokugawa period were embedded within their regions and beyond through cooperative organizations, legal norms, and the growth of commercial ties. Even when examining water flowing into and out of villages through regional rivers and irrigation systems, too few of these scholars have grasped the wider environmental relations upon which these villages were predicated.

Since the 1980s, historians of Japan have increasingly recognized the interconnected character of villages and expanded their research beyond rice farming to include fishing, forestry, and other forms of livelihood. Until recently, however, few have seldom investigated these topics with an eye on environmental issues. Despite giving attention to soil, rivers, fish, and forests, historians have typically done so with the aim of explaining the historical contexts of specific events, such as village disputes and agreements, or institutions, such as taxation and rural merchant associations. As described in the introductory chapter, most scholars who have offered descriptions of rural life and local environments in premodern Japan have consciously and unconsciously tended to write these histories from a progressive, declensionist, or contextualist perspective. Unlike the people they write about, these scholars often assume a clear ontological distinction between humans and a singular nature and use this binary to structure their narratives.

In eschewing this modern dualism or positing a hybrid of it, this chapter argues for writing rivers and their life-giving waters back into the lives and livelihoods of rural commoners and doing so from an alternative approach. It focuses on the riparian relations that emerged along the waters of the Kantō

---

tightly knit and convoluted community structures. This resulting village mentality was skillfully manipulated and used as a means of social control from the Tokugawa period up to and including the period of modernization." Ui Jun, *Industrial Pollution in Japan* (Tokyo: United Nations University, 1992), 4.

9   Kelly, *Water Control in Tokugawa Japan*, 13–14.

10   Kimura Motoi, *Mura no kataru Nihon no rekishi* (Tokyo: Soshiete, 1983), 2:178.

region and constantly changed through the regular routines of boat pilots like Honda Kanosuke and others, including farmers and fishers. By beginning with people's everyday interactions with the Tone River and other bodies of water, and by not subsuming these entities into the modern category of nature, this chapter emphasizes how these people's lifeworlds were created through the daily, seasonal, and annual work involved in fishing, irrigating fields, and sailing between riverports. After all, it was largely their labor—their constant turning of soil, planting and harvesting crops, toiling in the waters, cutting of grass and brush, the building, extension, and repair of levees and irrigation networks—and the workings of water, sediment, plants, and other entities that generated and sustained their lives and the landscapes through which the Tone River coursed. Moreover, because these waters flowed and these people moved around, the fluvial activity of both proved instrumental in the formation of the Kantō region. In this way, village life in the Kantō and across the rest of the archipelago during this time was predicated on a complex tangle of local and regional environmental relations.

This attention to the quotidian role of waters in the making of the Kantō region and people's livelihoods also serves to take one across ontological and epistemological boundaries that have led many a historian to write of humans as separate from the environments within which they lived. To preclude the standard storyline by which histories often begin, one that places rivers within a passive geographical or environmental background in order to later foreground a more active history of humans, the first section begins by demonstrating how riverine and human activities together produced the Kantō region through which Kanosuke and his crew traveled in the mid-nineteenth century.[11] Having established how these riparian relations were *co-constituted* and *coeval*, this section next provides general information that is pertinent for understanding how factors like slope, seasons, soil, temperature, and precipitation influenced the formation, maintenance, and dissolution of riparian assemblages in the Kantō and elsewhere on the archipelago. Delving into specific riparian assemblages, the second section explores the riparian relations

---

11   As touched on in the introductory chapter, I argue that places like the Kantō region are produced by the combined activities of the objects, artifacts, humans, and other creatures that constitute discrete environmental relations. A place is not, as is often assumed, a point in a preexisting, infinite, and universal Cartesian space. A place is necessarily relational. It is bound or limited by the extent of the relations that are internal to and create it and those relations that are external to it and create other exterior places. Finally, a place is historical in that it is an event with a beginning and an ending. In this sense it is constantly changing along with the environmental relations through which it is constituted. This understanding of place draws on a number of writings, but especially Henri Lefebvre, *The Production of Space* (Cambridge: Blackwell, 1991); Jeff Malpas, *Heidegger's Topology: Being, Place, and World* (Cambridge: MIT Press, 2006).

established through riverboat transport and to a lesser degree freshwater fishing and irrigated farming. It highlights the relations formed through these commonplace activities, thereby showing how the everyday activity of work was a central means by which rural commoners participated in these disparate riparian relations and is suggestive of how agency was distributive and differentiated within these riparian assemblages.

1 Producing the Kantō Region and Its Riverscapes during the Seventeenth Century

1.1 *The Shifting Riverscapes of the Lower Tone River*

Well before Tokugawa Ieyasu (1543–1616; r. 1603–5) chose Edo as his headquarters in 1590, the encompassing Kantō region had a long history in literature and as an administrative territory.[12] Also referred to as Bandō in ancient and medieval times, the area was typically defined as a region composed of the eight provinces east of the gate at the Usui Pass along the mountainous 534 km highway, the Nakasendō.[13] While these earlier regional and provincial identities and boundaries continued beyond the medieval period, the direct control over the entire Kantō by the Tokugawa, the rapid construction and growth of the city of Edo, the increased settlement and reclamation throughout its hinterland, and the deepening commercial integration contributed to other processes of regional cohesion.[14] Flowing through all of these changes were the rivers upon which Edo, its hinterland, and the commerce that bound them together so depended. In fact, an emphasis on riparian relations reminds us that, until the centralizing efforts at national development in the modern period, rivers had an important place in shaping, but in no way determining, the geographies of the Kinai region in western Japan and the Kantō region in eastern Japan that

---

12   David Spafford, *A Sense of Place: The Political Landscape in Late Medieval Japan*, Harvard East Asian Monographs 361 (Cambridge: Harvard University Asia Center, 2013).

13   The Usui Barrier (*Usui sekisho*) is located in present-day Gunma Prefecture and the eight provinces to the east of it were Sagami, Musashi, Kōzuke, Shimotsuke, Hitachi, Shimōsa, Kazusa, and Awa. David Spafford points out that occasionally the peninsular Izu Province was also included in medieval configurations of the Kantō, thereby bringing the total to nine provinces. Spafford, *A Sense of Place*, 4.

14   Kären Wigen has thought more than most historians or geographers of Japan about the various meanings of region, suggesting that the region is a "fluid" concept that is less "product" or result than it is an ongoing "process." Similarly, I define the Kantō as a region less for its formal boundaries and more by the different historical processes and relations that held it together and gave it a distinctive character vis-à-vis other regions. Kären Wigen, "Culture, Power, and Place: The New Landscapes of East Asian Regionalism," *American Historical Review* 104, no. 4 (1999): 1198.

are the focus of this book. Moreover, the geographical extent of most people's lives in the Kantō often lay between the local villages and towns in which they called home and the regional transport, irrigation, mercantile, and other organizations within which they eked out their livelihoods.[15] In this sense, the nineteenth-century Kantō through which the boat pilot Kanosuke sailed was the coeval product of complex interactions between the Tokugawa regime and its retainers, the activities of commoners, and the region's rivers. Rather than start with the all too common narrative structure of describing the geography and environment of a place as the passive stage upon which the real drama of a human-centered history unfolds, this section begins by highlighting how seemingly distinct natural and social processes are better understood as being inextricably entwined environmental relations that helped produce the Kantō region during the Tokugawa period.

During his journeys to and from Edo, Kanosuke frequently commented on the changing winds and shifting shoals as he and his crew worked their boat from port to port along the lower Tone River where it branched into several streams and became indistinguishable from what is today called Lake Kasumigaura. Nearly two centuries earlier in the 1670s, this same shifting riverscape had contributed to a dispute between Sawara and Shinowara Villages and the downstream village of Tsunomiya. The disagreement stemmed from competing demands to fish the river and farm recently formed islands in the Tone. The headmen of the upstream villages cited a 1655 agreement for the river in front of the three villages to be fished as a commons, while Tsunomiya asserted they alone had a rights to the fishery. Similarly, the three villages had opposing assertions on paper and in the form of fields and paddy land on the islands emerging in the middle of the river. By 1678, two more villages downstream had joined the fray, claiming rights to land and water. The situation clearly had become quite vociferous because, rather than settle their differences among themselves, the local Tokugawa official was compelled to investigate and adjudicate the dispute.[16] The official's initial concern seems to have

15   Rivers were limited by the topographical regions through which they flowed, but people moved both literally and imaginatively beyond the often blurry boundaries that defined these regions. Many historians have acknowledged the strength of these local and regional ties and identities but in recent years have also explored the extent to which people experienced and expressed a protonational identity. See, for example, Mary Elizabeth Berry, *Japan in Print: Information and Nation in the Early Modern Period*, Asia: Local Studies/Global Themes 12 (Berkeley: University of California Press, 2006); Ronald P. Toby, *Engaging the Other: "Japan" and Its Alter-Egos, 1550–1850*, Brill's Japanese Studies Library 65 (Leiden: Brill, 2019).
16   "Shinshima-ryō iriai gijō torikae washi shōmon" [1655], in *Chiba-ken no rekishi: shiryō hen, kinsei*, ed. Chiba-ken Shiryō Kenkyū Zaidan (Chiba: Chiba-ken, 2004), 5:492; "Sawara, Shinowara, Tsunomiya shinsu iriai sōron saikyo-jō" and "Ōkura-mura, Yōrogo-mura,

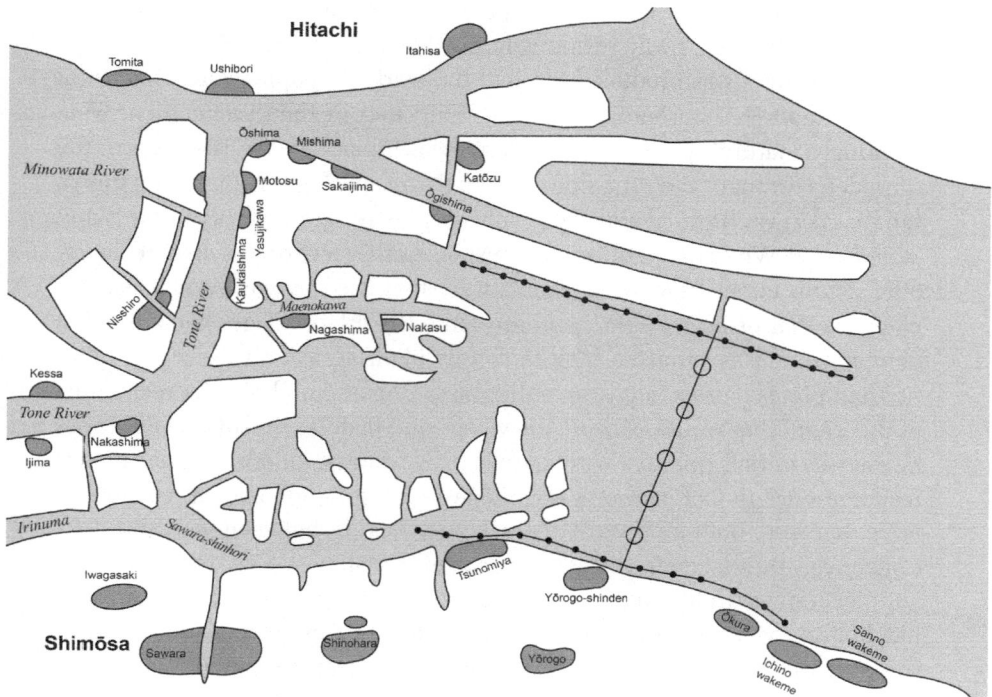

FIGURE 7   Map of boundaries between Tsunomiya's fishery and fields and those
of neighboring villages in 1678. Based on "Ōkura-mura, Yōrogo-mura,
Tsunomiya-mura jizakai umizakai saikyo ezu" [Map of Land and Sea Boundaries
for Ōkura, Yōrogo, and Tsunomiya Villages] (1678). In the Inō family documents,
National Museum of Japanese History, Sakura

been that new land was being cultivated and not included in the taxes of one of
the villages. In the end, the official found that no taxes were being avoided, but
reaffirmed the villages' obligations to submit taxes in exchange for the right to
fish the river.[17] He also drew up a detailed map that indicated the boundaries
of all of the surrounding villages and ordered the pounding of poles into the
riverbed to mark the extent of Tsunomiya's fishery (fig. 7).[18]

Tsunomiya-mura jizakai unasaka sōron saikyo ezu" [1678], in *Chiba-ken no rekishi: shiryō
hen, kinsei*, ed. Chiba-ken Shiryō Kenkyū Zaidan (Chiba: Chiba-ken, 2005), 6:225–27.

17   The following two articles use the documents produced from this incident to explain how
the Tokugawa's system of taxation worked along the lower Tone River: Hara Junji, "Kinsei
zenki Tonegawa ryūiki no gyogyō," *Umikami-chō shi kenkyū*, no. 31 (1990): 1–25; Gotō
Masatoshi, "Shōtoku-Kyōhō-ki ni okeru shimo-Tonegawa chū-ryūiki no gyogyō to muramura," *Kokuritsu rekishi minzoku hakubutsukan kenkyū hōkoku*, no. 115 (2004): 161–76.

18   "Ōkura-mura, Yōrogo-mura, Tsunomiya-mura jizakai unasaka sōron saikyo ezu" [1678], in
Chiba-ken no rekishi: shiryō hen, kinsei, 6: frontispiece and 228–29.

   This late seventeenth-century dispute provides us with one of the earliest maps of the area's waters and is indicative of how the Kantō's riverscape
during this time was produced through the work of people *within* their local
environments.[19] The islands that lay at the center of the disagreement were
seemingly "natural" phenomena, emerging at a place in the river where the
silt-laden current of the Tone slowed enough to deposit grain after grain until a
sandbar (*su*) was formed and eventually became recognizable as a new island
(*shinjima*).[20] While the petitions and responses that record this dispute do not
offer details about how these islands were first used by local residents, it is
plausible that peasants from Tsunomiya and the other villages had a hand in
helping "nature" secure the island's soil by planting it with reeds and other
riparian plants. For example, an earlier 1640 document about the reclaiming
of the island that would become the village and paddies of Isoyama describes
how it was initially planted with cattails to dry out the land in preparation for
reclamation.[21] In fact, Isoyama was the last of a group of sixteen "island" villages that were built atop similarly reclaimed islands between 1590 and 1640.
Collectively these sixteen villages were called the "Sixteen-Island Reclamation"
(Jūrokushima-shinden) and were largely settled by people from Sawara and
neighboring villages on the southern bank of the Tone.[22] The sum effect of
these riparian activities was the extension of the river through the formation
of a north bank where previously its waters had gently flowed through brackish tidelands into what at the time was called the Katori Sea (Katori no umi) or

---

19   The term "riverscape" derives from the following two articles: Kurt D. Fausch, Christian E.
      Torgersen, Colden V. Baxter, and Hiram W. Li, "Landscapes to Riverscapes: Bridging the
      Gap between Research and Conservation of Stream Fishes," *Bioscience* 52, no. 6 (2002):
      483–98; J. V. Ward, "Riverine Landscapes: Biodiversity Patterns, Disturbance Regimes, and
      Aquatic Conservation," *Biological Conservation* 83, no. 3 (1998): 269–78.
20   In describing different stretches of the Tone River, the geographer Koide Haku explains
      that the gradient of the river near its headwaters is as steep as 1/140, but at the lower
      reaches near Lake Kasumigaura it flattens to about 1/4350. Koide Haku, *Nihon no kasen
      kenkyū: chiikisei to kobetsusei* (Tokyo: Tōkyō Daigaku Shuppankai, 1972), 12.
21   Sawara Shiyakusho, ed., *Sawara-shi shi* (Sawara: Sawara Shiyakusho, 1966), 168.
22   The first of these reclaimed islands was the furthest upstream and called Kaminoshima. In
      1590, Tokugawa Ieyasu himself had granted his retainer Yoshida Satarō (dates unknown)
      the right to reclaim the island as a means of extending Tokugawa influence along the
      riparian border they shared with the powerful Satake family who were based just to
      the north in Hitachi Province. In addition to these reclamation projects, in 1626–27 an
      effort to dredge a channel through these marshy tidelands was also carried out in front of
      Kōzaki Village and further downstream in front of Tsunomiya and Ōkura Villages. Sawara
      Shiyakusho, *Sawara-shi shi*, 162–63.

Inner Sea (Uchi no umi).[23] Thus, in their endeavor to eke out and even improve their lives, these villagers were agents in the shaping of the very riverscape itself by engaging with sandbars, plants, fish, and the river. While this is a local example of the work of rural commoners to enlarge their village acreage and fisheries, elsewhere on the Kantō Plain in the early seventeenth century those with greater power and resources under their command also interacted with the Tone and other rivers in ways that led to even more profound changes to the riverscapes of the Kantō region.

During much of the first half of the seventeenth century, in fact, the Tokugawa regime expended much effort in transforming riverscapes throughout the Kantō region. The most notable of these many riparian projects was the moving of the middle and lower Tone River away from its historic southward channel into the bay near Edo to a new eastward channel that flowed into the Katori Sea and from there into the Pacific Ocean, where it continues to flow to this day. Just as with the late sixteenth-century changes to the Uji and other rivers of the Kinai region that are mentioned in the introductory chapter, the shifting of rivers in the Kantō region also started in an area of marshy, floodprone bottomlands. In this case, those bottomlands were formed at the confluence of the Tone and Watarase Rivers, which was the Tone's largest tributary and one of the Kantō region's bigger rivers (fig. 8).[24] From 1594, a vassal of the lord of nearby Oshi Castle began mobilizing peasants and materials to build a sizable 33 km long levee across a shallow valley where the Tone branched into two channels close to Honkawamata Village (present-day Hanyū City, Saitama Prefecture), thereby blocking the main channel, the Old Tone River (Furu-Tonegawa), and sending all of the river's waters to the east via the minor channel.[25] It was about this same time and further upstream where the Tone

---

23   The historian David Bello has similarly shown how these "interactions" between the Yangzi River, peasants, and Qing government officials played a decisive, if not contradictory, role in creating the "intermittent order" of the river's delta region. David Bello, "An Intermittent Order: Contrived on Sand: Managing Water, Siltage, Locusts, and Cultivators on the Lower Yangzi in the Early 1800s," in "Grassroots History: Global Environmental Histories from Below," ed. Robert Michael Morrissey and Roderick I. Wilson, special issue, *Resilience: A Journal of the Environmental Humanities* 3 (2016): 14–33.

24   Koide Haku notes that this area also has one of the lowest gradients (1/3040) for the entire Tone River. Koide, *Nihon no kasen kenkyū*, 11.

25   Compiled between 1810 and 1830, the provincial gazetteer *Shinpen Musashi fudokikō* explained that the levee running along this portion of the southern bank of the Tone River was 2 *jō* (6 m) in height. Ashida Koreto et al., eds., *Shinpen Musashi fudokikō* (Tokyo: Yūsankaku, 1996), 11:48; Koide, *Nihon no kasen kenkyū*, 46–48; Ōkuma Takashi, *Tonegawa chisui no hensen to suigai* (Tokyo: Tōkyō Daigaku Shuppankai, 1981), 5–7, 11–13; Tonegawa Hyaku-nen Shi Hensan Iinkai, ed., *Tonegawa hyaku-nen shi* (Tokyo: Kokudo Kaihatsu

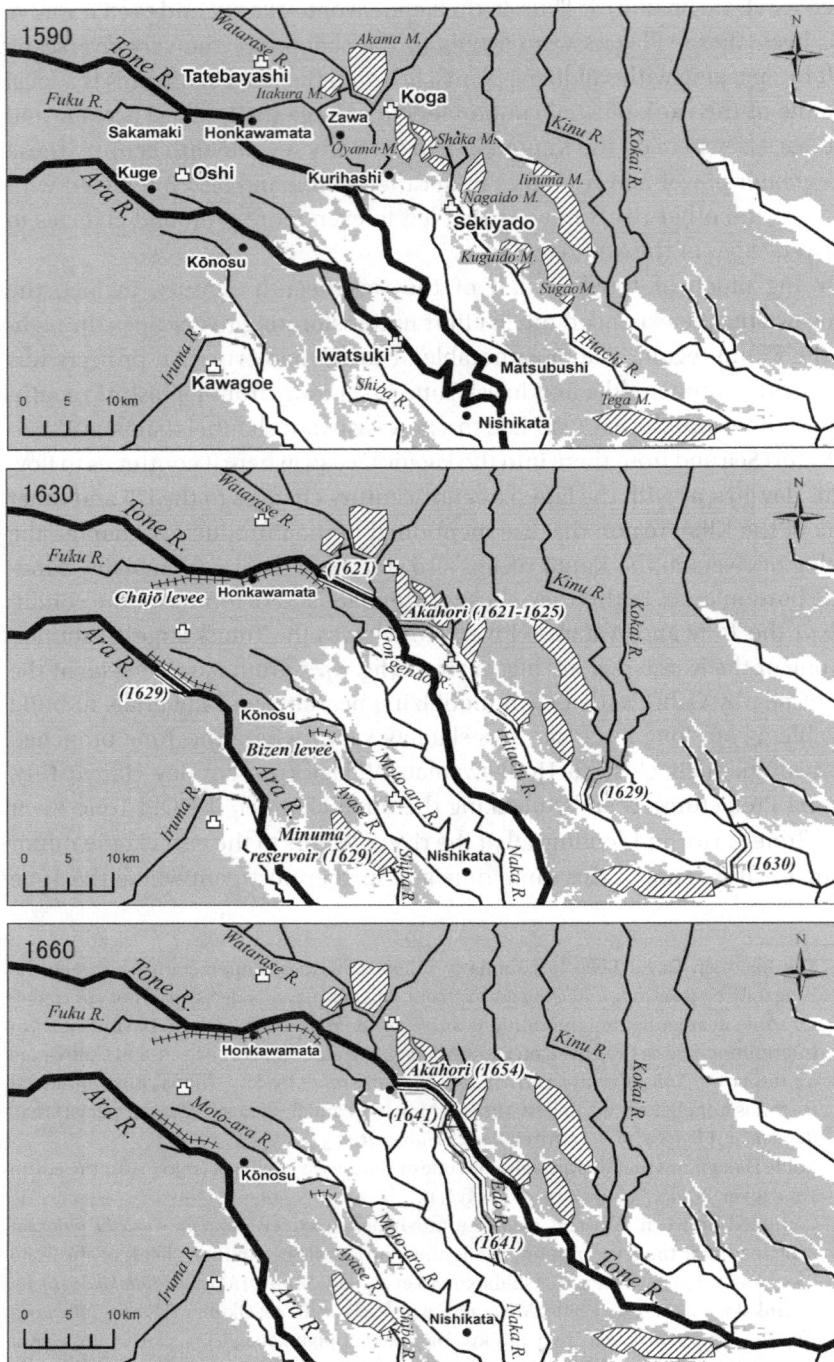

FIGURE 8   Map of seventeenth-century diversions along the Tone and Ara Rivers

River narrowed to just 400 m between Sakamaki and Sedoi Villages that the same castle lord also ordered the construction of the lengthy Chūjō Levee, which forced floodwaters to back up and spread out along the floodplains of the Tone and Fuku Rivers before entering the bottomlands of the middle Tone.[26] In 1621, Ina Tadaharu (1592–1653), the head intendant (*daikan-gashira*) of the area, initiated the next major project that again diverted the Tone to the east by overseeing the excavation of a new river channel from near Zawa Village across the marshy area where the Watarase River flowed into the Tone (the neighboring post town of Kurihashi would be established soon after in 1624) to the north of the medieval castle town of Sekiyado.[27] Unlike previous engineering works that utilized the river's own older channels to divert the Tone, this 13 m wide channel included an 8 km long portion called the Akahori, which cut across the low watershed that until then had separated the Tone-Watarase River basin from the rivers of Hitachi Province.[28] The Akahori was meant to channel the Tone into what was then known as the Hitachi River, which in that area was a slow-draining waterway that connected the southern ends of the fingerlike marshes (*numa*) of Ōyama, Shaka, Mitsukai, Nagaido, Kuguido, and Sugao Marshes.[29] Instead of allowing itself to be rerouted to the east, the Tone continued its southward flow into the Gongendō River and on occasion is recorded to have overflown its banks and inundated the surrounding bottomlands. Thereafter, Ina Tadaharu and later his son Tadakatsu (1617–65) oversaw several projects to better control the river. This involved widening and deepening the Akahori, digging new side channels, blocking the old channel of the Watarase River (present-day Nakagawa, or Naka River), and excavating another southward channel that was subsequently named the Edo River. It was not

Gijutsu Kenkyū Sentā, 1987), 309–10; Ōtani Sadao, *Edo bakufu chisui seisaku no kenkyū*, 271–73; Hashimoto Naoko, *Kōchi kaihatsu to keikan no shizen kankyōgaku Tonegawa ryūiki no kinsei kankyō o chūshin ni* (Tokyo: Kokin Shoin, 2010), 59–60; Matsuura Shigeki, *Tonegawa kingendai shi* (Tokyo: Kokon Shoin, 2016), 408–10.

26   Gradually lengthened and heightened over the years, the Chūjō Levee at Sakamaki was about 1 *jō* (3 m) in height according to the *Shinpen Musashi fudokikō*. Ashida, *Shinpen Musashi fudokikō*, 11:54–55; Ōkuma, *Tonegawa chisui*, 14–15; Tonegawa Hyaku-nen Shi Hensan Iinkai, *Tonegawa hyaku-nen shi*, 310.

27   Ashida, *Shinpen Musashi fudokikō*, 10:273, 2:218; Koide, *Nihon no kasen kenkyū*, 48–50; Ōkuma, *Tonegawa chisui*, 15–20; Tonegawa Hyaku-nen Shi Hensan Iinkai, *Tonegawa hyaku-nen shi*, 310–12, 326–31; Ōtani, *Edo bakufu chisui seisaku*, 273–77; Hashimoto, *Kōchi kaihatsu to keikan*, 60–61; Matsuura, *Tonegawa kingendai shi*, 412–16.

28   The Akahori apparently acquired its name from the thick layer of red (*aka*) loam through which the channel was cut. Tonegawa Hyaku-nen Shi Hensan Iinkai, *Tonegawa hyaku-nen shi*, 310–11.

29   Following the Home Ministry's reengineering of the Tone River in the 1910s, all but the Sugao Marsh were drained and transformed into rice paddies by the early 1940s.

until 1654 and a third round of widening and deepening the Akahori to nearly 50 m that most of the Tone River's water could reliably flow eastward toward the Katori Sea.[30] The massive, decades-long undertaking that rechanneled the archipelago's most voluminous river into what was during that period likely a more brackish Katori Sea therefore aided in producing the freshwater fisheries and islands over which Tsunomiya and its neighboring villages argued a few decades later. This reconfigured river system also enabled Kanosuke to sail his riverboat between Edo and Mito domain two centuries later. The shifting of the Tone River was certainly one of the most ambitious undertakings in the Kantō region during the Tokugawa period, but it was repeated time and again on a smaller scale with the region's other rivers.

Elsewhere throughout the Kantō region, Tokugawa government administered a variety of river excavation, diversion, and levee-building projects. In Hitachi Province between 1624 and 1643, the Kinu River was rerouted such that it flowed directly into the Hitachi River instead of first pouring into the Kokai River, which was moved in 1630 to join the Hitachi River further downstream.[31] More important to the nascent Tokugawa regime, however, were riparian projects undertaken in Musashi Province around the quickly expanding city of Edo. In 1629, it is believed that Ina Tadaharu ordered the diversion of the Ara River, the region's second largest river, away from its channel on the Saitama highlands where it flowed close to the Tone River.[32] As with the initial efforts to redirect the Tone, the Ara was altered from its former course by excavating a channel that led the river into an existing river channel. In order to prevent the Ara from reverting to its old channel during the next flood, a sizable 10 km long levee was constructed near Kuge Village across this previous channel and along its north bank.[33] After rechanneling the Ara so that it merged with the Iruma River, the now more voluminous river traveled southward and around what was then the northern and eastern limits of Edo where it was known as the Sumida River. To protect the city from the Ara's flooding, the Nihon Levee (Nihon-zutsumi), an imposing earthen embankment of 1.5 km in length, was constructed just to the north of the temple complex of Sensōji in

---

30   Beside regular dredging and levee repair, little additional work was done on the Akahori until 1809 when it was widened to about 72 m (40 *ken*). Ōkuma, *Tonegawa chisui*, 30–32; Tonegawa Hyaku-nen Shi Hensan Iinkai, *Tonegawa hyaku-nen shi*, 311–12, 326; Hashimoto, *Kōchi kaihatsu to keikan*, 61–63.

31   Ōkuma, *Tonegawa*, 21–25; Tonegawa Hyaku-nen Shi Hensan Iinkai, *Tonegawa hyaku-nen shi*, 313–15.

32   Koide, *Nihon no kasen kenkyū*, 58–62; Ōkuma, *Tonegawa chisui*, 25–26; Matsuura Shigeki, *Kokudo no kaihatsu to kasen: jōrisei kara damu kaihatsu made* (Tokyo: Kashima Shuppankai, 1989), 63–65; Saitama-ken, ed., *Arakawa* (Urawa: Saitama-ken, 1987), 2:368.

33   Matsuura, *Kokudo no kaihatsu to kasen*, 63–66.

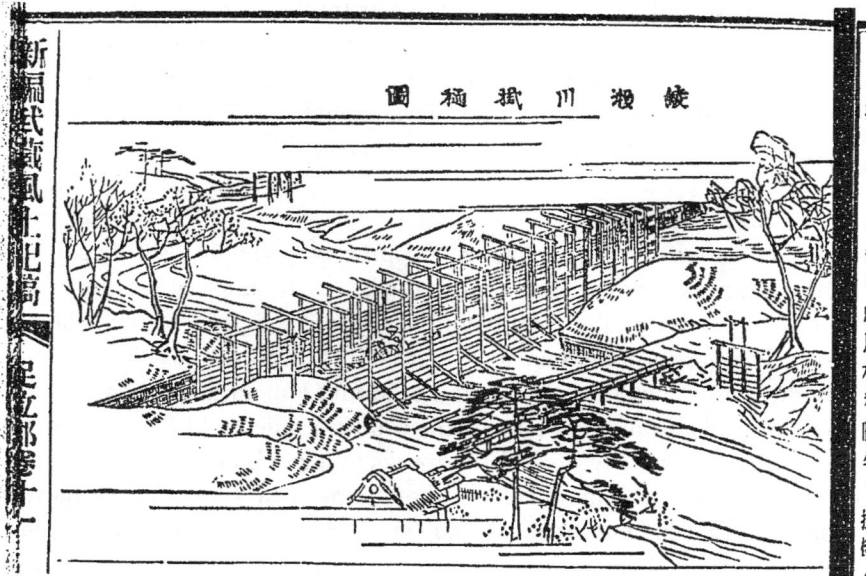

FIGURE 9   Early nineteenth-century illustration of the Minumadai Canal where it crosses
over the Ayase River in Kami-Kawarabuki Village. In *Shinpen Musashi fudokikō*
(Tokyo: Naimushō, 1884), 19
COURTESY OF THE NATIONAL DIET LIBRARY, TOKYO

the Asakusa area of the city.[34] In the same year that the Ara River was rerouted into the Iruma River channel, Tadaharu also ordered the building of the 870 m Hacchō Embankment across the Shiba River to transform the marshy areas along the river into the single 1,200 ha Minuma Reservoir (Minuma Tamei), which he apparently hoped would provide water for irrigation to the surrounding lands.[35] Beginning just south of the well-known Bizen Levee, the Ayase River was redirected at two points during the seventeenth century in order that this smaller but important river would flow into the new channel of the Ara just where the larger river turned southward along the eastern edge of Edo and into the bay (fig. 9).[36] The Ina intendants and other officials were able to

34   There was little need to extend the Nihon Levee further down the western bank of the Sumida because over the centuries the river had built up a natural levee. Tōkyō Shiyakusho, ed. *Tōkyō-shi shikō: shigai hen* (Tokyo: Tōkyō-shi, 1928), 4:54–59.
35   Minumadai Yōsui Tochi Kairyō-ku, ed., *Minumadai Yōsui enkakushi* (Urawa: Minumadai Yōsui Tochi Kairyō-ku, 1957), 77–78; H. I. H. Crown Prince Naruhito [Emperor Reiwa], "Edo and Water," in *Asia and the History of the International Economy: Essays in Memory of Peter Mathias*, ed. A. J. H. Latham and Heita Kawakatsu (New York: Routledge, 2018), 42.
36   The Ayase is believed to be the original lower channel of the Ara River before the Ara (later named the Moto-Ara River) was diverted to the east sometime during the Keichō

carry out these and many other river projects throughout the region because of developments in engineering technologies during the decades of warfare in the sixteenth century and the Tokugawa's consolidation of political authority in the early seventeenth century. But these intendants also relied on the historic and continuing fluvial work of the rivers themselves.

1.2   *The Role of Rivers*

Rivers and other nonhuman agents and processes significantly shaped the Kantō region as a whole and the particular environmental relations that emerged there during the seventeenth century. The Japanese archipelago is essentially a massive mountain range rising out of the western Pacific to a maximum height of 3,776 m at the summit of Mount Fuji, located just southwest of the Kantō Plain. Soaring alongside the country's tallest and most celebrated mountain are nearly two dozen other peaks that reach heights of over 3,000 m. Together these and hundreds of other shorter peaks form a long narrow archipelago that extends for about 3,500 km from north to south. At its widest point the biggest island, Honshū, is only 300 km across. Thus, compared with the size of continental rivers like the Huanghe (Yellow), Indus, Nile, Rhône, Rhine, or Mississippi, Japan's rivers may appear diminutive. But what they lack in length and volume, the Tone and other rivers of the archipelago make up for in speed—that is, Japan's rivers typically cover the same drop in elevation as these longer continental cousins, but do so in much less distance and therefore time (fig. 10).

With its headwaters high in the Mikuni Mountains, the 322 km Tone River descends from an elevation of over 1,800 m to 100 m near Takasaki City in just 130 km.[37] The Tone's 814 tributaries create a catchment area of 16,840 sq km, accounting for the most water of any river system on the archipelago.[38] Nonetheless, many of its fluvial features are characteristic of central Honshū's other primary rivers. For example, the 173 km Ara River has 127 tributaries in a drainage area of 2,940 sq km, and falls from an elevation of about 2,200 m to 100 m in a mere 55 km. Running along the southern edge of the Kantō Plain,

---

era (1596–1614) with digging of a short diversion canal and the building of the Bizen Levee. Ashida, *Shinpen Musashi fudokikō*, 7:346; Saitama-ken, *Arakawa*, 2: 368–70.

37   The gradient of the Tone over this distance changes from 1/140 to 1/400. Based on data published by the Water and Disaster Management Bureau, Ministry of Land, Infrastructure, Transport, and Tourism. Kokudo kōtsūshō. "Nihon no kawa: zenkoku no ikkyū kasen o shōkai," http://www.mlit.go.jp/river/toukei_chousa/kasen/jiten/nihon_kawa/index.html, accessed 19 August 2018.

38   The longest river on the archipelago is the 367 km long Shinano River (this includes 214 km Chikuma River that forms the upper Shinano) has a drainage area of 11,900 sq km. Its headwaters are just across the watershed from the Ara River at about 2,200 m, and it drops to 100 m elevation in about 240 km.

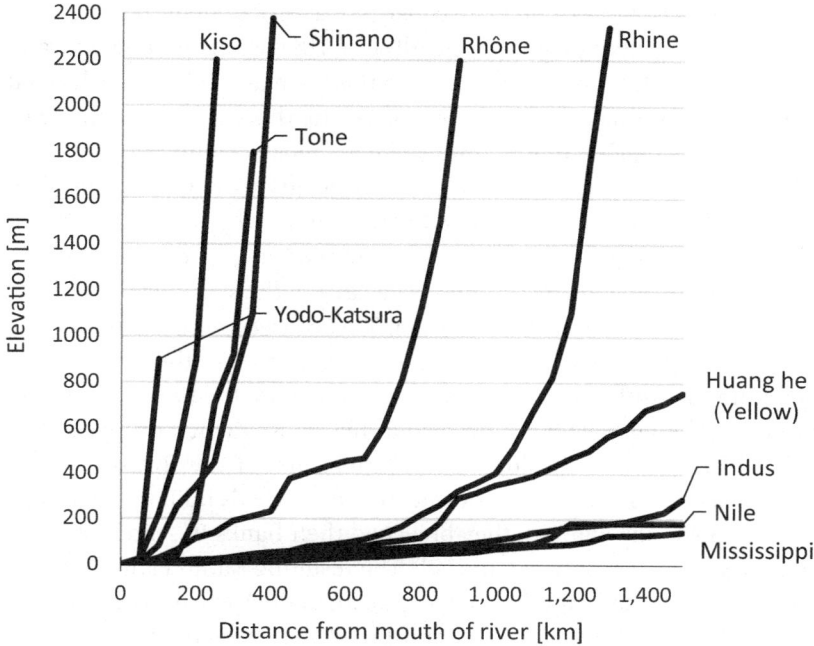

FIGURE 10   Comparison of river elevations and lengths

the Tama River is 138 km long, has a drainage area of 1,240 sq km, and descends from an elevation of more than 1,900 m to 100 m within 90 km. Although the mountains and main rivers of the Kinai region are considerably shorter than those of the Kantō region, the 114 km Katsura River, which is one of the Yodo's biggest tributaries, still has forty-seven tributaries in a drainage area of 1,100 sq km and falls from 900 m to 100 m in just 70 km.[39] In carving deep mountain valleys and building alluvial plains, these rivers have been an integral part of the geological processes that have been inexorably eroding and moving these mountains onto the Kantō and Osaka Plains.

Despite being surrounded by tall mountain ranges with peaks of over 3,000 m elevation, the vast Kantō Plain is the dominant feature of the region. It spreads west to east for over 17,000 sq km and is easily the archipelago's largest such lowland.[40] Formed over several millennia through the geological activity of rising tectonic plates, erupting volcanos, blowing wind, and flowing rivers,

---

39   The more mountainous 229 km long Kiso River has a drainage area of 5,275 sq km and drops from over 2,200 to 100 m over the course of 150 km.

40   The Kantō is much more expansive than the Osaka Plain, which covers an area of about 1,600 sq km, and the centrally located Nobi Plain, which is covers about 1,800 sq km. On the northern island of Hokkaidō, the Ishikari Plain is the archipelago's second biggest plain at about 4,000 sq km.

much of the surface of the Kantō Plain consists of a thick layer of volcanic loam that in many areas is over 30 m in depth. All across the plain, the Tone, Ara, and other rivers have etched shallow valleys into this loam and subsequently filled them with alluvial sediment. These rivers picked up this sediment as they cascaded through the region's mountains, which are mostly composed of granite and other kinds of igneous rock and covered to varying degrees in residual soils.[41] While dense forest canopies and other ground vegetation can absorb rainfall and hold this soil in place, a long history of logging trees for lumber and charcoal in the region's mountains, especially in the seventeenth and late nineteenth centuries, exacerbated erosion. This caused these rivers to carry heavy loads of silt and sediment downstream.[42] But once these waterways emerged from the confines of the mountain valleys onto the Kantō Plain, they quickly widened, their velocity slowed, and they consequently dropped their suspended load of sediment along these flatter parts of the riverbed. If not regularly dredged or scoured by floodwaters, the riverbeds built up over time, and where topography allowed, they breached their banks in search of lower ground to begin forming new channels.[43] The resulting Kantō Plain therefore resembles less a flat mathematical plane than an undulating landscape of low hills, small plateaus, shallow valleys, and broad bottomlands. More than in the lightly populated mountain valleys near the headwaters of the Tone, Ara, Tama, and other rivers of the region, it is on the Kantō Plain where much of this area's riparian history has occurred, and it is on these stretches of the river that the remainder of this chapter focuses.

1.3   *The Role of Riparian Assemblages*

This long history and its seemingly natural contours, boundaries, and integration along riparian corridors notwithstanding, the Kantō is more than a region defined by its physical geography. From the seventeenth century onward,

---

41   The archipelago is geologically young, volcanically active, and frequented by earthquakes. These geological factors together contribute to the making of a mountainside soil that is crumbly and easily erodes. The government forester Akiyama Tomohide discusses the soil quality and difficulty of reforesting the steep mountains around the Ashio Copper Mine in the Watarase River basin in his *A Forest Again: Lessons from the Ashio Copper Mine and Reforestation Operations*, trans. Shiro Okabe and Sadao Hatta (Tokyo: Food and Agriculture Policy Research Center, 1992).

42   For a classic study of the consequences of deforestation and afforestation in premodern Japanese history, see Conrad D. Totman, *The Green Archipelago: Forestry in Preindustrial Japan* (Berkeley: University of California Press, 1989).

43   For a definitive explanation of these channel dynamics in English, see Luna B. Leopold, "Sediment Load," in *A View of the River* (Cambridge: Harvard University Press, 1994), 183–218.

different kinds of riparian assemblages played key roles in helping to produce and continuously reproduce this region. A key factor in the formation
of these assemblages was the city of Edo. One of several regional castle towns
in 1590 when Tokugawa Ieyasu chose it as his headquarters, Edo had grown by
the 1720s into the country's preeminent castle town (*jōkamachi*) and arguably
the world's largest city at this time with over one million people. To assist in the
construction of Edo Castle and the surrounding city, the Tokugawa regime had
ordered numerous domain lords (*daimyō*) to oversee and assume the costs of
various building projects in and around Edo, such as the building of the central
keeps and excavation of the outer moat, a section of which is today the Kanda
River in central Tokyo.[44] In addition, in 1635 the regime also initiated the system of alternative attendance (*sankin kōtai*) that by 1642 required all of the
roughly 260 domain lords to maintain residences in the city of Edo where they
and their families lived for a portion of each year.[45] In the initial decades of the
seventeenth century, coastal ships laboriously carried from the Kinai region
much of the foodstuffs and processed goods that were consumed in Edo. By
the eighteenth century, however, the Kantō region itself had grown to supply
many, if not most, of those goods. The emerging bonds between the city and its
hinterland likewise created new riverscapes that were most clearly manifest in
the formation of three kinds of important riparian assemblages and their concomitant relations—namely, irrigation, water supply, and riverboat networks.

Irrigation systems exemplify the qualities characterizing riparian assemblages. On the Kantō Plain, the larger irrigation systems were heterogenous
organizations of wood and stone sluices, canals of compacted dirt and clay,
small reservoirs, water typically drawn from upstream rivers, and multivillage
associations that managed and maintained parts of the overall system.[46] The
biggest such system in the Kantō region at the time, one still in use, is what
today is known as the Kasai Canal (Kasai Yōsui), which took on much of its current configuration during the Kyōhō era (1716–36).[47] Before the Kasai Canal,

44 Naitō Akira, *Edo to Edo-jō* (Tokyo: Kashima Shuppankai, 1966); Kitahara Itoko, *Edo-jō sotobori monogatari* (Tokyo: Chikuma Shobō, 1999); Jinnai Hidenobu, *Tokyo: A Spatial Anthropology*, trans. Kimiko Nishimura (Berkeley: University of California Press, 1995).

45 Constantine Nomikos Vaporis, *Tour of Duty: Samurai, Military Service in Edo and the Culture of Early Modern Japan* (Honolulu: University of Hawai'i Press, 2008).

46 The anthropologist William W. Kelly argues that we must recognize the complexity of irrigation systems, or as he prefers "irrigation organizations," which necessarily include four
distinct "phases" (securing a water source, water delivery, in-field use, and drainage) and
"tasks" (modifying landscape and constructing canals, operation and maintenance, allo-
cation among users, and conflict resolution). Kelly, *Water Control in Tokugawa Japan*, 5–7.

47 Kasai Yōsuiro Tochi Kairyōku, ed., *Kasai Yōsui shi: tsūshi hen* (Kasukabe: Kasai Yōsuiro
Tochi Kairyōku, 1988); Hashimoto, *Kōchi kaihatsu to keikan*, 180–204.

there were many separate irrigation ponds and canals along the eastern edge of Musashi Province. In the summer of 1704, a large flood buried a key sluice with debris, and after several failed efforts to dredge and clear the area around the sluice, it could no longer provide the necessary volume of water to the many villages that depended on it.[48] Following repeated petitions from these villages to ameliorate the situation, in 1719 the Kantō Intendant (Kantō Gundai), Ina Tadamichi (d. 1756), ordered the construction of a canal that would draw water from the Tone into the already existing Satte and other irrigation systems. By 1729, the Kasai Canal was extended into the channel of the Naka River (another of the historic distributaries of the Old Tone River) that allowed its remaining waters to drain into the bay.[49]

Roughly 70 km in length and at its source nearly 4 m wide, the Kasai Canal supplied water to over three hundred villages that were organized into ten different irrigation districts.[50] But Musashi Province had other sizable irrigation systems—the Minumadai, Nobi, and Tama—that were all begun in the seventeenth century and expanded during the eighteenth century. In 1653, the Kantō Intendant, Ina Tadakatsu, commissioned two commoners to oversee the digging of the Tama River Aqueduct (Tamagawa Jōsui) from the distant Tama River to the west of Edo in an effort to furnish the city with a reliable source of drinking water. Completed the next year, this 43 km long aqueduct was enlarged in the 1720s to supply water to upwards of thirty new irrigation networks on the water-scarce Musashino highland. This enabled farmers to transform this once sparsely populated area into a landscape of grain fields and vegetable patches.[51] Within Edo, the Tama River Aqueduct and the smaller, older Kanda Aqueduct (Kanda Jōsui) first provided water to Edo Castle and the estates of warrior elites living atop the eastern edge of the highland. After

---

48   Kasai Yōsuiro Tochi Kairyōku, *Kasai Yōsui shi: tsūshi hen*, 289–91, 294–95.

49   The singular name Kasai Canal (Kasai Yōsui) for this irrigation system only became common in the nineteenth century. Prior to this time, different portions of the canal system had different names, often tracing back to their origin as separate smaller irrigation and drainage canals. For example, the Honjo Aqueduct (Honjo Jōsui) was excavated in 1675 to carry water from the Kawarazone Reservoir in the present-day city of Koshigaya to the new eastern districts of Edo. No longer tapped for drinking water after 1722, the canal continued to be used for drainage, irrigation, and water transport, for which it was popularly called the "Towboat River" or Hikifunegawa, until the early twentieth century. Itō Yoshiichi, *Edo jōsuidō no rekishi* (Tokyo: Yoshikawa Kōbunkan, 1996), 14–18, 126–29; Hashimoto, *Kōchi kaihatsu to keikan*, 195–96.

50   Kasai Yōsuiro Tochi Kairyōku, *Kasai Yōsui shi: tsūshi hen*, 295–97.

51   Itō, *Edo jōsuidō no rekishi*, 113–18; M. William Steele, "The History of the Tama River: Social Reconstructions," in *A History of Water: Water Control and River Biographies*, ed. T. Tvedt and E. Jakobsson (London: I. B. Tauris, 2006), 218–19.

serving the needs of status elites, both water supplies descended and ramified through a series of buried wood pipes that supplied wells in the commoner districts of Edo's low city (*shitamachi*) before allowing its remaining waters to pour into canals, the Sumida River, and the bay.[52] The builders of these irrigation canals often used the historical fluvial work of the region's rivers by using portions of old river channels that had either been abandoned by the river or through the above described efforts to shift their direction and flow. In the case of the main Kasai Canal, much of the trunk canal traced the channel of the Old Tone River from Honkawamata Village to Matsubushi Village (in present-day Matsubushi Town) where it branched into eastern and western canals. After 1729, this included a stretch of the original Ara River (Moto-Arakawa) channel before turning southward into the Naka River.[53] In addition to following old river channels, these regional irrigation systems literally extended their respective rivers beyond their historic and new channels, thereby assisting in shaping vital riparian relations between these rivers and hitherto distant villages and their environs.

By moving and tapping the region's rivers, the Tokugawa government and local villages transformed the Kantō region. These changes did not end at the river's edge. Rather, these excavated watery corridors became a vital part of the soil farmers tilled and planted, the organization within villages, and the interaction (and occasional conflict) between them. As such, throughout the seventeenth and early eighteenth centuries, these new river channels and canals enabled the tremendous increase in arable land.[54] Much of this arable land appeared along, and occasionally in, the rivers and the wetlands they fed. A clear example of this kind of expansion is the aforementioned "Sixteen-Island

---

52   Between 1659 and 1664, the Tokugawa regime also ordered the excavation of the smaller Aoyama, Mita, Senkawa, and the eastern Honjo (Kameari) Aqueducts to supply water to different parts of the city. Because of problems with water quality and quantity, after 1722 these four aqueducts were discontinued as sources of drinking water and instead used to supply water for irrigation and other purposes. Itō, *Edo jōsuidō no rekishi*, 23–36; Susan B. Hanley, "Urban Sanitation in Preindustrial Japan," *Journal of Interdisciplinary History* 18, no. 1 (1987): 6–8; Jun Hatano, "Edo's Water Supply," trans. Toshiko Kishida-Ellis, in *Edo and Paris: Urban Life and the State in the Early Modern Era*, ed. James McClain, John M. Merriman, and Ugawa Kaoru (Ithaca: Cornell University Press, 1994), 243–49; H. I. H. Crown Prince Naruhito [Emperor Reiwa], "Edo and Water," 47.

53   Kasai Yōsuiro Tochi Kairyōku, *Kasai Yōsui shi: tsūshi hen*, 304.

54   Distinguished from existing or primary fields (*honden*), cleared or reclaimed lands were typically described in contemporary documents as "new fields" (*shinden*) and often taxed differently and separately from a village's primary fields. Despite the use of the term "*den*," or "paddy," this arable land also included dry fields as well as the wet fields for rice cultivation. Fukuda Tōru, *Kinsei shinden to sono genryū* (Tokyo: Kokon Shoin, 1986); Kikuchi Toshio, *Zoku shinden kaihatsu: jirei hen* (Tokyo: Kokon Shoin, 1986).

Reclamation" where locals claimed and expanded the emergent islands in the Tone River and Katori Sea into which it flowed for farming. The region's expanding system of canals were also instrumental in irrigating (yōsui) hitherto dry upland areas and in draining (akusui) water from marshy bottomlands.[55] In fact, one of the earliest portions of what would become part of the trunk of the Kasai Canal was excavated in 1613 to drain water from Nishikata Village (present-day city of Koshigaya) to the nearby Ayase River.[56] Similarly, along what would become a section of the Minumadai Canal, areas within the post town Kōnosu were drained in the 1620s to create rice paddies.[57] After more than a century of expanding arable and tax revenue, the Tokugawa government was facing fiscal shortfalls, the Kyōhō Famine (1732–33), and the prospect of peasant protests over its taxation policies. In response to these and other problems, the Tokugawa initiated a variety of reforms. These included a concerted effort to encourage the additional clearance and reclamation of marginal lands, which in their unreclaimed state had provided vital fodder and firewood for farmers.[58] Compared with the end of the sixteenth century, the number of villages and arable land, as measured by reported yield (kokudaka) in the counties along the Tone, Edo, and Ara Rivers, had by the mid-seventeenth century dramatically increased.[59] In this way, the transformation of the region's rivers also created conditions by which large swaths of the Kantō Plain were transformed as woods and marshes gave way to fields that were planted with diverse crops ranging from rice and rapeseed to barley, buckwheat, and beans.[60]

Stimulating much of this expansion in arable lands and rural villages was the growth of the city of Edo. In order to provision the tens of thousands of

---

55   Ishizaki, "Nōgyō no hatten," 79–86.

56   Kasai Yōsuiro Tochi Kairyōku, Kasai Yōsui shi: tsūshi hen, 244–45.

57   Saitama-ken, Arakawa, 2:368.

58   In the largely Tokugawa-controlled Kantō region, officials sought to increase tax revenue for the regime by having villagers themselves or merchants from Edo reclaim land around the Tega, Inba, and other marshes as well as upland pastures (maki) and the floodplains (ryūsakuba) of the Tone and other rivers. Abiko-shi Kyōiku Iinkai, ed., Abiko-shi shi: kinsei hen (Abiko: Abiko-shi Kyōiku Iinkai, 2005), 106–22; Ōishi Manabu, Kyōhō kaikaku no chiiki seisaku (Tokyo: Yoshikawa Kōbunkan, 1996); Saitama-ken, Arakawa, 2:388–89.

59   The reported yield in the first countrywide survey of 1598 is problematic, but from the 1650 Shōhō gōchō onward the numbers are considerably more reliable. The reported yield for Katsushika County in Shimōsa Province, for example, totaled 57,742 koku in 1650, 97,626 koku in 1702, and 121,577 koku in 1834. Izumi Seiji, "Kinsei shoki ikkoku gōchō no kenkyū: Shōhō gōchō o chūshin ni," Chiiki seisaku kenkyū 8, no. 2 (2005): 1–19; Chiba-ken no rekishi: tsūshi hen, kinsei, ed. Chiba-ken Shiryō Kenkyū Zaidan (Chiba: Chiba-ken, 2007), 1:130.

60   Kōnosu-shi Shishi Hensan Chōsakai, ed., Kōnosu-shi shi: tsūshi kinsei (Kōnosu: Kōnosu-shi Shishi Hensan Chōsakai, 2004), 381–89; Abiko-shi Kyōiku Iinkai, Abiko-shi shi: kinsei hen, 254–68.

artisans, labors, servants, warriors, and others who within just a few decades had moved to Edo, Tokugawa officials and domain lords had to develop new transportation networks to deliver food, building materials, and tax revenue, which at the time was mostly paid in bales of rice and other in-kind forms of payment, from their home domains to Edo. With legal and geographical limits on the use of wheeled traffic and the costs of transporting overland by pack-horse, riverboats emerged as the most practical means for shipping heavy and bulky goods within the Kantō region and beyond.[61] While domain lords from the western regions of the country relied primarily on existing and expanded coastal shipping routes, those in the Kantō region and the northeastern domains had to create wholly new inland and coastal shipping networks. With the coastal route around the Bōsō Peninsula and into the bay to Edo being both dangerous and time consuming because they had to sail against the dominant Kuroshio Current and prevailing southwesterly winds, ships from the northern domains like Tsugaru, Nanbu, and Sendai began off-loading their cargo onto smaller boats at the port of Naka in Mito domain.[62] From Naka, these boats sailed southward on the Hi Marsh (Hinuma) to Ebisawa where they portaged their cargo overland to the Tomoe River. From there they sailed downstream to the riverport of Kushibiki.[63] It was not until 1654 when the Tone River was suc-cessfully rerouted into the Hitachi River system and Katori Sea that riverboats could sail directly from Kushibiki to Edo.[64] And two centuries later, in 1853, it was from this same riverport that Kanosuke began all four of his journeys carrying rice and supplies for the Edo estates of the Mito domain.[65] Although

---

61   In the nineteenth century, the *takasebune* that sailed the Tone River system could hold up to one thousand bales of rice (each weighing about 64 kg). By comparison, the small packhorses used in the Kantō region typically carried two bales each and additionally required handlers, feed, and time to rest.

62   Kawana Noboru, *Kinsei Nihon suiun shi no kenkyū* (Tokyo: Yūzankaku Shuppan, 1984), 5.

63   In 1655, Mito domain established an office at Ebisawa to regulate and tax (*tsuyaku*) these boats as they traversed its waters. Mito-shi Shi Hensan Iinkai, ed., *Mito-shi shi: chūkan* (Mito: Mito-shi, 1968), 1:610–11.

64   By the 1670s, the seaport of Chōshi at the mouth of the rerouted Tone River, where it poured into the Pacific Ocean, also became a viable port. Although infamous for its hid-den shoals and rocks, coastal ships from the northern domains began anchoring in this estuary harbor to off-load their cargo directly onto riverboats or onto lighters that would ferry the goods to shoreline storehouses. Chōshi-shi Shi Hensan Iinkai, ed., *Chōshi-shi shi* (Chōshi: Chōshi-shi Shi Hensan Iinkai, 1956), 240–47.

65   The Tokugawa regime, domain lords, and their respective officials and retainers regularly contracted with merchants to ship tax payments from rural riverports to the region's castle towns, including Edo. Tanji Kenzō, *Kantō kasen suiun shi no kenkyū* (Tokyo: Hōsei Daigaku Shuppankyoku, 1984), 13–20; Yoshida Nobuyuki, "Edo no tsumi tonya to hashike yado," *Kokuritsu rekishi minzoku hakubutsukan kenkyū hōkoku*, no. 103 (2003): 448.

outpaced by commercial boat traffic by the early eighteenth century, the shipment of tax-rice and supplies by river and coastal boat were vital in stimulating
the broader use of the rivers for transport and remained an integral part of the
infrastructure of governance throughout the Tokugawa period.

Following the ambitious riparian projects of the seventeenth century,
the Kantō region as a whole was becoming thoroughly commercialized and
increasingly centered on Edo.[66] Transporting the majority of crops-turned-
commodities from these rural villages to Edo and back again was an extensive
assemblage made up of rural and urban merchants, riverports and storehouses,
checkpoints and licenses, and riverboats and their crews. Along the Tone River,
for example, there were about eighty riverports (*kashi*) and an additional hundred or so such ports on the river's main tributaries like the Watarase, Edo,
and Kinu Rivers, and in the area of the Katori Sea.[67] These riverports were also
knots in an emerging net of riparian relations. At each of these ports, small and
large riverboats loaded goods from shoreline storehouses and unloaded their
cargo to local wholesalers or overland shipping agents. People from nearby
villages went to buy and sell goods, trade gossip, and work as stevedores in
the off-season. Boat pilots and other travelers gathered to bath, gamble, or
stop by local temples or shrines. And, wharf merchants (*kashi tonya*) sent and
received goods from merchants in the Edo-based Association of Inland River
Boat Loaders (Okukawa Funazumi Tonya).[68] In this way, despite often being
little more than a wharf or dock, these riverports brought a taste of the cos-
mopolitan culture of Edo and the region's other cities to the countryside.[69]
These relations and their accompanying accommodations were apparently
developed enough by 1687 that the peripatetic poet Matsuo Bashō (1644–94)

---

66   There is a voluminous history about the commercialization of Edo and its hinterland,
      the Kantō region. One of the earliest and most influential studies is Itō Yoshiichi, *Edo
      jimawari keizai no tenkai* (Tokyo: Kashiwa Shobō, 1966).

67   Aside from its use in the compound word *uo-gashi*, or "fish wharf," the term *kashi* (literally
      kawa no kishi or riverside) has largely disappeared with the riverboat traffic that had once
      made these places bustling centers of local activity and commerce. The term *kashi* was
      common throughout the Kantō and Tōhoku regions of Japan, but on the Kiso and other
      rivers of Chūbu region, these riverports were called *minato*. Along the Yodo River and its
      tributaries, these ports were known as *hama*. For the numbers and names of the Tone's
      riverports, see Kawana Noboru, "Kantō ni okeru kasen unyu kikō no seiritsu," *Rekishi chiri*
      89, no. 4 (1960): 54–64.

68   Tanji Kenzō, "Okukawa funazumi tonya no suitai to nobori nimotsu," in *Kantō kasen suiun
      shi no kenkyū*, 118–60.

69   In his classic social history of these riverports and the culture they supported, Kawana
      Noboru describes these ports as the "city in the midst of the village" (*mura no naka no
      toshi*). Kawana Noboru, *Kashi ni ikiru hitobito: Tonegawa suiun no shakai shi* (Tokyo:
      Heibonsha, 1982), 98–105.

and his companions were able to spend a night in the riverport of Fusa before catching a boat down the Tone to visit the three shrines of the eastern Kantō: the Katori, Kashima, and Ikisu.[70]

Just as along overland highways, the Tokugawa government established checkpoints (bansho) at two key riverside locations: in 1641 at the castle town and riverport of Sekiyado where the newly excavated Edo River flowed southward from the Tone and in 1678 at the intersection of the Naka River and Onagi Canal on the eastern edge of Edo.[71] To run these checkpoints, as well as issue and enforce regulations, in 1678 the Tokugawa created an office to oversee riverboat traffic (Kawabune Bugyōsho). This office supervised the shipment of tax-rice, the collection of annual taxes from boatowners, and the regulation of the building and use of riverboats through boat registers and licenses.[72] This combination of official and commercial river traffic played an important role in producing and reproducing the Kantō as an integrated region during the Tokugawa period.

While historians have detailed many aspects of these transformations in the Kantō region during the seventeenth and early eighteenth centuries, geologists and historical geographers have focused their analyses on soil deposits, land formations, and land use. Nonetheless, there is still much that remains unclear about the first century of Tokugawa rule over the hinterland of the Kantō region. This is especially true of the Kantō Intendant's intention in successively diverting the Tone, Ara, and other rivers. Owing in some extent to a paucity of early seventeenth-century documents, scholars have been left to speculate on the basis of the Tokugawa government's needs at the time and the actual results of these riparian projects. It was once widely believed, for example, that the diversion of the Ara and Tone was part of a regional plan to reclaim and clear more land through drainage and irrigation.[73]

Historians have since shown that during the seventeenth century Ina Tadaharu and subsequent intendants seldom followed through or succeeded with their reclamation projects.[74] It seems much more likely that the Tone

70   Matsuo Bashō, "Kashima mōde," in Matsuo Bashō shū, ed. Imoto Nōichi, Hori Nobuo, and Muramatsu Tomotsugu, Nihon koten bungaku zenshū (Tokyo: Shōgakukan, 1972), 41:305.

71   In 1720, the Tokugawa regime also established a checkpoint at Uraga on the Miura Peninsula where coastal ships were required to visit when entering the bay and sailing toward Edo. Nishikawa Takeomi, Edo naiwan no minato to ryūtsū (Tokyo: Iwata Shoin, 1993), 31–42; Katō Takashi, "Nakagawa bansho no kinō to sono tokushitsu," Kōtsūshi kenkyū, no. 12 (1984): 27–46.

72   Kawana, Kinsei Nihon suiun shi no kenkyū, 233–70.

73   Kikuchi Toshio, Shinden kaihatsu (Tokyo: Kokin Shoin, 1959), 51–67.

74   Ōtani, Edo bakufu chisui seisaku, 303.

and Ara were rerouted to improve flood control and water transport with the ancillary benefit of helping drainage and reclamation efforts by Tokugawa officials, Edo-based merchants, and local villagers. Yet even when limited to flood control and water transport, scholars continue to disagree about the primary aim of each project. The geographer Koide Haku, for instance, suggests that the Ara was diverted to run along the eastern edge of Edo so that logs for the construction of the shogun's new capital could be transported to lumberyards in the city from the river's headwaters in the Chichibu Mountains.[75] The historian Kawana Noboru argues that the primary purpose of redirecting the Tone River into the Hitachi River system was to enable Tokugawa retainers and domain lords to ship tax-rice and other supplies from the north via a safer inland route.[76] The engineering historian Matsuura Shigeki offers a contrasting view, arguing that the projects to shift the Tone and Ara Rivers belonged to a larger regionwide plan primarily intended to control flooding, especially along the Nakasendō, one of the vital circuits used by domain lords and their several hundred member retinues when traveling to and from Edo for their required residence in the city.[77]

Regardless of interpretation, one thing these seventeenth-century riparian projects demonstrate is that modern societies do not have a monopoly on the capacity to radically alter the landscapes and riverscapes in which people live. The Kantō has long been a site of human habitation whose very environment took form through centuries of logging, reclamation, and agriculture. In other words, the transformation of the seventeenth-century Kantō region does not support a story of a "first" pristine nature giving way to a "second" nature of human construction and contrivance. Rather, the transformation is perhaps better thought of as changes to specific riparian relations established through a *coeval* relationship between 1) various groups that fished, sailed on, and drew water from the rivers of the Kantō, 2) the ruling Tokugawa authorities that claimed suzerain rights over all the river and coastal waters within their domain, and 3) the rivers themselves. From the eighteenth century onward, the riparian relations that had developed along the waters of the Kantō during the seventeenth century became increasingly complex as reclamation projects continued to bring new lands under cultivation; farming became more intensive with the multiple cropping of fields; people foraged, fished, and hunted further into the region's marshes and lakes; and all became bound together

75   Koide Haku, *Nihon no kasen: shizen shi to shakai shi* (Tokyo: Tōkyō Daigaku Shuppankai, 1973), 74–75.

76   Kawana, *Kinsei Nihon suiun shi no kenkyū*, 11–12.

77   Matsuura, *Kokudo no kaihatsu to kasen*, 71–74.

through the expansion of transportation and commercial networks centered on the city of Edo.

2   Water Worlds of Farmers, Fishers, and Boat Pilots

For much of the low-lying areas of the Kantō Plain, rivers and the countless marshes, ponds, and lakes through which they coursed formed an essential and inextricable part of people's lives and livelihood. This was especially true of the villages located along the Tone and other large rivers of the region. Through the work of farming and fishing, these villages were deeply entangled within and contributed to broader environmental relations that aided in molding the region's riverscapes. Farmers drew water from the Tone and smaller rivers to fill both local and regional irrigation systems that ramified across the land delivering water to near and distant fields and paddies. Many in these villages also preyed on seasonal runs of trout and salmon as well as migrating ducks and geese to meet their tax obligations and provide for themselves and their families. In casting nets for fish and sowing seed for crops, they worked together with these waters and lands to coproduce commodities that were consumed in nearby towns and the city of Edo. And, carrying much of these goods to the region's towns and cities were riverboats like the one piloted by Honda Kanosuke. In this way, farmers, fishers, and boat pilots were entangled within and thereby shaped the material media of the Tone and the other rivers that constituted their water worlds. These mundane activities were also demonstrative of how historical agency works. All too frequently, historians abstract people and objects from these kinds of environmental relations, assuming the former is uniquely endowed with agency while the latter acts according to some kind of predetermined design or an inherent internal capacity for change.[78] In this and other sections, an examination of quotidian routines on and along the rivers of the Kantō affirms how agency was integral to and operated *within* and *through* these relations.

Honda Kanosuke's four journeys to and from Edo in 1853 therefore offer a poignant example of how entangled many like this boat pilot were in the riparian relations of the Kantō region. In sailing his large *takasebune* riverboat up and

---

78   For differing critiques of the so-called "realist" viewpoint, see, for example, Tim Ingold, *Being Alive: Essays on Movement, Knowledge and Description* (New York: Routledge, 2011), esp. chapter 2; Bruno Latour, *Pandora's Hope: Essays on the Reality of Science Studies* (Cambridge: Harvard University Press, 1999), esp. chapter 4; Jessica Riskin, *The Restless Clock: A History of the Centuries-Long Argument over What Makes Living Things Tick* (Chicago: University of Chicago Press, 2016).

down the region's rivers, Kanosuke navigated through a well-known, yet challenging, riparian landscape. Along the Tone and Edo Rivers between the lakeside village of Kushibiki and the metropolitan center of Edo, upstream weather conditions constantly affected downstream river situations. Rainstorms in the distant Chichibu or Mikuni Mountains caused rivers to flow faster and water levels to rise throughout much of the Kantō region. These swollen streams and rivers tore at riverbeds and banks to carry away silt and sand, which gathered downstream as potentially perilous shoals and sandbars. While the influence of upstream rainstorms may not have been felt for hours or even days, downstream changes in the weather and the seasons were immediately noticed. In fact, the literal translation of Kanosuke's logbook *Kawajō fūu tomari nikki* is *Daily Record of River Conditions, Wind and Rain Stops*.

Throughout his journeys, Kanosuke complained of drenching rains that must have numbed his body and required he and his crew to stop in order to bail water from their boat. He also recorded the southerly winds, which in the Kantō region were referred to as *inasa* and *fushi*, against which they would try to pole their boat with "bone-breaking" (*honeori*) effort and noted when northerly *narai* winds filled their sails and propelled them forward.[79] Meriting constant monitoring, the weather and waters within which Kanosuke was entangled clearly influenced, but did not determine, which channel he sailed or where and when he decided to moor his boat. Indeed, on occasion, his decision to moor his boat had less to do with these sailing conditions than being delayed by a fight between two other boat pilots or meeting a friend on the river and deciding to visit a nearby temple or shrine together.[80] In other words, these weather and water conditions about which Kanosuke was so concerned neither determined his or others' activities nor did they form a preexisting and passive natural landscape to be traversed by the knowing boat pilot or traveler. Rather, Kanosuke recorded what it meant to be in what the anthropologist Tim Ingold calls a "weather-world"—that is, to be fully part of an environment as it unfolded in time and space.[81]

---

79   Over just three days in the third month, for example, Kanosuke records first "good weather with *inasa* winds" then "good weather, morning westerly winds, later *narai* winds," and finally "*fushi* southerly winds that gradually blew into a heavy wind." See entries for 3rd month, 19th day; 3rd month, 20th day; and 3rd month, 21st day in Honda, "Kawajō fūu tomari nikki," 392.

80   For instances like these, see the entries on his first journey for 22 March (2nd month, 13th day) and 29 March (2nd month, 20th day). Honda, "Kawajō fūu tomari nikki," 392–93.

81   Tim Ingold, "Footprints through the Weather-World: Walking, Breathing, Knowing," *Journal of the Royal Anthropological Institute* 16 (2010): 121–39.

2.1   Riverboats

Kanosuke navigated his way in this particular weather-world aboard a river-boat. Although little is known about Kanosuke's life before or after 1853, at least during this year he was in the employment of Mito domain and demonstrated himself to be a seasoned boat pilot. Along with a crew of two to three boat-men, Kanosuke earned a stipend for sailing what was likely one of about ten Mito-owned riverboats for the domain.[82] Based on his logbook's inclusion of his crew members names, its description of his cargo, mention of parts of the boat, and comments on how they were sailing, Kanosuke was clearly aboard a *takasebune* riverboat.[83] To the uninitiated these riverboats may have all looked alike. Indeed, even government officials tasked with ensuring riverboats enter-ing and leaving Edo had paid their taxes and presented the correct permits apparently required a picture book to identify the various kinds of riverboats.[84] Dated 1802, the *Funakagami* included labeled illustrations of thirty-three kinds of boats that plied the waters of the Kantō region and is believed to have been used to help identify and discriminate between, for example, different kinds of small *chabune* and large *hiratabune* boats or high-bowed fishing boats (*ryōsen*) and the high-bowed and high-speed *oshiokuribune* delivery boat.[85] The twenty-fourth boat listed in the *Funakagami* was a *takasebune* that was likely similar to the one Honda sailed on the Tone and Edo Rivers in 1853 (fig. 11). By the early nineteenth century, the *takasebune*, their pilots, and crews had become the mainstays of the middle and lower Tone River and its tributaries.

---

82   In addition to the stipend Kanosuke would have earned from Mito domain, the histo-rian Watanabe Hideo explains that the boat pilot also would have been allowed to make additional income by buying goods in Edo and selling them along his return route to Kushibiki. Watanabe Hideo, *Kinsei Tonegawa suiun shi no kenkyū* (Tokyo: Yoshikawa Kōbunkan, 2002), 35–36.

83   By the nineteenth century, the most common riverboat plying the middle and lower Tone River system was the *takasebune*. Likely because it did not warrant recording, however, Kanosuke never mentions the name or kind of boat he was sailing. Watanabe, *Kinsei Tonegawa suiun shi no kenkyū*, 11.

84   Because Kanosuke was sailing a Mito-owned riverboat, he would have sailed under the seal of the domain (*gokuin*) and been exempted from the fees and taxes demanded of commoner-owned vessels. Watanabe, *Kinsei Tonegawa suiun shi no kenkyū*, 234–35.

85   The illustrations in figure 11 are from a copy of the *Funakagami* that is archived at the National Diet Library, Tokyo. This copy of the *Funakagami* is dated 1873 and notes that it is a copy of an earlier 1802 edition. The historian Kawana Noboru compares the four extant copies of this illustrated guide to boats and concludes that, while all are very simi-lar, the undated one held by the Museum of Maritime Science (Fune no Kagakkan) is the oldest and that it was probably first produced for the Riverboat Inspector (Kawabune Aratameyaku). Kawana Noboru, *Kinsei Nihon no kawabune kenkyū* (Tokyo: Nihon Keizai Hyōronsha, 2003), 1:439–48.

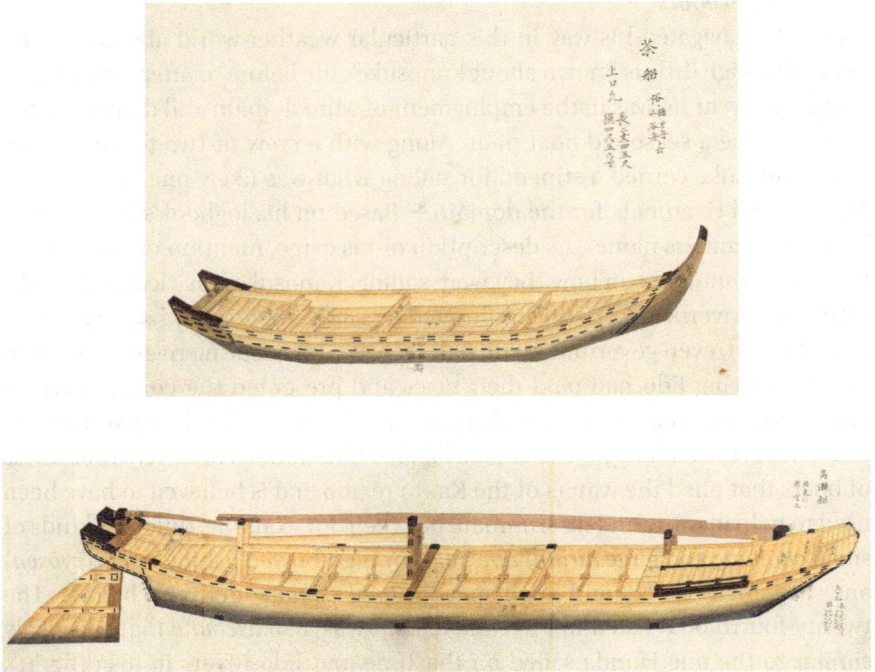

FIGURE 11   Examples of the small *chabune* (7–8 m long) and large *takasebune* (12–27 m long) riverboats as depicted in *Funakagami*, originally printed in 1802. Author and publisher unknown. Unpaginated
COURTESY OF THE NATIONAL DIET LIBRARY, TOKYO

With their tall masts and broad rectangular sails, the *takasebune* were also a ubiquitous element in the region's riverscape. As discussed in the introductory chapter, a riverboat was more than just an object in a preexisting landscape or a tool manipulated by Kanosuke and his crew; it was an integral part of the assemblage that required crew, gear, and river to operate. The varying depths, volumes, and lengths of the Tone and Yodo Rivers meant that the riverboat assemblages that emerged along each river over a long period of time also bore dissimilar features. While these differences were manifest in many ways, they can be seen in the distinct design of the Yodo's *sanjikkokubune* riverboat and the Tone's *takasebune*.

Where the *sanjikkokubune* regularly relayed passengers along the short and busy riparian corridor between Osaka and Kyoto, the *takasebune* hauled cargo over the longer more difficult routes between Edo and its hinterland riverports. Both boats were large and flat-bottomed, but the *sanjikkokubune* ordinarily had a crew of four who sailed downstream by riding the river's current and propelled it upstream through a combination of setting poles and towropes. These boats also enjoyed a deeper draft than the *takasebune* because the Yodo River itself was deeper year-round than the Tone River due to the constant flow of water draining from Lake Biwa. Moreover, by the nineteenth century, the *sanjikkokubune* mostly carried passengers so they usually had a boarded-over hull to make a flat deck for seating that was in turn covered with a wood-framed, thatched roof to protect passengers from both the rain and sun (see fig. 4).[86] In contrast, the *takasebune* was designed to transport sizeable volumes of cargo both across the deep open waters of the region's lakes and marshes as well as over the shallow sandbars that frequented certain parts of the Tone River system. Lacking a keel to keep them steady in deeper waters, the *takasebune* and their somewhat smaller upstream cousins the *hiratabune* relied on an oversized, adjustable rudder to both steady and steer the craft.[87] The *takasebune* was built mostly from straight-grained and rot-resistant cedar boards that were harvested from 130 to 200 year-old trees and assembled with special joinery and nails of up to 18 cm in length.[88] According to the *Funakagami*, the *takasebune* ranged in size from 3 *jō* and 12 *shaku* (12.7 m) to 8 *jō* and 8–9 *shaku* (27 m) in length and 7–8 *shaku* (2.4 m) to 1 *jō* and 6–7 *shaku* (5.2 m) in width.[89] Despite their shallow draft, these dimensions allowed the *takasebune* of the lower Tone River to typically carry a cargo of 900 to 1,200 *hyō* (57–76,000 kg).[90] The *takasebune* was also versatile for the many ways a pilot and its crew could

---

86 Ishii Kenji, *Zusetsu wabune shiwa* (Tokyo: Shiseidō, 1983), 229–32; Hino Shōshō, *Kinai Kasen kōtsū shi kenkyū* (Tokyo: Yoshikawa Kōbunkan, 1986), 229–30; Kawana, *Kinsei Nihon no kawabune kenkyū*, 2:614–21.

87 Ishii, *Zusetsu wabune shiwa*, 223–29; Kawana, *Kinsei Nihon no kawabune kenkyū*, 1:236–62, 445.

88 Watanabe Kōji, *Tonegawa takasebune* (Nagareyama: Ronshobō, 1990), 270–72, 279.

89 Based on an 1866 itemized estimate of lumber, nails, and other materials for the building of a new *takasebune* that was submitted by the boatwright Sajiuemon of Fusa Village to Tanaka domain, the proposed riverboat had a burthen or carrying capacity of 500 *hyō* (32,000 kg) and was likely about 20 m in length and 4.5 m wide. "Ofune uchikae shiyō-chō," reprinted in Abiko-shi Kyōiku Iinkai, *Abiko-shi shi: kinsei hen*, 367–69.

90 Kawana Noboru provides a chart listing the burthen of various kinds of riverboats navigating the Tone, Yodo, and Yamato Rivers with 1 *hyō* equaling 4 *to* or about 64 kg. Kawana, *Kashi ni ikiru hitobito*, 18. In his 1855 gazetteer of the Tone River, Akamatsu Sōtan specifies a smaller burthen for *takasebune* that likely reflected his inclusion of smaller versions of the vessel that were built to navigate further upstream: from 500 to 600 *hyō* (32–38,000 kg) to 800 to 900 *hyō* (51–57,000 kg). Using a different base measure, Sōtan also explains that 1 *hyō* equals 4 *to* and 2 *shō* (67.2 kg). Akamatsu Sōtan, *Tonegawa zushi* (Tokyo: Iwanami Shoten, 1936), 52.

propel their craft forward.[91] With its large sail, a good wind could push the *takasebune* at a fast clip, even upstream against the current of a river.[92] When the winds were absent or unfavorable, the pilot and crew could also rely on long bamboo setting poles and plenty of "bone-breaking" effort to push their boat forward.[93] Finally, where the river allowed and conditions necessitated it, a crew could also use ropes to walk on the bed or banks of the river to slowly pull their boat toward its destination. Thus, although the *sanjikkokubune* and *takasebune* resembled one another in materials and construction, each of these riverboats also differed in ways that reflected their being part of specific riparian assemblages.

2.2   *Rural Riverports*

Whether rain or shine, northerly or southerly winds, Kanosuke invariably measured the progress of his journey by the riverside ports where he and his crew paused or moored their boat. After leaving Kashima on the morning of 30 July 1853, at the start of the journey described at the beginning of this chapter, Kanosuke recorded in his logbook, "Good weather. Morning wind. Worked the pole to push the boat up the Hitachi [Tone] River. Arrived at Tsunomiya."[94] As noted above in this chapter, the fishing village and riverport of Tsunomiya was the same village that two centuries earlier had been embroiled in a conflict with its neighboring villages over access and control of the waters and land that Kanosuke now poled and sailed his boat through. In his 1858 *Tonegawa zushi*, a gazetteer of the Tone River, Akamatsu Sōtan (1806–62), a doctor from the riverside village of Fukawa, began his short entry on the fishing and wayfaring village of Tsunomiya by mentioning its namesake—the large partially submerged *torii* gate under which visitors would pass when disembarking from their boats and walking to the nearby Katori Shrine (fig. 12).[95] While unusual

---

91   Where Kawana Noboru explains that the largest *takasebune* had a burthen of 1,200 *hyō* (76,000 kg) and required six to seven people to sail, Akamatsu Sōtan explains that typically the *takasebune* had a crew of four and the bigger vessels had a crew of six. Kawana, *Kashi ni ikiru hitobito*, 18; Akamatsu, *Tonegawa zushi*, 52.

92   The mast on a *takasebune* was also detachable to enable it to pass beneath bridges in Edo and other towns in the Kantō region.

93   The *takasebune*, *hiratabune*, and *sanjikkokubune* were all built with wide gunwales that allowed their crews to walk from bow to stern while pushing their boat forward with their bamboo setting poles, which could be as long as 5 m in length.

94   Entry for 6th month, 6th day on the intercalary calendar. Honda, "Kawajō fūu tomari nikki," 405.

95   Akamatsu, *Tonegawa zushi*, 314–17.

FIGURE 12   An 1855 illustration of the riverport of Tsunomiya. In Akamatsu Sōtan, *Tonegawa zushi* (Tokyo: Iwanami Shoten, 1938), 314–15

for its proximity to one of the most renowned pilgrimage sites in the Kantō region, Tsunomiya was but one of hundreds of such riverports in the Kantō. Sometimes, these riverports were little more than a riverside village with mooring poles and reinforced embankments for wharves, but often they were more substantial and lay near fording or ferry points for overland roads and highways. In this way, these ports tied together complimentary routes for water and land transport to form networks through which people, goods, and information flowed throughout and beyond the Kantō region.

One of the region's busiest and largest riverports was Tsunomiya's neighbor, Sawara Village. Both exemplary of many of the riverside ports frequented by Kanosuke and other boat pilots and extraordinary for its size and regional influence, a close examination of Sawara reveals much about rural riverside life in the Kantō region at that time. It also shows how riparian relations shaped and were shaped by the geography and organization of these riverports and how agency was unevenly distributed between wealthy merchant families and other villagers and worked through complex relations within and between this and other riverports.

A 1745 map of Sawara that was reproduced in Sōtan's 1857 *Tonegawa zushi* is of interest for what it can tell us about how water flowed through the village and was thoroughly entangled in all aspects of village life (fig. 13).[96] As Sōtan, a rural doctor-turned-author, described in his gazetteer:

> Sawara is the most prosperous area along the lower Tone [River]. There is a river [the Ono] in the middle of the village, and a bridge crosses between Shinjuku and Honjuku [districts] (it is called the "Big Bridge" [Ōhashi]). From the mouth of the Ono to this place, rice, other grains, and various other goods are loaded and unloaded, boat passengers vie for the front [of the line] and resent the narrowness of both banks. Without pausing for day or night, this is truly a gathering of water and land traffic (*suiriku ōrai*).[97]

Situated 2 km from the Tone River along the banks of the Ono River where it crossed the Katori Highway (Katori-kaidō), Sawara was a crossroads for overland and water transport. Protected from all but the greatest floods from the Tone River, Sawara sustained a regional marketplace that village documents claim began in the Tenshō era (1573–92).[98] This Rokusai Market (Rokusai-ichi) was held six times each month at different locations within the village, attracting merchants and others from the surrounding countryside.[99] At some point, both banks of the Ono River in Sawara had been reinforced with stone embankments that included broad staircases to ease in the loading and unloading of boats moored along them. Running atop these stone embankments were what look like "narrow" streets on the map, however, these strips of land were labeled "*kashi*" (wharf) and would have been strictly regulated and used to move both goods and passengers on and off waiting boats. Facing the Ono River on the other side of these wharves were the shophouses of many of Sawara's merchant families.[100] With access to the waterfront being a premium, these narrow two-story wood shophouses were tightly packed together and extended

---

96   "Shimōsa no kuni Katori-gun Sawara-mura bunken ezu" [1857], in *Chiba-ken no rekishi: shiryō hen, kinsei*, 6:frontispiece.

97   Akamatsu, *Tonegawa zushi*, 313.

98   *Chiba-ken no rekishi: tsūshi hen, kinsei*, ed. Chiba-ken Shiryō Kenkyū Zaidan (Chiba: Chiba-ken, 2008), 2:81.

99   Using the "three and eight" (*sanpachi*) calendar, the market opened on days of the month that included the numbers three and eight—that is, 3rd, 8th, 13th, 18th, 23rd, and 28th. *Chiba-ken no rekishi: tsūshi hen, kinsei*, 2:81–82.

100   In a brief explanation on his 1857 copy of the 1745 map, Sōtan notes that he added the shophouses (*machiya*) to his map. They can be seen lining the wharves along the Ono River and the Katori Highway where it passed through Sawara.

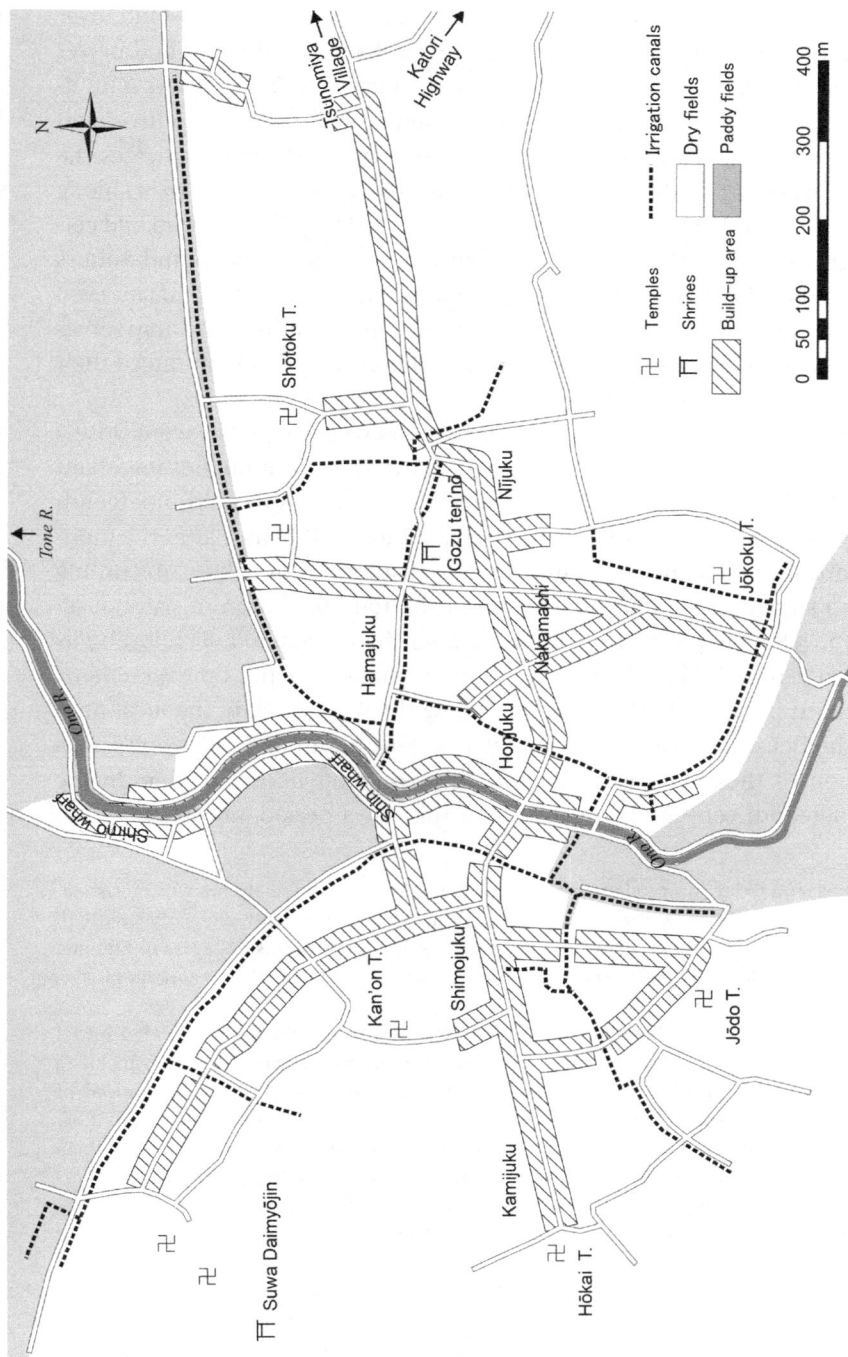

FIGURE 13 Map of Sawara, c. 1745. Based on "Shimōsa-no-kuni Katori-gun Sawara-mura bunken ezu" [Survey map of Sawara Village, Katori County, Shimōsa Province]. In *Chiba-ken no rekishi: shiryō hen, kinsei*, ed. Chiba-ken Shiryō Kenkyū Zaidan (Chiba: Chiba-ken, 2005), 6: frontispiece

back from the wharves for some distance.[101] As noted by Sōtan, the Ono River also bifurcated Sawara with the older Honjuku district to the east and newer Shinjuku district to the west.[102] Moreover, the map in figure 13 shows a number of small irrigation canals draining into and away from the Ono River and the village center. And, just beyond the village center, the map indicates the slightly raised dry fields (*hatake*) and the low-lying rice paddies (*den*) along the Ono River and between Sawara and the nearby Tone River. Sawara had certainly grown during the century between the original 1745 map and Sōtan's 1857 copy, but the basic layout of the village remained unaltered and can even be identified today in aerial photographs of the city. In this way, the map serves as a cartographic representation of how riparian relations also produced their own local spatial relations.[103]

The riparian relations that Sawara shaped and were shaped by were closely tied to the wealth and commercial activity of the village's numerous merchant houses. While nominally and administratively a "village," by the mid-nineteenth century Sawara was the third largest town in Shimōsa Province after the maritime port of Chōshi and the administrative castle town of Sakura. According to a 1710 survey, Sawara already had a substantial population of 958 households and 3,819 people. By 1838, those numbers had grown to 1,163 households and 5,647 people.[104] Among these households, many were full-time merchants who ranged from local fishmongers hawking the day's catch in the local market to the rich and powerful Inō family. The most prominent of Sawara's merchant houses, the Inō were divided into seven separate branch families by the mid-nineteenth century. Throughout the Tokugawa period, however, the Inō

---

101   In Sawara today (now a district within the city of Katori), there are many extant shop-houses as well as newer ones that were built in the late nineteenth and early twentieth centuries. For a similar analysis of the spatial structure of watersides areas in Edo and Tokyo, see, for example, Jinnai Hidenobu, ed., *Edo Tōkyō no mikata shirabekata* (Tokyo: Kashima Shuppankai, 1989).

102   Although not noted by Sōtan, each of these districts was further subdivided into a total of five groups (*kumi*) each with its own administrative leader. Honjuku included Honjuku-gumi, Hamajuku-gumi, and Niijuku-gumi, and Shinjuku was comprised of Kamijuku-gumi and Shimojuku-gumi. *Chiba-ken no rekishi: tsūshi hen, kinsei*, 2:318.

103   This observation is similar to Yoshida Nobuyuki's often stated argument about how "societies in traditional cities" gave shape to the "segmented quality of their spatial structure" (*kūkan kōzō no bunsetsuteki na tokushitsu*). See, for example, Yoshida Nobuyuki, "Soshiabirite to bunsetsu kōzō," in *Dentō toshi: bunsetsu kōzō*, ed. Yoshida Nobuyuki and Itō Takashi (Tokyo: Tōkyō Shuppankai, 2010), v.

104   By comparison, in 1806 Chōshi had 2,654 households and 12,519 people, and at mid-century Sakura had a combination of 1,238 warrior and commoner households and an estimated population of 10,000 people. Ishii Susumu and Uno Shun'ichi, eds. *Chiba-ken no rekishi* (Tokyo: Yamakawa Shuppansha, 2000), 209–11.

Saburōemon branch remained the main family line with one of its patriarchs being the well-known surveyor and cartographer Inō Tadataka (1745–1818).[105] From its position as head (*nanushi*) of the central Honjuku group of Sawara, the Inō Saburōemon extended its influence and affluence by overseeing land reclamation efforts during the seventeenth century. This included the previously discussed sandbars and islands in the Katori Sea that led to the dispute between Sawara and neighboring Tsunomiya Village.[106] In addition to earning a reliable income in rent from their extensive holdings of land both in and outside of Sawara, the Inō Saburōemon also entered the shipping business by collecting, carrying, and storing tax-rice from nearby villages for the Tokugawa and its high-ranking bannermen (*hatamoto*) who had fiefs in the surrounding area. In recognition of the Inō's crucial role in tax collection, in 1690 the Tokugawa designated Sawara as an official tax-handling wharf. By the eighteenth century, the Inō had turned its collection, distribution, and storage of tax-rice into a lucrative sake-brewing business, shipping this product by boat throughout the surrounding area as well as to Edo.[107] Although nearly a century later and having become an important moneylender to other merchants and Tokugawa retainers, in 1784 the Inō also opened a branch store named Kanōya along the Kamakura wharf in central Edo. There they handled the tax-rice collected from villages within the sizable fief of Lord Tsuda, a powerful *hatamoto* retainer with a substantial enfeoffment of 6,000 *koku*.[108] Through these various activities, the Inō and the village's other merchants played a prominent role in making Sawara a key node in a network of riparian relations that tied the rural riverport to Edo and the surrounding countryside. In doing so, it helped produce the Kantō as a region.

---

105   The youngest child of the village head's family in Ozeki Village (south of Chōshi in present-day Kujūkuri Town), Tadataka married into and became the official heir of the Inō Saburōemon at seventeen years of age in 1762. At forty-nine, he officially relinquished his position as patriarch to his eldest son Kagetaka and moved to Edo where he studied astronomy, surveying, and cartography. From 1800 and until his death in 1818, he received permission from the Tokugawa to travel throughout the country to survey and create the first accurate map of the archipelago's coastline from Kyushu in the south to Ezo (Hokkaidō) in the north. Suzuki Junko, "Seeking Accuracy: The First Modern Survey of Japan's Coast," in *Cartographic Japan: A History in Maps*, ed. Sugimoto Fumiko, Kären Wigen, and Cary Karacas (Chicago: University of Chicago Press, 2016), 129–32; Inō Tadataka Kenkyūkai, ed., *Tadataka to Inō-zu* (Tokyo: Awa Puran'ningu, 1998), 14–15.

106   *Chiba-ken no rekishi: tsūshi hen, kinsei*, 2:322–24.

107   In 1744, the Inō opened its own branch store handling rice and sake in Edo's shipping and wharf district of Koami-chō. *Chiba-ken no rekishi: tsūshi hen, kinsei*, 2:328–34.

108   *Chiba-ken no rekishi: tsūshi hen, kinsei*, 2:334–36.

Its short distance up the Ono River may have prevented central Sawara from being flooded from the Tone River, but this smaller river also shaped the arrangement and operations of the port. A 1756 petition provides a summary of the state of water transport in the village. According to this document, the leaders of Sawara stated that, "from the tenth through second month" the Ono grows shallow because its source is in the nearby "hills and valleys" and thus only drains a small river basin. They noted that from early spring farmers draw water from upstream in order to irrigate their downstream paddy fields. Moreover, they pointed out that in "rare years" the river gets "somewhat buried" (*shōshō umari*) and requires dredging. As if to forestall concerns about the viability of Sawara's status as an official tax-handling wharf, they clarified that these conditions were not so difficult as to "impede the shipping of tax-rice and other goods."[109] Another document from 1759 described how boats from "various places in nearby provinces" delivered firewood, planks, vinegar, sake, soy sauce, rice and other grains, and dried sardines used for fertilizer by farmers throughout the region. Some of these boats, like that piloted by Kanosuke, would stop in or near the mouth of the Ono as they passed Sawara on their routes between Edo and more distant riverports in order to off-load part of their cargo to a lighter (*hashike*) or to seek shelter when encountering "difficult winds" (*nanpū*).[110] In other words, seasonal differences in rainfall and the diminutive size of the Ono River meant that only smaller riverboats could regularly navigate up the Ono to dock directly at Sawara's wharves while bigger *takasebune* like Kanosuke's had to load and unload their goods onto lighters that sailed out of the riverport. Despite these limitations, Sawara remained a bustling riverport until the early twentieth century.

A set of complex arrangements at Sawara's riverport thus shaped the loading and unloading of boats, use of wharves and storehouses, and the payment of fees and taxes. Although little is known about the organization of the riverport before the mid-eighteenth century, a 1770 document explains that there were about ninety boats of various sizes working out of Sawara.[111] Three years later, it was recorded elsewhere that about half of these boats travelled regularly between Sawara and Edo.[112] Many of the other boats in Sawara were likely

109   "Sawara-mura Jinzō funa-tonya shutsugan ni tsuki Sawara-mura hentōgaki" [1756], in *Chiba-ken no rekishi: shiryō hen, kinsei*, 6:550.
110   "Hamajuku-kumi Gohei funa-tonya shutsugan ni tsuki Sawara-mura hentōgaki" [1759], in *Chiba-ken no rekishi: shiryō hen, kinsei*, 6:551.
111   "Sawara-mura Gonzaburō goyōfune ukeoi gansho oyobi Shimojuku kumigashira mōshiagegaki" [1770], in *Chiba-ken no rekishi: shiryō hen, kinsei*, 6:563.
112   In 1773, there were forty-four riverboats listed as sailing between Sawara and Edo. Of these, Nishinomiya Rinpei owned three boats and employed a different pilot for each. Inō

lighters that operated locally.[113] Between 1772 and 1774, the Tokugawa's Finance Office (Kanjōsho) carried out a series of river wharf inspections (*kashi ginmi*) throughout the entire Kantō region with the aim of broadening its tax base to include more mercantile activity. Following these investigations, the Finance Office began collecting an annual wharf tax (*kashi unjō*) from these villages in exchange for the issuance of a license to act as an officially recognized wharf merchant (*kashi tonya*). In Sawara, the prominent Inō Saburōemon and another Inō branch family, the Mozaemon, became the village port's only two wharf merchants. While the two Inō families collected a commission (*kōsen*) when boats were loaded and unloaded as well as storage fees (*niwasen*) for goods held in wharf storehouses, they exercised their power within the village to pass on the burden of paying the new tax to their less influential fellow merchants. With the initiation of this wharf-merchant system, eighty merchant households in Sawara paid a specific fee to jointly settle the village's annual wharf tax.[114] Whether due to the growth of Sawara as a whole or just its merchant population, by 1863 the number of merchants contributing toward the payment of the annual wharf tax rose to 276 merchant households.[115] This information about boats, boatowners, boat pilots, and merchants who paid taxes on and used the village's wharves is suggestive of just how central the riverport was to Sawara and how by the nineteenth century the village had become deeply entangled in the region's broader riparian networks.

Besides Sawara, by the nineteenth century there were other busy riverports along the Tone River route that lay between Edo and the towns and villages of Shimōsa and Hitachi Provinces. These included the castle town of Sekiyado, the fishing village and packhorse station of Fuse, Ōhori with its seven licensed wharf merchants and its seasonal fleet of lighters, and Kioroshi with its

---

Saburōemon and seven others owned two boats apiece with individual pilots for each. Twenty others each owned only one boat and employed one pilot. The remaining thirteen riverboats were owned by their own pilots. These numbers are based on the following table: "1793 (Kansei 5) nen, Edo kara Sawara aida no yusō ni jūji suru fune no funanushi," in *Chiba-ken no rekishi: tsūshi hen, kinsei*, 2:62.

113 Although there is little documentation about the lighter system in Sawara, by the nineteenth century the operators of these small boats appear to have belonged to a "lighter association" (*hashike nakama*) that was under the authority of the office of the acting village head (*nenban yakusho*). According to an 1842 petition from a local merchant group to the office of the acting village head, they desired to halt the recent lottery practice of determining the order in which lighters could take on jobs and return to the system where boatowners and merchants could freely contract with individual lighters. *Chiba-ken no rekishi: tsūshi hen, kinsei*, 2:37–38.

114 "Kashi yakusen waritsuki hikae" [1775] in *Chiba-ken no rekishi: shiryō hen, kinsei*, 6:570–73.

115 "Kashi unjō toritate-chō," [1863] in *Chiba-ken no rekishi: shiryō hen, kinsei*, 6:573–87.

well-known *chabune* passenger boats for tourists and pilgrims from Edo and beyond. For the pilots of the sizable *takasebune* with which Kanosuke and others sailed their heavy cargos of tax-rice and other goods for Edo's lordly estates and storehouses, the riverport of Ōhori was a necessary stop on most journeys. They did not pause for its bathhouses, eateries, or other entertainments since nearly every other riverport had these amenities. Rather, *takasebune* dropped anchor at Ōhori for the port's lighter services.[116] Just upstream from this riverport and as far as Sekiyado the Tone grew dangerously shallow as it widened and slowed when flowing through the marshy bottomlands into which the Ōyama, Nagaido, and other large marshes drained. When mooring at Ōhori, for example, Kanosuke like many other boat pilots contracted with one or more of these lighters to carry a portion of his cargo upstream, around Sekiyado, and down the Edo River as far as the riverport of Matsudo.[117] By off-loading a portion of his cargo in this way, his *takasebune* sat higher in the water enabling it to sail with the hired lighter along the shallower stretches of the Tone and Edo Rivers. During the summer months, these rivers ran deeper so there was less need for lighters, many of which relocated during this time of year to work the waters of Edo.[118] Riverboats that could sail as far upstream as Fuse Village on the south bank of the Tone also had the option of off-loading a portion of their load onto waiting packhorses. From Fuse, "load agents" (*niyado*) led trains of up to twenty small packhorses overland to Ka Village on the eastern bank of the Edo River where their goods were typically loaded on to a different riverboat. While more expensive, this overland portage route was favored for shipping fresh tuna and other perishables from the fishing grounds on the Pacific coast. As the historian Nagahara Tatehiko points out, although the packhorse trains that carried goods overland between riverports were technically a form

---

116   Unlike Sawara where the port and village were generally synonymous with each other, Ōhori was separated by about 3 km of dry fields and winding paths from the administrative village of Ino to which it belonged. Where the center of Ino lay on higher ground near the Mito Highway, Ōhori stretched out along the levee on the north bank of the Tone for a full kilometer. During the summer months, most of Ōhori's residents earned much of their living by fishing and farming, but during the dry months of winter they worked as stevedores and crew for the many lighters operating out of the port. Watanabe, *Kinsei Tonegawa suiun shi no kenkyū*, 165–67.

117   At Ōhori on 25 March 1853 (2nd month, 16th day), for example, Kanosuke off-loaded 100 bails of rice and 280 bundles of boards to a lighter. Two days later at the riverport of Sakai, he also hired a laborer (*kako*) to help pull his *takasebune* with a towrope. Once he passed Sekiyado the next day, he transferred the cargo from the lighter back to his *takasebune* and continued sailing for Edo. Honda, "Kawajō fūu tomari nikki," 393.

118   Watanabe, *Kinsei Tonegawa suiun shi no kenkyū*, 163.

of "land transport" (*riku'un*), they were also integral to the region's "water transport society" (*suiun no shakai*).[119]

2.3   *River Fishing Villages*

In addition to water transport, fishing and the hunting of waterfowl were also illustrative of local and regional riparian relations that emerged through river-related activities from the seventeenth century. More than just individuals fishing to fill out a family's diet, it was the emergence of commercial fishing that shaped the riparian relations of entire waterside villages. With its many interconnected marshes, lakes, and the brackish waters of the downstream Katori Sea, the Tone River was home to carp, trout, and several other kinds of fish.[120] Throughout this time, however, salmon remained the most prized of all river fish. Integral to this valuation of Tone River salmon and other fish was the growing population of Edo and the surrounding region, increasingly efficient fishing gear, and the heightened commercialization of fishing and related activities. These factors worked together to transform those riparian relations centered on fishing along the lower Tone River.

Whether along the coast or rivers, the commercial fishing operations in the Kantō followed a seasonal cycle. In his 1855 gazetteer, for example, Sōtan explained that on the Tone River the salmon season ran every year between the seventh and tenth months as these large anadromous fish returned from the Pacific Ocean to spawn in the upper reaches of the river's tributaries.[121] While up and down the river, villages with recognized fishing rights caught this prized fish as they swam upstream, Sōtan describes in detail the changing color and flavor of salmon caught at different stretches of the Tone and its tributaries. Between Chōshi and Sawara, he remarked, the flesh of the salmon was "salty" (*shioke ari*) and therefore its color was light red and its "taste awfully inferior" (*ajiwaitaku otoreri*).[122] Perhaps not too surprising, Sōtan extolled the salmon caught by the fishers from his home village of Fukawa (fig. 14). He praised how these salmon had, after swimming upstream in fresh water, completely lost their saltiness, had fattened up, their flesh becoming deep red, and their flavor peerless. Sōtan extolled his local fish, but by the time he was

---

119   Nagahara Tatehiko, "Niyado," in *Mibunteki shūen to kinsei shakai 2: umi to kawa ni ikiru*, ed. Saitō Yoshiyuki (Tokyo: Yoshikawa Kōbunkan, 2007), 107.

120   In his visual encyclopedia of freshwater fish and fishing along the lower Tone River and its connecting marshes and lakes, the local historian Ashihara Shūji describes dozens of fish, shellfish, and other riparian creatures of the region as well as the different ways to catch and cook them. Ashihara Shūji, *Kawazakana zushi* (Nagareyama: Ronshobō, 1984).

121   Akamatsu, *Tonegawa zushi*, 62.

122   Akamatsu, *Tonegawa zushi*, 63.

FIGURE 14   An 1855 illustration of salmon fishing in the Tone River near Fusa Village. In
Akamatsu Sōtan, *Tonegawa zushi* (Tokyo: Iwanami Shoten, 1938), 164–65

writing in the mid-nineteenth century, salmon were also increasingly scarce
and thereby expensive. Even when writing about salmon in his home province
of Echigo, the wealthy merchant-turned-writer Suzuki Bokushi (1770–1842)
wrote in his 1841 collection of essays that: "Although it is said that Edo has the
Tone River, [salmon] is so rare that the value of the first salmon of the year
compares to that of the first bonito!"[123]

There are many examples of shifting riparian relations surrounding the fishing of salmon and other fish along the Tone River, but the riverside villages
of Fukawa and Fusa and their common fishery offer a representative case.
Located on the north and south banks of the Tone River where it narrowed
to pass between low bluffs on either side of the river, Fukawa and Fusa shared
and occasionally contested the fishery that lay between them. To catch fish
whose habits varied as much as carp, trout, and salmon, fishers in both villages used several kinds of lines, nets, traps, weirs, and even spears. The documentation included in an 1844 agreement shows that these two villages had at

---

123   Suzuki Bokushi, *Hokuetsu seppu*, ed. Okada Takematsu (Tokyo: Iwanami Shoten, 2001),
119. On Suzuki's life and times, see Takeshi Moriyama, *Crossing Boundaries in Tokugawa
Society: Suzuki Bokushi, a Rural Elite Commoner*, Brill's Japanese Studies Library 41 (Leiden:
Brill, 2013).

different times over two centuries contested each other's and their neighboring villages' access to their river fishery as well as the kinds of gear that could be used to fish this stretch of the river.[124] Similar to the dispute between the downstream villages of Sawara, Shinowara, and Tsunomiya that was discussed at the beginning of this chapter, the dispute between Fukawa and Fusa also dated back to the mid-seventeenth century when the Tone River was diverted eastward into the Hitachi River. These upstream villages apparently had no new islands over which to argue but, like those downstream villages, they quarreled with nearby villages over the boundaries of their fishery. In the Tenwa era (1681–84), Fukawa and Fusa affirmed an earlier obligation to pay an annual tax on each boat employed for fishing and that their fishery extended upstream to Omonma Village (just below Ōhori) and downstream as far as Ajiki Village. As with other river fisheries in the region, this Fukawa-Fusa fishery had historically been divided between a spring trout run and the autumn salmon run. Because of increased fishing and likely declining numbers of salmon, Fukawa and Fusa acceded in the Tenwa agreement to adopt a "bidding" (nyūsatsu) system that granted the exclusive right to one or the other village to fish for salmon within the fishery for a single season and shoulder the obligation to pay the annual fishery tax. By the 1820s, however, Ōhori and two other upstream villages had begun encroaching on Fukawa's and Fusa's shared fishery and all parties had begun using the ruthlessly efficient beach seines (jibiki-ami) and dragnets called ikuri. In the 1844 agreement, the two villages just upstream gained the right to fish the river in front of their respective villages with the obligation to pay their annual fishery tax. Moreover, all villages agreed to a prohibition on the use of beach seines and dragnets in the fall salmon fishery.[125] Although this represented only a short 10 km stretch of the Tone River, the resulting riparian relations between Fukawa, Fusa, and their fishery can be seen elsewhere along the river and its tributaries. It is difficult to know what the severe decrease in salmon populations meant for the broader riparian assemblage, but their scarcity in the Tone River led villagers to prey more upon other kinds of commercially viable fish like carp, trout, and sweetfish (ayu).

These quotidian activities, as well as the riparian relations and assemblages they constituted, also created their own geographies and temporalities. By carrying goods between Edo and hinterland riverports, assemblages of riverboats, crews, and rivers helped form complex riparian relations that entwined with commercial and vassal relations to produce particular places and geographies

---

124   "Tonegawa gyoryō ni tsuki Tenwa-ki yori no saikyo utsushi" [1844], in Tone-machi shi: shiryō shū, ed. Tone-machi Shi Hensan Iinkai (Tone: Tone-machi, 1983), 2:205.

125   Tone-machi Shi Hensan Iinkai, Tone-machi shi: shiryō shū, 2:205.

at local and regional levels. Their repeated passage and stopping by specific ports brought goods and people to and from bustling rural villages and towns like Sawara. Whereas Sawara with its many merchants, markets, lighters, and wharves was an extraordinary example of such a rural riverport, its physical layout and the interaction between different groups in and outside the village exemplified the kinds of activities that could found elsewhere throughout the Kantō region. Moreover, with their seasonal rotations and combinations of fishing, farming, and wharf work, villages like Tsunomiya, Fukawa, and Fuse demonstrate how each of these villages also had their own temporalities. As noted above, rice farming in Sawara began annually in early spring with the diversion of upstream river water into irrigation canals that flooded downstream paddy fields. These preparations were followed by a series of regular activities from transplanting rice stalks to the draining of paddy fields. Even after the fall harvest, the Inō Saburōemon and similarly positioned merchants adhered to a regular calendar of collecting the dried, threshed, and sacked rice; transporting it to their riverports for sale, storage, or processing into sake and other products; and at fairly consistent times of the year shipping the rice, and goods made from it, to Edo and other destinations. While the shipping of tax-rice and other goods corresponded with these harvest and storage schedules, they were also shaped by seasonal differences in rainfall and therefore water levels in the region's rivers. In the same way, the seasonal runs of salmon, trout, and other fish affected both the organization of labor within villages and their relations with each other. As these various examples suggest, villages in the Kantō region were neither enclosed nor autonomous. Rather, these communities were entangled within complex and constantly changing sets of riparian and other relations.

3   Conclusion

This chapter has focused on the role of riparian relations in the formation the Kantō region and its riverscapes through a myriad of fluvial activities carried out by the Tokugawa government, rural commoners, and the rivers themselves between the seventeenth and nineteenth centuries. Although already discussed in the introductory chapter, it is worth emphasizing again that there was no mention in the sources from this time of terms like *shizen* (nature), *kankyō* (the environment), or their numerous synonyms. None of the documents, be they Kanosuke's logbook, petitions and agreements issued by village leaders, or even Sōtan's contemplative writing about the Tone River, described the river, with its brush-covered banks and sandbars or the fish that swam and spawned in its waters, in terms of the modern, unified concept of "nature" or "environment." Instead, Kanosuke noted where the river was shallow or when the winds were blowing favorably. Villagers commented on the payment of fees and taxes, access to parts of the river, the seasonal runs of fish, and kinds of nets employed to catch them. And, even when recounting local "climes" (*tenkō*) or "products" (*bussan*), Sōtan quoted the Chinese classics and commented on the kinds of winds, preparations for rain, varieties of fish, and even the elusive and mysterious water goblin known as a *kappa*.[126] All of these people of the region commented on the river and their diverse relations with it without use of the modern concept of nature that abstracts humans from the lifeworlds in which they were so thoroughly entangled.

By jettisoning a historical ontology based on the clear separation of humans from the worlds within which they lived, this chapter (and book) call into question common assumptions about the notion of agency in historical narratives. Most histories about the rerouting of the seventeenth-century Tone, Ara, and other rivers and the subsequent transformations of the Kantō region tend to assume that some humans, such as the Tokugawa's intendants, were "agent-full." At the same time, they assume these rivers and the tens of thousands of people who also assisted in the transformation of the Kantō region and its riverscapes somehow possessed little if any historical agency (fig. 15). Throughout the Kantō region, however, many river diversions and irrigation canals followed channels already carved into the land through the historical fluvial work of the rivers themselves. These projects frequently began with an upstream levee or sluice that directed a river in a different direction and then relied on the river itself to excavate much of the remainder of the new channel. Moreover, despite the Ina intendants role in designing and overseeing these projects, it was tens of thousands of typically nameless commoners who actually labored on these diversion and excavation projects. As seen with Sawara, Tsunomiya, and nearby villages, it was local farmers and fishers, often under the direction of a village leader or wealthy merchant family like that of the Inō Saburōemon, who along with riverine reeds and shrubs and sediment-bearing rivers, transformed wetlands into farmlands and therein helped define the banks of the region's rivers. Similarly, boat pilots like Kanosuke did not simply command a riverboat to sail through a preexisting riverscape. They worked with their crews, their boats, and the vagaries of seasonal winds and waters and therein continuously contributed to the formation of the Kantō region's

---

126   Akamatsu, *Tonegawa zushi*, 53–73. For a discussion of the modern transformation of the *kappa*, see Michael D. Foster, "The Metamorphosis of the Kappa: Transformation of Folklore to Folklorism in Japan," *Asian Folklore Studies* 57, no. 1 (1998): 1–24.

FIGURE 15   Early nineteenth-century illustration of levee work, most likely on the outskirts of
             Edo. Katsushika Hokusai, no title for print, c. 1824–26
             COURTESY OF THE BIBLIOTHÈQUE NATIONALE DE FRANCE, PARIS

riverscapes. Instead of limiting historical agency to a few elite authorities or
even more generally to humans, the examples set out in this chapter demonstrate that it is more accurate to view agency as being distributed between
the different parts of these assemblages. This does not, however, mean that
agency was evenly exercised within these riparian assemblages. As discussed
in the following chapter it was in fact unevenly distributed within and between
these assemblages, with some actors, such as the Ina intendants and the Inō
Saburōemon of Sawara, clearly being more powerful and exercising more
agency than others.

CHAPTER 2

The Kantō River Regime under the Tokugawa Government

The one who governs the rivers, governs the country.

Kawa o osameru mono ga kuni o osameru
河を治める者が国を治める

∵

Drawn from classical Chinese thought, the above undated maxim reflects the Tokugawa regime's approach to governing the rivers within its dominion and even today continues to be routinely cited by politicians and government officials in Japan.[1] Pithy in its formulation, this passage expresses the importance of controlling a country's rivers and waters in order for a ruler or government to maintain their legitimacy and authority over their realm. It also suggests that a ruler's failure to regulate the waters of their realm is a sign of broader failings in their administration—a clear reminder that governance extends beyond the common focus on state-society relations to necessarily involve the nonhuman water, land, and creatures that make life and government possible. During the Tokugawa period, this maxim not only encapsulated the relative power of successive shogunal and domain rulers within riparian and other assemblages but also their waning capacity to rule from the nineteenth century onward.

More powerful than any previous regime on the Japanese archipelago, the Tokugawa government exercised its power through a variety of relations, including those formed within and between riparian assemblages. As described in chapter 1, from its earliest years the Tokugawa expended much effort and expense to transform the riverscapes of the Kantō region and

---

1 In addressing broader issues of river and water management, this maxim is also frequently modified by substituting "river" with "water" (*mizu*). Examples of both contemporary usages of this maxim can be found by searching the following official websites of the Japan's House of Representatives (Shūgiin) and the Ministry of Land, Infrastructure, Transport, and Tourism (Kokudokōtsūshō): http://www.shugiin.go.jp/internet/index.nsf/html/index.htm, accessed 12 October 2019, and http://www.mlit.go.jp/, accessed 12 October 2019.

beyond. The Kantō was the most critical and vital region for the Tokugawa. It was produced with the country's preeminent castle town of Edo at the center of a network of rivers and sea lanes that supplied it with valuable tax-rice and much of its other foodstuffs and commodities.[2] Both the Tokugawa government and rural communities alike worked with the Tone, Ara, and other rivers of the Kantō region to shift, narrow, and extend their channels in old and new directions. Whether for flood control, water transport, or land reclamation, these river projects helped locals to grow, ship, and sell greater amounts and varieties of crops. Moreover, it enabled the Tokugawa to govern more fully, drawing resources and revenue from the entire Kantō region. Elsewhere in the archipelago, the Tokugawa and domain governments ordered the rerouting, narrowing, and tapping of large and small rivers to improve water transport or to increase and protect arable land. On the lower Kiso River system in central Japan, for example, the Tokugawa ordered the 1619 excavation of the Ōgure River and the building of multiple levees that contributed to the delta's characteristic polder (*wajū*) landscape.[3] Similarly, along the Yodo River, Tokugawa retainers oversaw a number of riparian projects to strengthen flood controls and facilitate navigation to and from the port of Osaka including the 1684 excavation of the Aji River and 1704 diversion of the Yamato River.[4] While the Tokugawa directly administered river engineering and management in the Kantō region and in areas around the cities of Osaka and Nagoya, from 1703 onward it also compelled domain lords to annually supervise village dredging and erosion-prevention efforts within the Yodo River basin. And, in 1754, it infamously ordered Satsuma domain to undertake the costly Hōreki flood-control project along the lower Kiso River.[5]

Although of hitherto unprecedented power and capacity, the Tokugawa government was not a modern state. Both Japanese and English-language scholarship on the Tokugawa period maintain that the now decades-old "state debate" (*kokkaron*) began by jettisoning the once dominant view of the Tokugawa as an

2   Murakami Tadashi, "Kinsei Kantō no chiikiteki tokushitsu to kadai," in *Bakuhan shakai no tenkai to Kantō*, ed. Murakami Tadashi (Tokyo: Yoshikawa Kōbunkan, 1986), 1–18.
3   Gifu-ken, ed., *Gifu-ken shi: tsūshi hen, kinsei 2* (Gifu: Gifu-ken, 1972), 166–71.
4   Murata Michihito, *Kinsei Yodogawa chisui* (Tokyo: Yamakawa Shuppansha, 2009), 31–34, 75–81.
5   Patricia G. Sippel, "*Chisui*: Creating a Sacred Domain in Early Modern and Modern Japan," in *Public Spheres, Private Lives in Modern Japan, 1600–1950: Essays in Honor of Albert M. Craig*, ed. Andrew Gordon, Gail Lee Bernstein, and Kate Wildman Nakai, Harvard East Asian Monographs 238 (Cambridge: Harvard University Asia Center, 2005), 167–72; Mizumoto Kunihiko, *Kinsei no mura shakai to kokka* (Tokyo: Tokyo Daigaku Shuppankai, 1987), 237–57; Nakanishi Tatsuharu, *Hōreki chisui to Hirata Yukie: Shijitsu to kenshō no ayumi* (Nagoya: Arumu, 2015).

absolute state ruling over a feudal society to instead provide a more accurate and complex view of its governing institutions and its relations with domain lords, the imperial household, and rural and urban commoners.[6] By the 1980s, historians had reevaluated and discovered new primary sources that revealed an array of anachronisms, inaccurate chronologies, and many misunderstandings of the Tokugawa period.[7] This research also revealed the patchwork and often ad-hoc character of Tokugawa institutions and raised significant questions about the nature and extent of Tokugawa authority (kōgi) vis-à-vis villages, merchant houses, the imperial household, temples and shrines, and especially domain lords. In the 1990s, for example, three separate English-language studies of large domains collectively argued for a greater recognition of the local autonomy, power, and hence disparity between domain policies regarding demographics, finances, and governing institutions.[8] In a more recent authoritative series on Japanese history by the publisher Iwanami, historians address

---

6   The historian Philip Brown points out that this view of Tokugawa absolutism and feudalism was both inaccurate and followed a "Eurocentric conceptualization of states." Philip C. Brown, *Central Authority and Local Autonomy in the Formation of Early Modern Japan: The Case of Kaga Domain* (Stanford: Stanford University Press, 1993), 27. For an early example of this revised view of Tokugawa governance, see Hara Hidesaburō, Minegishi Sumio, Sasaki Junnosuke, and Nakamura Masanori, eds., *Taikei Nihon kokka shi: kinsei* (Tokyo: Tōkyō Shuppankai, 1975).

7   Two of the most important correctives were of the *sakoku* paradigm, which inaccurately viewed the Tokugawa government as having secluded Japan from the outside world from the seventeenth century onward, and of what might be called the "status" paradigm which incorrectly viewed the Tokugawa as enforcing an orthodox view of Confucianism to divide society into four classes or estates (i.e., warrior-scholars, peasants, artisans, and merchants). The following English-language books provided clear reevaluations of these respective paradigms and initiated many subsequent studies of Tokugawa foreign relations and social status: Ronald P. Toby, *State and Diplomacy in Early Modern Japan: Asia in the Development of the Tokugawa Bakufu* (Princeton: Princeton University Press, 1984); Daniel Botsman, *Punishment and Power in the Making of Modern Japan* (Princeton: Princeton University Press, 2005); David L. Howell, *Geographies of Identity in Nineteenth-Century Japan* (Berkeley: University of California Press, 2005).

8   In his review essay of Ravina's and Roberts' books, the historian Ronald P. Toby cautions against their more ambitious arguments about the nation and state-like qualities of the largest domains: "Japan, I shall argue, was 'the Nation' and the [Tokugawa] bakufu 'the State' in early modern Japan, while domains were neither 'states' (except in the sense that Texas and Massachusetts are 'states') nor 'nations,' but local or regional units within the political and discursive bounds of 'Japan.'" Ronald P. Toby, "Rescuing the Nation from History: The State of the State in Early Modern Japan," *Monumenta Nipponica* 56, no. 2 (2001): 200; Brown, *Central Authority and Local Autonomy*; Mark Ravina, *Land and Lordship in Early Modern Japan* (Stanford: Stanford University Press, 1999); Luke S. Roberts, *Mercantilism in a Japanese Domain: The Merchant Origins of Economic Nationalism in 18th-Century Tosa* (Cambridge: Cambridge University Press, 1998).

a wide range of topics related to the "state debate" and demonstrate how this dialog continues to shape the field. Of the chapters on Tokugawa governance, for instance, the authors in the Iwanami series collectively pursued the previous generation's corrections of anachronisms and variously reexamine the following topics: the processes by which the Tokugawa created its governing institutions and extended its authority, differences between domain lords and the Tokugawa's highest-ranking bannermen (*hatamoto*), the Tokugawa's basic institutions of rule from the perspective of the Kinai region, relations with the other countries of East Asia, and the intent and effect of major Tokugawa reforms.[9] These suggest that most research on the Tokugawa and domain governments continues to overlook or minimize nonhuman factors and actors like rivers.[10]

Despite its absence in this recent scholarship, the Tokugawa government and its officials displayed a keen interest in the governance of riparian activities like irrigation, fishing, water transport, and flood control. Chapter 1 has already shown how, from the early seventeenth century, rivers in the Kantō region became entrained in the Tokugawa's governing institutions through its leaders' efforts to increase arable land and thus tax revenue, to develop new transport routes, and to limit the damage caused by flooding.[11] This chapter continues to examine the riparian history of the Kantō region. In addition to the region being centered on the archipelago's largest plain (the Kantō Plain), traversed by its largest river (the Tone River), and the location of what became its largest city (Edo), the Kantō was also the core region under Tokugawa authority. Accordingly, Tokugawa rule over the Kantō region has the clearest temporal and administrative boundaries, lending itself to a historical inquiry into how between the early seventeenth and mid-nineteenth centuries this preeminent power conditioned and was conditioned through the region's complex riparian relations.[12] Whereas the modern state in Japan came to concentrate its

---

9   Ōtsu Hide, Sakurai Eiji, Fujii Jōji, Yoshida Yutaka, and Li Sonshi, eds., *Iwanami kōza Nihon rekishi* (Tokyo: Iwanami Shoten, 2014), vols. 10–14.

10   Of the thirty-seven chapters included in these four volumes dedicated to the Tokugawa period, the two notable exceptions to this generalization are: Murata Michibiko, "Yoshimune no seiji," in *Iwanami kōza Nihon rekishi: kinsei 3*, ed. Ōtsu Hide et al. (Tokyo: Iwanami Shoten, 2014), 12:1–34; and Takahashi Yoshitaka, "Gyogyō," in *Iwanami kōza Nihon rekishi: kinsei 4*, ed. Ōtsu Hide et al. (Tokyo: Iwanami Shoten, 2015), 13:137–65.

11   Andrew M. Bauer and Steve Kosiba, "How Things Act: An Archaeology of Materials in Political Life," *Journal of Social Archaeology* 16, no. 2 (2016): 122–24.

12   An investigation of how domain lords governed riparian relations within their dominions is beyond the scope of this study. For examples of domain efforts at various forms of riparian governance, see Yokoyama Akio, *Kinsei kasen suiun shi no kenkyū: Mogamigawa suiun no rekishiteki tenkai o chūshin to shite* (Tokyo: Yoshikawa Kōbunkan, 1980); Saitō

energies on flood control and related projects, the Tokugawa was consistently concerned with regulating the wider ways in which urban and rural communities interacted with the rivers of the Kantō region.[13] Furthermore, unlike the territorially contiguous, nested, and typically scalable institutions of the modern state, the Tokugawa regime ruled through territorially segmented, composite, and often nonscalable institutions. The historian Yoshida Nobuyuki has analyzed the fractured character of authority and governance under the Tokugawa to reveal how urban and rural societies were organized along complex "segmented structures" (*bunsetsuteki na kōzō*) that connected "particular places" (*tokutei no ba*) to produce specific regions.[14] For these reasons, the Kantō region is exemplary *and* illustrative of how rivers became entrained in the institutions and practices of Tokugawa governance. The first section of this chapter focuses on river transport. It discusses how initial military concerns with the role of rivers in security and supply routes eventually gave way to the more bureaucratic concerns of securing taxes, settling disputes, and safeguarding transportation routes. Section two examines the reforms that began in the Kyōhō era (1716–36) and the Tokugawa government's efforts to deal with systemic problems in its approach to riparian governance. The concluding section commences with the 1783 eruption of Mount Asama and considers why the Tokugawa increasingly lacked the capacity to maintain and govern the riparian infrastructure upon which its rule had become so reliant.

1   Establishing Tokugawa Governance over the Waters of the Kantō
         Region, 1590–1700

The Tokugawa began its rule over the Kantō region in 1590 through institutions that had served its military needs during many years of intermittent warfare. These military origins shaped the Tokugawa's occupation of the territory in the Kantō region and its governance of the region's rivers in ways

---

Yoshiyuki, "Umi to kawa ni ikiru: Sendai-han no sakana no michi to ryūtsū shoshūdan," in *Mibunteki shūen to kinsei shakai 2: umi to kawa ni ikiru*, ed. Saitō Yoshiyuki (Tokyo: Yoshikawa Kōbunkan, 2007), 201–31.

13   I agree with the historian Patricia Sippel's argument that the twentieth-century Japanese government's focus on *chisui* (flood control, literally the "controlling of water") as a "sacred domain" of interaction between the Tokugawa government and local communities dates to the eighteenth century. It should also be emphasized that until the late 1880s the Tokugawa and later Meiji governments were *also* concerned with fishing, irrigation, and especially water transport. Sippel, "*Chisui*," 156–57, 182–83.

14   Yoshida Nobuyuki, "Soshiabirite to bunsetsu kōzō," in *Dentō toshi: bunsetsu kōzō*, ed. Yoshida Nobuyuki and Itō Takeshi (Tokyo: Tōkyō Daigaku Shuppankai, 2010), v, x.

that would have a lasting influence. Chapter 1 in this study outlined the fact that the new Tokugawa government expended great effort in the first half of the seventeenth century rechanneling and tapping into the region's rivers to secure and provision the preeminent castle town of Edo and the overall region. By the end of the seventeenth century, however, the exigencies of ruling the Kantō region had much less to do with military preparedness and more to do with the statecraft of keeping the peace, maintaining infrastructure, expanding its tax base, and balancing its budgets. In order to accomplish these goals, the Tokugawa government gradually developed practices and institutions that sought to render the region's riparian relations more legible and thereby governable. In villages along the rivers of the Kantō region, commoners complied with and a times passively resisted the Tokugawa's efforts to extract ever more wealth from them. Consequently, by the end of the seventeenth century, the region's rivers had become thoroughly entrained in the segmented and stratified structure of the region's governing institutions.

Fundamental to the Tokugawa governance of the region's rivers was its claim of ultimate authority (*kōgi*) over all the country's seas and rivers.[15] In writ, the Tokugawa declared as early as 1593 that "all forests, meadows, mountains, and rivers" (*rinya sansen mina*) lay within its dominion.[16] More importantly, in practice, the Tokugawa repeatedly exercised this authority over the rivers of the realm to demand payment of taxes for their use and delineate usufruct rights in navigation, irrigation, fishing, and other riparian disputes between villages, fiefs, and domains. As with the long-running dispute discussed in chapter 1 between Tsunomiya and its neighboring villages over fishing and the cultivation of newly formed islands in the waters near their villages, the Tokugawa regime intervened to ensure that taxes were paid for the rights to fish in the sea and river and farm the recently reclaimed islands. While its security and legitimacy depended on the maintenance of peace, the Tokugawa regime also recognized that these adjacent riparian areas provided villages with the water and green manure required to keep their fields fertile and productive.[17] These

---

15   Niwa Kunio, "Kinsei ni okeru san'ya kakai no shoyū-shihai to Meiji no henkaku," in *Nihon no shakai shi: kyōkai ryōiki to kōtsū*, ed. Asao Naohiro (Tokyo: Iwanami Shoten, 1987), 173–213; Takagi Shōsaku, "'Shōgun no umi' to iu ronri: kujira unjō o tegakari to shite," in *Suisan no shakai shi*, ed. Gotō Masatoshi and Yoshida Nobuyuki (Tokyo: Yamakawa Shuppansha, 2002), 171–93.

16   Document Nos. 306–37 in *Tokugawa kinrei kō*, ed. Shihōshō Hōseishi Gakkai (Tokyo: Sōbunsha, 1959), 1:153.

17   The agricultural historian Niwa Kunio, for example, argues that the Tokugawa government broadly understood that marginal riparian and littoral areas as well as meadows and wooded mountains were a precondition for the continued agricultural productivity

issues of securing the peace and an agrarian tax base shaped the Tokugawa's approach to governing the Kantō region and its rivers.

Soon after his entrance into the Kantō and choice of Edo as his headquarters in 1590, Tokugawa Ieyasu began reassembling the region's preexisting geographies of power. In order to secure the transport of tax-rice and control the movement of troops and their supplies, Ieyasu and his advisors enfeoffed retainers at strategic locations within two-days travel from Edo (about 10–20 *ri* or 40–80 km). Concentrated in Kōzuke, Musashi, Shimōsa, and Kazusa Provinces, the more than sixty retainers whose fiefs were greater than 10,000 *koku* occupied existing castles or built new strongholds near regional highways and along the Ara and Tone Rivers. Similarly, at the region's important castle towns, such as Oshi and Sekiyado, the Tokugawa also installed vassal lords (*fudai*) with modest domains of 10,000–20,000 *koku* and charged them with the same task of managing their lands and defending the region against potential attacks and uprisings.[18] In the years following the Battle of Sekigahara in 1600, the Tokugawa moved most of its senior retainers and some domain lords from the Kantō region to rule over territories in distant provinces. In their place, the Tokugawa created smaller fiefs (*chigyō*) controlled by a greater number of high-ranking bannermen, who even after being ordered to relocate their residences to Edo continued to receive their stipends from these nearby fiefs.[19] The Tokugawa also retained large areas across the Kantō region as its own direct holdings and appointed reliable retainers to oversee these villages, lands, and waters. By the end of the seventeenth century, the Tokugawa's system of governance for the Kantō region had mostly been established. Of the more than 1,600 villages in Shimōsa Province, for example, 24 percent were

---

of the country's villages. Niwa, "Kinsei ni okeru san'ya kakai no shoyū-shihai to Meiji no henkaku," 178.

18   One *koku* is a measurement of unpolished rice that equals about 180 liters. With Toyotomi Hideyoshi's 1582–98 cadastral survey and registration (*Taikō kenchi*), the *koku* became the standardized unit by which to measure the harvest yield and therefore tax rate for villages of vastly different sizes and degrees of productivity. Under the Tokugawa, both the village as an administrative unit and its *koku* value became the accepted measures by which to enfeoff retainers and domain lords. For examples of the limitations and role of local officials in shaping these yield results and tax rates, see Philip C. Brown, "The Mismeasure of Land: Land Surveying in the Tokugawa Period," *Monumenta Nipponica* 42, no. 2 (1987): 115–55.

19   According to a late eighteenth-century report, there were 5,200 *hatamoto* of whom 11 percent held fiefs of between 3,000 and 10,000 *koku*, 25 percent held fiefs of between 1,000 and 3,000 *koku*, 35 percent held fiefs of 500 and 1,000 *koku*, and the remaining roughly 30 percent held fiefs of less than 500 *koku*. Fukai Masaumi, "Hatamoto gokenin," in *Kokushi daijiten*, ed. Kokushi Daijiten Henshū Iinkai (Tokyo: Yoshikawa Kōbunkan, 1990), 11:582–83.

directly governed by Tokugawa intendants, 34 percent belonged to domain lords, and 35 percent were in the fiefs of Tokugawa bannermen.[20] In this way, the Tokugawa had fully reassembled the structures of power throughout the Kantō region from the hundreds of elite and increasingly urban warrior families down to thousands of rural villages. The result was one of a segmented series of interrelated yet distinct hierarchies of governing institutions that emerged through an entwining of old military organizations from the preceding period of persistent warfare and the new bureaucratic ones that had arisen during this sustained era of peace. While this segmentation of regional governance was clearly focused on the control of villages, the Tone, Ara, and the region's other rivers were also critical to the area's governing institutions.

The Tokugawa's principle of having authority over all rivers and seas and its segmented structure of administration shaped the institutions and practices that governed riparian relations across the Kantō region from the seventeenth century onward. In broad terms, the Tokugawa government established two general institutions to administer these rivers and the complex relations surrounding them. The first of these institutions was its system of intendants. By 1642 the Tokugawa's four head intendants (*daikan-gashira*) were consolidated into the single office of the Kantō Intendant (Kantō Gundai) that was held by Ina Tadaharu.[21] As described in chapter 1, Ina Tadaharu, his son Ina Tadakatsu, and their progeny persisted in this position for generations while pursuing policies and engineering projects across the Kantō Plain that aimed to expand the Tokugawa government's agrarian tax base. After the mid-seventeenth century, there were no projects in the Kantō region that approached the size and difficulty of the earlier rechanneling of the Tone and Ara Rivers; nonetheless,

---

20   Although these percentages in Shimōsa Province are based on a mid-nineteenth-century report, the ratio between these three forms of governance in the province date back to the late seventeenth century. *Chiba-ken no rekishi: tsūshi hen, kinsei*, ed. Chiba-ken Shiryō Kenkyū Zaidan (Chiba: Chiba-ken, 2007), 1:131–32. These percentages, however, obscure the system of *aikyū* by which villages often paid differing portions of their annual taxes to more than one domain lord, bannerman, or Tokugawa official. In 1677, for example, Sawara Village was assessed at 1,817.5 *koku*, of which 1,000 *koku* was paid to Okutsu Naiki, 350 *koku* to Kondō Jūbei, 350 *koku* to Amakata Shume, and 117.5 *koku* to the Matsudaira of Sakura domain. In addition, for land reclaimed (*shinden*) by Sawara in the proceeding decades, the village paid the area's intendant (*daikan*), Moriya Seihō, 1,775.4 *koku*. Sakai Yūji, "Kinsei zenki Shimōsa ni okeru kumiai-mura to kenchi," *Rekishi chirigaku*, no. 121 (1983): 2–4.

21   Murakami Tadashi, "Kantō gundai no seiritsu ni kan suru ichikōsatsu," in *Bakuhansei kokka seiritsu katei no kenkyū: Kanei-ki o chūshin ni*, ed. Kitajima Masamoto (Tokyo: Yoshikawa Kōbunkan, 1977), 108–18. See also Ōta Naohiro, *Bakufu daikan Ina-shi to Edo shūhen chiiki* (Tokyo: Iwata Shoin, 2010).

the Kantō Intendant continued to supervise smaller levee, dredging, and irrigation projects. Within their respective jurisdictions and often in smaller bannerman fiefs, the duties of regular intendants (*daikan*) ranged from policing and adjudicating disputes between villages to carrying out cadastral surveys, sponsoring irrigation and reclamation projects, supervising the building of new river works and repairing existing ones, and in particular the collecting of taxes.[22] The largest portion of village taxes were typically collected in the form of rice and other grains from surveyed fields, but intendants also determined the amount of miscellaneous taxes (*komononari*) to be collected for fishing, hunting, and collecting grasses in and along the region's rivers.[23] Moreover, they oversaw the shipment of tax-rice from hundreds of rural villages throughout the Kantō region to the Tokugawa's storehouses in Edo. Over the course of the seventeenth century, the shipment of tax-rice changed as old military procurement practices gave way to a system of contracted shipping agents and standardized shipping rates.[24] For tax-rice shipped from Sawara Village to Edo in 1634, for example, the shipping rates differed depending upon whose tax-rice was being shipped, with the locally enfeoffed bannerman Amakata Shume being charged a 3 percent commission (three bales of rice per hundred shipped) and the intendant governing the area being charged a 5 percent commission.[25] Throughout this period, the governance of the region's rivers by the Kantō Intendant and regular intendants fixated on increasing tax revenue through the building and maintaining of river works, expanding irrigation and reclamation, and overseeing the collecting and shipping of annual taxes.

The Tokugawa government also created a second institution for administering another of its main riparian policies in the Kantō region—the regulation of riverboat and coastal shipping. In the early seventeenth century, the Tokugawa appointed riverboat magistrates (*kawabune bugyō*) to administer

---

22   Murakami Tadashi, *Edo bakufu no daikan gunzō* (Tokyo: Dōseisha, 1997), 3–10; Izumi Seiji, *Bakufu no chiiki shihai to daikan* (Tokyo: Dōseisha, 2001), 72–112.

23   As noted in chapter 1 regarding the dispute over the Fusa-Fukawa fishery, the taxation of fishing along the lower and middle Tone River was governed by what historians call a "tax river" (*unjō kawa*) arrangement with annual rights to fish a designated fishery being granted to the bidder offering the highest tax payment. Hara Junji, "Kinsei zenki Tonegawa ryūiki no gyogyō," *Umikami-chō shi kenkyū*, no. 31 (1990): 1–25; Gotō Masatoshi, "Shōtoku-Kyōhō-ki ni okeru shimo-Tonegawa chūryūiki no gyogyō to muramura," *Kokuritsu rekishi minzoku hakubutsukan kenkyū hōkoku*, no. 115 (2004): 162, 166–68.

24   In principle, villages were responsible for the shipping of tax-rice for distances within 20 km (5 *ri*), and the local intendants and bannerman covered the cost for distances greater than 20 km. Kawana Noboru, *Kinsei Nihon suiun shi no kenkyū* (Tokyo: Yūzankaku Shuppan, 1984), 152–53.

25   Kawana, *Kinsei Nihon suiun shi no kenkyū*, 153–55.

all cargo-hauling riverboats that sailed on the waters of the eight provinces of the Kantō region. As with many of the Tokugawa government's early institutions, these magistrates had their origins in the demands for military preparedness. Initially two to three bannermen were appointed to serve as river magistrates and charged with maintaining a registry of river and seaworthy boats that could be mobilized in the event of attack. They also oversaw the riverboats entering and leaving Edo and ensured the secure and reliable shipment of tax-rice and other goods between the countryside and the quickly growing city. To monitor the movement of riverboats along the changing Tone River system, the Tokugawa government established checkpoints at the strategic locations of Sekiyado, where the Edo River branched off the Tone River, and along the Naka River at the eastern edge of Edo (fig. 16).[26] At the Naka River Checkpoint, for example, typically some six officials supervised the inspection and passage of all boats entering and leaving Edo. To regulate passage through this checkpoint, these officials followed a set of rules first issued in 1661, and subsequently reissued in later years, which demanded that all riverboat pilots, crew, and passengers remove their hats and scarves and required the opening of all hatches and containers large enough to hide a person. These rules also stipulated that departure by boat was forbidden at night (nighttime entry was allowed), transport of more than "two or three" firearms or other weapons required documentation, and women were prohibited from leaving or entering Edo by boat.[27]

---

26   The Sekiyado Checkpoint (*Sekiyado bansho*) was established in 1641 with the rechanneling of the Tone River into the what would later be called the Edo River. The Naka River Checkpoint (*Nakagawa bansho*) was originally located along the Sumida River and was called the Fukagawa Checkpoint, but as Edo rapidly expanded across the Sumida, in 1661 the checkpoint was moved eastward to the intersection of the new Onagi Canal and Naka River. Later in 1720, a checkpoint was also established at Uraga in Sagami Province for the similar purpose of monitoring the ships entering and leaving the bay leading to Edo. Kawana, *Kinsei Nihon suiun shi no kenkyū*, 325–64; Katō Takashi, "Nakagawa bansho no kinō to sono tokushitsu," *Kōtsū shi kenkyū*, no. 12 (1984): 27–46; Nishikawa Takeomi, *Edo naiwan no minato to ryūtsū* (Tokyo: Iwata Shoin, 1993), 31–42.

27   Document No. 2188 in *Tokugawa kinrei kō*, ed. Shihōshō Hōseishi Gakkai (Tokyo: Sōbunsha, 1959), 4:208–9. These riparian checkpoints operated in many ways like their well-researched terrestrial counterparts (*sekisho*), including prohibitions on the passage of women. The authorities typically granted women permission to travel when they were young and traveling with family, fulfilling special obligations like weddings or funerals, or venturing on a pilgrimage with permission from the intendant's office administering their area. It was also part of the local lore in Edo that women could circumvent this prohibition by disembarking from their boat before the Naka River Checkpoint, walking around the bamboo grove behind it, and again boarding their boat on the other side of the checkpoint. For more discussion of restrictions on women's mobility and highway barriers, see

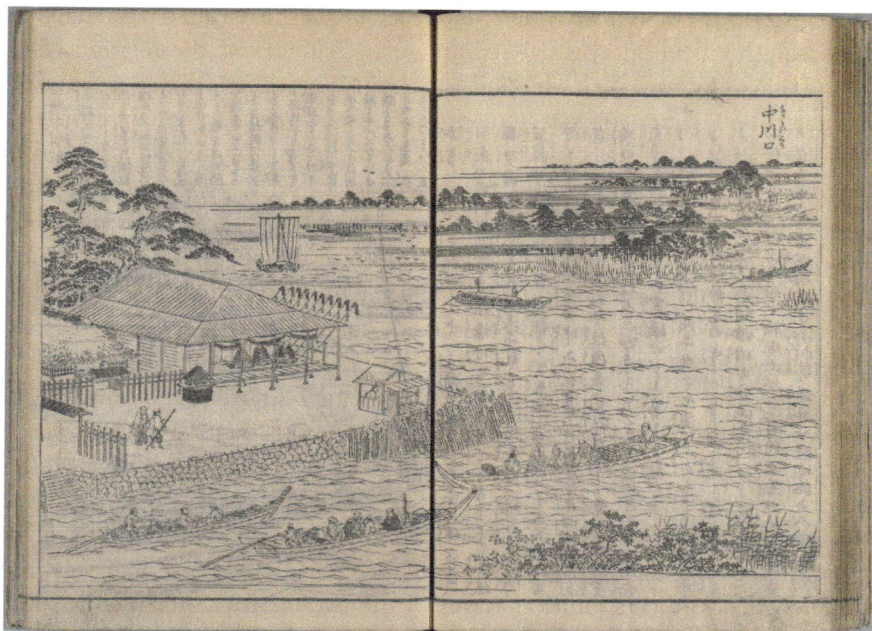

FIGURE 16   Early nineteenth-century illustration of the Naka River Checkpoint.
"Nakagawa-guchi," in Saitō Gesshin, *Edo meisho zue* (Edo: Subaraya Mohei,
1834–36), vol. 7, unpaginated
COURTESY OF THE NATIONAL DIET LIBRARY, TOKYO

A series of reforms were initiated from 1678, beginning with setting the number of Riverboat Magistrates at three and placing them under the authority of the Finance Magistrate (Kanjō Bugyō).[28] From the first month of that year, the magistrates required that the heads of all districts (*chō*) in Edo submit a list of the number of boats within their districts and that all boatowners receive a new stamp (*gokuin*) burned onto the side of their boats as proof of tax payment on them.[29] With many of the boats in Edo sailing to the city from the surrounding countryside, the magistrates soon expanded this registration requirement by ordering boats in villages facing the bay near Edo as well as those along all rivers, estuaries, lakes, and marshes throughout the Kantō region to sail to Edo for

Laura Nenzi, *Excursions in Identity: Travel and the Intersection of Place, Gender, and Status in Edo Japan* (Honolulu: University of Hawai'i Press, 2008), 46–55.

28   Kawana, *Kinsei Nihon suiun shi no kenkyū*, 242–69; Tanji Kenzō, *Kantō kasen suiun shi no kenkyū* (Tokyo: Hōsei Daigaku Shuppankai, 1984), 202–21.

29   For districts without any boats, a statement to that effect had to be submitted. Document No. 1433 in *Edo machibure shūsei*, ed. Kinsei Shiryō Kenkyūkai (Tokyo: Hanawa Shobō, 1994), 1:425.

the registering of their tax payment and receiving of the required new stamp.[30] Reflecting both the increasingly commercial character of the relations that bound Edo to its growing hinterland and the Tokugawa government's faltering finances, the Finance Magistrate continued to seek ways to collect more tax revenue. Starting in late 1689, it mobilized twenty-seven intendants to investigate shipping rates for tax-rice from riverside wharves (*kashi*) and seaside ports (*minato*) to Edo throughout the eight Kantō provinces and in Izu and Suruga Provinces. Based on the findings of these investigations, the Finance Magistrate set shipping rates for each village with the twofold aim of limiting potential corruption by individual intendants and shifting more of the cost of governing shipping to the villagers who were actually paying the taxes.[31]

In a related effort, in 1689 the Finance Magistrate ordered all owners of "riverboats" (*kawabune*) to pay a tax and have their boats branded with a new stamp.[32] A number of villages failed to comply with this order, which led the Riverboat Magistrates to dispatch a pair of officers (*tedai*) in 1692 to visit riverports along the Tone River to look for boats lacking the magistrate's stamp. During an inspection of the boats in Fuse Village that year, for instance, these officers found that one of the two boats at the Shichiri Ferry (Shichiri-ga-watashi) did not bear the required stamp. In a written order admonishing those involved, they demanded the boat to be quickly sailed to Edo to pay the required tax and receive its stamp.[33] When these same officials arrived a week later at the busy riverside port of Sawara, they discovered 151 boats whose owners had failed to have their boats stamped as proof of having paid the boat tax. While most of these boats were later identified to be local farm boats (*kōsakubune*) and therefore exempted from the tax, eight riverboats were judged as needing tax payment and a stamp. To ensure that these boats received their stamps, the officers insisted on written promises from the leaders of the districts (*juku*) and groups (*kumi*) to which the boatowners belonged.[34] This example is typical of many at the time wherein Edo-based officials pressed

---

30 Document No. 1479 in *Edo machibure shūsei*, 1:435; Ōta Nanpo, ed., *Chikkyō yohitsu* (Tokyo: Kokusho Kankōkai, 1917), 88–89. The earliest extant example for the Kantō region of a receipt for this boat tax is the 700 *mon* tax paid by a boatowner in Fuse Village in early 1679. "Enpō roku-nen kawabune nengu tegata," in *Kashiwa-shi shiryō hen: Fuse-mura kankei monjo*, ed. Kashiwa-shi Hensan Iinkai (Kashiwa: Kashiwa Shiyakusho, 1971), 6:24.

31 Kawana, *Kinsei Nihon suiun shi no kenkyū*, 165.

32 Document Nos. 2661 and No. 2662 in *Edo machibure shūsei*, 1:189–90.

33 The document is dated 5th year of Genroku, 7th month, 10th day according the old luni-solar calendar. This is 21 August 1692 in the Common Era calendar. "Watashibune gokuin aratame ni tsuki ukegaki," in *Kashiwa-shi shiryō hen: Fuse-mura kankei monjo*, 6:25–26.

34 "Kawabune oaratame otsūji," in *Sawara-shi shi: shiryō hen, betsu hen*, ed. Sawara-shi Hensan Iinkai (Sawara: Sawara Yakusho, 1996), 1:136–39.

village heads to accept the additional obligations and responsibility for their communities. In other cases, it appears the very materiality of the registration process hindered compliance with "boats whose stamps have become faded" (*gokuin usuku nari sōrō fune*).[35] It is perhaps not surprising that constant exposure to the elements caused some of these stamps burned into the side of wooden riverboats to fade beyond recognition. Similar to boats without stamps, in 1696 the magistrates ordered these boats with unverifiable markings to sail to Edo to be stamped; the leaders of the districts and villages where these boats were registered also had to submit a list of all the boats in their community. Likely encouraged by a combination of an ingrained instinct to require commoners to bear the burden of much of their own governance and the apathy of its own officers, these riverboat magistrates permitted contractors to register boats (*funeuke*) and others to collect taxes (*yakugin ukeoi*) on their behalf.[36] After nearly two decades of plodding implementation and passive resistance, the riverboat magistrates achieved both a greater amount of tax revenue and legibility over this riparian infrastructure of riverboats and riverside wharves.

By the end of the seventeenth century, the Tokugawa had created a complex set of institutions to rule over the Kantō region and its waters. By broadly shifting its concerns from defense to maintenance, the Tokugawa had melded old military institutions with new bureaucratic ones to produce a compound set of segmented and stratified governing institutions. By century's end, rivers had become thoroughly entrained in the Tokugawa's governance of the region. They supplied water that fed irrigation networks and paddy fields of rice, provided the fish and waterfowl that locals caught and for which they paid annual taxes to the intendant governing their area. After great effort and expense to alter the region's riverscape, they offered a ready infrastructure upon which vital tax-rice and a growing variety of commodities could be shipped between Edo and its expanding hinterland. Moreover, in its determination to redirect specific rivers and their waters and to render the resulting riparian infrastructure of boats and ports more legible and governable, the Tokugawa government also delineated tangible boundaries for the Kantō region that included Izu and Suruga Provinces. This suggests how the extent of the Kantō's "rivers" had less to do with modern scientific distinctions between rivers, lakes, marshes, and seas and more to do with the flow of boats and the taxes and later the commodities they carried. In this way, by the end of the seventeenth century, the Tokugawa government had exercised its authority to shape the

35   Document No. 3228 in *Edo machibure shūsei*, 2:325.
36   Kawana, *Kinsei Nihon suiun shi no kenkyū*, 246, 254.

regional riparian assemblage that increasingly tied distant villages in dispersed fiefs and domains to the city of Edo.

2   **Maintaining Riparian Governance in the Kantō Region, 1700–1783**

The Tokugawa leadership's reassessment of its governance of the Kantō region's rivers and their concomitant riparian relations belonged to a broader series of reforms undertaken between 1716 and 1745 under the direction of the vigorous Tokugawa Yoshimune (1684–1751; r. 1716–1745). Collectively referred to by historians as the Kyōhō Reforms, the various initiatives carried out during Yoshimune's reign sought to deal with chronic corruption, budgetary short-falls, and the declining value of warrior stipends amidst the steady growth of the commercial economy.[37] Although the Kyōhō Reforms succeeded only in patching over and passing on the contradiction inherent in using rice as both foodstuff and warrior stipend, they represented a wholehearted effort to grapple with enduring administrative and budgetary difficulties.[38]

Regarding the Tokugawa's governance of rivers, the first phase of reforms focused on long-identified problems concerning corruption and incompetence within its administration. During the 1720s, the following initiatives were undertaken with mixed results: the removal of venal and inept intendants, inauguration of a system of burden-sharing for river work called *kuniyaku-fushin* (discussed below), expansion of the boat tax and registration system to include more kinds of boats and an additional system requiring boatwrights to submit paperwork about newly built and refurbished boats, replacement of the three Riverboat Magistrates with a single Riverboat Inspector (*kawabune aratameyaku*), and the establishment of the short-lived position of Four River Magistrate (Shisen Bugyō) to oversee river and canal work on the lower Tone,

37   Ōishi Manabu, "Kyōhō kaikaku to shakai henyō," in *Kyōhō kaikaku to shakai henyō*, ed. Ōishi Manabu (Tokyo: Yoshikawa Kōbunkan, 2003), 9; Fujita Satoru, *Kinsei no sandai kakumei* (Tokyo: Yamakawa Shuppankai, 2002), 17–29; Hayami Akira and Miyamata Matarō, "Gaisetsu 17–18 seiki," in *Keizai shakai no seiritsu: 17–18 seiki*, ed. Hayami Akira and Miyamata Matarō, *Nihon keizai shi*, ed. Umemura Mataji et al. (Tokyo: Iwanami Shoten, 1988), 1:47–52.
38   Reiko Hayashi, "Provisioning Edo in the Early Eighteenth Century: The Pricing Policies of the Shogunate and the Crisis of 1733," in *Edo and Paris: Urban Life and the State in the Early Modern Era*, ed. James L. McClain, John M. Merriman, and Ugawa Kaoru (Ithaca: Cornell University Press, 1994), 211–33; Murata Michibiko, "Yoshimune no seiji," in *Iwanami kōza Nihon rekishi: kinsei 3*, 12:5, 26; Ōishi, "Kyōhō kaikaku to shakai henyō," 22–23.

Edo, Kinu, and Kokai Rivers between 1728 and 1731.[39] For a government still fundamentally fixated on agrarian production, the Tokugawa leadership likewise promoted the clearing of arable woodlands and reclaiming of marshes, coastal areas, and riverside wetlands (ryūsakuba) throughout the Kantō region and elsewhere in the country.[40] The Kyōhō era marked a general shift from riparian policies that aimed to expand the tax base through reclamation to those more intent on maintaining what had already been gained. Furthermore, as farmers' fields pressed in upon rivers and expenditures for the maintenance and repair of this complex riparian infrastructure grew, Tokugawa officials sought ways to reduce their part of this burden by requiring others to shoulder much of the cost of dredging rivers and repairing levees.[41]

What brought the limits of the Tokugawa's governance of riparian relations into high relief was the increased flooding in the Kantō region during the eighteenth century. In the previous century, existing villages had expanded, with new ones being established throughout the region. As the number of people and villages grew, they reclaimed much of the region's bottomlands and began encroaching on the banks and floodplains of the Ara, Tone, and other rivers. Villages upstream in the surrounding mountains similarly expanded further up into deeply crevassed river valleys. Despite having less area for commercial crops, these upland villages had nonetheless become deeply entwined in Edo's growing economy by meeting the city's tremendous need for lumber as well as charcoal and firewood for heating and cooking.[42] One of the unintended results of all this activity was a worsening of upstream erosion and downstream flooding. By the early eighteenth century, "deforestation reduced the land's capacity to retain precipitation," explains the historian Conrad Totman, "thereby increasing the rate of runoff after rains and snow melt and, as a

---

39   Izumi, Bakufu no chiiki shihai to daikan, 102–8; Ōishi, "Kyōhō kaikaku to shakai henyō," 28–38; Kawana, Kinsei Nihon suiun shi no kenkyū, 270–99; Ōtani Sadao, Edo bakufu chisui seisaku no kenkyū (Tokyo: Yūzankaku Shuppan, 1996), 93–109.

40   Murata Michibito shows that, from the time of the 1682–87 river projects carried out in the Kinai region, the Tokugawa had already begun allowing the conditional reclamation of wetlands along the Yodo and other large rivers. Murata, "Yoshimune no seiji," in Iwanami kōza Nihon rekishi: kinsei 3, 12:8–11.

41   Although the Tokugawa and domain governments promoted reclamation, Sippel points out that villages often undertook reclamation even along historically flood-prone rivers, such as the Ibi, Nagara, and Kiso Rivers. Sippel, "Chisui," 159.

42   Kimizuka Yoshihiko, "Bakufu goyō sumi-yaku no tenkai to sonraku," Shikai 33 (1986): 29–48; Conrad D. Totman, The Green Archipelago: Forestry in Preindustrial Japan (Berkeley: University of California Press, 1989), 60–68; Yoshida Nobuyuki, "Shūun to takigi: Edo no butsuryū infura to nenryō," in Yoshida Nobuyuki, Toshi: Edo ni ikiru (Tokyo: Iwanami Shoten, 2015), 197–244.

corollary, intensifying soil erosion, silting of streams, and risk of flooding."[43]
While these conditions are common to most mountain streams, they were
exacerbated by the geology of the Kantō's rivers, which had historically dumped
large amounts of eroded sediment onto their riverbeds and caused them to
frequently meander and change course across the Kantō Plain. These riparian
relations between upstream and downstream areas were not lost upon people
at the time. This awareness can be seen, for example, in the writings of the village head Tanaka Kyūgu (1662–1729), who in 1721 was appointed by the Finance
Office to oversee flood-control work along the Ara, Tama, and other rivers
in the Kantō region.[44] A generation earlier, Kumazawa Banzan (1619–91), a
Confucian scholar and advisor to the domain lord Ikeda Mitsumasa (1609–82)
in the western province of Bizen, had written that: "Mountains and rivers are
the core of the country. In recent years, mountains have become desolate and
rivers shallow. This is the desolation of the country."[45] As described in chapter
1, widespread transformation of the riverscape of the Kantō region during the
seventeenth century meant that thereafter the Tokugawa government, domain
lords, and thousands of villages had to expend more effort and resources to
repair levees and dredge riverbeds and irrigation sluices in order to keep these
rivers confined to their newly prescribed channels.

The historian Ōtani Sadao has correlated a number of documents about various calamities, such as flooding, drought, wind damage, volcanic eruptions,
and crop failures, with the recording of the annual rice tax submitted by five
different villages on the Kantō Plain over a 265-year period from 1603 to 1867.[46]

---

43   Conrad D. Totman, "Preindustrial River Conservancy: Causes and Consequences,"
      Monumenta Nipponica 47, no. 1 (1992): 61.
44   Tanaka Kyūgu was forty-three when adopted into the Tanaka family, merchants who
      served as the hereditary heads of Kawasaki Station (Kawasaki-juku), the second such sta-
      tion south of Edo along the Tōkaidō where it crossed the Tama River. Fukaya Katsumi,
      "Tanaka Kyūgu: Jikata kōsha no minsei gijutsu," in *Kōza Nihon gijutsu no shakai shi: jin-
      butsu hen kinsei*, ed. Nagahara Keiji, Yamaguchi Tetsuji, and Fukaya Katsumi (Tokyo:
      Nihon Hyōronsha, 1986), 155–79; Murakami, *Edo bakufu no daikan gunzō*, 82–90.
45   Kumazawa Banzan, "Daigaku wakumon," in *Kumazawa Banzan*, ed. Gotō Yōichi and
      Tomoeda Ryūtarō, *Nihon shisō taikei* (Tokyo: Iwanami Shoten, 1971), 30:432–33. While
      he was visiting Koga near the Watarase River in 1685, the Tokugawa authorities order
      Kumazawa Banzan's confinement as punishment for his published criticism of the policy
      of alternative attendance (*sankin kōtai*). During his confinement to a room in Koga Castle
      for the last four years of his life, Banzan is said to have advised the Koga officials about
      how to deal with flooding at the confluence of the Watarase and Omoi Rivers. Okuya
      Kōichi, "Tanaka Shōzō no kasen to chisui no shisō (2)," *Sapporo Gakuin Daigaku Jinbun
      Gakkai kiyō*, no. 101 (2017): 24.
46   These five villages are Shimotoda and Nakaikemori villages in Musashi Province and
      Tachigi, Haneno, and Isobe villages in Shimōsa Province. Ōtani, *Edo bakufu chisui seisaku*,
      13–40.

Based on this survey, he concludes that nearly 70 percent of these calamities (fifty-four instances) were caused by typhoons or long, heavy rains (*nagame*).[47] While the sources for the early seventeenth century do not lead to conclusive statements, those from later that century and after show that on average severe flooding occurred somewhere on the Kantō Plain about once every four years. For example, after days of rain in the summer of 1704, levees gave way along the Tone, Ara, and Edo Rivers with a breach in a levee in Sarugamata Village along the Naka River. This allowed floodwaters to inundate eastern Edo in what was reported to be 6–7 *shaku* (2 m) of water above the floorboards.[48] Another calamity struck at the end of 1707 when Mount Fuji erupted for sixteen days, covering areas of Suruga, Sagami, and Musashi Provinces in as much as 30 m of tephra.[49] In addition to the immediate and long-term destruction of vegetation covered in volcanic material, subsequent rains washed this material downstream causing riverbeds to rise and chronic flooding along the Sakawa and other rivers for many years.[50] While it required decades for parts of Sagami and Suruga to fully recover from Mount Fuji's eruption, there was severe flooding elsewhere in the Kantō region in 1717, 1728, and 1730. By far the most destructive flood of the eighteenth century occurred in 1742.

In late August 1742, several days of rain saturated the entire area from the Kinai region in the west to the Kantō region in the east. With rivers already rising and flooding their banks, a large typhoon approached the Kantō region from the south, passing directly over Sagami, Musashi, and Kōzuke Provinces as it traveled across the widest part of the country and into Shinano and Echigo Provinces.[51] The typhoon released a tremendous amount of rain on the saturated catchments that included the Tone and Ara Rivers.[52] Fed by freshets

---

47 Ōtani, *Edo bakufu chisui seisaku*, 40.

48 The following chronicles recount the 1704 flood and its effects on Edo and its environs. Saitō Gesshin, *Bukō nenpyō*, ed. Imai Kingo (Tokyo: Chikuma Shobō, 2003), 1:242–43; Inobe Shigeo, Maruyama Jirō, Kuroita Katsumi, and Umasugi Tarō, eds., *Tokugawa jikki*, vol. 43, *Shintei zōho kokushi taikei* (Tokyo: Yoshikawa Kōbunkan, 1965), 543.

49 Matsuo Mieko, "Fujisan funka to Asamasan funka," in *Kyōhō kaikaku to shakai henyō*, ed. Ōishi Manabu (Tokyo: Yoshikawa Kōbunkan, 2003), 149–64; Totman, "Preindustrial River Conservancy," 65–66; Beatrice M. Bodart-Bailey, "Pyroclastic Rivers: The Hōei Fuji Eruption (1707)," in *Local Realities and Environmental Changes in the History of East Asia*, ed. Ts'ui-jung Liu (New York: Routledge, 2016), 158–61.

50 Matsuo, "Fujisan funka to Asamasan funka," 156–57, 164; Bodart-Bailey, "Pyroclastic Rivers," 161–62, 170–71.

51 According to the old lunisolar calendar, the date of this typhoon's passage over Edo and the Kantō region was the 2nd year of Kanpō, 8th month, 1st day. On the Common Era calendar this was 30 August 1742.

52 My account follows that provided by the geographer Machida Takahisa who has recently examined fourteen extant diary accounts of these weather events from various regions and compared them to subsequent known weather events and patterns to reconstruct

pouring off the mountains, the Tone, Ara, and other rivers quickly rose and
burst through the Chūjō, Bizen, and other crucial levees.[53] Along the Tone
River at Honkawamata Village, for instance, flood waters washed away the
highway barrier (sekisho) atop the levee before making a massive breach in
the levee itself, sending the churning waters southward through the river's historic channel (see fig. 8).[54] The head of Nishikata Village, which was located
near the historic confluence of the Tone and Ara Rivers, recorded that the
flood waters were as high as the statue of the Fudōson in the nearby temple,
Daishōji, and did not recede for nearly two weeks.[55] Like the 1704 flood before
it, the 1742 flood also inundated Edo. In a desperate effort to save the central
part of the city from the full onslaught of the flooding, the Kantō Intendant,
Ina Tadamichi, ordered the breaching of the levee at Sarugamata Village in
order to divert floodwaters into the low-laying eastern areas of the city.[56] The
strategy likely had some effect, but it was not enough to save the city from its
worst flood in history. Compounding the problem for Edo was the tidal flood
that swept into the city from the bay as the typhoon passed over the region.
The result was successive flooding first from the bay and then from the region's
rivers. In a number of neighborhoods on both sides of the Sumida River, flood
waters are documented as having risen as high as the eaves of many buildings,

the five-day period of heavy rains and winds that led to the catastrophic flooding in the
summer of 1742. In doing so, he offers a corrective of previous hypotheses that variously
explained the flooding was caused by a series of heavy rainstorms, a single typhoon
crossing from the Kinai to the Kantō region, or the appearance two successive typhoons.
Machida Takahisa, "Kanpō ni-nen saigai o motorashita taifū no shinro to tenkō no fukugen," Chigaku zasshi 123, no. 3 (2014): 363–77.

53   Ōkuma Takashi, Tonegawa chisui no hensen to suigai (Tokyo: Tōkyō Daigaku Shuppankai,
1981), 54; Matsuura Shigeki, Kokudo no kaihatsu to kasen: jōri-sei kara damu kaihatsu made
(Tokyo: Kashima Shuppankai, 1989), 51; Ōtani, Edo bakufu chisui seisaku, 52–62; Takasaki
Tetsurō, Ten issai o nagasu: Edo-ki saidai no kanpō suigai saikoku daimyō ni yoru tetsudai-
bushin (Tokyo: Kashima Shuppan, 2001), 19–48.

54   "Kanpō nenjūki," quoted in Hanyū-shi shi, ed. Hanyū-shi Shi Henshū Iinkai (Hanyū:
Hannyū Shiyakusho, 1971), 1:547–48.

55   "Inu-doshi ōmizu nangi konkyū no koto," in Koshigaya-shi shi: zoku shiryō hen, ed.
Koshigaya-shi Shishi Hensanshitsu (Koshigaya: Koshigaya Shiyakusho, 1981), 1:286–90. See
also "Suinan ikken," in Koshigaya-shi shi: shiryō, ed. Koshigaya-shi Shishi Hensanshitsu
(Koshigaya: Koshigaya Shiyakusho, 1973), 1:825–27.

56   Tōkyō Shiyakusho, ed. Tōkyō-shi shikō: hensai hen (Tokyo: Tōkyō-shi, 1915), 2:270–316;
Matsuura, Kokudo no kaihatsu to kasen, 51; Ōtani, Edo bakufu chisui seisaku, 62–64; "Ina
Tadamichi," in Tokugawa bakufu zen-daikan jinmei jiten, ed. Murakami Tadashi et al.
(Tokyo: Tōkyōdō Shuppan, 2015), 59–60; Takasaki, Ten issai o nagasu, 48–53.

sweeping away several bridges, and taking the lives of nearly four thousand people.[57]

The increased flooding of the eighteenth century challenged the Tokugawa's efforts to govern the Kantō region's rivers. These recurring inundations, however, did not lead to the adoption of an array of new engineering techniques or technologies for preventing or controlling future flooding. The engineering historian Matsuura Shigeki, for instance, explains that the changes that did occur between the seventeenth and eighteenth centuries had less to do with new knowledge or technologies and more to do with an overall shift from large-scale river and reclamation projects to small-scale projects carried out in more marginal and flood-prone areas.[58] The rerouting of the Tone and Ara Rivers were, as noted in chapter 1, signature projects of the early seventeenth century that mostly used excavation and the river's own scouring power to redirect these waters into older channels. These earlier endeavors at river control and diversion sought to keep these rivers in their channels by blocking alternative routes with enormous earthen embankments like the Chūjō and Bizen levees. These larger levees were often built atop or extended existing levees and were designed to cause floodwaters to back up into bottomlands that served as flood-plains (fig. 17). In other places, levees were designed at differential heights to ensure that once floodwaters reached a dangerous level, they spilled through a reinforced section of the shorter levee and into an area that could be sacrificed to flooding. Similarly, the main irrigation canals at the time mostly followed abandoned river routes and employed the simple technology of earthen dams to make ponds (*tameike*) in order to deliver a more consistent supply of water throughout the year. Even though there was a general understanding regarding the relationship between upstream deforestation and weather events contributing to downstream flooding, eighteenth-century designers and builders of

---

57   Ishiyama Hidekazu, "Toshi Edo ni okeru suigai shi kenkyū no genjō to kadai," *Tōkyō-to Edo Tōkyō hakubutsukan kenkyū hōkoku*, no. 16 (2010): 5–18.

58   Matsuura Shigeki also dismisses the overwrought distinction made by engineering historians of the so-called seventeenth-century Ina or "Kantō approach" (*Kantō-ryū*) and the later eighteenth-century Izawa or "Kishū approach" (*Kishū-ryū*) by explaining that the Finance Inspector Izawa Yasobē, a native of Kii Province (hence Kishū), largely used extant technologies and worked within the system of rivers, levees, and irrigation canals that had been developed by the Ina intendants during the previous century. Matsuura, *Kokudo no kaihatsu to kasen*, 82–100. For a discussion of Izawa and the growing numbers and role of these engineering officers, see Ōtani, *Edo bakufu chisui seisaku*, 109–23.

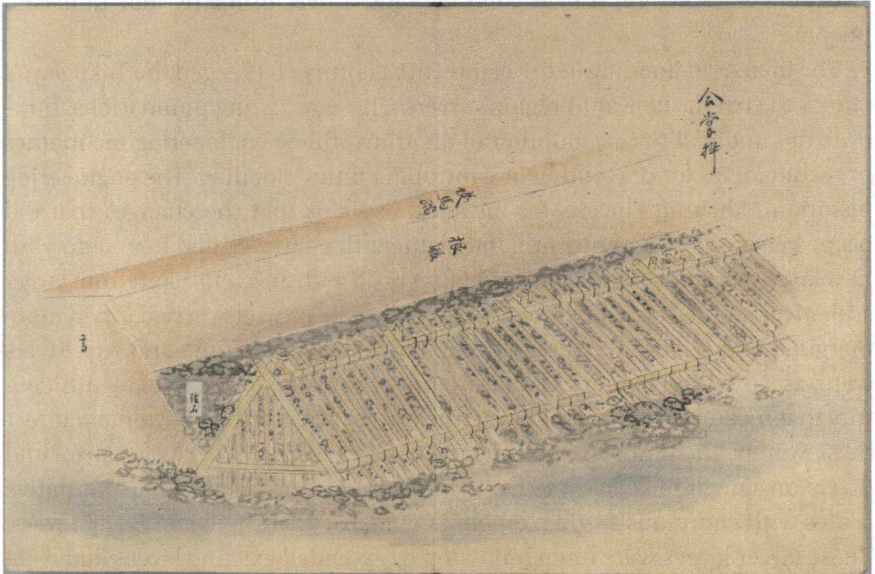

FIGURE 17   Diagram modeling levee design with lumber and stone reinforcement. *Kawayoke toihashi-zu*. c. 19th century. No author, publisher, or pagination
COURTESY OF THE NATIONAL DIET LIBRARY, TOKYO

levees, weirs, and sluices lacked the instruments and mathematical formulae required to measure and predict water levels, volume, and speed.[59]

In the absence of significant technological changes, the Tokugawa government focused on improving its administrative and accounting practices. It also commenced a series of reforms to reduce its expenditure on river works.[60] Until the end of the seventeenth century, most riparian projects like levee-building or repair were small scale and had been undertaken independently by villages, domains, and Tokugawa officials.[61] Following the flood of 1704, however, the Tokugawa government broadened its existing military-duty system of *tetsudai-bushin* by ordering four domain lords to pay and supervise contractors who were hired to dredge rivers and repair levees along the Kantō's

59   Ōkuma Takashi, "Hajime ni," in *Kawa o seishita kindai gijutsu*, ed. Ōkuma Takashi (Tokyo: Heibonsha, 1994), 7–8.

60   The historian of technology Chino Yasuaki notes that, as river work became more expensive during the eighteenth century, the corpus of writings about river engineering also demonstrates a parallel shift from concerns about riparian technology to a focus on advice for procuring materials, estimating costs, and managing accounts. Chino Yasuaki, "Kinsei monjo ni miru chisui risui gijutsu," in *Kawa o seishita kindai gijutsu*, 122–23, 140.

61   Ōtani, *Edo bakufu chisui seisaku*, 277; Totman, "Preindustrial River Conservancy," 59.

largest rivers.[62] The first use of *tetsudai-bushin* for river work had only occurred in the previous year (1703) when the Tokugawa ordered six domain lords to supervise and cover the cost to reroute the Yamato River from the north to the south of Osaka.[63] Prior to this time, the Tokugawa had primarily relied on *tetsudai-bushin* to order domain lords to "assist" (*tetsudai*) in the "construction" (*fushin*) of large and expensive projects, such as repairs to Tokugawa castles or the rebuilding of Tokugawa-affiliated temples.[64] After having utilized the system of *tetsudai-bushin* only four times for river work in Kantō region, in 1720 and amidst the broader Kyōhō Reforms the Tokugawa suspended further application of *tetsudai-bushin* for river projects in favor of a policy known as *kuniyaku-bushin*.

The *kuniyaku-bushin* policy (literally "provincial construction duty") aimed to standardize and limit Tokugawa government expenses for river projects while protecting village farmlands and therefore essential tax revenue.[65] The policy also sought to address a problem particular to the Kantō region: the difficulty of governing rivers that flowed across the multiple territories whose governance was segmented between lords of small domains, bannermen's fiefs, and intendants' jurisdictions. The policy was promulgated and administered by the Tokugawa's Finance Office (Kanjōsho), whose officers likewise supervised the activities of a new corps of designated engineering officers (*fushinyaku*). It assessed a levy (*kuniyakukin*) on temples, smaller domains, and intendant-administered villages within specified provinces to pay the estimated cost of specific large riparian projects above the 10 percent that the Finance Office

---

62 In the months after the 1704 flood, the following four domain lords carried out *tetsudai-bushin* along the main rivers of the Kantō region: Yamauchi Toyofusa of Tosa, Satake Yoshitada of Kubota, Matsudaira Chikatomo of Hirose, and Sagara Yoritomi of Hitoyoshi. *Shinpen Saitama-ken shi: tsūshi hen, kinsei*, ed. Saitama-ken (Urawa: Saitama-ken, 1989), 2:577–78; Ōtani, *Edo bakufu chisui seisaku*, 140–41; Matsuo Mieko, "Tetsudai-bushin ichiran-hyō," *Gakushūin daigaku bungakubu kenkyū nenpyō* 15 (1968): 101. In his study of the Tosa domain, Luke Roberts explains that the additional burden of the *tetsudai-bushin* duty in 1704–5 led the domain leaders to impose a special levy (*kariage*) on all domain residents even as they grappled with a regionwide famine. Roberts, *Mercantilism in a Japanese Domain*, 93.

63 Murata Michihito, "Hōei gannen Yamatogawa tsukekae tetsudai-bushin ni tsuite," *Ōsaka Daigaku Daigakuin Kenkyūka* 20 (1986): 21–44; Shinshū Ōsaka-shi Shi Hensan Iinkai, ed., *Shinshū Ōsaka-shi shi* (Osaka: Ōsaka-shi, 1989), 3:625–34.

64 Matsuo, "Tetsudai-bushin ichiran-hyō," 87–119.

65 The term *kuniyaku* predates the Tokugawa government. The sixteenth-century warlord Oda Nobunaga, for instance, commanded craftsmen in the building trades in Omi Province to provide corveé as *kuniyaku*. Wakita Osamu, "The Emergence of the State in Sixteenth-Century Japan: From Oda to Tokugawa," *Journal of Japanese Studies* 8, no. 2 (1982): 361.

itself covered.[66] While domains of more than 20,000 *koku* continued to shoulder all expenses related to their own river work, the Finance Office apparently hoped that the limiting of its assistance to a set rate would reduce its own overall expenditures.[67] Used most frequently for flood-damaged rivers in the Kantō region, the new policy initially brought in significant additional revenue for these rehabilitation projects. In 1725, for example, the Finance Office collected 21,122 *ryō* from Kōzuke, Musashi, Hitachi, Shimōsa, Kazusa, and Awa Provinces for work on the Tone, Ara, and other sizable rivers flowing through these provinces.[68] Following the flood and wind damage of 1728 and in 1730, however, the Finance Office found its expenditures far outweighed any income realized through the *kuniyaku* levies. In 1730, the Finance Office collected 16,448 *ryō* in revenue through this special levy in the Kantō region, but ended up spending 49,000 *ryō* on dredging and the repair of damaged levees and sluices along rivers in the Tōkai and Kantō regions.[69] Two years later, in 1732, the Finance Office suspended the *kuniyaku-bushin* policy after having to contend with mismanagement, mounting expenses, and a widespread famine. It returned fiscal responsibility for river projects to the villages and domains, assisting only on an ad-hoc basis.[70] In place of the more centralized approach to riparian governance that the *kuniyaku-bushin* policy sought to achieve, the Finance Office resumed delegating the supervision of river work to the Edo city magistrates, the Kantō Intendant, and Izawa Yasobē (1654–1738), a finance inspector (*kanjō ginmiyaku*), and their respective intendants.

Both the *tetsudai-bushin* and the *kuniyaku-bushin* policies had been designed to deal with repair and recovery efforts following devastating floods. But most river work was preventative in nature—dredging rivers, maintaining canals and sluices, attending to levees, weirs, and wing-dams—and was carried out annually by local villages. In 1732, the year that the Finance Office suspended its *kuniyaku-bushin* policy it also issued a ten-point decree setting out village obligations (*murayaku*) for regular preventative river work.[71] This

---

66   "Kantō kawagawa fushin kuniyakukin toritatekata," in *Nihon zaisei shiryō*, ed. Ōkurashō (Tokyo: Zaisei Keizai Gakkai, 1923), 9:89–92.

67   Nishida Masaki, "Kawayoke to kuniyaku-bushin," in *Kōza Nihon gijutsu no shakai shi: doboku*, ed. Nagahara Keiji and Yamaguchi Tetsuji (Tokyo: Nihon Hyōron-sha, 1984): 235–39; Totman, "Preindustrial River Conservancy," 67–69; Ōtani, *Edo bakufu chisui seisaku*, 247–53.

68   Ōtani, *Edo bakufu chisui seisaku*, 258.

69   Ōtani, *Edo bakufu chisui seisaku*, 259.

70   "Kuniyaku tōbun teishi," in *Nihon zaisei keizai shiryō*, ed. Ōkurashō (Tokyo: Zaisei Keizai Gakkai, 1922), 4:827.

71   Document No. 4008 in *Tokugawa kinrei kō*, ed. Shihōshō Hōseishi Gakkai (Tokyo: Sōbunsha, 1959), 6:324–25.

decree remained in effect until the collapse of the Tokugawa government more than a century later, and it stipulated that villages must supply corveé for spring river work at a set rate of fifty persons per one hundred *koku* of the village's assessed annual crop yield. In addition, villages were obliged to supply money for unpolished rice used in the meals provided to corveé laborers as well as construction materials (e.g., lumber, straw sacks, rope) or their cash equivalency.[72] By the eighteenth century, many of these villages belonged to regional flood-prevention associations (*fushin kumiai*) that often overlapped with irrigation associations to carry out the seasonal work of dredging and repairing levees and irrigation sluices along nearby rivers.[73]

Following the devastation from the flooding in 1742, the Tokugawa's Finance Office revived earlier attempts to standardize and defray its contribution toward the recovery effort. The most substantial policy change was the resumption of the *tetsudai-bushin* and *kuniyaku-bushin* policies. Within months of the regionwide flooding in 1742, the Tokugawa used the policy of *tetsudai-bushin* to order ten domain lords from unaffected areas in western Japan to cover the costs and to supervise, together with the intendants of the affected areas, the dredging of buried navigation channels and irrigation canals. In addition, these domain lords oversaw the rebuilding of levees, bridges, embankments, and sluice gates on the upper and lower Tone, Ara, Edo, and other rivers in the Kantō region.[74] As the Finance Office grew to rely on *tetsudai-bushin*, it streamlined the process by using its own officials to supervise the repairs and rebuilding while requiring reluctant domain lords to pay for upwards of 95 percent of the costs.[75] Many of these lords, often already in debt to Osaka-based merchants, struggled to pay for this river work and were forced to take out new loans, slash stipends to retainers, and increase taxes within their domains. In 1757, the Finance Office also resumed the regular use of its *kuniyaku-bushin* policy of collecting an annual levy in exchange for funding 10 percent of significant riparian recovery projects along rivers whose administrative structure was segmented among smaller domains, bannerman fiefs, and different Tokugawa administered areas. From the early nineteenth century, however, it dealt with budget shortfalls by selecting fewer projects for funding, raising its levy rate, and for a few decades providing this assistance only to domains and

---

72   Ōtani, *Edo bakufu chisui seisaku no kenkyū*, 246.
73   Ōtani, *Edo bakufu chisui seisaku no kenkyū*, 289–355.
74   "Gofushin tetsudai daimyo kasho tsuki," in *Shinpen Saitama-ken shi: shiryō hen, kinsei*, ed. Saitama-ken (Urawa: Saitama-ken, 1983), 4:935–36; Matsuo, "Tetsudai-bushin ichiran-hyō," 102.; Ōtani, *Edo bakufu chisui seisaku no kenkyū*, 172–73.
75   Ōtani, *Edo bakufu chisui seisaku no kenkyū*, 246.

fiefs of less than 10,000 *koku*.[76] In contrast to the reinstitution of these preexisting policies, subsequent adjustments to village obligations for preventative work were minimal. The only substantive reform appears to have been a shift in the second half of the eighteenth century in the oversight of individual multivillage flood-prevention associations by intendants to designated engineering officers directly supervised by the Finance Office.[77]

3   Losing Ground against Continued Flooding, 1783–1868

The single most significant change to the rivers and their riparian relations of the Kantō region during the eighteenth century, however, had nothing to do with the efforts of villages or Tokugawa officials to manipulate and control the flow of water. It was the 1783 eruption of Mount Asama. After a few months of rumbling and regular smoke plumbs, in August 1783 the residents of the north Kantō likely felt that demons from the deepest bowels of the earth had burst forth from the nearby mountains.[78] When the 2,568 m tall Mount Asama finally erupted, it spewed ash and rock high into the summer sky (fig. 18).[79] In the immediate vicinity of the mountain, large fiery rocks fell from the sky, crushing people and their homes. At the post town of Karuizawa on the Nakasendō, where it followed the valley just to the south of the mountain, it was reported that of its 186 buildings, fifty-one had burned, seventy had been crushed, and the remaining sixty-five were badly damaged.[80] Along the Agatsuma River that snaked around the north side of Mount Asama, a logjam burst to send a "mountain tidal wave" (*yama-tsunami*) of hot mud, rock, and tephra through the narrow valley and into the Tone River. As it made its way downstream, the wave of debris swept away or buried fields, farms, and families from sixteen

---

76   Bokuryū Katsumi, "Kinsei kuniyaku-bushin taisei no seiritsu to tenkai," *Hōsei daigaku daigakuin kiyō* 10 (1983): 20–25; Nishida, "Kawayoke to kuniyaku-bushin," 243–60; Ōtani, *Edo bakufu chisui seisaku no kenkyū*, 261–62.

77   Ōtani, *Edo bakufu chisui seisaku no kenkyū*, 268.

78   On the old lunisolar calendar, the eruption of Mount Asama occurred over two days on 3rd year of Tenmei, 7th month, 7th and 8th days. This is 4–5 August 1783 in the Common Era calendar. For two contemporary accounts of the 1783 eruption of Mount Asama, see the following five-volume collection of transcribed and published documents: Hagiwara Susumu, ed. *Asamayama Tenmei funka shiryō shūsei* (Maebashi: Gunma-ken Bunka Jigyō Shinkōkai, 1985–95).

79   One of the most active volcanos in the archipelago, Mount Asama is recorded as having also erupted on this kind of large scale in 1108. Watanabe Takashi, *Asamayama daifunka* (Tokyo: Yoshikawa Kōbunkan, 2003), 2.

80   Matsuo, "Fujisan funka to Asamasan funka," 164–65.

FIGURE 18   1783 eruption of Mount Asama. From Isaac Titsingh, *Illustrations of Japan*
(London: Printed for R. Ackermann, 1822), 126

villages. Even the distant coastal town of Chōshi at the mouth of the Tone recorded 12 cm of tephra. Edo escaped major damage thanks to prevailing winds that prevented all but 3 cm of the volcanic material from falling within the city.[81] The Tone, Edo, and Ara Rivers, however, quickly brought some of the upstream destruction to the downstream areas of these rivers by leaving debris and the bodies of dead people and animals along their banks and the bay in and around Edo.[82]

The Mount Asama eruption had immediate and long-term effects on the rivers of the Kantō region. In the near term, the volcano ravaged the surrounding area by filling rivers with volcanic debris and destroying much of the farmland and animals that locals needed to survive. Dispatched to the area more than a month after the eruption, the Finance Inspector Negishi Yasumori (1737–1815) visited many of the most affected villages to survey the damage

---

81   Ōishi Shinzaburō, *Tenmei san-nen Asama daifunka: Nihon no Ponpei Kanbara-mura hakkutsu* (Tokyo: Kadokawa Shoten, 1986) 74; Watanabe, *Asamayama daifunka*, 10.

82   The Shingon temple, Zenyōji, along the Edo River in present-day Tokyo, for example, erected a stone memorial for the repose of the many nameless victims whose bodies had washed up on nearby riverbanks.

and recommend a response.[83] In his report, Negishi noted that the village of Kanbara on the north side of the mountain had suffered the greatest loss with 466 people, 76 percent of the village's residents, having died in the eruption. At Naka Village where the Agatsuma flows into the Tone River, he observed that one sturdy two-story house had withstood the slurry of mud and volcanic debris, but that it had been buried up to the second floor where some lucky locals and a few of their horses had found refuge.[84] In his final account, the inspector tabulated that in that area alone the volcano had ruined 6,012 *koku* of crops, destroyed 1,482 homes, and took the lives of 1,453 oxen and horses and 1,124 people. It is clear that the massive mudflow along the Agatsuma led to much of the loss of home and life with 1,105 dwellings being recorded as having been "swept away" (*ryūshitsu*) and 522 oxen and horses and all 1,124 people having been "swept away to their deaths" (*ryūshi*). While the Agatsuma River valley undoubtedly bore the brunt of Mount Asama's destructive power, other contemporary sources from nearby areas overlooked by Negishi during his inspection suggest that the devastation and loss of life was far greater than that officially reported to the Finance Office. Further downstream and downwind, the eruption caused flooding and, as tephra blanketed the region, widespread crop failures.[85] Just accounting for this immediate destruction, the eruption was the worst volcanic disaster in the country's history.[86]

The silting, sedimentation, and gradual rise in riverbeds had presented a problem even before the 1783 Mount Asama eruption.[87] Mount Fuji had wrecked similar damage upon the countryside when it erupted in 1707, but Asama's location meant that rain washed ash and debris into the Kantō

---

83   Born into a low-ranking bannerman family, Negishi Yasumori served as a finance inspec-
       tor between 1776 and 1784 before being promoted to Magistrate of Sado Island and
       eventually in 1798 to the position of city magistrate (*machi bugyō*) in Edo. Negishi is also
       well known for his collection of essays and hearsay that he wrote over a three-decade
       period; it was published at the end of his life under the title *Mimibukuro*. Negishi's 1783
       report was submitted under the name Negishi Kurōzaemon and has been republished as
       "Asamayama yaki ni tsuki kenbun oboegaki," in *Asamayama Tenmei funka shiryō shūsei*,
       ed. Hagiwara Susumu (Maebashi: Gunma-ken Bunka Jigyō Shinkōkai, 1986), 2:332–47.

84   Ōishi Shinzaburō notes that in 1982, when constructing the Shibukawa-Ikaho Interchange
       for the new regional expressway, a team of archeologists found the remains of the old Naka
       Village and its fields at a depth of 3 to 3.5 m. Ōishi, *Tenmei san-nen Asama daifunka*, 73–76.

85   *Shinpen Saitama-ken shi: shiryō hen, kinsei*, 4:55.

86   Matsuo, "Fujisan funka to Asamasan funka," 164.

87   In the spring just before the Mount Asama eruption, for example, twenty-two villages
       were engaged in a dispute over the increasingly scarce supply of water entering the
       Hoshi River, a part of the Minumadai Canal, due to a large sandbar that had developed in
       front of its intake sluice along the Tone River. "Kamisaki sekidai deiri saikyo ukegaki," in
       Shinpen Saitama-ken shi: shiryō hen, kinsei, 4:896–97.

region's streams and rivers and eventually into the Tone and Ara river systems. In 1786, just three years after Mount Asama's explosion, the Kantō experienced one of its worst floods in history. In August that year, the *Bukō nenpyō* records that, "mountain waters overflowed and flooded ... the Kantō's eight provinces and nearby provinces." The flood waters remained for so long that "shipping routes from the northeastern provinces were cut and goods became increasingly expensive."[88] On par with the devastation of the 1742 flood, the 1786 flood also marked the beginning of the enduring problem of rising riverbeds along the main rivers of the Kantō region. Working its way downstream with each annual rainy season over several decades, the mass of volcanic debris acted like a slow-moving landslide. The extraordinary amount of sediment and tephra entered the region's rivers systems, which gradually raised riverbeds by as much as 3 m and rendered levees relatively shorter or even obsolete. This required the frequent dredging or even the abandoning of irrigation sluices, the reduction of the amount of water flowing into and out of existing irrigation canals. Together this caused canals and smaller tributaries flowing into the larger and now higher Tone and Ara Rivers to back up and flood fields that had previously not needed protective levees.[89] Over the next eighty-four years until the Tokugawa's collapse in 1867, the Ara River alone is recorded as having flooded fifty-seven times. That number is two-thirds more than the thirty-six documented floods for the preceding one hundred years.[90] The engineering historian Ōkuma Takashi describes how along the Tone River the "peak" height of these raised riverbeds slowly shifted downstream from the river's upstream confluence with the Tori River from 1790s to the 1820s to the middle stretch of the river near Honkawamata Village from the 1820s to the 1860s. Meanwhile, he explains that the low gradient of the bottomlands around the Tone's confluence with the Watarase River and the Tone's distributary with the Edo River meant that the problem of rising riverbeds that began at the start of the nineteenth century was not resolved until the early twentieth century. Moreover, the narrowness of the Akahori Channel, which had been excavated between

---

88   This flood is recorded to have started on the old lunisolar calendar on in the 6th year of
      Tenmei, the 12th day, 7th month. This is 5 August 1786 in the Common Era calendar. Saitō,
      Bukō nenpyō, 2:105–6.

89   Ōkuma, *Tonegawa chisui no hensen to suigai*, 66–94; Ōtani, *Edo bakufu chisui seisaku no
      kenkyū*, 346–47.

90   These numbers are compiled from chronologies in the two institutional histories:
      Kensetsushō Kantō Chihō Kensetsukyoku Arakawa Jōryū Kōji Jimusho, ed., *Arakawa jōryū
      kaishū rokujū-nen shi* (Kawagoe: Kensetsushō Kantō Chihō Kensetsukyoku Arakawa Jōryū
      Kōji Jimusho, 1979); Arakawa Karyū Kōji Jimusho Nanajūgo-nen Shi Henshū Iinkai, ed.,
      Toshi o yuku Arakawa: Arakawa karyū kōji jimusho nanajūgo-nen shi (Tokyo: Kensetsushō
      Kantō Chihō Kensetsukyoku Arakawa Karyū Kōji Jimusho, 1990).

1624 and 1654, meant that much of this sediment and debris remained in these bottomlands until the modern state with its greater resources and new industrial technologies widened the channel in the early twentieth century.[91] Following the Mount Asama eruption, Ōkuma points out there was a marked increase in flooding all along the Tone River but especially for areas upstream of the Akahori Channel.[92]

The relatively fast and dramatic rise in riverbeds presented a host of intractable problems for local villages and Edo-based authorities due to these rivers being entrained in the Tokugawa governance of the Kantō region. In addition to the rising incidence and severity of flooding described above and its consequent demands on government finances, two of the clearest problems were that of sediment filling irrigation sluices and canals and a greater number of ever-shifting sandbars and shallows that made navigation slower and more dangerous. In some places during the rainy summer months, the rising riverbed resulted in a swollen Ara or Tone Rivers flowing into and for a short time reversing the current of smaller streams and canals that ordinarily drained into these major rivers. In other places, these rivers changed course within their broad riverbeds. When a river significantly shifted its route within its wider channel, it could either move away from existing irrigation sluices or fill them with the silt and sediment that reduced the amount of water they could deliver and subsequently drain. In bad years this could block them all together. In the fall of 1792, for example, three village heads representing a group of forty-one villages along an upstream portion of the Kasai Canal explained in a petition to the area's intendant that the Tone River's high waters during the summer had for the second consecutive year caused water to back up and breach a recently repaired levee protecting their irrigation sluice and threatened the larger levee protecting the entire area. While the intendant initially demurred by explaining that repairs to the levee in question were the responsibility of the villages, approval was finally granted in the spring of 1793 to supplement

91   Nakayama Masatami, "Chūsei kinsei no Tonegawa chūryū chiiki ni okeru chikei kankyō to shakai shi: Asamayama no daifunka to Tonegawa no sekae," *Rekishi chirigaku* 39, no. 3 (1997): 1–24. Ōkuma also speculates that the Home Ministry's widening of the Akahori Channel during its first phase of river improvement work that began in 1896 allowed the trapped debris from the 1783 Mount Asama eruption to finally continue its way downstream. This led to a notable rise in incidents of flooding below the Akahori Channel during the early twentieth century. Ōkuma, *Tonegawa chisui no hensen to suigai*, 91.

92   Above the Akahori Channel, Ōkuma counts only eight large floods between 1624 and 1783, but he counts thirty-seven large floods following the eruption of Mount Asama until 1950. Ōkuma, *Tonegawa chisui no hensen to suigai*, 91.

the work that had already been undertaken by the villages themselves during the winter.[93] With hundreds of villages relying on the Kasai Canal to grow their crops every year, this kind of maintenance and repair of the Tone's levees and irrigation sluices was a critical and increasingly costly operation for villages and the Tokugawa government. Although less apparent, the Tone and other rivers of the region also required considerable effort and expenditure to dredge and keep them navigable throughout the year. As was seen in chapter 1, by the time Honda Kanosuke sailed these rivers on his four journeys between Kushibiki and Edo in 1853, the stretch of the Tone River above Ōhori had grown so shallow that the bigger boats, such as his *takasebune*, had to lessen their draft by temporarily unloading a portion of their cargo onto the waiting lighters that accompanied them as far as Matsudo or Ka Villages along the Edo River. Further upstream from Sekiyado, sandbars had become common enough as to render the river nearly impassible for bigger boats.[94]

In the face of these rising riverbeds and increased flooding, the Tokugawa government continued to rely on its existing policies as they sought long-term solutions. During the eight decades between the 1783 Mount Asama eruption and the end of shogunal rule in 1867, Tokugawa leaders employed *tetsudai-bushin* eleven times to order domain lords from other parts of the country to repair levees and dredge rivers in the Kantō region.[95] That is more than twice the five times the Tokugawa relied on *tetsudai-bushin* in the previous eight decades between 1704 and 1783. The most extensive use of *tetsudai-bushin* throughout the entire period of Tokugawa rule was in the aftermath of the 1786 flooding when nineteen domain lords were instructed to contribute a total of 421,250 *ryō* to the recovery efforts along the rivers throughout the Kantō region as well as in Izu and Suruga Provinces.[96] As noted above, the Tokugawa's powerful Finance Office depended upon the resumed policy of *kuniyaku-bushin* for much of the other riparian recovery and repair work. These policies and projects were largely reactive and often carried out in a piecemeal manner. Moreover, they failed to fundamentally address or alter the primary problem presented by the Mount Asama eruption—that is, the massive amount of new sediment and debris that was slowly moving its way into and through the complex riparian assemblages of the Kantō region.

---

93   "Kawaguchi-sekitei fushin negai ikken hikaegaki," in *Kasai Yōsui shi: shiryō hen*, ed. Kasai Yōsuiro Tochi Kairyōku (Kasukabe: Kasai Yōsuiro Toshi Kairyō-ku, 1989), 2:874–98.

94   Watanabe Kōji, *Tonegawa takasebune* (Nagareyama: Ronshobō, 1990), 264.

95   Matsuo, "Tetsudai-bushin ichiran-hyō," 88–119.

96   Iijima Chiaki, "Tenmei-Kansei-ki no 'Kinō tedai' fushin: kasen fushin no baai," *Shinano* 54, no. 4 (2002): 233–60.

Given the gravity of the problem for shipping, irrigation, and flood control, it is not surprising that there were many proposals and plans that offered to ameliorate the situation. By 1822, for example, a partial barrage (*bōdashi*) had been constructed across the mouth of the Edo River to limit the amount of water flowing into this distributary when rains engorged the Tone River.[97] Where the *bōdashi* succeeded in reducing floods along the Edo River, its associated project to widen the Akahori Channel was abandoned due to limited financing and progress.[98] The most ambitious of these projects was the navigable Inba Canal, which had it been completed would have connected the lower Tone River through the Inba Marsh to the bay near Edo.[99] Responding to fears about a possible blockade of Edo by the Western powers, the Tokugawa's senior councilor (*rōjū*), Mizuno Tadakuni (1794–1851), ordered the excavation of this canal, but when Mizuno fell from favor in 1845 so also did this expensive project.[100] While never finished, the plan for the Inba Canal did receive revived interest in 1853–54 as a means of preventing the United States Navy from blockading Edo. In the end, most of these proposals and plans were as transient as Kamo no Chōmei's foam on a river's current.

4   Conclusion

Although the most ambitious of these mid-nineteenth-century plans never came to fruition, the Tokugawa government had before and throughout this time demonstrated an enduring commitment to maintaining the riparian infrastructure of the Kantō region. The 1783 eruption of Mount Asama and its long-term effects on the Tone River system clearly strained the capacity of the Tokugawa to "govern the rivers" of the region, but there was no alternative: failure to keep up this complex system of levees, shipping channels, and irrigation sluices was tantamount to failing to "govern the country." As the two chapters in Part 1 of this book have shown, successive Tokugawa leaders invested in the maintenance of the Kantō's rivers and the riparian relations within which they

---

97   Ōtani Sadao, "Kinsei ni okeru Sekiyado-atari no chisui jijō," *Chiba-ken shi kenkyū* 19 (2002): 9–15.

98   *Shinpen Saitama-ken shi: shiryō hen, kinsei*, 4:296–99.

99   *Chiba-ken no rekishi: tsūshi hen, kinsei*, 1:855–76; Chiba-shi Shi Hensan Iinkai, ed., *Tenpō-ki no Inba-numa horiwari fushin* (Chiba: Chiba-shi, 1998); Fujita Satoru, *Bakuhansei kokka no seiji shiteki kenkyū: Tenpō-ki no chitsujo gunji gaikō* (Tokyo: Azekura Shobō, 1989), 222–60.

100   Fujita Satoru also notes that this canal-digging project has often been mischaracterized as a government-promoted reclamation project. Fujita, *Kinsei no sandai kakumei*, 79–80.

were entangled because these waterways were so thoroughly entrained in the institutions of Tokugawa rule. From the catching of fish and growing of crops to the shipment of tax-rice and other goods, the rivers of this vast and vital region were critical to people's livelihood and the operations of government.

The segmented and stratified structure of Tokugawa governance in the Kantō region, however, was very unlike that of the centralized and national organization of Japan's modern government that would come to rule the country's rivers from the late nineteenth century onward. This older segmented approach to governance meant that rivers and their riparian relations often flowed across the multiple territorial and hence jurisdictional boundaries of Tokugawa intendants, bannermen fiefs, and small domains. One aspect of Tokugawa rule in the Kantō that was common to these different kinds of territories, however, was the relegation of much of the adjudication of fishing, hunting, and shipping disputes and onsite supervision of levee and irrigation work to village headmen. These educated village elites also oversaw, either as a single village or in cooperation with several villages, much of the land reclamation that occurred throughout the seventeenth and first half of the eighteenth century. The result of their cumulative efforts was a significant expansion in arable land and a concomitant increase in the number of peasants and villages in the Kantō region. As the population and agricultural production expanded, villages opened new fields and paddies that encroached upon the banks and floodplains of nearby rivers. Villages grew and multiplied upstream as well. Earning less of their livelihood from farming, they logged and otherwise removed vegetation from the region's uplands and steep mountainsides to supply lumber, charcoal, and other products to Edo. These activities, however, inadvertently reduced the capacity of the region's highlands to retain soil and water, leading to widespread erosion and downstream flooding. As a consequence, especially after the 1783 Mount Asama eruption, the Kantō river regime that had been developed for over 150 years became more unstable as the occasional flood gave way to regular inundations and requisite expenditures for repair and recovery.

While the Tokugawa did not survive the instability of the mid-nineteenth century, parts of the river regime it had helped create in the Kantō region did.[101] Even several years after the 1868 Meiji Restoration, village leaders with their updated titles and allegiance to the recently founded government continued in their capacity as the administrative frontline for many aspects of

---

101   In another example of continuity, the new national government also kept on collecting the *kuniyaku* levy until 1875. Matsuo Mieko, "Kuniyaku-bushin," in *Kokushi daijiten*, 4:733; Nishida, "Kawayoke to kuniyaku-bushin," 259–60.

life, including those related to rivers. In 1878, for instance, Subara Tokutada (dates unknown), heir to the village headman's position, was appointed to the position of Levee and Water Warden (*teibō suihai kakari*) for an area that encompassed his native Sasagasaki Village along the Tokyo prefectural side of the Edo River.[102] He kept a year-long log of his communications with higher officials about various river-related issues, such as petitions to move an irrigation intake, remove sandbars from the river, and most concerning to report about trouble along the nearby levee. Until at least the 1890s and the growth of a nationwide cadre of engineering professionals, most river projects in Japan proceeded to take place on the cusp between duty and livelihood and between formal and tacit knowledge. Village leaders relied on books, oral traditions, and their own experience to oversee the condition and upkeep of local levees, irrigation works, and shipping channels.[103] Moving away from a focus on the Kantō region, Part 2 of this book examines the national and global contexts within which the modern engineering profession emerged and how these university-educated engineers eventually replaced these village headmen and contributed to the formation of an entirely new national river regime under the aegis of the powerful Home Ministry.

---

102   "Teibō nisshi," in *Subara monjo*, ed. Edogawa-ku Kyōiku Iinkai (Tokyo: Edogawa-ku Kyōiku Iinkai, 1988), 6:171–86.

103   Gregory Clancey examines the relationship between builders (*daiku*) and the new profession of architecture in late nineteenth-century Japan to argue in a similar vein that nearly all buildings (Japanese, Western, and eclectic) during this period continued to be designed and built by "traditional" *daiku*. Gregory Clancey, *Earthquake Nation: The Cultural Politics of Japanese Seismicity, 1868–1930* (Berkeley: University of California Press, 2006), esp. chapter 1.

PART 2

Techno-politics of River Engineering in Imperial Japan

∴

CHAPTER 3

Engineering and River Engineers in the Age of Imperialism

> I am sure that our attentive hosts [in San Francisco, California] thought they were showing us something entirely unknown, naturally looking for our surprise at each new device of modern engineering. But on the contrary, there was really nothing new, at least to me.... I had been studying nothing else but such scientific principles ever since I had gone to Ogata [Kōan]'s school [in Japan].
>
> 亜米利加人の考にさう云ふものは日本人の夢にも知らない事だらうと思て見せて呉た所が此方はチャント知て居る……先方では爾う云ふ事は思ひも寄らぬ事だと斯う察して懇ろに数へて呉れるのであらうが此方は日本に居る中に数年の間そんな事はかり穿鑿して居たのであるからソレは少しも驚くに足らない。
>
> FUKUZAWA YUKICHI, *The Autobiography of Fukuzawa Yukichi*[1]
> 福澤諭吉『福翁自傳』[2]

∴

In his autobiography, the publicist and intellectual Fukuzawa Yukichi (1835–1901) reflected on what most amazed him and his compatriots when stopping over in San Francisco, California, at the start of the Tokugawa government's 1860 diplomatic mission to the United States. The Tokugawa's first such official visit to the United States, the delegation was given a tour of various parts of the city where Fukuzawa recalled being astonished by the high prices for basic commodities (particularly jarred oysters), the "enormous waste of iron

---

1 This is Eiichi Kiyooka translation. Although he has liberally translated "things that Japanese did not even know in their dreams" (*Nihonjin no yume ni mo shiranai koto*) as "each new device of modern engineering," Fukuzawa's meaning in this passage is unambiguous—he was not the least surprised by the technology he was shown by his American hosts. Yukichi Fukuzawa, *The Autobiography of Fukuzawa Yukichi*, trans. Eiichi Kiyooka (New York: Columbia University Press, 1966), 115.

2 Fukuzawa Yukichi, *Fukuō jiden* (Tokyo: Jiji Shinpōsha, 1899), 191.

everywhere" in the form of "old tins, empty cans, and broken tools" that were left in garbage piles and along the seashore, and especially at the "social, political, and economic" institutions of the country.[3] He did not, however, register "surprise at each new device of modern engineering," such as the telegraph system or a sugar refinery about which they were given detailed explanations. As he notes, he and others in the delegation were well-versed in the "scientific principles" that explained electroplating, chemical reactions, and the workings of vacuums.[4] Although Fukuzawa recounted these experiences toward the end of his colorful life and likely embellished parts of his personal story, his visit to the United States and his lack of surprise at the technology he saw there is suggestive of how scientific and technological information was flowing around the globe and even through Japan during the last decades of Tokugawa rule. This chapter examines how, in the years that followed Fukuzawa's journey, river engineers from the Netherlands traveled with their books and equipment to Japan to help build what was hoped would become a national infrastructure of rivers, canals, and coastal ports. At the same time, the nascent national government in Tokyo sent a number of young, well-educated Japanese men to Europe and the United States to further their education in engineering and other fields. Upon their return to Japan, many joined the country's growing cadre of educators, engineers, and technocrats. And, more than the Dutch engineers, it was these returning Japanese engineers who played a decisive role in reframing relations between the nascent national government and the country's rivers from the late nineteenth century onward.

This was a time of great turbulence and transformation both inside and outside Japan. Industrialization and imperialism were transforming Europe and the United States in ways that enabling them to create an international order centered on their political economies. It was through this uneven geography of formal and informal empires that engineers from the Netherlands, France, Great Britain, the United States, and elsewhere traveled in search of employment and adventure.[5] Due to the industrial and nationalist character of that era's "new imperialism," these individuals could readily offer their expertise to their respective consular authorities at port cities throughout Asia, Africa, and Latin America.[6] In Japan and in response to the threat posed by Great Britain,

---

3 Fukuzawa, *Fukuō jiden*, 115–16.
4 Masao Miyoshi, *As We Saw Them: The First Japanese Embassy to the United States* (Berkeley: University of California Press, 1979).
5 For an example of British engineers, see R. A. Buchanan, "The Diaspora of British Engineering," *Technology and Culture* 27, no. 3 (1986): 501–24.
6 Michael Adas, *Machines as the Measure of Men: Science, Technology, and Ideologies of Western Dominance* (Ithaca: Cornell University Press, 1989); Timothy Mitchell, *Rule of Experts: Egypt,*

France, Russia, and the United States, the Tokugawa and individual domain governments hired experts during the 1860s from some of these very same countries to build dockyards and factories, conduct geological and other surveys, and teach subjects ranging from languages and medicine to mathematics and military drill.[7] Following the 1868 Meiji Restoration, the new national government created a hierarchy of nested administrative units centered on Tokyo and established what the historian Jeffery Hanes calls a "fixed frame" within which the government directed scarce resources toward specific rail, road, river, and port projects that it deemed to be of particular significance.[8] In order to introduce the latest industrial technologies and sciences from the imperial powers, the government in Tokyo continued the Tokugawa practice of hiring foreign experts to initiate and supervise these infrastructure projects.[9] The result was the production of an uneven geography fixed within an emerging national framework. Seemingly remote places like the Fudō River worksite discussed below achieved temporary relevance through their relation to an infrastructure project deemed to be of national importance, such as the improvement of navigation along the Yodo River. Thus, between the 1870s and 1920s, the central government, together with individuals and companies who had the capital to invest in railways, mines, and other rural and urban enterprises, affected what the historical geographer Kären Wigen argues became

Techno-Politics, and Modernity (Berkeley: University of California Press, 2002); Maria Paula Diogo and Dirk van Laak, eds., *Europeans Globalizing: Mapping, Exploiting, Exchanging* (London: Palgrave Macmillan, 2016).

7   Graeme J. N. Gooday and Morris F. Low, "Technology Transfer and Cultural Exchange: Western Scientists and Engineers Encounter Late Tokugawa and Meiji Japan," in "Beyond Joseph Needham: Science, Technology, and Medicine in East and Southeast Asia," ed. Morris F. Low, special issue, *Osiris*, 2nd ser., 13 (1998): 99–128; Hazel J. Jones, *Live Machines: Hired Foreigners and Meiji Japan* (Vancouver: University of British Columbia Press, 1980), 1–5; Unno Fukuju, "Josetsu: gairai to zairai," in *Seiō gijutsu no inyū to Meiji shakai*, ed. Unno Fukuju (Tokyo: Yuhikaku, 1982), 2–27.

8   Jeffrey E. Hanes, "Contesting Centralization? Space, Time, and Hegemony in Meiji Japan," in *New Directions in the Study of Meiji Japan*, ed. Helen Hardacre (Leiden: Brill, 1997), 485–95.

9   In the case of Dutch engineers, the continuity from the Tokugawa to the Meiji period was embodied in the form of Anthonius Franciscus Bauduin (1820–85), who between 1862 and 1873 served in Japan as a medical instructor and advisor. After returning to the Netherlands, he was integral to the hiring of the first Dutch engineer, Cornelis Johannes van Doorn. Harm Stevens, "Naar Japan," in *In een Japanse stroomversnelling: Berichten van nederlandse watermannen—rijswerkers, ingenieurs, werkbazen—1872–1903*, ed. L. A. van Gasteren (Amsterdam: Euro Books, 2000), 123–24; Kamibayashi Yoshiyuki, *Nihon no kawa o yomigaeraseta gishi de Reike* (Tokyo: Sōshisha, 1999), 45–46.

a "geographical revolution" wherein previously prominent regions became peripheries to the new "national core" in Tokyo.[10]

Engineering technology was instrumental in producing this fixed frame of national development and in transforming riparian relations along the country's largest waterways.[11] As the above quote from Fukuzawa's autobiography suggests, some in Japan clearly understood the scientific principles these foreign experts were teaching and using or were themselves already applying similar technologies and techniques along the Tone, Yodo, and other rivers. Part 1 of this book demonstrates the existence of a long history before the arrival of these foreign experts of manipulating the flow of water for irrigation, reclamation, navigation, and flood control along the Tone, Yodo, and elsewhere on the archipelago. This history is a reminder that prior to the 1868 Meiji Restoration, people in Japan had gained an eclectic knowledge of Chinese classics, mathematics, and nature studies (honzōgaku) under private tutelage or at relatively small private, domain-sponsored schools in towns and cities scattered throughout the archipelago.[12] People improved their numerical literacy, balanced their accounts, studied the stars and constructed calendars, surveyed and drew maps, designed buildings and calculated the materials required to build them.[13] By the collapse of the Tokugawa regime, thousands of students and scholars within Japan also had access to a century's worth of "Dutch Studies" (rangaku) when setting out to study topics ranging from meteorology

10   Kären Wigen, The Making of a Japanese Periphery, 1750–1920 (Berkeley: University of California Press, 1995), 296.

11   Although the role of engineering and technology may seem tangential to environmental history, I agree with the notion of "envirotech," in which the "boundary" between environment and technology is "illusory" because the two categories are fundamentally "interdependent." See Martin Reuss and Stephen H. Cutcliffe, eds., The Illusory Boundary: Environment and Technology in History (Charlottesville: University of Virginia Press, 2010), 1.

12   Kurasawa Gō, Shohan no kyōiku seisaku (Tokyo: Yoshikawa Kōbunkan, 1986); Richard Rubinger, Popular Literacy in Early Modern Japan (Honolulu: University of Hawai'i Press, 2007), chapter 4.

13   Hidetoshi Fukagawa and Tony Rothman, Sacred Mathematics: Japanese Temple Geometry (Princeton: Princeton University Press, 2008); Matthias Hayek and Annick Horiuchi, "The Jinkōki Phenomenon: The Story of a Longstanding Calculation Manual in Tokugawa Japan," in Listen, Copy, Read: Popular Learning in Early Modern Japan, ed. Matthias Hayek and Annick Horiuchi, Brill's Japanese Studies Library 46 (Leiden: Brill, 2014); Tsukane Ogawa, Mitsuo Morimoto, and Seki Kowa, Mathematics of Takebe Katahiro and History of Mathematics in East Asia (Tokyo: Mathematical Society of Japan, 2018); Mark Ravina, "Wasan and the Physics That Wasn't: Mathematics in the Tokugawa Period," Monumenta Nipponica 48, no. 2 (1993): 205–24.

and vaccinations to foreign relations and surveying methods.[14] For these reasons and as a consequence of the preindustrial character of construction around the world at the time, it is not surprising that in the 1870s and 1880s Dutch and Japanese engineers approached the task of improving river navigation and flood control in a like manner. They possessed comparable tools and were equipped with the common materials of sand, clay, lumber, rope, and rock.

Despite these similarities in engineering technologies and techniques, the Dutch engineers did introduce novel practices and perspectives to their Japanese counterparts and assistants. Foremost among them were those related to measuring the changing level, velocity, and volume of water. Dutch engineers installed peils, for example, at the mouths of large rivers to measure rivers as they rose and fell with each tide in an effort to determine the local mean sea level and hence zero-level elevation. This standard measurement of zero for an entire river basin was immensely important to river engineers. It enabled them to measure the slope of a riverbed and the relative height of everything from upstream levees and sluices to downstream jetties and docks in the estuaries of these rivers. Just as Dutch engineers were installing peils in Japan in the 1870s, in the Netherlands the Normaal Amsterdam Peil (NAP) was being approved as the national standard and being gradually accepted elsewhere in Europe, such as by the New Berlin Observatory in 1879.[15] While some of the technologies and techniques associated with one locale like Amsterdam were being adopted within Europe and beyond, others emerged in Europe's colonial territories before being implemented in their home countries.[16] These colonies also served as incubators for the engineers who were applying and

---

14   Aoki Toshiyuki, "Kagakuteki shikō no hattatsu to rangaku," in *Jugaku kokugaku yōgaku*, ed. Rai Ki'ichi (Tokyo: Chūō Kōronsha, 1993), 320–29; Nakamura Tsuko, "Inō Tadataka ga Seto naikai sokuryō de shiyō shita tenmon sokki to 'yachū sokuryō no zu' no kansokuchi," *Kagakushi kenkyū* 273 (2015): 3–15; Yulia Frumer, "Translating Words, Building Worlds: Meteorology in Japanese, Dutch, and Chinese," *Isis* 109, no. 2 (2014): 785–820; Terrence Jackson, *Network of Knowledge: Western Science and the Tokugawa Information Revolution* (Honolulu: University of Hawai'i Press, 2016); Ann Bowman Jannetta, *The Vaccinators: Smallpox, Medical Knowledge, and the Opening of Japan* (Stanford: Stanford University Press, 2007).

15   Today, the Normaal Amsterdam Peil (NAP) provides the standard measure of sea level for the European Union. For a history of its adoption within the Netherlands and elsewhere in Europe, see Pieter Izaak van der Weele, *De geschiedenis van het N.A.P. [I.E. Normaal Amsterdams Peil]* (Delft: Rijkscommissie voor Geodesie, 1971).

16   Jessica B. Teisch, *Engineering Nature: Water, Development, and the Global Spread of American Environmental Expertise* (Chapel Hill: University of the North Carolina Press, 2011), 17–37; David Gilmartin, *Blood and Water: The Indus River Basin in Modern History* (Oakland: University of California Press, 2015), 151.

adapting what they learned through formal schooling, mentorship at worksites, and a proliferating number of professional and trade publications.

As this circulation of similar and dissimilar approaches for manipulating and measuring the flow of water suggests, the movement and improvement of technologies is ill described by terms, such as "diffusion" and "technology transfer," that often assume a unilinear relationship between an advanced scientific and technological center and a less developed periphery. In other words, rather than equate whole nations like the Netherlands and Japan or continent-sized areas like Europe and Asia with particular levels of technological attainment, it is more useful to follow the trail left by specific technologies and techniques as they moved across the uneven landscapes *between* and *within* nations and empires.[17] More than the larger diplomatic interaction between nations and empires, it was these transnational networks of personal and professional relations, the sale and purchase of equipment, and the circulation of technical and trade publications that introduced different ways of knowing and interacting with rivers into Japan. Once in Japan, these Dutch and returning Japanese engineers, their new tools and equipment, and novel practices and approaches all became part of a process of reassembling preexisting riparian assemblages at worksites on the Yodo and other rivers, lecture halls of the country's top universities, and eventually in the planning and policy-making occurring within the Home Ministry and its regional offices. And, as the historian Ian Miller has shown with animals in his study of Tokyo's Ueno Zoological Garden, it was in part through this assemblage of engineers, educational institutions, the Home Ministry, and their gradual reshaping of riverscapes throughout the country that rivers were increasingly seen as belonging to a "natural order" of physical, fluvial phenomena and as ontologically distinct from the communities and relations they helped constitute.[18]

---

17   Discussing the scholarly shift away from Eurocentric views on the history of science and technology, for instance, David Chambers and Richard Gillespie comment that, "modern science is better understood, both metaphorically and actually, as a polycentric communications network." David Wade Chambers and Richard Gillespie, "Locality in the History of Science: Colonial Science, Technoscience, and Indigenous Knowledge," *Osiris* 15 (2000): 223.

18   Ian Jared Miller, *The Nature of the Beasts: Empire and Exhibition at the Tokyo Imperial Zoo* (Berkeley: University of California Press, 2012), 28–30. Similarly, the historian Robert Stolz describes how Obata Tokujirō in his well-known 1868 pamphlet, *Tenpen no chii*, sought to educate his readers about the underlying principles of "natural phenomena," such as lightning, earthquakes, and comets, and to disassociate them from other older explanations like "divine punishment." Robert Stolz, *Bad Water: Nature, Pollution, & Politics in Japan, 1870–1950* (Durham: Duke University Press, 2014), 1–3.

1   The Home Ministry's Early Riparian Policies

Before the administrative and conceptual changes to river engineering and management in the 1890s, the national government in Japan had pursued a policy of both preventing flooding and maintaining a constant stream flow for year-round navigation. This policy of trying to balance the needs of flood control with those for irrigation, and especially navigability, had emerged as a practical solution for a national government seeking to develop and integrate its regional economies despite the lack of resources to invest in building a completely new national infrastructure of highways or railways. In the years immediately following the Meiji Restoration, the administrative apparatus of the country's rivers had passed from one short-lived bureau or department to another.[19] In November 1873, however, this unsettled situation changed with the establishment of the Home Ministry (Naimushō), whose broad authority grew to include the appointment of both local and prefectural officials (notably all governors); the administration of the national census and land tax assessment surveys; the control of the national mail service; the supervision of the national police force that included a special organization for policing Tokyo (Keishichō); and the coordination and oversight of all river, road, and port projects.[20] Under its first minister, the influential Ōkubo Toshimichi (1830–78), the Home Ministry saw in the country's rivers a viable and affordable means to further integrate and develop the nation's economy through water transport. In a May 1874 proposal, for instance, the Home Ministry countered rival plans for highway and railway construction by extolling the benefits of river and coastal shipping, concluding that, "Water transport should come first and land transport later."[21]

Over the next few years, this 1874 proposal became a key part of the national government's policy that was collectively referred to by the slogan "promotion of production and encouragement of industry" (*shokusan kōgyō*). Under Ōkubo's vigorous leadership, the Home Ministry used the 1874 proposal to guide its approach to the management of the nation's many rivers. In a petition submitted a few months later, Ōkubo argued that Japan should follow the

---

19   Ogawa Makoto, "Chisui, risui, tochi kairyō no taikeiteki seibi," in *Nihon nōgyō hattatsu shi: Meiji ikō ni okeru*, ed. Nōgyō Hattsu-shi Chōsakai (Tokyo: Chūō Kōronsha, 1954), 117–232, 121–27; Osumikai Naimushō Shi Henshū Iinkai, ed., *Naimushō shi* (Tokyo: Chihō Zaimu Kyōkai, 1971), 3:21–23.

20   Soeda Yoshiya, *Naimushō no shakai shi* (Tokyo: Tōkyō Daigaku Shuppankai, 2007), esp. chapter 2.

21   "Dobokuryō kengi suisei kōsei no gi utagai," in Kōbunroku Collection [May 1874], National Archives of Japan, #01-2A-009-00.

example of the "small island nation" of Great Britain and build upon its existing networks of waterways and ports. In doing so, he exhorted the government
to initiate a policy to "encourage industry" and "increase production" by utiliz-
ing the country's "natural advantages" (ten'nen no ri).[22] The Home Minister,
however, did not provide details for how an infrastructure of waterways might
accomplish these goals until after the government had crushed a series of
costly rebellions by frustrated former warriors on the southwestern island of
Kyushu between 1874 and 1877. When Ōkubo did furnish details about his ideas
in March 1878, it was in the form of an inquiry addressed to Sanjō Sanetomi
(1837–91), the Chancellor of the Central Chamber (Sei-in). Ōkubo explained
that in order to "foster the vitality of the nation" the government should promote production by further developing the system of rivers, canals, and ports
that link the northern Tōhoku region to Tokyo.[23] While this water-based infrastructure certainly appeared cheaper than comparable schemes for railways
or roads, Ōkubo's proposition offered no explanation for how the indebted
national government would plan and pay for the dredging of rivers, the digging
of new canals, and the deepening and expansion of coastal ports.[24]

It was these questions of cost and oversight that had been central to the
debate on public works three years earlier during the 1875 Osaka Conference,
a meeting of the Assembly of Prefectural Governors (Chihōkan Kaigi).
Established in part to placate those demanding the creation of a national
assembly and constitutional government, the assembly met three times in
1875, 1878, and 1880 to discuss and vote on legislation for taxation, education,
policing, administrative duties and boundaries, and the formation of prefectural assemblies. These issues were all essential to the ongoing negotiation of
political authority between the new national and prefectural governments.[25]
Of the numerous topics addressed during the first meeting in 1875, the assembled governors and ministry officials focused on whether the prefectures or the

22   Ōkubo Toshimichi, "Shokusan kōgyō ni kansuru kengisho" (5–6 July 1874), in *Ōkubo
     Toshimichi monjo*, ed. Nihon Shiseki Kyōkai (Tokyo: Nihon Shiseki Kyōkai, 1929), 5:561–65.
23   Ōkubo Toshimichi, "Sanjō e no ukagai-gaki" (6 March 1878), in *Ōkubo Toshimichi monjo*,
     9:39–55.
24   Masuda Hiromi, "Shokusan kōgyō seisaku to kasen shū'un," *Shakai keizai shigaku* 48, no. 6
     (1982): 6–22.
25   Nishikawa Makoto, "Kaisetsu: Dai ikkai chihōkan kaigi kaisai o meguru seiji jōkyō," in
     Meiji zenki chihōkan kaigi shiryō shūsei, ed. Gabe Masao, Hirose Yoshihiro, and Nishikawa
     Makoto (Tokyo: Kashiwa Shobō, 1997), series 2, 6:487–515; Kyu Hyun Kim, *The Age of
     Visions and Arguments: Parliamentarianism and the National Public Sphere in Early Meiji
     Japan* (Cambridge: Harvard University Press, 2007), 116–19; Michio Umegaki, *After the
     Restoration: The Beginning of Japan's Modern State* (New York: New York University Press,
     1988), 150–54.

national government would be responsible for planning, funding, and maintaining critical public works projects like port improvements, highway construction, and river dredging.[26] In its Levee Measure (Teibō Hōan), the Home Ministry criticized both the Tokugawa government's reliance on village corveé as a "feudal" (*hōken*) remnant and the new government's continued division of rivers into three grades wherein a river's main channel was effectively categorized as a separate river from its tributaries and distributaries.[27] Despite this criticism, the government's efforts in the early 1870s to create a standardized system to administer all of the country's rivers was a dramatic change from the highly segmented approach to riparian governance that characterized the period of Tokugawa rule. As shown in chapter 2, along the Tone River, for instance, the Tokugawa government had relied variously on its own officials, pan-village associations, small local domains, and large distant domains to carry out river work. It also attempted little or no coordination between upstream and downstream projects. In place of this piecemeal approach to river management, the assembly quickly approved the Home Ministry's proposal to improve navigability and flood control by administering rivers as single riparian systems.[28] The responsibility for covering the expense and carrying out river work, however, proved to be thornier issues.

In the second and third articles of its Levee Measure, the Home Ministry recommended an administrative division of labor for all river work. The ministry, it explained, would oversee all "preventative work" (*yobō no kō*), such as the designation and maintenance of floodplains, building of diversionary canals, dredging and clearing of shipping channels, and the control of erosion along the country's biggest rivers. Prefectures and local governments, on the other hand, would oversee all "defensive work" (*bōgyo no kō*), which primarily entailed the localized but expensive maintenance, extension, and repair of levees and embankments.[29] Not surprisingly, many of the prefectures balked at being asked to cover all costs related to levee upkeep and repair, especially when flood damage from larger rivers could easily exceed their meager budgets.[30] After two more days of deliberation about the costs and inequities of the measure, a majority of the assembly eventually stood in favor of

---

26   A facsimile of the handwritten preparations, proposals, petitions, minutes, and other documents from these meetings have been published under the title *Meiji zenki chihōkan kaigi shiryō shūsei*.

27   "Teibō hōan" [2 July 1876], in *Meiji zenki chihōkan kaigi shiryō shūsei*, ed. Gabe Masao, Hirose Yoshihiro, and Nishikawa Makoto (Tokyo: Kashiwa Shobo, 1997), series 1, 4:235–42.

28   "Teibō hōan," in *Meiji zenki chihōkan kaigi shiryō shūsei*, series 1, 4:283.

29   "Teibō hōan," in *Meiji zenki chihōkan kaigi shiryō shūsei*, series 1, 4:238–42.

30   "Teibō hōan," in *Meiji zenki chihōkan kaigi shiryō shūsei*, series 1, 4:313–35; 5:13–66.

an amended version of the proposal wherein the administrative separation of preventative and defensive work remained, but the Home Ministry agreed to provide national funding for defensive works when damage from a single flood exceeded a prefecture's ability to repair its levees.[31] While the Home Ministry retained ultimate authority over the country's rivers, it was this agreement to divide the funding, responsibility, and kinds of river work between the national and prefectural governments that for the next two decades furnished the framework for administering the nation's waterways.[32]

Throughout the discussions of the Levee Measure at the Assembly of Prefectural Governors, there was a conspicuous absence of the engineers who would later come to dominate river administration from the 1890s onward.[33] This absence is evident only in hindsight, however. At the time, different government ministries employed foreign engineers to accommodate the country's treaty obligations of building lighthouses and improving ports. Others also taught in Japan's new universities as well as planned and oversaw various river, railway, and mining projects. But it was not until the early 1880s that the country's first engineering students started graduating from the recently established Imperial College of Technology (Kōbu Daigakkō), the country's first engineering school, or began returning from their studies in Europe and the United States.[34] The administrative framework that governed Japan's rivers began to change after 1875, but as emphasized at the end of chapter 2, the actual work of dredging channels and sluices, inspecting and repairing levees, and regulating shipping, fishing, and irrigation continued to be carried out much as it had under the Tokugawa government.

---

31   "Teibō hōan," in *Meiji zenki chihōkan kaigi shiryō shūsei*, series 1, 6:101–19.

32   Fujii Mikio and Matsuura Shigeki, "Furuichi Kōi to kasen jigyō," in *Furuichi Kōi to sono jidai*, ed. Doboku Gakkai Dobokushi Kenkyu Iinkai (Tokyo: Doboku Gakkai, 2004), 150–51.

33   In the meeting minutes, it is recorded that there was a motion to create a survey team of water experts (*suiri no senmonka*). In addition, for 2 July 1875, it is recorded that an instructor from the Tōkyō Kaisei Gakkō by the name of Smith was present, but no comments by him or about him are included in the meeting minutes. This instructor was likely the youthful Robert Henry Smith (1851–1916), who taught mechanical engineering at the school from 1874 until 1878 when he returned to Great Britain. "Teibō hōan," in *Meiji zenki chihōkan kaigi shiryō shūsei*, series 1, 4:235.

34   Kyū-Kōbu Daigakkō Shiryō Hensankai, ed., *Kyū-Kōbu Daigakkō shiryō dō furoku* (Tokyo: Seishisha, 1977).

2   The Fudō River Worksite

An unlikely site in the emergence of a nationwide assemblage of institutions, personnel, technologies, and ideas about rivers was the Fudō River in Kabata and Hirao Villages in southeast Kyoto Prefecture. Snaking eastward from the Kizu River into the mountains near the ruins of the ancient temple, Kōmyōsen, the Fudō is barely 6 km in length and only drains an area of about 430 ha (see fig. 1). The Fudō attracted the attention of the new national government, less for its clearly diminutive size than for the momentous problem it represented. Intent on deepening and straightening the channel of the Yodo River for navigation, engineers of the recently founded Home Ministry had quickly identified the Fudō as an example of the broader problem of the Kinai region's rivers—namely, deforestation, erosion, and the sedimentation of downstream riverbeds and the port at Osaka. Located just upstream from the confluence of the Kizu and Yodo Rivers, the Fudō was well known at the time as one of the region's "ceiling rivers" (*tenjōgawa*) whose riverbeds were higher than the surrounding countryside and only kept in place through the vigilant upkeep of its levees. The elevation of the Fudō's riverbed above neighboring farmlands owed to the heavy sediment load eroding from what were called "bald mountains" (*hageyama*). These mountains had been so heavily logged and picked over for fuel that it is was difficult for new trees and even grasses to establish themselves. Owing perhaps to its convenient location and its notoriety as a dangerous ceiling river, the Fudō became in 1875 one of the government's first riparian worksites where Home Ministry engineers and technicians experimented with various afforestation and erosion-control techniques.

In serving the new government's efforts to use and enhance the navigability of the country's bigger regional rivers, the Fudō also became an important local eddy in the global flow of engineers, technology, and riparian knowledge during the second half of the nineteenth century. Between March and June of 1875, the Home Ministry dispatched one of its employees—the thirty-two-year-old Dutch engineer Johannis de Rijke (1842–1913)—to oversee work in the Fudō River basin. Under De Rijke's supervision was the forty-eight-year-old engineer Ichikawa Yoshikata (1826–?).[35] At the Fudō River worksite, these two men of different generations and distinctly dissimilar backgrounds found themselves working together to improve downstream navigation by addressing the intractable problem of upstream erosion. Over the course of four months, De Rijke and Ichikawa, their technicians, and teams of laborers installed straw bundles

---

35   Yamashiro-chō, ed., *Yamashiro-chō shi: honbun* (Yamashiro: Yamashiro-chō Yakuba, 1987), 839–45.

(Dutch: *landwiep*; Japanese: *warataba*) across the area's steep mountain slopes, experimented with the planting of a variety of trees, and built sixteen kinds of erosion-control dams on streams feeding into the Fudō.[36] In 1878, the Home Ministry also established a testing and administrative office in Kabata Village from which it oversaw the erosion-prevention efforts in much of the Kizu River basin in both Kyoto and Nara Prefectures.[37]

The Fudō River experimental projects were carried out on a small scale on an otherwise unremarkable mountain stream. Nonetheless, they had an outsized influence because other engineers and technicians in the Home Ministry and other prefectures replicated some of their techniques and structures at the headwaters of large rivers elsewhere in the country. Moreover, in 1881, the Home Ministry published some of the techniques tested at the Fudō worksite in its influential *Doboku kōyōroku*, which despite being described as a selection of sample levee, bridge, and other designs compiled by the previous Tokugawa government also included a few of what it termed "Dutch methods" (*Oranda kōhō*) (fig. 19).[38] In his own 1895 *Suiri shinpō*, Ichikawa was more critical of the results of the experiments implemented at the Fudō worksite by explaining that seven out of ten failed within a few years.[39] Recognized as being intimately related to the ministry's downstream efforts to improve navigation along the Yodo River and in the port of Osaka, this upstream erosion-control work executed along the Fudō River is a reminder of the geographic extent of the riparian relations that constituted the Yodo River.

Ichikawa's and De Rijke's approaches to erosion prevention were surprisingly similar, but the two engineers clearly took different routes to arrive on the banks of the Fudō River in the spring of 1875. Their activities before, during, and after their work together on the Fudō reflected the wider world in which each was engaged. Perhaps owing to the tumult resulting from the collapse of

36   Johannis de Rijke, "Dosha-yama ikken ni tsuki mōshiide" [3 April 1875], reprinted in *Yodogawa Oranda gishi monjo: Oubun kanren hen*, ed. Yodogawa Kindai Kaishū no Akebono Kenkyūkai (Hirakata: Kensetsushō Kinki Chihō Kensetsukyoku Yodogawa Kōji Jimusho, 1997), 184–87.

37   Leaving his position with Kyoto Prefecture, Ichikawa joined the Home Ministry to head this office, which in 1884 was renamed the Kabata Erosion Prevention Camp (Kabata Sabō Kōeisho). Yamashiro-chō, *Yamashiro-chō shi: honbun*, 840–41.

38   Volume 3, *Hito no bu*, also includes a reprint of the following essay by De Rijke: "Mizuhane sunawachi shiba-kō no gitei," in *Doboku kōyōroku*, ed. Naimushō Dobokukyoku (Tokyo: Yūrindō, 1881), 3:2–9.

39   Originally published in 1895 under the title of *Suiri shinpō*, Ichikawa issued a slightly revised version of the book two years later with the publisher Hakubunkan. Ichikawa Yoshikata, *Zukai: suiri shinpō* (Tokyo: Hakubunkan, 1897), 2:29. See also Chino Yasuaki, "Kinsei chisui gijutsu o tsutaeru kindai no bunken," in *Kawa o seishita kindai gijutsu*, ed. Ōkuma Takashi (Tokyo: Heibonsha, 1994), 159–61.

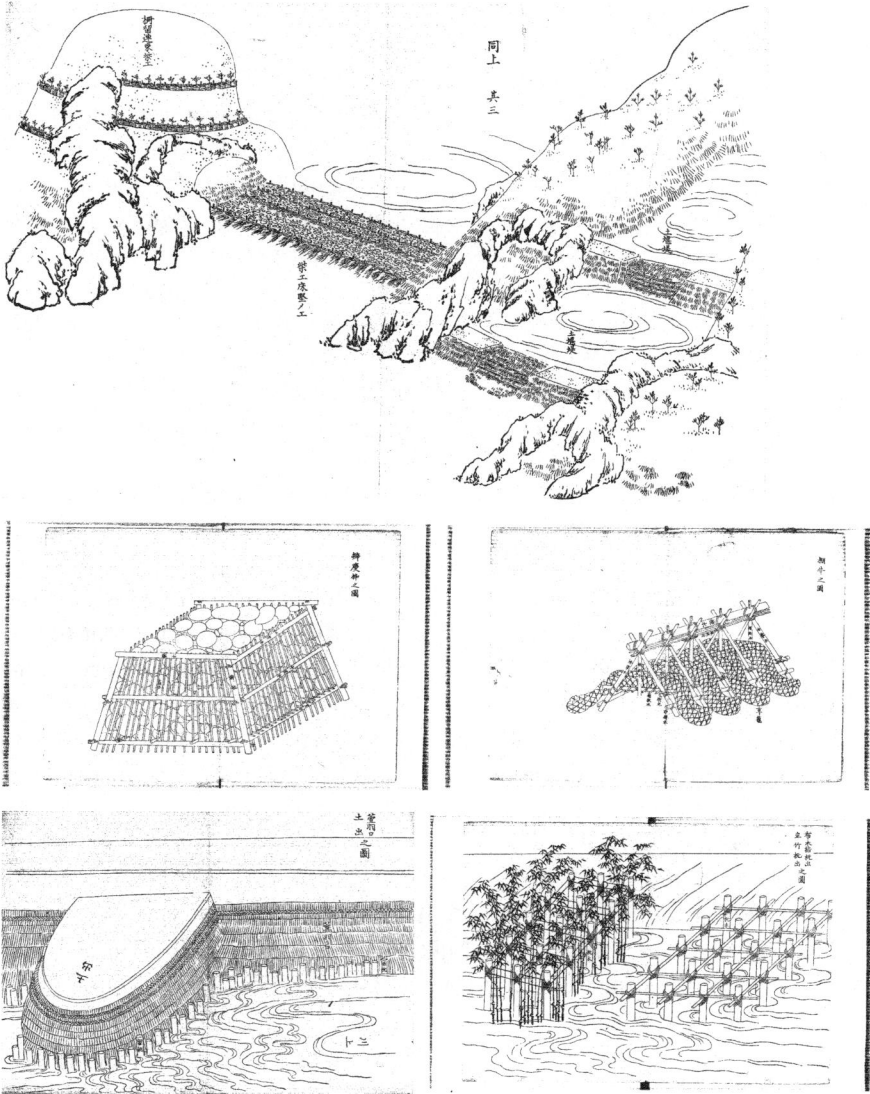

FIGURE 19   Top image: landscape showing methods of replanting "bald mountains"
(*hageyama*) and erosion controls for mountain streams. Central two images:
common designs for cribs (*benkeiwaku* and a large *hijiriushiwaku*) employed to
protect downstream embankments. Bottom two images: two kinds of groynes
(*tsuchidashi* and *nunokiyuikuidashi* / *tatetakekuidashi*) used for protecting
riverbanks and for slowing and channeling the flow of water to make rivers
more navigable. All images are from the *Doboku kōyōroku*, a Home Ministry
compilation of river-related engineering designs. Naimushō Dobokukyoku,
Doboku kōyōroku (Tokyo: Yūrindō, 1881)
COURTESY OF THE NATIONAL DIET LIBRARY, TOKYO

the Tokugawa regime and formation of a new government in 1868, very little is known about Ichikawa's life and career. Aside from his 1895 book, his name only surfaces occasionally in the Kyoto prefectural and Home Ministry documents. He is believed to have been a native of nearby Fushimi, yet little else is known about his education and upbringing or what happened to him following the publication of his book. Nonetheless, he had knowledge and training before 1868 when at the age of forty-two he was hired as an engineer (*doboku gakari*) by the recently established Kyoto prefectural government.[40] From that year until 1870, the prefecture assigned him to river-related projects, including the 1868–70 shifting of the mouth of the Kizu River to the south of the old castle town of Yodo.[41] In 1870, he was dispatched for about one year to a mountainous area about 20 km east of the Fudō River where he was tasked with supervising the building of roads, an irrigation system, and homes for the new village of Dōsenbō.[42] Prior to his employment at the Fudō River worksite, Ichikawa's experience as an engineer had involved everything from supervising the digging of an irrigation pond and ditches to the building of houses and levees. And all of that within the Yodo River basin.

Ichikawa's younger Dutch counterpart on the Fudō River, De Rijke, was entirely new to the Yodo and Kizu Rivers and their environs, but not to the realm of engineering. Born in 1842 to a long lineage of levee builders in the small town of Colijnsplaat in the Netherlands' southwestern province of Zeeland, De Rjike never formally studied engineering at a technical school or university. Rather, while his father Pieter was employed on a levee-building project on South Beveland Island (now peninsula) in Zeeland, the younger De Rijke learned the principles of hydraulic engineering by apprenticing under Jacobus Lebret (1819–1906), who at the time was the levee project's supervising engineer for the Rijkswaterstaat.[43] After serving as a foreman during the building of a lock in Katerveer, De Rijke was hired in 1865 as a construction foreman for the building of the much larger Orange Locks on the 27 km North

40   Fujii Hatsuo, "Ichikawa Yoshikata," in *Doboku jinbutsu jiten* (Tokyo: Atena Shobō, 2004), 36.
41   Kumiyama-chō Shi Hensan Iinkai, ed., *Kumiyama-chō shi* (Kumiyama-chō: Kumiyama-chō, 1989), 2:347–51.
42   Minamiyamashiro Sonshi Hensan Iinkai, ed., *Minamiyamashiro-son shi: honbun hen* (Minamiyamashiro: Minamiyamashiro-mura, 2005), 419–47.
43   Established in 1798, the Rijkswaterstaat (Waterstaat until 1848) was charged with the construction, maintenance, and management of the rivers, canals, polders, and levees in the Netherlands. Following his employment with the Rijkswaterstaat, Jacobus Lebret became a professor of hydraulic engineering at the Royal Academy of Delft. Bert Toussaint, "Johannis de Rijke," in *In een Japanse stroomversnelling*, 180–81; Kamibayashi, *Nihon no kawa*, 18–21.

Sea Canal.[44] During his seven years on this project, De Rijke learned much and made a favorable impression on his supervisors, including the engineer Cornelis Johannes van Doorn (1837–1908). Having already left to work on river and port projects in Japan in 1872, Van Doorn received approval from the Japanese government to hire De Rijke and four others to join him in Japan. One of these Dutch engineers was Van Doorn's former university classmate George Arnold Escher (1843–1939), father of the well-known artist M. C. Escher (1898–1972).[45] De Rijke arrived in Osaka on 25 September 1873 and was appointed a fourth-class engineer with a handsome salary. Along with Escher, he was quickly tasked with drawing up plans for the port of Osaka and improving navigation on the Yodo River. Over the next two years, these Dutch engineers and their Japanese assistants, including Ichikawa, carried out numerous surveys of Osaka Bay and the Yodo River and hiked the river's distant headwaters to evaluate for themselves the challenges posed by the region's steep terrain and bald mountains. As unusual as their collaboration may have been, Ichikawa's and De Rijke's relationship was far from unique during the 1870s and 1880s.

3   Dutch Engineers in Japan

As was seen along the Yodo River and its upstream tributaries like the Fudō, officials in the Home Ministry and elsewhere in the national government believed the country's existing approaches to river management and engineering were insufficient. To ameliorate the situation, they sought to hire engineers from Europe who could introduce different engineering techniques and technologies and could train a new generation of Japanese technicians and engineers in these novel approaches. As was agreed upon during the 1875 Assembly of Prefectural Governors, the national government thereafter significantly increased the amount of "preventative" work executed along some of the country's largest and most flood-prone rivers. Between the 1875 assembly and the promulgation of the 1896 River Law (Kasenhō), the national government directly administered various kinds of improvement projects at sites on fourteen rivers nationwide in conjunction with the excavation of two lock-operated

---

44   Gerard P. van de Ven, ed., *Man-Made Lowlands: History of Water Management and Land Reclamation in the Netherlands* (Utrecht: Matrijs, 1993), 203.

45   The three other Dutchmen were the brick mason Dick Arnst (1843–86), the engineer third-class Alphonse Th. J. H. Thissen, and the metal worker Johannes Nicolaas Westerviel (1840–1924). Bert Toussaint, "Cornelis Johannes van Doorn," in *In een Japanse stroomversnelling*, 140, 196–97; Harm Stevens, "Alphonse Theodore Jozef Hurbert Thissen," in *In een Japanse stroomversnelling*, 260; Kamibayashi, *Nihon no kawa*, 49–53.

TABLE 1   Dates and cumulative costs for all river projects directly administered by the
           national government before the promulgation of the 1896 River Law. These
           fourteen rivers are listed in the order they appear in the following 1937 annual
           report published by the Civil Engineering Bureau of the Home Ministry. Based
           on Naimushō Dobokukyoku Kasenka, ed., *Dobokukyoku daisanjūkai tōkei nenpyō:
           zenhen* (Tokyo: Naimushō Dobokukyoku Kasenka, 1937), 61–70. National Diet
           Library, Tokyo

River	Years before 1896	Expenses (yen)
Yodo	1875–95	770,150
Tone	1869–70 and 1875–95	1,416,775
Shinano	1869–95	1,943,879
Kiso	1877–95	1,383,061
Kitagami	1880–95	716,959
Agano	1882–95	44,016
Fuji	1883–95	440,874
Shō	1883–95	53,230
Abukuma	1883–95	55,351
Chikugo	1882–95	491,621
Mogami	1882–95	345,852
Yoshino	1882–95	236,200
Ōi	1882–95	38,725
Tenryū	1884–95	449,020

canals and the building and expansion of several ports (Table 1).[46] Different in
scale and purpose from local "defensive" river work, these bigger improvement
projects were chosen by the Home Ministry for their importance to national
economic development by preventing further flooding and facilitating inland
navigation.

To plan and supervise these river, canal, and port projects, the national
government employed a total of eleven Dutch engineers and technicians
between 1872 and 1903. Officially referred to by the title "hired foreigner"
(*oyatoi gaikokujin*), the Dutch engineers Van Doorn, De Rijke, and Escher were
only three of the over two thousand foreign experts the national government

46   Before the establishment of the Home Ministry in 1873, the national government had
      already initiated some work along the Tone and Shinano Rivers. Naimushō Dobokukyoku
      Kasenka, ed., *Dobokukyoku daisanjūkai tōkei nenpyō: zenhen* (Tokyo: Naimushō Dobo-
      kukyoku Kasenka, 1937), 61–70.

employed between 1868 and 1889.[47] During this time, various ministries paid a premium salary to 146 engineers from Great Britain, France, Finland, Germany, the Netherlands, and the United States to teach in Japan's new universities as well as plan and supervise infrastructure projects throughout the archipelago.[48] The hiring of these engineers reflected a combination of personal relations, treaty obligations, inter-ministerial rivalries within the Japanese government, and competition among imperial powers. The national reputation of the Dutch was also significant.[49] The historian of the Rhine and Oder Rivers, David Blackbourn, notes that from the eighteenth century, "the Dutch were Europe's acknowledged experts in the engineering of waterways."[50] And this reputation, although somewhat dated, was not lost on Japanese leaders who as early as 1870 began soliciting for Dutch engineers to oversee Japan's river and port projects.[51] It was not until 1872, however, that the first two Dutch engineers— Van Doorn and Isaac Anne Lindo (1848–1941)—arrived in Japan.

The thirty-five-year-old Van Doorn and the twenty-three-year-old Lindo landed at the port of Yokohama in February 1872. They brought with them the

---

47   The word *oyatoi gaikokujin* was the official term for all foreigners hired by the govern-
      ment during this period of unequal treaties, including several thousand Chinese workers
      who helped develop tea and sericulture industries for the export market. The following
      volume contains bibliographic information for nearly all the foreign experts from Europe
      and the United States who were employed in Japan between 1868 and 1889. It also has a
      number of essays about the origins of this term and practice of hiring foreign experts in
      China, Japan, Thailand, and Turkey following the 1840–1842 Opium War between Great
      Britain and the Qing Empire. UNESCO Higashi Ajia Bunka Kenkyū Sentā, ed., *Shiryō: oya-
      toi gaikokujin* (Tokyo: Shōgakukan, 1975).

48   Muramatsu Teijirō, "Oyatoi gaikokujin to Nihon no doboku gijutsu," *Doboku Gakkaishi* 61
      (1976): 9–16.

49   In the 1870s, for example, Americans dominated the Development Agency (Kaitakushi)
      on the northern island of Hokkaidō, and British engineers held sway in the railway-
      building Public Works Ministry (Kōbushō).

50   David Blackbourn, "'Time is a Violent Torrent': Constructing and Reconstructing the
      Rhine in Modern German History," in *Rivers in History: Perspectives on Waterways in
      Europe and North America*, ed. Christof Mauch and Thomas Zeller (Pittsburgh: University
      of Pittsburgh Press, 2008), 14.

51   In his description of the visit of the Iwakura Embassy to the Netherlands in February 1873,
      Kume Kunitake (1839–1931) bemoaned what he saw as misplaced praise for Dutch river
      engineering. After explaining how the geography and "hydrological techniques" of the
      Netherlands with its flat landscape and slow-moving rivers were completely different
      from Japan, he wrote, "Anyone who does not know this, yet talks of controlling water
      in Japan by importing Dutch technology just because he has heard they are masters of
      hydrology, may be compared to the man who climbs a tree hoping to catch a fish!" Kume
      Kunitake, *The Iwakura Embassy, 1871–73: A True Account of the Ambassador Extraordinary
      & Plenipotentiary's Journeys of Observation through the United States and Europe*
      (Princeton: Princeton University Press, 2002), 3:227–29.

engineer's portmanteau of general textbook knowledge and practical work-site experience. After graduating from the Royal Academy of Civil Engineers in Delft, Van Doorn was employed for three years by the colonial government in the Dutch East Indies to survey and design port and rail facilities in the mountainous terrain of Java. After returning to the Netherlands, Van Doorn continued applying his technical skills on railway and other projects, including the abovementioned North Sea Canal.[52] A recent graduate of the Royal Military Academy in Breda, Lindo had also worked in the Netherlands for a few years before joining Van Doorn for their journey to Japan.[53] Thus, while being trained and experienced engineers, the two Dutchmen had actually spent little time on river or port projects. Perhaps it was to compensate for this relatively limited employment on river projects that Van Doorn, Lindo, and later Dutch engineers brought with them numerous books and essays about new techniques and technologies being used on river and port projects in various European countries and their colonies.[54] Nonetheless, the short-lived Civil Engineering Department (Dobokuryō) of the Finance Ministry apparently found that Van Doorn's and Lindo's nationality and profession were reason enough to hire them to supervise the surveying and planning of river and port projects throughout the Japanese archipelago. As it turns out, this trust was not misplaced.

Assigned to the Tokyo office of the Civil Engineering Department, both Van Doorn and Lindo took up residence in the rapidly changing post-restoration city and quickly set about their work. Within weeks of their arrival, the government dispatched them to inspect and draw up plans for the country's most voluminous waterway, the Tone River. After traveling and surveying the length of the river, they installed peils to determine the mean sea level at the mouths of the Tone, Edo (Yedo), and Ara (Sumida) Rivers in order to measure the daily

52   In 1864, the Royal Academy of Civil Engineers in Delft became the Polytechnic University of Delft, which has since expanded into today's Delft University of Technology. Toussaint, "Cornelis Johannes van Doorn," in *In een Japanse stroomversnelling*, 140; Kokudo Seisaku Kikō, ed., *Kokudo o tsukutta doboku gijutsushatachi* (Tokyo: Kashima Shuppankai, 2000), 90–95.

53   Doboku Gakkai, ed., *Meiji igo: honpō doboku to gaijin* (Tokyo: Doboku Gakkai, 1942), 170–72.

54   Though the exact titles and number of books Van Doorn and Lindo brought with them is not known, their contents are suggested by the small library of 398 engineering books that the engineer George Arnold Escher donated to the Home Ministry before returning to the Netherlands in 1878. Itō Yasuo, ed., *Ranjin kōshi Esseru Nihon kaisō-roku/Memoirs of G. A. Escher: Japan 1873–1878* (Mikuni: Mikuni-chō, 1990).

and seasonal fluctuations in water levels.[55] Upon completing these preliminary surveys, Van Doorn drew up and submitted a pair of influential essays containing textbook-like information on the terms and concepts of river hydrology, the design and material for embankments and levees, and examples and diagrams from his and Lindo's survey of the Tone and Edo Rivers (fig. 20).[56]

Following their work in the Kantō region, Van Doorn and Lindo split up and supervised teams of Japanese technicians on separate surveys of the port in Osaka and the Shinano River in Niigata. Overwhelmed by the immensity of the port project for Osaka, in 1873 Van Doorn requested that the Japanese government hire additional engineers from the Netherlands.[57] Therefore, despite Lindo returning home in 1875, he was replaced by others like De Rijke, Escher, Anthonie Th. L. R. Mulder (1848–1901), and Alphonse Th. J. H. Thissen (1843–78). Like Van Doorn and Lindo, and in keeping with the Home Ministry's policy of promoting both water transport and preventative floodworks, all of these engineers were employed on port and river improvement projects in different parts of the country. After working on the Yodo River and port for Osaka, for instance, Escher was sent to survey and plan a number of port improvement projects, including one at Mikuni on the Japan Sea where he experimented with and submitted a report on the local materials available to make hydraulic cement.[58] Elsewhere, Mulder designed and supervised several projects including the nearly 9 km Tone Canal, which was built between 1887 and 1890 to connect the Edo and Tone Rivers.[59] This shortcut essentially traced the two-century-old overland packhorse route and significantly reduced the shipping time between Tokyo and the eastern Kantō region. Heavily used during its first two decades of operation, the canal handled a dwindling number of boats until 1941 when a typhoon caused the Tone River to flood the canal and render it impassible.[60] Although not as costly a failure as the canal and jetties

---

55   For a brief history of the Arakawa Peil (AP) and Yedo Peil (YP), see the report by the office by the Kantō regional office of the Home Ministry: "Reiganjima ryōsuihyō reii to Tōkyō wanjū nado chōi narabi ni Horie ryōsuihyō reii to no kankei" [January 1927], Naimushō Tōkyō Dobokukyoku Shucchōjo, National Diet Library, Tokyo.

56   C. J. van Doorn, "Kasui kaishū no kōan," 4 February 1873; C. J. van Doorn, "Chisui sōron," 5 February 1873. Both documents are archived at the library for the Japan Society of Civil Engineers, Tokyo.

57   Doboku Gakkai, *Meiji igo*, 158–59.

58   G. A. Escher, "Hydraulishe Mortel/Esseru-shi 'semento' shikenki" [24 October 1876], *Yodogawa Oranda gishi monjo*, 288–97.

59   Aihara Masayoshi, "Meiji-ki no Kamedagawa tenchū Tone unga kaisaku ni miru chiiki to hito no haikei," *Hōsei chiri* 33 (2002): 1–15.

60   Morimura Gyōta et al., "Songai baishō seikyū ni tai suru kaitō" [27 September 1941], in *Nagareyama-shi shi: Tonegawa unga shiryō shū*, ed. Nagareyama Hakubutsukan

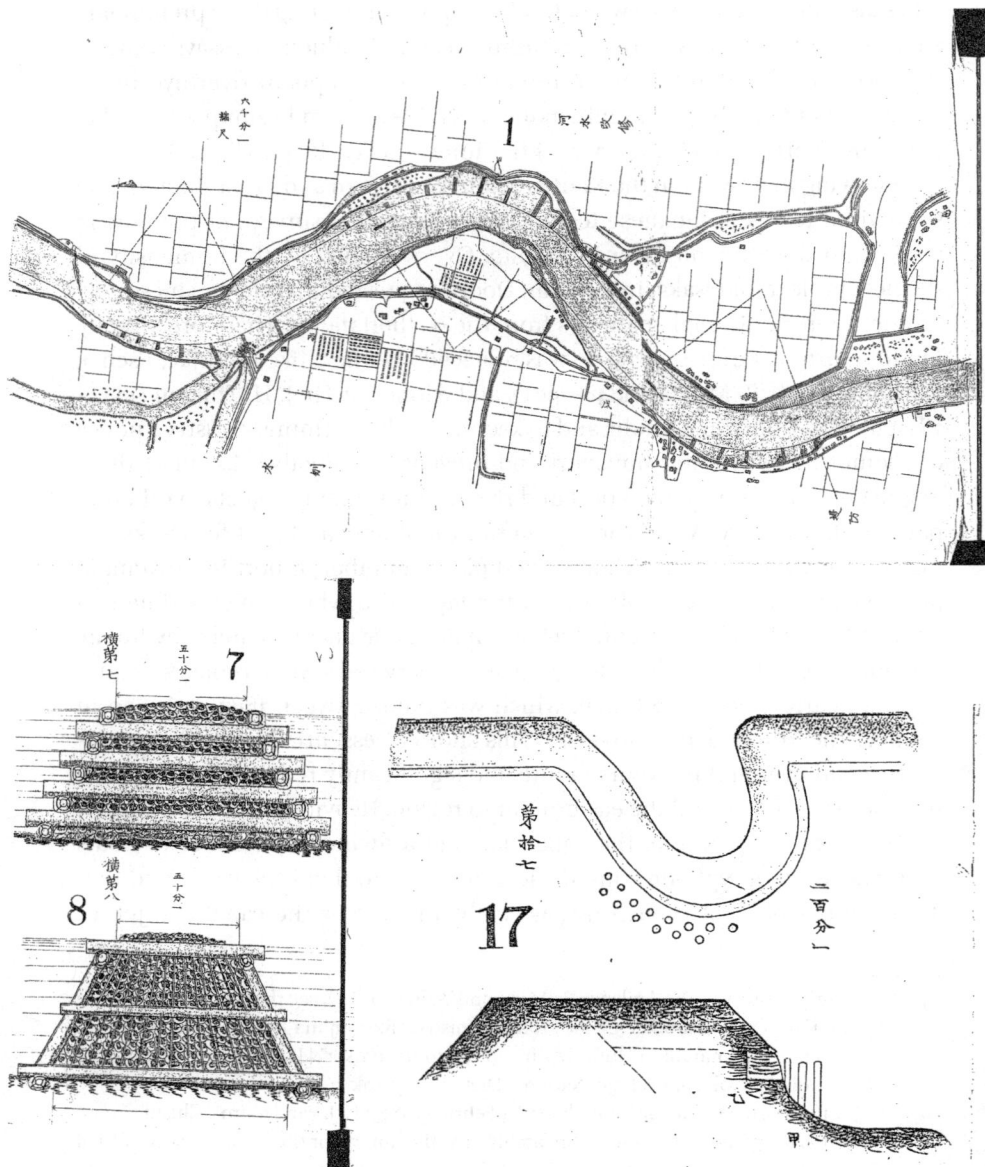

FIGURE 20   Top: survey map displaying Cornelis Johannes van Doorn's and Isaac Anne Lindo's plan
to remove a meander from the Edo River near Tokyo. Bottom left: two cribs similar to
the *benkei-waku* presented in Figure 19. Bottom right: a groyne much like the *tsuchidashi*
presented elsewhere. The use of scale, cross-sections, and orthographic projection (not shown
here) set these diagrams apart from those in the *Doboku kōyōroku*. C. J. van Doorn, "Chisui
sōron" (1873)

Van Doorn designed for the port at Nobiru (north of Sendai), the Tone Canal turned out to be less successful than its sponsors had promised as railways and eventually highways replaced regional waterways as the primary means of moving goods and people throughout the country.[61] And, as discussed at the beginning of this chapter, De Rijke, who remained in Japan until 1903, had more success and lasting influence with his calls for upstream erosion prevention and downstream use of fascines—long bundles of wood tightly wrapped with vines or willow and anchored with stakes or stones—to protect riverbanks and create a narrower river channel.[62] During their time in Japan, the Dutch engineers worked on most of the Home Ministry's directly administered port, canal, and river projects. In doing so, they played a significant role in translating European riparian technologies and adapting local ones to the specific conditions of riverside worksites throughout Japan.

Of the many river, canal, and port projects that engaged the Dutch engineers, the Home Ministry came to prioritize the Yodo River and bustling port of Osaka. During this era, Osaka was Japan's busiest commercial center and the Yodo River flowing through the city was the country's busiest inland waterway, carrying hundreds of riverboats every day to and from Kyoto and other inland cities. The Yodo also drained Japan's sixth largest river basin, including its biggest body of fresh water, Lake Biwa. As suggested at the beginning of this chapter, the Yodo received a heavy sediment load from the surrounding mountains

---

(Nagareyama: Nagareyama-shi, 1985), 189–91. Its long use aside, the Tone Canal also suffered from its share of problems related to flooding, sedimentation, insufficient water, and, with the continued rise of the Tone's riverbed, a reversal in the direction water flowed through the canal. Morimura Gyōta and Tatsuma Kenzō, "Sekiyado kōmon suiryō chōsetsu ni kansuru chinjō" [17 August 1936], in *Nagareyama-shi shi: Tonegawa unga shiryō shū*, 182.

61   Before his 1880 return to the Netherlands, Van Doorn had been instrumental in choosing the location and designing the complicated inner port facilities at Nobiru. Plagued from the beginning by budget overruns, strong winds, and sedimentation of the canal and port, in September 1884 a powerful typhoon struck the area, destroyed the port's protective jetties, and forced the government to abandon the entire project. Matsuura Shigeki, *Meiji no kokudo kaihatsushi: kindai doboku gijutsu no ishizue* (Tokyo: Kashima Shuppankai, 1992), 70–82.

62   In Japan, fascines were long called *soda*, but with the adaptation of Dutch-style fascines to Japan's rivers, they also came to be known as *soda chinshō* and by the Dutch loan-word *kereppu* (from *krib* or *kribbe*). Johannis de Rijke, "Soda-hane gaisoku/de Rēke-shi shibakō mizuhane" [November 1873], *Yodogawa Oranda gishi monjo*, 45–61. For two contemporary descriptions of the different uses, required materials, and installation of these fascines and similar erosion controls in Japan and the Netherlands. See also Tsujimura Yōkichi, "Soda-kō," *Kōgakkaishi* 5, no. 57 (1886): 1357–1405; Thomas Colclough Watson, "On the Use of Fascines in the Public Works of Holland," *Minutes of Proceedings of the Institution of Civil Engineering* 41 (1875): 158–70.

due to the rampant problem of deforestation in the river's headwaters. Much of this sediment eventually settled in the Yodo's estuary to form massive, shifting sandbars across a wide area where the current of the river met the tides of Osaka Bay. Consequently, only small lighters and fishing boats were able to navigate over or around these often hidden obstacles. "As the river was the only means of getting on board ships from old Japan's chief commercial center," explained the British engineer Richard Brunton (1841–1901) in 1870, "the existence of this sand bar apparently nullified the long and wearisome negotiations and infinite labor from which its opening resulted. Nature seemed to have been victorious over [the] diplomacy [used to open the port]."[63]

Hired specifically to work on the Yodo River and port for Osaka, Escher and De Rijke arrived in Osaka and immediately began surveying the Yodo and its tributaries. Over several months in 1873 and 1874, they examined how and where cargo was being shipped in and out of Osaka, measured the deepest and shallowest draft for boats at various points on the river, and hiked along the Yodo's tributaries to observe and measure the severity of upstream erosion. As noted above, De Rijke experimented upstream with erosion-control dams and afforestation methods and together with Thissen tested different kinds of fascines along the downstream portion of the river. To accomplish all these tasks, the Dutch engineers relied on a cadre of Japanese engineers and technicians like Ichikawa Yoshikata to survey, draw maps, install measuring devices, and supervise construction. Typically younger than the experienced Ichikawa, these Japanese specialists were employed by individual prefectures and the Home Ministry's Civil Engineering Bureau (Dobokukyoku) to assist the Dutch engineers and also to study under them formally as technical assistants.[64] In the course of their work, these young men received training in European methods of cartography and surveying that included the proper handling of equipment, such as theodolites, peils, sounding rods, and current meters, and the calculating of river discharge, horizontal and vertical dimensions, and low- and high-water stages.[65] Under the direction of Escher, De Rijke, and other Dutch

63   Richard Henry Brunton, *Schoolmaster to an Empire: Richard Henry Brunton in Meiji Japan, 1868–1876* (New York: Greenwood Press, 1991), 21.
64   The Civil Engineering Bureau of the Home Ministry appears to have officially called these assistants *kōsei* (technical students), but often referred to them in documents as *minarai* (apprentice). The Dutch engineers were less standardized, referring to them variously as students (*leerlingen*), assistants (*assistentent*), or trainee engineers (*aspirant-Ingenieurs*). The following letter provides examples of the use of some of these terms in Dutch and their translation into contemporary Japanese: G. A. Escher to Ono Gishin [29 January 1875], *Yodogawa Oranda gishi monjo*, 161–62.
65   A. Thissen to Ono Gishin [4 December 1874], *Yodogawa Oranda gishi monjo*, 142–45. See also Kiso Sansen Rekishi Bunka Shiryō Henshū Kentōkai, *Meiji kaishū kansei hyaku-shūnen*

engineers, these Japanese assistants then translated these measurements into tables, diagrams, and maps that effectively produced a representation of the river as a hydraulic process abstracted from the complexity of its broader riparian relations. Language, however, appears to have been an area of concern for the Dutch engineers. In order to study the fundamentals of engineering Escher explained to his supervisor that their students would need to read books written in either Dutch or English.[66] Although the Civil Engineering Bureau employed upwards of eight translators, they clearly spent most of their time translating letters, reports, and other missives between the foreign engineers and their supervising officials in the bureau and had little time to translate technically difficult books into Japanese.[67] Some of these technical assistants had some knowledge of European languages, but probably had like Ichikawa acquired much of their technical know-how from jobsite experience before and after working under the tutelage of the Dutch engineers. And when foreign technical articles or books were read and consulted, they were very likely sources translated into Japanese.[68] Or, as discussed in the next section, they

---

tokubetsu-gō: Kiso sansen rekishi bunka no chōsa kenkyū shiryō (Kuwana: Kokudo Kōtsūshō Chūbu Chihō Seibikyoku Kisogawa Karyū Kasen Jimusho Chūsaka, 2013), 20.

66   G. A. Escher to Ono Gishin [29 January 1875], *Yodogawa Oranda gishi monjo*, 161–62. The Dutch engineers also evidently approved of and appreciated having their own students. For example, Thissen requested that one of his more capable apprentices (*leerling*) be hired and later asked that this same student be transferred with him to his new assignment in Tokyo. Thissen called the apprentice Ouigara, but in the Japanese translations of the Dutchman's letters he is named Uehara (given name and dates unknown). A. Thessin to Ono Gishin [4 December 1874] and A. Thessin to Ono Gishin [1 February 1875], *Yodogawa Oranda gishi monjo*, 142–45, 163–64.

67   Escher suggested that a textbook in English would be most appropriate because that was the European language in which their Japanese assistants were most proficient. He recommended an English translation of Charles-Eugène Delaunay's *Cours Élémentaire de mécanique* and that a "very good book" (*zeer goed boek*) in Dutch is D. J. Storm Buysing's *Handleiding tot de Kennis der Waterbouwkunde*. Apparently unknown to Escher, Atsumi Teiji (1836–84) had in 1871 already translated the third edition of Buysing's book, published in 1864, under the Japanese title of *Chisuigaku shuka hen*. Buysing's treatises was undoubtedly one of the earliest European books about river engineering to be translated into Japanese.

68   Van Doorn wrote two influential essays on hydraulic engineering that were translated into Japanese in 1873 for his students. Soon afterward, translators made available to a wider audience in Japan other British and American civil engineering manuals, for example, William J. M. Rankine, *Manual of Civil Engineering* (London: Charles Griffin, 1861) and James Leffel & Co., *Construction of Mill Dams, Comprising also the Building of Race and Reservoir Embankments and Head Gates, the Measurement of Streams, Gauging of Water Supply, &c.* (Springfield, Ohio: O. J. Leffel & Co., 1874). From 1881, *Kōgakkaishi* (*Journal of the Engineering Society* (of Japan)) also began publishing articles on a variety of topics, including the use of tacheometers in surveying, methods of measuring water flowage,

read articles and books written in Japanese by a growing number of authors like Ichikawa who were deeply concerned with the country's riparian policies.

Following the departure from Japan of the majority of Dutch engineers by the early 1880s, their technical assistants and students continued to survey and oversee projects on the Yodo and other rivers. Many enjoyed long careers in the Home Ministry, and a few even managed to make names for themselves. After working on the Fuji and Yodo Rivers with the Dutch engineers, for instance, in 1891 Inoue Seitarō (1852–1936) published a well-regarded treatise on approaches to erosion prevention.[69] After the flooding of the Yodo River in 1885, Ichikawa left his post in Kyoto Prefecture to join the Home Ministry as an engineer of the fifth rank.[70] These career paths of technicians in Japan shared similarities with those in Europe and the United States at the time. This is seen in the case of De Rijke who with no formal engineering education was promoted to construction foreman in the Netherlands before being hired by the Home Ministry in Japan, upon Van Doorn's advice, as a fourth-rank engineer. While the formal study of engineering at military institutes and universities was increasingly common in continental Europe, until the late nineteenth century in Great Britain and the United States most technicians and engineers had learned their trade while apprenticing jobs for several years.[71] "The great engineers of nineteenth century Britain," notes the historian J. A. Buchanan, "remained essentially the same as the diligent artisans, millwrights, surveyors, and craftsmen, from whom the engineering profession had sprung in the previous century."[72] By century's end in Europe and Japan, however, a university degree would become a prerequisite of advancement to the professional status of engineer or *gishi*.

---

design and installation of fascines, and reports on different engineering projects in Japan and abroad.

69   Inoue Seitarō, *Sabō-kō daii* (Osaka: Naimushō Ōsaka Doboku Shucchōjo, 1891).

70   Fujii, "Ichikawa Yoshikata," *Doboku jinbutsu jiten*, 37.

71   R. A. Buchanan, "Institutional Proliferation in the British Engineering Profession, 1847–1914," *Economic History Review* 38, no. 2 (1985): 42–60; Colin Divall, "A Measure of Agreement: Employers and Engineering Studies in the Universities of England and Wales, 1897–1939," *Social Studies of Science* 20, no. 1 (1990): 65–122; Eda Kranakis, "Social Determinants of Engineering Practice: A Comparative View of France and America in the Nineteenth Century" *Social Studies of Science* 19, no. 1 (1989): 5–70; Terry Shinn, "The Industry, Research, and Education Nexus," in *The Modern Physical and Mathematical Sciences*, ed. Mary Jo Nye The Cambridge History of Science 5 (Cambridge: Cambridge University Press, 2002), 133–53; Cecil O. Smith, Jr., "The Longest Run: Public Engineers and Planning in France," *American Historical Review* 95, no. 3 (1990): 657–92.

72   R. A. Buchanan, "Science and Engineering: A Case Study in British Experience in the Mid-Nineteenth Century," *Notes and Records of the Royal Society of London* 32, no. 2 (1978): 215.

Having carried out months of survey work on the Yodo River and its tributaries in late 1873 and 1874, De Rijke, Escher, and Thissen began submitting
reports and plans to the Home Ministry. These plans called for better surveys
of boat traffic and measurements of water levels at various points along the
river, the building of upstream erosion dams, the installation downstream of
levee and bank protecting fascines, and the dredging of the river to a navigable
depth of five feet.[73] While the more comprehensive and costly aspects of their
plans were never acted upon, the Home Ministry, as well as Osaka and Kyoto
Prefectures, later requested De Rijke to supervise the fortification and repair of
collapsing riverbanks, the removal of vegetation from and dredging of the riverbed, the restriction of the river to a single channel, and as examined earlier,
erosion-prevention efforts for mountain streams.[74]

In the decades after the devastating flooding of the Yodo and Kiso Rivers in
1885, the Home Ministry's initial focus on the "preventative" work of balancing
water transport needs with flood prevention was retroactively dismissed as an
ineffective "low-water" (teisui) policy. As explained earlier, the Home Ministry's
riparian policies during the 1870s and 1880s mostly reflected its nascent authority, limited fiscal resources, and Home Minister Ōkubo's early vision of developing the country's riparian corridors for commerce. Nonetheless, as addressed
in the conclusion to this chapter, it has been the Dutch engineers carrying out
this policy who have been blamed by later engineers and historians for the
1885 floods and other inundations along the country's largest rivers. But as discussed in chapter 4, it was De Rijke who played a significant role in formulating
this abandonment of the Home Ministry's earlier emphasis on "preventative"
work in favor of greater attention to the "defensive" work of flood protection.
Regardless of who was responsible for the limitations of these earlier policies,
the devastating flooding of 1885 signaled an explicit shift toward what became

---

73   Two reports summarize much of the work on the Yodo River that Escher and De Rijke
      were planning and supervising: Escher and De Rijke, "Yodogawawerken" [15 May 1875];
      De Rijke, "Waterverdeeling Yodogawa" [5 June 1876], Yodogawa Oranda gishi monjo, 201–4,
      268–70.

74   In a later 1890 report, De Rijke summarized that his previous plans and work on the Yodo
      River and harbor facilities for Osaka were undertaken in accordance with the low-water
      policies then pursued by the Home Ministry: "The plan which I made for the Central
      Government years ago, which is now nearly executed, was only to regulate the low water-
      bed along the main river, i.e., to form a uniform and navigable channel instead of the
      irregular and shifting boat track intersected, as it was when I took the river in hand, by
      numerous shallows and sandbanks." Elsewhere in this report, he also emphasized his ear-
      lier suggestions for how to address downstream flooding and repeat his warnings about
      the continued problem of upstream erosion. De Rijke, "With Reports Concerning the
      Yodogawa and Yamatogawa" [1 July 1890], Yodogawa Oranda gishi monjo, 314.

known as a "high-water" (*kōsui*) policy with its primary objective of defending against high river waters during floods.

4   Educating Japanese Engineers: The French Connection

As we have seen, after the Restoration, the young government in Japan sought out and paid handsomely for European and American expertise in matters ranging from the construction of lighthouses to the creation of a modern army and navy. The government not only employed Van Doorn, De Rijke, and other Dutch engineers to plan and supervise port and river projects but it also hired a number of American, British, and other Europeans to teach engineering and related subjects in Japan's first colleges and universities. Eager to reduce its dependence on foreign experts and the tremendous cost of employing them, in 1875 the Ministry of Education decided to send promising students to study in universities in Europe and the United States in the hope that they would replace these foreign specialists and teachers upon their return.[75] Unlike the varied educational background of students sent abroad in the 1860s by the Tokugawa and several domain governments, however, the cohort of 1875 were all graduates of the new Tōkyō Kaisei Gakkō, the successor to the Tokugawa regime's school for foreign studies, the Kaiseisho. Like other students at this institution, they had enrolled in courses ranging from mining and engineering to law and language, taught for the most part by foreign instructors in either French or English. Destined to study law, medicine, science, and engineering at universities in the United States, Germany, and France, the young men who made up this first cohort of overseas students were in effect retracing the steps of the foreign experts who had come to Japan. In joining this transnational flow of expertise, these students reinforced the status of Europe and the United States as the central node of what was seen as "modern civilization." But they also contributed to the ongoing movement of experts and expertise that in time would see Japan strengthen its governance over its people and resources, gain its own empire, and redefine itself as an "alternative" to the West.

---

75   For the 1877–78 school year, for instance, the new Tokyo University (Tōkyō daigaku) allocated a full third of its annual budget to pay the salary of foreign instructors. For a discussion of the government's decision to send students abroad, see Ishizuki Minoru, *Kindai Nihon no kaigai ryūgaku shi* (Tokyo: Chūō Kōron, 1992), 133–41. For a brief overview of the government's policies regarding overseas studies in English, see Ishizuki Minoru, "Overseas Study by Japanese in the Early Meiji Period," in *The Modernizers: Overseas Students, Foreign Employees, and Meiji Japan*, ed. Ardath W. Burks (Boulder: Westview Press, 1985), 161–83.

Among the eleven young men who boarded a steamship in Yokohama on 18 July 1875, the twenty-year-old Furuichi Kōi (1854–1934) was the only one destined for France.[76] During his five years abroad, Furuichi proved himself to be an astute student of the sciences and mathematics of engineering. Within two weeks of arriving in Paris on 1 September he began classes at the École Monge in preparation for advanced study.[77] The following summer, he placed sixth out of two hundred on the entrance exam for the École Centrale des Arts et Manufactures and soon afterward was allowed to enroll as a regular university student. At this time, he also shared an apartment with three new Japanese classmates: Yamada Torakichi (1854–1927), Okino Tadao (1854–1921), and Yamaguchi Hanroku (1858–1900). After the collapse of the Tokugawa government, Yamada, a student from Kokura domain on the southern island of Kyushu, first studied in Great Britain and then in France. Like Furuichi, Okino and Yamaguchi were recent graduates of the Tōkyō Kaisei Gakkō, but belonged to the Ministry of Education's second cohort of overseas students.[78]

Although the students at the École Centrale came from diverse backgrounds, together they immersed themselves in the progressive ideals of acquiring expertise in mathematics and the industrial sciences and applying that knowledge to improve the world. As Furuichi fondly recounted years later, students at the École Centrale received an "encyclopedic education" (*insaikuropedekaru ejukēshon*) that emphasized a mastery of engineering principles and required all students to attend classes outside their chosen specialization.[79] Accordingly, during their first year at the École Centrale, the four Japanese students and their 215 classmates from countries throughout Europe enrolled in compulsory courses in architecture, geology, calculus, differential mechanics, and descriptive geometry before choosing one of four fields of specialization

---

76   Hatoyama Kazuo was among this first cohort of government-sponsored students. He kept a diary that recorded the group's travels by steamship from Yokohama to San Francisco and by train to Chicago, Niagara Falls, and New York. After returning from the United States where he studied Columbia and Yale Universities, Hatoyama became a law professor at Tokyo Imperial University, the first president of Waseda University, an official with the Foreign Ministry, and member of the Tokyo City Assembly and Imperial Diet. Hatoyama Haruko, *Hatoyama no isshō* (Tokyo: Ōsorasha, 1997, originally published 1929).

77   The École Monge was designated a national preparatory school and renamed Lycée Carnot in 1894. Haraguchi Masato, "Furuichi Kōi to kyōiku," in *Furuichi Kōi to sono jidai*, ed. Doboku Gakkai Dobokushi Kenkyu Iinkai, 19–21.

78   In terms of social status, all four of these students had been born into warrior families from domains in Western Japan. Haraguchi, "Furuichi Kōi to kyōiku," 34.

79   Furuichi Kōi, "Doboku Gakkai dai ikkai sōkai kaichō kōen," *Doboku Gakkai zasshi* 1, no. 1 (1915): 2.

for their second and third years.[80] When it came time to specialize in their second year, all four of the Japanese students chose civil engineering. Accordingly during their second and third years, they took courses ranging from applied mechanics and metallurgy to steam engines and railway engineering.[81] During their three years of coursework at the École Centrale, all students also undertook a number of experiments, surveys, and projects that require each to design and explain the operation of boilers, train stations, and other industrial technologies.[82] By the end of their education, the students were meant to have a broad understanding of how to conduct preliminary surveys, use specific instruments, gather usable data, analyze this abstracted information, and prepare summary plans and reports. In short, this regimen of courses, projects, and assignments sought to equip students with the calculative skills of engineers and the ability to apply them in a variety of working environments.

During their studies in Paris, Furuichi and his roommates also had ample opportunity to observe the many roles that engineers and engineering had come to play in French society. If Paris in the 1870s was the "capital of modernity," it owed this modernity to the inventive public financing and ambitious engineering used to redesign the city after the 1852 declaration of the Second Empire by Napoleon III (Charles-Louis Napoleon Bonaparte, 1803–73).[83] Part of the wide-ranging economic and infrastructural reforms called for by Napoleon III was the renovation of Paris, a task assigned to the newly appointed Prefect of the Seine, Baron Georges-Eugène Haussmann (1809–1891). Through the 1850s and 1860s, Haussmann's administrators and architects rent open the city's premodern urban fabric by ordering the expropriation of land and demolition of thousands of buildings to make way for broad boulevards, city parks, public monuments, and rail stations.[84] Below ground, Haussmann delegated the improvement of Paris's water supply and sewer system to the engineer Eugène Belgrand (1810–78), who subsequently expanded the entire system by tapping nearby rivers and building numerous reservoirs to meet the

---

80   Although starting earlier than his three roommates, Yamada enrolled in many of the same courses as the other students.

81   In his lengthy essay about the Furuichi's education, the engineering historian Haraguchi Masato provides a table showing all the courses the four Japanese students enrolled in as well as the grades they received while studying at the École Centrale. Haraguchi, "Furuichi Kōi to kyōiku," 36, 39–48.

82   Haraguchi, "Furuichi Kōi to kyōiku," 43–50.

83   David Harvey, *Paris, Capital of Modernity* (New York: Routledge, 2003), 93–124.

84   David P. Jordan, *Transforming Paris: The Life and Labors of Baron Haussmann* (New York: Simon and Schuster, 1995).

city's growing thirst.[85] In the 1830s, the French Parliament had begun financing several public works projects that by 1870 had grown into a nationwide system of complimentary railways and canals.[86] Although having made Paris the central hub in this national infrastructure may have proved a liability when needing to transport troops and supplies along the frontlines during its war against Prussia in 1870, it succeeded in cementing the capital city's preeminent place in French society and economy.

While in Paris, Furuichi appears to have made numerous excursions around France to tour various engineering projects. He broadened the scope of these study tours after graduation from the École Centrale in August 1879 by inspecting facilities in Great Britain, Ireland, Belgium, and the Netherlands. His handwritten account of these tours describes meetings with engineers and includes multiple sketches and explanations of wharves, docks, breakwaters, lighthouses, canals, embankments, railways, railcars, stations, platforms, and signal flags.[87] His accounts reveal the twenty-five-year-old's keen interest in understanding how these large "public engineering projects" (kōkyō doboku jigyō) functioned, especially the linkage between rail and maritime transport systems at port cities. This early concern with the role of engineering in building a national infrastructure and economy anticipated Furuichi's and his roommate Okino's later activities and influential careers at the Home Ministry.

Furuichi and his peers also imbibed the philosophical draft that had stimulated the reengineering of Paris and the building of a new national infrastructure for France. These projects had emerged through the work of graduates of the state-centered École de Ponts et Chaussées and École Polytechnique, as well as the more industry-focused École Centrale. Furuichi and his roommates were immersed in and gained an appreciation for the Saint-Simonian belief in the progressive influence engineers could have on society.[88] In 1840, for

85   Jordan, *Transforming Paris*, 267–77; Matthew Gandy, "The Paris Sewers and the Rationalization of Urban Space," *Transactions of the Institute of British Geographers* 24, no. 1 (1999): 23–44.

86   Smith, "The Longest Run," 665–80.

87   Furuichi Kōi, *Motes des mes voyages d'étude* (1879). Held in the Furuichi Bunko, Civil Engineering Library, Tokyo University. Iguchi Shōhei has translated Furuichi's notebooks into Japanese with a short introduction. See Iguchi Shōhei, "Furuichi Kōi no kengaku ryokōki," pts. 1–3, *Nihon no kawa* 30 (October 1984): 54–74; 31 (April 1985): 33–62; 33 (March 1986): 35–65.

88   The historian Antoine Picon also explains that engineers in nineteenth-century France differed from their more pragmatic peers in Great Britain for their "generalist" ("encyclopedic" in Furuichi's words) and "messianic" perspective of themselves and their burgeoning profession. Antoine Picon, "French Engineers and Social Thought, 18th–20th Centuries: An Archeology of Technocratic Ideals," *History and Technology* 23, no. 3

instance, a student at the École Polytechnique described what he had learned about the virtues of the theoretic, deductive approach: "These abstract studies develop a rational and independent mind ... Analysis has torn away the veil from the mysteries of nature. Mechanics, clarified and complemented by differential calculus, permits us to ... regulate natural forces more advantageously."[89] In other words, through the application of their "abstract studies," engineers gained knowledge of a real "nature" that could be regulated and controlled to the advantage of French society. In this way, Furuichi and his roommates returned to Japan equipped with lessons about the place of engineering in society: the importance of studying and applying advanced mathematics to understand the "mysteries of nature," the engineer's service to society through the state, and a progressive belief in the positive application of science and technology to improve upon society and nature.

The paths of Furuichi and his roommates began to diverge following their graduation in 1879. After his month-long tour of public works projects in several western European countries, Furuichi returned to Paris for the remaining year of his government scholarship, taking advanced mathematics courses at the University of Paris, courses he would later teach in Tokyo. Okino seems to have stayed in Paris for two more years of self-study before returning to Japan in 1881.[90] Furuichi's and Okino's choice of furthering their education upon graduation was highly unusual. Nearly all of the other 146 classmates who managed to graduate from the École Centrale that year went on to put their education to remunerative use in factories and on construction sites throughout Europe.[91] Indeed, this was the direction that Yamaguchi and Yamada chose. Yamaguchi was employed for a year as an engineer in a factory near Paris before returning to Japan to supervise a number of public works projects, including the municipal improvement plans for Osaka and Nagasaki.[92] After having spent a decade in Europe, Yamada returned to Japan and entered the Agriculture and Commerce Ministry before moving to the Home Ministry,

---

(September 2007): 200–3. In contrasting French and American engineers, another historian explains that, "The French devoted much attention to mathematical, engineering theory, but tended to ignore experimental, industrial research." Eda Kranakis, "Social Determinants of Engineering Practice," 5. For an overview of Henri de Saint Simon (1760–1825), his science-based idealism, and his influence on intellectual elites in nineteenth-century France, see Richard G. Olson, *Science and Scientism in Nineteenth-Century Europe* (Urbana: University of Illinois Press, 2008), 41–61.

89   Quoted in Smith, "The Longest Run," 661.
90   Matsuura Shigeki, "Okino Tadao to Meiji kaishū," *Suiri kagaku* 40, no. 6 (1997): 97.
91   Haraguchi, "Furuichi Kōi to kyōiku," 51–52.
92   Fujimori Terunobu, *Meiji no Tōkyō keikaku* (Tokyo: Iwanami Shoten, 1982, reprinted 1990), 308.

where he planned and supervised several irrigation and river projects. While their education abroad ensured all four engineers an elite career track once back in Japan, their immediate employment at government universities and ministries was typical of the new engineering profession as a whole in Japan where at the time nearly all civil engineers were employees of prefectures or the national government.[93]

Furuichi and his roommates returned to Japan beginning in 1880 to witness a country undergoing rapid social and economic change as well as unmet expectations for greater participation in local and national government. Amidst this social and political turbulence, the Home Ministry was growing into one of the most powerful institutions in the national government and was quickly replacing its foreign engineers with qualified Japanese engineers. The ministry quickly offered positions to young returnees from abroad, albeit at much lower salaries than the foreign engineers in its employ. This included the four graduates of the École Centrale and others, such as Tanabe Gisaburō (1858–89) and Miyanohara Seizō (1847–88), who had studied in Germany and the United States, respectively.[94] Moreover, from 1878, the ranks of the emerging engineering profession were bolstered by graduates of the new engineering program at Tokyo University (Tōkyō Daigaku) and the recently founded Imperial College of Technology (Kōbu Daigakkō).

Among the Home Ministry's many university-educated employees, however, few were as influential as Furuichi and Okino. Joining the Home Ministry's Civil Engineering Bureau in 1880, over the next few years Furuichi was dispatched to supervise river and port projects in Niigata, Hokkaidō, and other parts of the country. And in 1890, after just ten years of service, the ministry promoted him to head the bureau itself. During the 1880s, the young engineer sat on sanitation and city planning committees in Tokyo. He also became a pivotal figure in engineering education through his position at the newly established Tokyo Imperial University (Tōkyō Teikoku Daigaku), where in 1886 he was appointed the first chair of the Engineering Department.[95]

---

93   After a number of years with the Home Ministry, Yamada resigned to work as the country's first private consulting civil engineer. This mid-career change to private consulting is notable for how unusual it was. Matsuura Shigeki, "Wasurerareta gijutsusha—Yamada Torakichi," *Suiri kagaku* 43, no. 5 (1999): 96–113.

94   Fujii, "Tanabe Gisaburō" and "Miyanohara Seizō," *Doboku jinbutsu jiten*, 192–93, 304.

95   In 1877, Tōkyō Kaisei Gakkō merged with Tokyo Medical School (Tōkyō Igakkō) to create Tokyo University, which in turn merged in 1886 with the Imperial College of Technology to form Tokyo Imperial University. For the circuitous origins of the University of Tokyo, see Tōkyō Daigaku Shuppankai, ed., *Tōkyō Daigaku: sono hyaku-nen* (Tokyo: Tōkyō Daigaku Shuppankai, 1977).

Okino's thirty-five-year career was marked by similar ambition and achievement. After he returned to Japan in 1881, he taught for two years at the new Tokyo Vocational University (Tōkyō Shōkō Gakkō) before entering the Home Ministry where he surveyed, planned, and supervised a number of river projects in eastern and central Japan before being promoted in 1890 to lead the Fourth Regional Engineering District, which until it was reorganized in July 1894 included Osaka, Kyoto, Nagoya, and the important Kiso and Yodo Rivers. During this transitional period, both Mulder and De Rijke continued to work for the Home Ministry, with the former supervising the building of the Tone Canal and the latter planning and overseeing projects along the Kiso and Yodo Rivers. As discussed in chapter 4, it was also in 1890 that De Rijke, Okino, and Furuichi all became directly involved in the reframing of the Yodo River, and through that project, in formulating a new framework to govern the rivers of Japan.

5   Conclusion

The first decades following the 1868 Meiji Restoration were in many ways transformative—the riparian assemblages of the Japanese archipelago were not immune to these changes. But these shifts occurred unevenly and had little effect on the quotidian riparian relations that had emerged during the previous period of Tokugawa rule. Where the efforts at reform most clearly began to intersect with the country's existing riparian assemblages during the 1870s and 1880s was in the debates and overlapping discourses about nation building. The leaders of the nascent national government in Tokyo chafed at Japan having been consigned to second-rank status by the imperial powers from Europe and the United States who had compelled the Tokugawa government to sign unequal treaties. To address its continuing vulnerability to their imperial ambitions and overcome regional rivalries within country, these leaders sought to strengthening Japan through policies like Home Minister Ōkubo's "promotion of commerce and industry." Central to their endeavors was an investment in the science and technology deemed necessary to build the infrastructure that would further integrate the country and rein in the centrifugal forces of the country's various regions. Large rivers and coastal shipping routes had long been the regional conduits upon which commerce was carried and seemed to offer the promise of prosperity without the peril and cost of creating a completely new infrastructure centered on roads and railways. First through the hiring of a handful of Dutch engineers and later through a combination of European-educated and homegrown engineers, the Home Ministry dispatched these men to work on the fourteen rivers listed at the beginning of this chapter that were deemed to be of national importance. The recalcitrant character of the country's finances and rivers, however, ensured that this effort did not proceed without turbulence. As the newly centralized government tried to utilize these regional rivers as a "national" infrastructure, local politicians and the communities to which they belong clamored for more assistance in maintaining and developing these waterways.

Given the critical involvement of the Dutch engineers during this formative period of river administration in Japan, historians have had much to say about the influence of these men and the European culture they represented. For some, the failures of the Dutch engineers overshadowed their successes. They contend that the Dutch contribution was negligible because the technologies these Dutch engineers sought to introduce were either too expensive to implement or resembled indigenous methods already in use, such as with stone-anchored fascines.[96] Citing the destruction caused by flooding along the Yodo River in 1885, the historian Yamazaki Yūkō makes an argument bordering on environmental determinism. He posits that, because the natural environments of Japan and the Netherlands are fundamentally different, it was "dangerous" to introduce into Japan the "flood-control technology of the flat country of the Netherlands."[97] Another historian, Matsuura Shigeki, is more sanguine in his assessment, asserting that the Dutch engineers succeeded in introducing a whole range of scientific methods for river engineering and tutoring an entire generation of Japanese engineers. "The modern science that is focused on hydrology," he explains, "objectively quantifies phenomena and formulates river plans not only through intuition and individual experience but with a universalizing method (*fuhenka shita hōhō*)."[98] Often overlooked in the biographies of these Dutch engineers and the new national government's efforts at river administration are the less pedigreed Japanese engineers and technicians like Ichikawa Yoshitaka and Inoue Seitarō who enabled these Dutchmen to

96   Sanada Hidekichi, *Nihon suiseikō ron* (Tokyo: Iwanami Shoten, 1932), 249–50; Chino, "Kinsei chisui gijutsu," 161–64.

97   Despite being a well-researched essay with interesting observations about the development of river administration in Japan, Yamazaki assumes that before arriving in Japan these Dutch engineers spent their whole lives working in the polder-lands of the Netherlands. Needless to say, this argument does not account for these engineers' education, travels, and work elsewhere in Europe and the Dutch empire or their capacity to experiment and learn in the field and from the Japanese engineers and technicians with whom they closely worked. Yamazaki Yūkō, "Naimushō no kasen seisaku," in *Michi to kawa no kindai*, ed. Takamura Naosuke (Tokyo: Yamakawa Shuppansha, 1996), 96.

98   Matsuura Shigeki, "Gaikokujin gijutsusha no hatashita yakuwari," in *Kawa o seishita kindai gijutsu*, 151.

carry out much of their work. Not lost in these histories, however, are the first generation of professional Japanese engineers, such as Furuichi Kōi and Okino Tadao, who had a central role in designing and building what I describe in subsequent chapters as Japan's modern river regime.

Most biographies of Furuichi Kōi, Okino Tadao, and their Japanese peers and professional progeny gravitate toward hagiography, stressing their extraordinary abilities and contributions to the building of modern Japan. Whether Okino's mastery of mathematics and engineering or Furuichi's ubiquitous presence on government advisory and planning committees, historians have highlighted the individual and collective acumen and accomplishments of these "men of the Meiji era."[99] Undoubtedly, they had influential roles as the lead engineers of several large infrastructural projects that were and still are acclaimed as hallmarks of Japan's rapid modernization. But in lauding their particular abilities and contributions to modern Japan, what these historians often neglect to provide is a critical examination of the broader contexts—social, global, environmental—within which these engineers made their mark. The importance and success of their work, as expressed in their writings and individual worldviews, are frequently taken at face value while simultaneously being shorn of their occasional elitist and nationalistic overtones. Historians have therefore tended to ignore or diminish the accomplishments of both Dutch and Japanese engineers in helping to build the empires of their respective countries. Instead of pigeonholing Van Doorn and De Rijke or Furuichi and Okino into a particular-culture versus universal-science binary, it is perhaps more useful to focus on how these engineers sought to introduce specific hydrological approaches and thinking into their reframing of Japan's rivers.

By the nineteenth century, the professions of hydrology and engineering were transnational in scope, exceeding the boundaries of any one language or country. Within Europe, the field of hydrology had matured slowly from the sixteenth century when the basic mathematics of water flow were formulated and tested along waterways in Italy's Po River valley.[100] Thereafter, new

99   Scholars tend to depict Furuichi and Okino as exemplars of what can be described as a gendered "men of Meiji" narrative, wherein these engineers developed their innate and individual intellect and abilities to help construct a masculinized modern Japan. Jason G. Karlin, *Gender and Nation in Meiji Japan: Modernity, Loss, and the Doing of History* (Honolulu: University of Hawai'i Press, 2014). See, for example, Takahashi Yutaka, *Gendai Nihon doboku shi* (Tokyo: Shōkokusha, 1990); Doboku Gakkai Dobokushi Kenkyu Iinkai, ed., *Furuichi Kōi to sono jidai*; Okino Tadao Kenkyū Shiryō Chōsa Iinkai, ed., *Okino Tadao to Meiji kaishū* (Tokyo: Doboku Gakkai, 2010).

100 Cesare S. Maffioli, "Italian Hydraulics and Experimental Physics in Eighteenth-Century Holland: From Poleni to Volta," in *Italian Scientists in the Low Countries of the XVIIth and XVIIIth Centuries*, ed. C. S. Maffioli and L. C. Palm (Amsterdam: Rodopi, 1989), 243–75.

ways of observing and measuring the flow of water grew increasingly more sophisticated as mathematicians and later engineers in Paris, London, Delft, Berlin, and elsewhere established what became the field of hydrology by incorporating important variables like hydrostatic pressure and surface friction.[101] This transnational character of hydrology and engineering is exemplified by the Karlsruhe-born engineer Johann Gottfried Tulla (1770–1828), who was formally educated in Gerabronn (then in the Kingdom of Prussia) and visited and studied hydraulic works in other German states, Scandinavia, France, and the Netherlands before, in 1817, initiating decades of work that eventually "tamed" the Rhine River.[102]

The scientific field of hydrology and engineering more broadly, however, did not grow within a laboratory scrubbed of political and ideological influence— it was deeply intertwined with the imperial expansion of European countries, later the United States, and even Japan. Although the new national government successfully extended its control over the whole of Hokkaidō and the Ryukyu Islands, Japan remained impotent in its attempts to renegotiate its unequal treaties with the United States and several European countries.[103] In addition to this real diplomatic unevenness in the nineteenth-century international system, Japanese statesmen, educators, and intellectuals also agonized over discrepancies in perceived levels of civilization. This can be seen in the shifting aims of the 1871–73 Iwakura Mission, which first visited the United States and then Great Britain and other countries in Europe with the initial goal of renegotiating the unequal treaties. When the drafting of new treaties proved impossible, the mission refocused its energies on learning what "civilizational" benchmarks would have to be met before these treaties could be revised and inspecting the institutions and industries that had enabled these countries to assert their authority globally.[104]

---

101   Mark Cioc, *The Rhine: An Eco-Biography, 1815–2000* (Seattle: University of Washington Press, 2002), 38; Willi H. Hager and Corrado Gisonni, "Henry Bazin—Civil Engineer," *Journal of Hydraulic Engineering* 129, no. 3 (2003): 171–75; Willi H. Hager and Corrado Gisonni, "Henry Bazin—Hydraulician," *American Society of Civil Engineers Conference Proceedings* (June 2003): 90–115.

102   While acting as the Chief Water Construction Engineer for Baden, in 1807 Tulla helped found an engineering school that later became a part of the Technical University of Karlsruhe. David Blackbourn, *The Conquest of Nature: Water, Landscape, and the Making of Modern Germany* (New York: W. W. Norton, 2006), 87–93; Cioc, *The Rhine*, 48–49.

103   In 1876, Japan also compelled the Joseon court in Korea to sign the similarly unequal Ganghwa Treaty. Eiji Oguma, *The Boundaries of "the Japanese": Korea, Taiwan and the Ainu 1868–1945*, trans. Leonie R. Stickland (Melborne: Trans Pacific Press, 2017).

104   Michael R. Auslin, *Negotiating with Imperialism: The Unequal Treaties and the Culture of Japanese Diplomacy* (Cambridge: Harvard University Press, 2004), 176–94.

Increasingly crucial and integral to the operation of these empires was a corresponding expansion of scientific networks made up of universities, research centers, academic societies, and journals. In contrast to the Eurocentric view, whereby modern science and technology diffused or transferred outward to the rest of the world, recent research has emphasized how technology and scientific knowledge circulated in both directions between the colonies and the metropole, and often directly from one colony to another. Knowledge about the relationship between climate and vegetation, for instance, grew as British, Dutch, and French colonial officials learned from locals and postulated conservationist explanations for ecological problems in the sensitive environments of St. Helena, Mauritius, and other islands in the Caribbean, Atlantic, and Indian Oceans.[105] In the same way, many of the foreign experts in Japan used their unusual location and influence not only to benefit their ministerial employers but also to make names for themselves as scholars and scientists. Edward Sylvester Morse's writings on zoology, John Milne's studies in seismology, and Henry Dyer's contributions to engineering education are all well-known examples.[106] Among the Dutch engineers, Mulder published a number of articles and reports in the Netherlands based on his ten years of working on rivers, canals, and ports in Japan.[107] In other cases, engineers adapted or localized their knowledge and technologies to the conditions of a given bay or river, such as with Escher's experiments using hydraulic cement and De Rijke's experiments with various erosion controls.[108] These examples indicate that

105   Richard Grove, *Green Imperialism: Colonial Expansion, Tropical Island Edens, and the Origins of Environmentalism, 1600–1860* (Cambridge: Cambridge University Press, 1995). See also Kapil Raj, "Beyond Postcolonialism ... and Postpositivism: Circulation and the Global History of Science," *Isis* 104, no. 2 (2013): 337–47.

106   Henry Dyer, "Engineering in Japan," *The Times*, Engineering Supplement, 18 March 1908, 3; Henry Dyer, *The Education of Civil and Mechanical Engineers* (London: E. & F. N. Spon, 1880); John Milne, "Seismometry and Engineering in Relation to the Recent Earthquake in Japan," *Nature* 45, no. 1154 (1891): 127; John Milne, *Seismology* (London: Kegan Paul, Trench, Trübner & Co., 1898); Edward Sylvester Morse, *First Book of Zoölogy* (New York: D. Appleton and Co., 1879); Edward Sylvester Morse, "Traces of Early Man in Japan," *Nature* 17, no. 89 (1877): 89.

107   See, for example, the following three articles, which Mulder published in the journal of the Royal Institute of Engineers, *Tijdschrift van het Koninklijk Instituut van Ingenieurs*: "Het Nederlandsche handelsestablissement te Port-Said," no. 287 (1877): 288–92; "Korte mededeelingen over Japan en meen bepaald over de voornaamste havens die in dat rijk gevonden worden," no. 91 (1887): 92–102; "Over een drietar zeestraten in den Japanschen archipel," no. 205 (1892–1893), 205–28.

108   Wim Ravesteijn discusses how, as a part of the Dutch "Ethical Policy," colonial officials and engineers were encouraged to adopt and use indigenous technologies and organizations in their irrigation, reclamation, and other developmental schemes. Wim Ravesteijn,

the continued imperial expansion of the United States and European countries certainly shaped the flow and direction of engineering knowledge and engineers in the nineteenth century. As underscored throughout this chapter, however, this flow was neither unidirectional nor, as some have suggested, were the Dutch and Japanese engineers limited to employing only those technologies developed within their countries of origin.[109]

The emphasis on the transnational or global character of engineering in the nineteenth century should not be conflated with arguing for universalism. As explained at the beginning of this concluding section, Matsuura maintains that despite their occasional mishaps, Dutch engineers succeeded in eroding away at the individualistic and intuitive approach once common to Tokugawa and domain technicians by introducing "universalizing methods" to the study of rivers. Matsuura's view is not unusual. He expresses what is known in the philosophy of science as a "naïve realist" belief that properly followed scientific methods reveal objective truths about the natural world. As scholars from gender studies to science studies have asserted, however, this view is untenable on at least two counts. First, objectivity is not a reflection of some universal "truth"—it is fundamentally an agreement. The idea that there is a universally accorded reality in the humanities, the sciences, or even the relatively small field of hydrology is tainted by the very subjectivity of those who would hold such a view.[110] All other forms of objectivity involve degrees of negotiated agreement among the participants about legitimate procedures and truth-claims.[111]

The second problem with Matsuura's view is more pertinent for understanding how Dutch and Japanese engineers participated in reframing rivers in Japan during the 1870s and 1880s. When measuring and surveying the Tone and Yodo Rivers, Ichikawa, De Rijke, Okino, and others did not simply reveal preexisting facts about water flow, soil conditions, and erosion. They engaged

---

"Between Globalization and Localization: The Case of Dutch Civil Engineering in Indonesia, 1800–1950," *Comparative Technology Transfer and Society* 5, no. 1 (2007): 32–64.

109   In the following 1897 report, a leading engineer in the Home Ministry at the time, toured engineering works on the island of Java in the Dutch East Indies and observed the use of De Rijke's erosion control techniques: Kondō Toragorō, *Ranryō Indo Jyawa-tō doboku jigyō shisatsu fukumeisho*, [1897], MS A-2-91, Yodogawa Shiryōkan, Hirakata City, Osaka Prefecture. Cited in Itō Yasuo, "Ranjin yatoi kōshi to sono chisui shisō," *Kyōto rekishi saigai kenkyū* 2 (2002): 5.

110   Ian Hacking, "What about the Natural Sciences?," in *The Social Construction of What?* (Cambridge: Harvard University Press, 1999): 63–99.

111   See, for example, Allan Megill, "Objectivity for Historians," in *Historical Knowledge, Historical Error: A Contemporary Guide to Practice* (Chicago: University of Chicago Press, 2007), 107–24.

with a whole host of other people, organisms, and objects to produce those facts. By tromping along the banks of these rivers, observing vegetation, sampling soil conditions, installing instruments, and taking measurements of the water, engineers abstracted various kinds of data. Once back in their offices in Tokyo and Osaka, the engineers organized this information into tables, maps, diagrams, and texts to generate two-dimensional representations of the rivers that they then submitted to Home Ministry officials. In this way, it was through measuring, recording, transporting, and representing that the engineers created scientific knowledge about these rivers.[112] In the process, they also reduced the totality of these river's riparian relations to those factors that were measurable and most accorded with theirs and the Home Ministry's goals of improving navigation and decreasing flooding and erosion. The limits of this kind of reductionism have been amply demonstrated when, even after having been thoroughly "studied" and then "improved," these rivers continued to burst through levees, rip out bridges, and dump tons of sediment onto downstream riverbeds and bays.

Instead of a reliance on particularistic and universalizing arguments, which have been at the heart of the social sciences since their inception in the nineteenth century, the experiences of these Dutch and Japanese engineers are evidence of their entanglement within the broader environmental relations of the Tone, Yodo, and other rivers and bays. Through their activities and decisions, these engineers embedded themselves into a series of environmental relations that included a government policy focused on maintaining and improving the navigability of select rivers, the location of farmers' fields and paddies along those rivers, existing means and routes for transport, heavily logged mountains, the design and material of fascines and levees, and summertime monsoons and typhoons. Moreover, it was through their work that these engineers, like their contemporary village leaders and riverboat pilots, gained an understanding about local waters, shoals, and embankments.[113] The difference in the resulting knowledge about rivers was not one of universality versus particularity—it was a difference in means and authority, one that enabled Dutch and Japanese engineers to have their reports reproduced, widely distributed, and, as is shown in the next two chapters, acted upon.

112   Bruno Latour, *Pandora's Hope: Essays on the Reality of Science Studies* (Cambridge: Harvard University Press, 1999), 36–39.

113   This is one of the main arguments Richard White makes in his history of the Columbia River. Richard White, *The Organic Machine: The Remaking of the Columbia River* (New York: Hill and Wang, 1995).

CHAPTER 4

Confluence along the Yodo River

Regarding the Lake Biwa Canal [in Kyoto Prefecture], members of water boards in the counties in the [Osaka] prefecture that are along the main channel and tributaries of the Yodo River have for some time been holding frequent meetings about ways to prevent flood damage in the affected areas.

琵琶湖疎水に付き澱川本支流に沿る府下各郡の水理委員ハ其が爲めに被る所の水害を豫防する方法に關する過般來各郡にて屡次會議を開きし由なる……

> *Osaka asahi shinbun* (13 August 1885)[1]
> 『大阪朝日新聞』（明治 18 年 8 月 13 日）

∵

The above quote from the beginning of an 1885 article in the *Osaka asahi shinbun* is suggestive of how upstream changes to a river, such as deforestation or the digging of a new canal, were of deep concern to downstream communities. Published a month after a devastating flood had inundated areas all along the Yodo River, this article discusses how water boards in many riverside counties in Osaka Prefecture had been meeting regularly for a few years to discuss how to respond and petition the prefectural and national governments to better address the perennial problem of flooding. In the meeting discussed in this newspaper article, water board members expressed their distress over how the planned excavation of the Lake Biwa Canal (*Biwa-ko sosui*) to bring boats and drinking water to the urban areas of Kyoto would worsen flooding for downstream rural areas and recommended the money would be better spent by dredging the Yodo River and heightening and widening vulnerable levees in Osaka Prefecture. In other articles on the same page of this newspaper, reporters wrote about areas where the waters had still not drained in the month since the flood, delays in planting a second crop of rice that year, the appearance of an unknown swarming insect (apparently neither a mosquito nor a fly)

---

1 "Biwa-ko sosui ni kan suru suiri iin no iken," *Osaka asahi shinbun*, 13 August 1885, 2.

following the flood, an example of how landowners in the area had fed and offered relief to their tenant farmers, and the ongoing efforts to recover from the flooding.

These articles and others like it are also a reminder that, in late nineteenth-century, rivers remained a vital part of the environmental relations that sustained people's livelihoods in rural and urban communities throughout Japan. These waterways still connected farming villages and regional towns to the country's growing metropolises. They supplied these communities with drinking water and filled irrigation networks that two to three times per year submerged vast plains of rice paddies.[2] They recharged subterranean aquafers and replenished the inland ponds and lakes where locals preyed on fish and migrating waterfowl.[3] Where these waters ran fast, they turned waterwheels that lifted water over banks, turned millstones, and powered some of the country's first textile factories.[4] As railways began to augment and eventually replace river transport and coal-burning and later hydroelectric plants started powering the country's factories and trains, the scope and role of these rivers in people's lives gradually changed, but their importance continued unabated.[5] Consequently, people's ongoing use of these rivers, and their propensity to flood, persisted as common concerns for riverside communities throughout the country.

The response to the shifting place of these rivers in people's lives and livelihoods led to a confluence of factors along the Yodo River in late nineteenth century that would transform the country's riparian relations. In 1885 and 1889, the Yodo and its tributaries twice breached their levees to flood the surrounding countryside in Shiga, Kyoto, and Osaka Prefectures. More than with previous floods, the 1885 flood also inundated large portions of the city of Osaka, the country's historic commercial center. As discussed in chapter 3, throughout this period the Home Ministry and its engineers had a limited budget with which to carry out the goal of improving the navigability of the Yodo and other sizable rivers in support of the stated policy of "Promotion of Industry and Commerce" (*shokusan kōgyō*). Later dismissively dubbed the "low-water"

---

2   "Shosen gensui no keikyō," *Osaka asahi shinbun*, 5 August 1886, 1; "Tenmabashi jōryū koshimizu no keikaku," *Osaka asahi shinbun*, 8 April 1887, 1.

3   "Yōgyojō no mizu o Shirakawa ni gōryū o shutsugan," *Osaka asahi shinbun*, 8 July 1883; "Unagi to suppon," 6 October 1885, 2; "Furyō no genin," *Osaka asahi shinbun*, 1 May 1886, 1.

4   "Suisha kikai o seishiba," *Osaka asahi shinbun*, 11 August 1881, 2; "Yoshinogawa e suisha kikai o suetsuke," *Osaka asahi shinbun*, 4 June 1882, 2.

5   "Yodogawa no shinkisen kaisha," *Osaka asahi shinbun*, 10 March 1888, 1; "Yodogawa suiriku no renraku," *Osaka asahi shinbun*, 26 June 1898, 2; "Suiryoku denki kyoka iken," *Osaka asahi shinbun*, 4 December 1897, 2.

policy, this initial approach tended to use a river's average flowage as a construction standard when balancing the need to repair and strengthen levees with the need to dredge and maintain the river's year-long navigability. In reaction to the increasing propensity of these rivers to flood due to upstream deforestation and other factors, from the early 1890s onward the Home Ministry's engineers developed what came to be called a "high-water" approach to riparian engineering and administration. With this new approach, engineers sought the "improvement" (*kairyō, kaishū*) of portions of the Yodo from its headwaters at Lake Biwa to its mouth in the city of Osaka with the principal aim of containing its historically highest flood level. These engineers not only directly addressed the Yodo's recent flood activity, but they were also influenced by the growing political influence of rural elites and their downstream urban allies. With the 1889 promulgation of the Constitution of the Empire of Japan and their right to vote and run for parliamentary office, wealthy male landowners, together with activists in villages and towns along the country's largest rivers, moved from petitioning the government to outright political lobbying to garner the resources and expertise required to improve navigation, expand irrigation, and especially to prevent further flooding of their farms and communities. In this way, this confluence of rivers, technical expertise, local and national politics came together along the Yodo River in the early 1890s in a manner that would have profound consequences for riparian relations throughout the country.

Histories in Japan or elsewhere about the modern transformation of rivers tend to stress the position and perspective of the state as well as its technocratic engineers.[6] This chapter argues that these histories are incomplete unless they also account for other actors and broader riparian relations. It shows how the Home Ministry and its engineers, together with local politicians and their communities, the Yodo River and its tributaries, were crucial actors in the development of a new approach to governing the Yodo and eventually all of Japan's major rivers. Because these waterways were so entangled in people's lives and the economic well-being of the Kinai region in the nineteenth century, any significant changes to them affected fishing, shipping, and

---

6   Itō Yasuo, *Kōzui to ningen: sono sōkoku no rekishi* (Tokyo: Kokin Shoin, 2010); Matsuura Shigeki, *Kokudo-zukuri no ishizue: kawa ga kataru Nihon no rekishi* (Tokyo: Kashima Shuppankai, 1997); Ōkuma Takashi, *Kōzui to chisui no kasen shi: suigai seiatsu kara juyō e* (Tokyo: Heibonsha, 1988); Takahashi Yutaka, *Kawa to kokudo no kinki: suigai to shakai* (Tokyo: Iwanami, 2012); Karen M. O'Neill, *Rivers by Design: State Power and the Origins of U.S. Flood Control* (Durham: Duke University Press, 2006); David A. Pietz, *The Yellow River: The Problem of Water in Modern China* (Cambridge: Harvard University Press, 2015); Sara B. Pritchard, *Confluence: The Nature of Technology and the Remaking of the Rhône* (Cambridge: Harvard University Press, 2011).

farming communities. An emphasis of the importance of these riparian relations in the Kinai region does not suggest that there was common agreement about the role of these rivers in people's lives. In fact, this chapter highlights the diverse ways individuals and communities interacted, valued, and sought to maintain or improve parts of these rivers depending on their occupations and their location upstream, downstream, along or afar from these rivers. It was only through the widely felt effects of catastrophic flooding along the Yodo River in the 1880s, the increasing political activity associated with the Movement for Freedom and Popular Rights (Jiyū Minken Undō), and the establishment of prefectural and national assemblies that these occupational and geographic differences were overcome.

The confluence of Yodo flood events, reports by its own engineers, and activism by locals compelled the Home Ministry to make drastic changes to its approach to river management. The result of this new approach to river management focused almost exclusively on flood control as the hallmark of Japan's "modern river regime," a notion that will be discussed in greater depth in chapter 5. Before this river regime could be produced in the early twentieth century, however, flooding was constructed as a problem of singular regional and national significance that required a techno-political solution that only the national government would have the capacity to address.

1   The Yodo River

Although in the 1870s and 1880s the Kinai region was principally rural and agricultural, it was also conceivably the most urban and thoroughly integrated region in Japan through its centuries-old commercial ties centered on the cities of Kyoto and Osaka.[7] Flowing through the middle of this region is the Yodo River. On a map, the Yodo and its primary tributaries appear like a tree (see fig. 1), with the Yodo forming a short stout trunk that measures only about 50 km in length but nearly an entire kilometer wide at its mouth. It has the capacity to carry 12,000 m³/s of water.[8] Such a volume of water is perhaps not surprising considering the Yodo drains the sixth most voluminous river basin in Japan, receiving much of its water from two of the region's biggest rivers—the

---

7   Ethan Isaac Segal, *Coins, Trade, and the State* (Cambridge: Harvard University Press, 2011); James L. McClain and Osamu Wakita, eds., *Osaka: The Merchant's Capital of Early Modern Japan* (Ithaca: Cornell University Press, 1999).

8   The geologist Koide Haku provides a dated but still worthwhile overview of the geomorphology and history of flood control and water use in the Yodo river basin. Koide Haku, *Nihon no kasen kenkyū: chikisei to kobetsusei* (Tokyo: Tōkyō Daigaku Shuppankai, 1972), 187–211.

Katsura and Kizu—and through the Uji River drains Lake Biwa, the so-called "water jug" (*mizugame*) of the region and the country's largest lake.[9] These tributaries draw their water from deep in the low, albeit steep, Tanba Highlands to the west, the Takami Mountains to the south, and the Suzuka Range to the east.[10] As described in detail in the introductory chapter these three tributaries meet at what used to be Ogura Lake in the marshy bottomlands of the Kinai region. Only 15 m in elevation at that point, the Yodo passes through a narrows between Mount Otoko and Mount Tennō as it historically meandered to the southwest across the alluvial Osaka Plain before draining into what is today called Osaka Bay. Over the centuries, riverside and inland communities, shipping and nonshipping, upstream and downstream interests have worked with and against each other on the issues of logging, dredging, reclamation, irrigation, and water transport. From the late nineteenth century, these preexisting relations and rivalries shifted with the advent of party politics, industrial technology, and new approaches to river management. Thus, as with the rivers of the Kantō region that are the subject of chapters 1 and 2, the history of riparian relations along the Yodo has similarly been a turbulent one.

Together with Home Ministry engineers and protesting locals, the Yodo River was also instrumental in its own reframing as a flood problem and the subsequent formation of Japan's modern river regime. Although other factors and other rivers did come into play, the Yodo River's flooding in 1885 and again in 1889 was key in the Home Ministry's decision to abandon its earlier policies of trying to balance continued water use (*risui*) with greater flood control (*chisui*). Moreover, the river demonstrated the weaknesses of the former agreement reached at the 1875 Osaka Conference (chapter 3) wherein "defensive work"—principally the repair or improvement of levees—was determined to be the administrative *and* budgetary responsibility of municipal and prefectural governments. Even though the Yodo River was not among the country's largest rivers, it nonetheless had the agential capacity to shape national river policy because of its importance to the country's most economically developed region. Integral to shipping and commerce, irrigation and farming, and fishing and other livelihoods, the Yodo was part of the material media that sustained life and livelihood along its banks and beyond. Flooding was a relatively rare occurrence but during its most violent torrents the Yodo was capable of

9   Until it was rerouted in 1704, the Yamato River also flowed into the Yodo River at present-day Higashi-Osaka. Murata Michibito, *Kinsei no Yodogawa chisui* (Tokyo: Yamakawa Shuppan, 2009), 75–98.

10   The highest mountains in these ranges are only between 1,000 and 1,200 m in elevation, but their steepness resulted in considerable erosion and regular landslides.

bringing both death and destruction to those who inhabited its banks and the bottomlands of the region. In the late nineteenth century, the river flooded with greater violence than in previous decades because unchecked deforestation throughout its extensive basin meant the region's mountains quickly shed the water that fell upon their slopes.[11] Swelling with this additional runoff and eroded sediment, the Yodo steadily exceeded the capacity of the extant system of levees and floodplains that had been built piecemeal over several centuries.

The Yodo's riverside communities were not strangers to flooding. Even with broad floodplains on either side of the Yodo between the levees, severe storms and typhoons could quickly fill the riverbed and begin eroding portions of these mostly earthen levees. Once the floodwaters burst through a levee, they could spread southward unimpeded across the relatively flat Osaka Plain. For these reasons, flooding was a recurrent if not regular experience of communities near the Yodo and its tributaries, and this gave rise to a flood culture along the Yodo and similarly large rivers.[12] Residents located their villages atop natural levees and other kinds of high ground, constructing their houses and storehouses on mounded dirt with higher floorboards and with small boats often hung from the eaves.[13] Despite these precautions and being accustomed to an occasional flood, the deluge of 1885 surpassed everyone's lived and inherited memories of flooding.

From 15 June 1885, two successive storms, one from the Japan Sea to the west and the other from the Inland Sea to the south, drenched the entire Kinai region. Three days later, the Ōtsu weather station near the headwaters of the Seta River had already measured 218.8 mm of rain. Downstream from the river at Mukōjima Village where water from the Uji River could overflow into the Ogura Lake, officials recorded that the Yodo rose by over 3 m. Later that same day and further downstream near the confluence with the much smaller Amano River, the Yodo rose over 4 m before bursting through the levee in two locations (fig. 21). The resulting flood inundated over 4,000 ha and nearly

---

11   In his 1897 book about flood and erosion control techniques, the engineer Ichikawa Yoshikata describes the chronic problem of topsoil erosion in the headwaters of the Kizu River and elsewhere in Kyoto Prefecture. Ichikawa Yoshikata, "Kuzure hageyama no jikkyō zusetsu," *Suiri shinpō* (Hakubunkan, 1897), 2: unpaginated. See also Yamashiro-chō, ed., *Yamashiro-chō shi: honbun* (Yamashiro: Yamashiro Machiyakuba, 1987), 839–45.

12   With the earliest known floodworks dating to the early fifth century, the Yodo or its tributaries are known to have flooded well over one hundred times. Kumiyama-chō Shi Hensan Iinkai, ed., *Kumiyama-chō shi* (Kumiyama: Kumiyama-chō, 1986), 1:101, 822.

13   Kumiyama-chō Shi Hensan Iinkai, ed., *Kumiyama-chō shi* (Kumiyama-chō: Kumiyama-chō, 1989), 2:246; *Uji-shi shi*, ed. Hayashi Tatsusaburō and Fujioka Kenjirō, vol. 6, *Ujigawa no seikatsu to kankyō* (Uji: Uji Shiyakusho, 1981), 405–6.

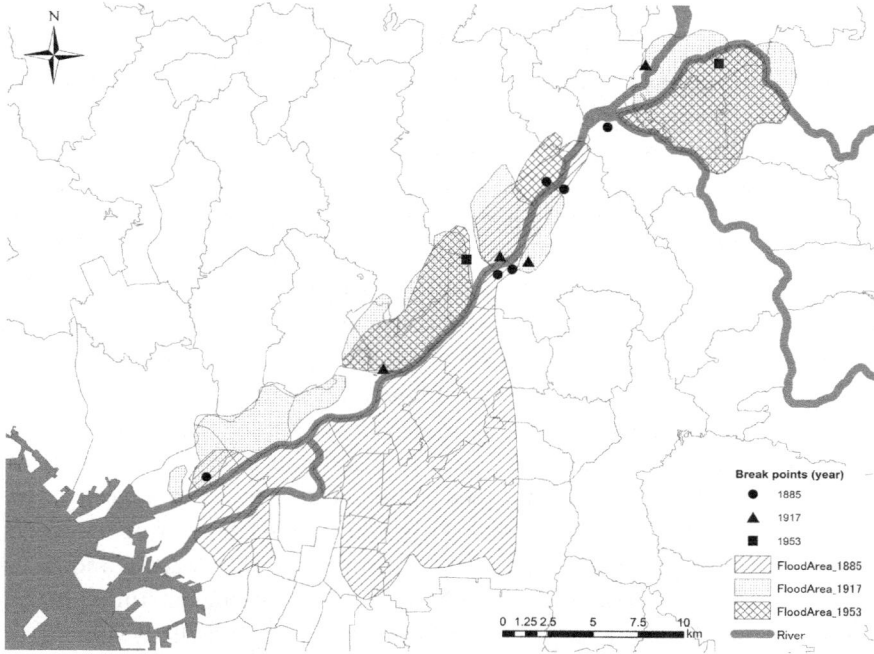

FIGURE 21   Map of the 1885 flooding of the Yodo River

10,000 houses.[14] On 25 June, just as the Yodo had begun to subside and the breached levees had been temporarily patched with sandbags and fascines, the rains recommenced and continued until 1 July. This time the Ōtsu weather station recorded 368.3 mm of rain over a seven-day period, and at Mukōjima the Uji River rose by 3.7 m. Further downstream the situation grew even more dire as the swollen Yodo broke through one levee after another as it pushed its way toward the sea. In the end, much of the city of Osaka and surrounding countryside lay under water. The government later calculated that over 15,000 ha had been flooded, over 70,000 houses submerged, thirty-one bridges washed away, more than 90,000 people forced to evacuate, and thirty-seven people died or were unrecovered.[15]

The power of the Yodo during full flood was awesome. Within hours of the torrential rainfall during the first storm, the Yodo and its tributaries swelled inexorably to several times their normal size. Churning and brown with all

---

14   Kensetsushō Kinki Chihōkyoku, ed., *Yodogawa hyaku-nen shi* (Osaka: Kensetsushō Kinki Chihōkyoku, 1974), 303–5.

15   Kensetsushō Kinki Chihōkyoku, *Yodogawa hyaku-nen shi*, 305–8.

the soil they had stripped from upstream hillsides, these fast-flowing rivers steadily rose against the levees that were meant to contain them. The waters assaulted these thick floodworks from top and bottom, as if probing for weaknesses in this long defensive line of pounded earthen levees and occasional fascines. While occasionally overtopping the levees, the rivers caused most of their damage below the waterline by saturating, softening, and eroding away at their bases. All along its length, the sheer volume of water draining into the Yodo from upstream also forced minor downstream rivers and drainage canals to back up and dangerously threaten to overflow banks and minor levees. On the evening of 17 June, it was the backing up of the much smaller Amano River and a nearby drainage sluice that breached the levees in the present-day city of Hirakata. Over the next several hours, the Yodo's floodwaters rushed through these holes in the levee system, widening them even further while sending an expanding muddy deluge southward and into northern parts of Osaka. Although the upstream levees had succeeded in containing this first bout of flooding, they failed disastrously two weeks later during a second round of flooding that began on 1 July. This time the Uji, Katsura, and Yodo Rivers all rose higher than they had two weeks earlier, easily bursting through the already sodden levees at many locations. Across the particularly vulnerable area of southern Kyoto Prefecture where the Katsura and Uji Rivers flowed into the Yodo, the official tally of levee breaches was an unbelievable 2,248. Once through the levees, the flood waters continued their destruction by inundating about 70 percent of the habitable land in Kuse County, where they submerged 1,514 ha of rice paddies, flooded 14,657 houses, destroyed another 810 houses, washed away or damaged 1,123 bridges, eroded roads in 1,870 different places, and killed thirteen people.[16] Although this event was catastrophic, the Yodo had previously flooded to a lesser extent in 1868, 1871, and 1876. And parts of it would do so again in 1889 and 1896.

This description of the flooding of 1885 permits a number of observations about historical agency of nonhuman entities, such as the Yodo River. First, if agency is defined as the power of one entity to impact another, then the river plainly demonstrated its agential capacity by wreaking destruction on the levees and lives that lay in its path. This agency equally highlights the spatial and temporal dimensions of the riparian relations that the river co-constituted. Because of the intensity of the 1885 flooding, the Yodo acted through these extended relations to affect the fields and livelihoods of farmers from Shiga in the north to Osaka in the south. The river similarly disrupted the movement of people and goods crossing its channel by sweeping away so many important

16   *Kyōto-fu shi*, ed. Kyōto-fu (Kyoto: Kyōto-fu, 1915), 2:156.

and newly built bridges.[17] The effects of the 1885 flood reached beyond the moment the river breached a levee or washed away a farmhouse. In the immediate aftermath, the government and private groups organized relief efforts to feed and house those who had lost their livelihoods and homes. Months later, people continued to patch levees, repair roads, rebuild bridges, clear buried sluices, and dredge the enlarged sandbars in the port of Osaka.[18] And for the next several years, Home Ministry engineers used the 1885 flood as the benchmark when reconsidering infrastructural projects along the entire length of the river and in the port of Osaka.

It should be clarified that as a nonbiological entity, the river could not and did not intend to flood and cause all of that downstream damage. Simply because the Yodo did not act with intent like humans or other organisms does not exclude it from exercising historical agency through its riparian assemblages that affected and was affected by the other entities and assemblages with which it interacted.[19] The 1885 flood is a clear example of how a relational approach to history can better account for the significant historical roles played by nonhuman entities, such as the Yodo River. As noted in the introductory chapter, it is nonetheless useful to retain a distinction between intentional and unintentional agency because intent lies at the crux of attributing responsibility and, in legal terms, liability.[20]

17 A report published in *Kōgakkaishi* (*Journal of the Engineering Society* (of Japan)) lists twenty-seven of the bridges destroyed in the 1885 flooding of the Yodo River and its tributaries. "Yodogawa kōzui no sai ryūshitsu kyōryō," *Kōgakkaishi* 5, no. 53 (1886): 1056–58.

18 In this short report, the engineer Sugiyama Shūkichi (1855–1939) lists the plans and estimated costs for rebuilding nineteen bridges over the Yodo River and its tributaries between 1885 and 1888. Sugiyama Shūkichi, "Ōsaka shinki kasetsu kyōryō oyobi kōhi yosan kettei," *Kōgakkaishi* 5, no. 53 (1886): 1058–60.

19 The manner in which agency was distributed across a number of entities—heavy rain, denuded mountain slopes, river channel, levees—during the 1885 flooding of the Kinai region can be understood in much the same way as the political theorist Jane Bennett describes for the 2003 blackout of another large, complex assemblage—the North American electrical grid. That is, the water in the river flowed through its system of heavily managed riparian channels much like the electricity did through its grid, but during an unanticipated event like the two successive rainstorms of 1885, the Yodo behaved in an unexpected manner. Jane Bennett, *Vibrant Matter: A Political Ecology of Things* (Durham: Duke University Press, 2010), 24–28.

20 For late nineteenth- and early twentieth-century Japan, the historian Carol Gluck shows how the modern word "responsibility" (*sekinin*) was freighted with a mixture of old and new meanings. From a relational perspective, responsibility for the 1885 flood and resulting destruction can be found across the riparian assemblage that was co-constituted by the Yodo River. Nonetheless, chapter 5 demonstrates that the politics surrounding the Yodo and the country's other large rivers in the 1890s focused on efforts to determine specifically human and institutional obligations and responsibilities for forest

2   Home Ministry Engineers

Prior to the 1885 flooding of the Yodo, engineers and technicians in the Home Ministry had already invested considerable effort in trying to improve the river and its tributaries. The Home Ministry was an enormous institutional assemblage that shaped the decisions of its engineers and the scope of their activities. These engineers were not powerless apparats. They molded the Home Ministry and its policies through their scientific reports, proposals, and their positions as administrators within the ministry's Civil Engineering Bureau.[21] Two engineers in particular, Johannis de Rijke and Okino Tadao, drew up similar plans for the Yodo River in the aftermath of the 1885 and 1889 floods. One of the results was the narrowing of the Yodo and its diverse riparian relations to one principally defined by the problem of flooding. In the process, they also looked upon the Yodo a passive entity to which they, with their calculative abilities and the resources of the Home Ministry, could study, predict, and ultimately control.

Since its founding in 1873, the Home Ministry had grappled with the problem of flooding while also trying to maintain the country's existing water transport system in the interest of promoting commerce and industry. Owing to its own limited resources and the precedent of levee upkeep and repair being primarily a local responsibility, in 1875 the national government negotiated an agreement wherein the Home Ministry would focus on facilitating inland navigation, and prefectural governments would bear most of the burden of preventing flooding.[22] As a result, along the Yodo River in the 1870s and 1880s, the Home Ministry concentrated its efforts on improving the port of Osaka and the concomitant task of preventing sediment from entering and accumulating in the Yodo and Osaka Bay into which it flowed.

---

administration, erosion prevention, and river engineering and maintenance. Carol Gluck, "*Sekinin*/Responsibility in Modern Japan," in *Words in Motion: Toward a Global Lexicon*, ed. Carol Gluck and Anna L. Tsing (Durham: Duke University Press, 2009), 91–94.

21   In his history of the Home Ministry, the historian Soeda Yoshiya explains that the ministry became so influential that it was referred to as being the "government within the government" (*yakusho no naka no yakusho*). He emphasizes that within the ministry the Civil Engineering Bureau was one of its five most important bureaus, together with those for policing, public health, prefectural governance, and Shinto shrines. Soeda Yoshiya, *Naimushō no shakai shi* (Tokyo: Tōkyō Daigaku Shuppankai, 2007), 3.

22   Following the 1868 Meiji Restoration and before the 1873 establishment of the Home Ministry, local authorities managed to carry out a few large river projects along the Yodo, such as the rerouting of the lower portion of the Kizu where it flowed into the Yodo. *Kumiyama-chō shi*, 2:347–51.

From as early as 1873, Johannis de Rijke, his countrymen Cornelis Johannes van Doorn, and George Arnold Escher (see chapter 3), together with several mostly unnamed Japanese technicians and surveyors, carried out successive surveys and experiments to determine the depth of the river at different seasons of the year, narrow the river to a single channel, and limit the silting of the riverbed and bay.[23] Central to these endeavors was the installation fascines along many sections of the Yodo River between Osaka and Fushimi, which were positioned perpendicular to the river flow in order to protect vulnerable levees, slow the river current, and channel its waters toward the middle of the river where it would over time scour a deeper channel. Before the installation of these fascines, for example, De Rijke and Alphonse Th. J. H. Thissen experimented with the use of Dutch-style fascines along the left bank of the river at Shōgijima near Tenma Bridge in Osaka.[24] These efforts succeeded in creating a narrower and deeper channel that could handle riverboats of up to 100 *koku* (10 ton) in size, including the recently inaugurated steamboat service between Osaka and Fushimi.[25] Following the 1885 and 1889 floods, however, some local leaders complained that these fascines slowed flood waters and made their communities more susceptible to inundation.[26] Many argued that the Home Ministry's plans and projects had proven ineffective and called for the abandonment of upstream projects like the Lake Biwa Canal, more commitment to the study and control of the Yodo, and more national government funding.

---

23   George Arnold Escher, "Yodogawa shūji sokuryō iriyō yōgu no mōshiide" [18 November 1873], and Cornelis Johannes van Doorn, "Soda bassai no ken" [8 January 1874], both reprinted in *Yodogawa Oranda gishi monjo: Oubun kanren hen*, ed. Yodogawa Kindai Kaishū no Akebono Kenkyūkai (Hirakata: Kensetsushō Kinki Chihō Kensetsukyoku Yodogawa Kōji Jimusho, 1997), 44–5, 71–3. See also Shinshū Ōsaka-shi Shi Hensan Iinkai, ed., *Shinshū Ōsaka-shi shi* (Osaka: Ōsaka-shi, 1991), 5:405–19; Kensetsushō Kinki Chihōkyoku, *Yodogawa hyaku-nen shi*, 311–17.

24   Earlier that year, De Rijke had already submitted his proposal for these experimental fascines. Johannis de Rijke, "Tenmabashi soda-kō shiken mokuromi senbun no ichi shazu (Plan van een 3 tal kribben bij Temmabashi—1/1000)" [1 August 1874], *Yodogawa Oranda gishi monjo*, 120–22; Shinshū Ōsaka-shi Shi Hensan Iinkai, *Shinshū Ōsaka-shi shi*, 5:407–8.

25   *Uji-shi shi*, ed. Hayashi Tatsusaburō and Fujioka Kenjirō, vol. 4, *Kinsei no rekishi to keikan* (Uji: Uji Shiyakusho, 1978), 215–17.

26   In 1890, for example, representatives from seven communities in Kii and Kuse Counties petitioned the governor of Kyoto Prefecture to remove recently installed fascines, which they claimed were causing the river to damage riverside farmland. In response, the head of the prefecture's civil engineering office and an engineer visited the affected areas to inspect the fascines and meet with residents. "Soda-kō tekkyo no seigan," *Hinode shinbun*, 26 July 1890, "Soda-kōji no jicchi kenbun," *Hinode shinbun*, 27 July 1890, and "Yodogawa junshi no moyō," *Hinode shinbun*, 1 August 1890.

In response to the rising costs related to flooding as well as the increasingly strident demands from communities located near the Yodo River for assistance, the Home Ministry continued to develop its approach to governing the country's biggest rivers. Two successive plans for the Yodo River are illustrative of the changing views held by the Home Ministry and its engineers about the Yodo and the country's other large rivers. De Rijke presented the first of these under the title "With Reports Concerning the Yodogawa and Yamatogawa" on 1 July 1890, after, in his words, being requested to "design a new plan by which the whole river could be made safe against disastrous freshets."[27] After more than two months of careful surveying and years of experience working on the Yodo and its tributaries, De Rijke submitted his report to his recently appointed supervisor—the Paris-trained and prominent engineer Furuichi Kōi (see chapter 3). Unlike his and other earlier reports on the Yodo, the Dutch engineer's latest recommendation discussed the improvement of the port in Osaka and the Yodo River as separate projects with the priority shifting to flood prevention.[28] Also different from previous reports, which had focused on the downstream portion of the Yodo where it flowed through Osaka Prefecture, De Rijke's 1890 plan emphasized the need for flood control along the entire length of the river, including its mountainous tributaries like the Fudō River.[29] De Rijke argued for better upstream erosion controls, maintaining that greater efforts were required to curtail deforestation and new regulations to prevent the private use of "floodbanks" and the riverbed for farming.[30]

De Rijke's plan for the delta area around the city of Osaka outlined how the Yodo should be fixed to a single channel by eliminating secondary channels, meanders, distributaries, and excavating a more direct route to the sea.[31] To slow the flow of floodwaters into the downstream portion of the Yodo, he also called for the continued use of the Ogura Lake and its surrounding marshes to temporarily retain and gradually release floodwaters.[32] Aiming to prevent a recurrence of the 1885 and 1889 floods, which De Rijke calculated at less than

---

27   Johannis de Rijke, "With Reports Concerning the Yodogawa and Yamatogawa" [1 July 1890], *Yodogawa Oranda gishi monjo*, 307.

28   At the beginning of this report, De Rijke includes a summary of his earlier report on the Yodo River (dated 18 April 1887) and possible objections to it. De Rijke, "With Reports Concerning the Yodogawa and Yamatogawa," 307–11. The 1887 and 1890 reports were republished in Kensetsushō Kinki Chihōkyoku, *Yodogawa hyaku-nen shi*, 312–15, 317–28.

29   De Rijke, "With Reports Concerning the Yodogawa and Yamatogawa," 322.

30   De Rijke, "With Reports Concerning the Yodogawa and Yamatogawa," 317. Some farmers in the villages of Sayama, Ta'i, and Shimotsuya along the Kizu River, for example, planted portions of the floodplain with tea bushes. *Kumiyama-chō shi*, 2:294.

31   De Rijke, "With Reports Concerning the Yodogawa and Yamatogawa," 318–20.

32   De Rijke, "With Reports Concerning the Yodogawa and Yamatogawa," 318.

"200,000 cub. ft. per second" (5,663 m³/s) of water, the engineer contrasted the earlier "L. W. [low-water] regulation" with what he identified as the new "H. W. [high-water] regulation plan" and only suggested once that navigation might improve as a result of better measures to prevent upstream erosion.[33] After being reviewed by a twelve-member committee, De Rijke's report was accepted with only minor changes.

The second new plan for the Yodo River was presented in 1894 by the engineer Okino Tadao. As noted in chapter 3, Okino had been a roommate and classmate of Furuichi at the École Centrale in Paris before returning to Japan and joining the Home Ministry. After overseeing the ministry's projects on the Fuji, Shinano, Kitagami, and other rivers, Okino was appointed in 1890 to head the office of the Fourth Regional Engineering District in Osaka, which administered work on the Yodo and other rivers of the Kinai region. In this capacity, he was also one of the twelve reviewers of De Rijke's 1890 plan for the Yodo River. In the following year, Home Minister and later Prime Minister Yamagata Aritomo (1838–1922) requested Okino to undertake another survey of the Yodo. Between April and September 1892, the Fourth Regional Engineering District carried out an extensive study and survey of soils and water throughout the entire river basin. On 28 June 1894, Okino submitted his report "Proposal for High-Water Defensive Construction on the Yodo River" to Home Minister Inoue Kaoru (1836–1915).[34] After review by Furuichi and a committee of other engineers, Okino took their suggestions into account and resubmitted his report with an addendum in August 1895.[35]

Okino's plan generally agreed with that submitted earlier in 1890 by De Rijke in recommending the excavation of a new, straighter channel through the delta along the Nakatsu River and the building of taller, stronger levees along the whole of the river's length (fig. 22). Explaining that he was following an earlier proposal by De Rijke and his fellow Dutch engineer Anthonie Th. L. R. Mulder, Okino called for a massive barrage to be constructed just above Osaka at Kema Village to direct most of the Yodo's floodwaters away from the city and into the enlarged drainage channel. Because this barrage would effectively barricade Osaka proper from the Yodo, he included a lock that could lift or lower ten to twenty riverboats together four times daily.[36] Where De Rijke had expressed content with his earlier work to improve the navigability of the

33   De Rijke, "With Reports Concerning the Yodogawa and Yamatogawa," 314–17, 318–22.

34   Okino's plan has been reprinted as follows: "Yodogawa kōsui bōgyo kōji keikaku ikenshō," in Kensetsushō Kinki Chihōkyoku, *Yodogawa hyaku-nen shi*, 345–82.

35   A portion of Okino's addendum has been reprinted as "Yodogawa kōsui bōgyo ni kansuru tsuishin," in Kensetsushō Kinki Chihōkyoku, *Yodogawa hyaku-nen shi*, 383.

36   Okino, "Yodogawa," 363–66.

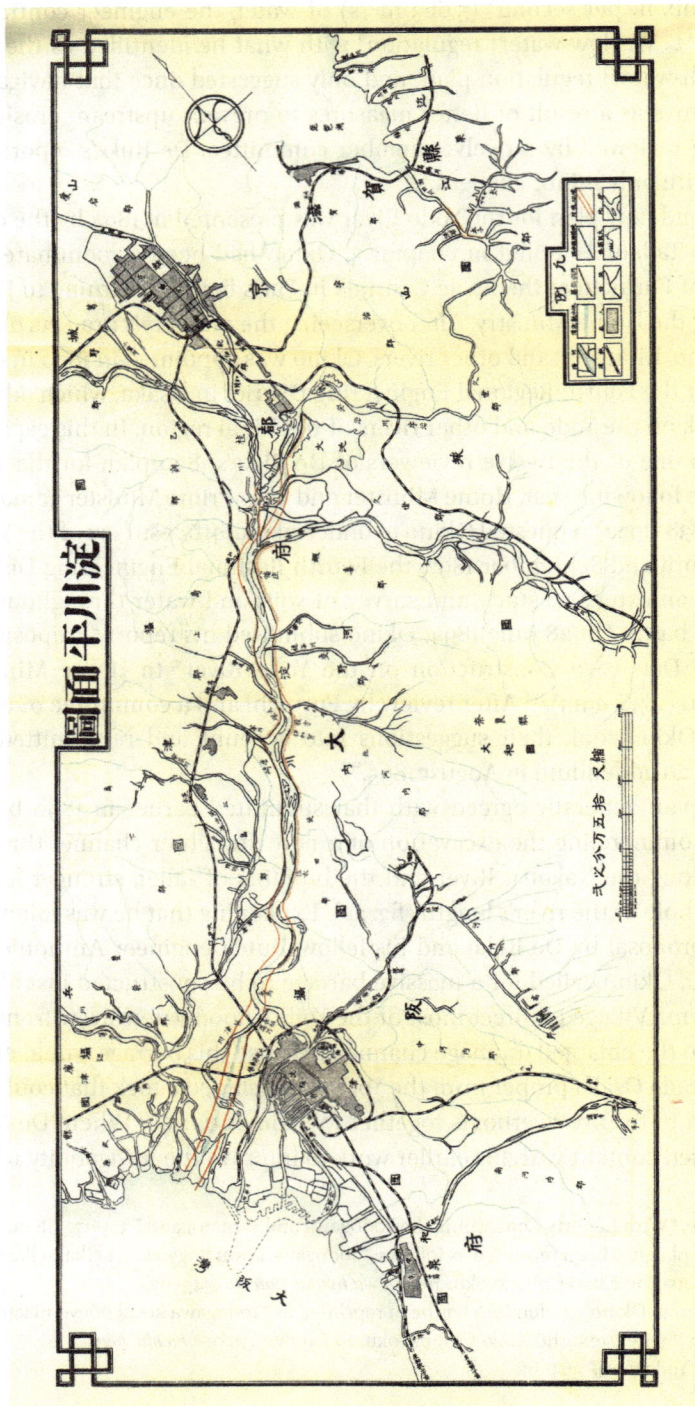

FIGURE 22   1894 plan for the reengineering of the Yodo River. Reprinted in Takeoka Mitsutada, *Yodogawa chisuishi* (Osaka: Yodogawa Chisuishi Kankōkai, 1931), frontispiece

Yodo, Okino recommended the addition of a 5.56 km long shipping channel that would start at the port and run parallel to the main stream of the Yodo at a depth of 2–3 m above the Osaka Peil (OP).[37] Although Okino briefly discussed the navigability of the Yodo and portions of its tributaries, his inclusion of the Kema shipping lock and channel were his sole provisions for boat traffic.

Like De Rikje, Okino's report did not mention any specific allowances for fishing, irrigation, or other common uses of the river. Nor did his plan address the previous primary objective of improving the port. In short, both plans focused on reengineering the river in accordance with engineers' calculations of the maximum "high-water" level achieved in the floods of 1885 and 1889. By the early 1890s, the Home Ministry's top engineers had begun the process of narrowing the calculative framework through which they would govern and maintain the country's rivers by largely reducing river management to a problem of financing and building for flood control. Unbeknownst to Okino and his colleagues at the time, they were contributing to the techno-political framework that would eventually be used to fashion Japan's modern river regime.

De Rijke's and Okino's plans diverged in terms of scientific knowledge, technology, and presentation. Having spent years designing and testing various kinds of erosion-control technologies at worksites along the Kiso and Yodo Rivers, De Rijke naturally emphasized their importance in his 1890 report. Through replanting denuded mountainsides, installing inexpensive straw nets and mats to slow runoff, supervising the building of small erosion-control dams across mountain streams, and looking "sharply after the owners of the land," he hoped to reduce the amount of sediment deposited on downstream riverbeds.[38] A mostly self-educated Dutch engineer (see chapter 3), De Rijke spent many years trekking along and studying Japan's rivers, talking with locals (albeit through a translator), and gaining what the political scientist James C. Scott calls *mētis*: "a wide array of practical skills and acquired intelligence in responding to a constantly changing natural and human environment."[39] By contrast, the highly educated Okino spared few words for erosion prevention and instead offered a bird's-eye view of the entire river basin with a keen eye for where and to what depth dredging should take place. More significantly, he argued against De Rijke's idea of retaining excess

---

37   The actual measurements of Okino's proposed shipping canal were a length of 51 *chō* (5.56 km), width of 36 *shaku* (10.9 m), and a navigable depth between 6 *shaku* 7 *sun* and 9 *shaku* 8 *sun* (2.03–2.97m). Okino, "Yodogawa," 366–67.

38   De Rijke, "Doshayama ikken ni tsuki mōshiide" [3 April 1875], *Yodogawa Oranda gishi monjo*, 184–86, and De Rijke, "With Reports Concerning the Yodogawa and Yamatogawa," 321.

39   James C. Scott, *Seeing Like a State: How Certain Schemes to Improve the Human Condition Have Failed* (New Haven: Yale University Press, 1998), 313.

FIGURE 23   Completed in 1905, this barrage built on the Seta River regulated water from
             Lake Biwa into the Yodo River system. In Biwa-ko Chisuikai, ed., *Biwa-ko chisui
             enkaku-shi* (Ōtsu: Biwa-ko Chisuikai, 1925), frontispiece

floodwaters in Ogura Lake, calculating that the shallow lake and surrounding
marshes would be too small to contain the overflow from another flood like
that of 1885.[40] Okino focused instead on regulating the flow of floodwaters
with a large concrete-and-masonry barrage at the southern end of Lake Biwa,
where that big body of water pours into the Seta River and from there into the
Uji and Yodo Rivers. The barrage, he contended, would allow a greater amount
of water to be released from Lake Biwa during the dry winter season and would
more importantly allow water to be retained in the lake during peak summertime rainfall (fig. 23).[41]

---

40   Okino, "Yodogawa kōsui bōgyo kōji keikaku ikenshō," 359–62.
41   De Rijke's and Okino's differing emphases on upstream erosion prevention and water
      retention rather than controlling the downstream channel are suggestive of what Wim
      Ravesteijn explains were contrasting colonial Dutch East Indies and French approaches
      to irrigation and river engineering: "A Dutch East Indies irrigation tradition developed
      that was part of a broader colonial civil-engineering culture, which to a certain extant sur-
      vived into the post—Second World War period in, for example, the form of Indonesian—
      Dutch upstream water control, as opposed to the French form of downstream control."
      Wim Ravesteijn, "Between Globalization and Localization," *Comparative Technology
      Transfer and Society* 5, no. 1 (2007): 51, and Okino, "Yodogawa," 351–58.

Okino's emphasis on a single sizable, upstream structure to regulate the water level of the Yodo River is suggestive of the even more ambitious engineering structure of the Aswan Dam then being planned for the Nile River in Egypt. Where Okino envisioned a massive masonry-built barrage across the main tributary of the Yodo, between 1898 and 1902 British engineers in colonial Egypt used very similar technologies to erect what was at the time the world's largest dam to store some of that river's famous floodwaters for the promotion of year-round irrigation and farming.[42] "The new scale of twentieth-century engineering," the political scientist Timothy Mitchell explains about the Aswan Dam, "turned the bizarre religion of the Saint-Simonians into an everyday belief: that 'human ingenuity' could now dominate the 'mighty elements' of nature. In manufacturing the dam, the engineers also manufactured nature."[43] Mitchell's observation about the British engineers and the Aswan Dam can also readily be applied to the plans and projects of the Paris-trained Okino (see chapter 3) and most of the other engineers in the Home Ministry. Together they demonstrate how both the dam on the Nile River and the barrage on the Seta River were part of the broader transnational process of global modernity that is addressed in chapter 5. In addition to their employment as technical experts, many engineers in Japan, Britain, France, and their respective colonies at the turn of the century held prominent positions as government administrators—they were in effect technocrats (*gijutsu kanryō*).[44] And, it was in their technical and administrative roles, that engineers like Okino and Furuichi proved instrumental in producing "flooding" as a problem requiring a technocratic solution.[45] Moreover, in concentrating much of this flood-control

---

42   After the building of the Aswan High Dam just upstream between 1956 and 1970, this older dam has been called the Aswan "Low" or "Old" dam. Sir William Willcocks and James Ireland Craig, *Egyptian Irrigation* (London: E. & F. N. Spon, 1913).

43   Timothy Mitchell, *Rule of Experts: Egypt, Techno-Politics, and Modernity* (Berkeley: University of California Press, 2002), 35.

44   The historian Hiromi Mizuno offers the best account in English of the emergence of these technocrats in early twentieth-century Japan. Hiromi Mizuno, *Science for the Empire: Scientific Nationalism in Modern Japan* (Stanford: Stanford University Press, 2009), esp. part one. See also Ōyodo Shōichi, *Gijutsu kanryō no seiji sangaku: Nihon no kagaku gijutsu no makuaki* (Tokyo: Chūō Kōronsha, 1997), esp. chapters 1, 2. For France's long history of technocratic governance, see Bruno Belhoste and Konstantinos Chatzis, "From Technical Corps to Technocratic Power: French State Engineers and Their Professional and Cultural Universe in the First Half of the 19th Century," *History and Technology* 23, no. 3 (2007): 209–25; Antoine Picon, "French Engineers and Social Thought, 18th–20th Centuries: An Archeology of Technocratic Ideals," *History and Technology* 23, no. 3 (2007): 197–208.

45   As explained in chapter 3, Johannis De Rijke worked in Japan for thirty years (until 1903). Although he was eventually granted an imperial appointment (*chokuninkan*) in 1891, the Dutchman remained a technical expert and never served in the same kind of

technology in a single location, these engineers sought to rearrange key elements of the riparian assemblage in such a way that the Home Ministry could
better extend its authority over the maintenance and use of the Kinai region's
most important river system.

As in Europe and the United States and their respective colonies, in the
late nineteenth century Japanese government officials also granted ever more
authority to numbers and statistics for their seeming ability to objectively
represent natural and social processes as well as the government budgets to
which they were inevitably linked. Both De Rijke's and Okino's plans for the
Yodo River reflected this new emphasis on quantitative measures and explanations. For his part, Okino presented information and arguments with greater
weight on the scientific bases of his results. He highlighted the collection and
use of numerical data with appended tables, which provided information
about instrumentation, gradients, surface areas of the primary waterways,
and low- and high-water discharge at different locations for different years.[46]
Furthermore, Okino took pains to explain how he generated mathematical
variables and utilized formulae, such as Bazin's average velocity equation, by
which he estimated the amount of water flowing into the Yodo and its main
tributaries.[47] Thus, with its statistical tables and mathematical formulae,
Okino's plan illustrates the growing authority attributed to science among
Japan's governing elite.[48] With parallels in Europe, the United States, and their

administrative positions as his Japanese peers. Kamibayashi Yoshiyuki, *Nihon no kawa o
yomigaeraseta gishi de Rijke* (Tokyo: Sōsōsha, 1999), 288.

46   Okino, "Yodogawa," 373–80.

47   Interestingly, although Okino included this data and formulae in the report, many of
his main measurements agreed with those presented with less explanation by De Rijke.
For example, De Rijke's report explained that the main channel of the Yodo will have
to be "improved" to handle "200,000 cub. ft. per second" (5,663 m³/s) of water whereas
Okino called for "200,000 cubic *shaku* per second" (5,560 m³/s). De Rijke, "With Reports
Concerning the Yodogawa and Yamatogawa," 319; Okino, "Yodogawa," 350.

48   The importance of these numbers and statistics can also be seen in the bulging amount
of data presented in statistical yearbooks published by municipal and prefectural offices
in the late nineteenth and early twentieth centuries. On the malleable role of these
yearbooks in representing a place in the Meiji period, see Kären Wigen, "The Poetry of
Statistics," in *A Malleable Map: Geographies of Restoration in Central Japan, 1600–1912*
(Berkeley: University of California Press, 2010), 139–66. Although James Bartholomew, a
historian of science in Japan, criticizes the lack of scientists in high government posts
in Japan during the late nineteenth century, he does highlight their marked increase
and influence compared to a few decades earlier under the Tokugawa government.
James R. Bartholomew, "Modern Science in Japan: Comparative Perspectives," *Journal of
World History* 4, no. 1 (1993): 111–13.

colonies, this authority lay in science's purported universality and its claim to be able to accurately represent the Yodo River in this universal language.

It would be mistaken to assume that this relatively new notion of scientific universality replaced the fundamentally qualitative and political character of technocratic decision-making.[49] Nonetheless, by believing they correctly measured and understood the Yodo's hydraulic behavior during these two historic floods, Okino, De Rijke, and their fellow engineers contended that this data held the promise of predicting the river's future behavior during severe floods. In the words of James C. Scott, these engineers rendered key aspects of the Yodo "legible," but as "builders of the modern nation-state" they did not "merely describe, observe, and map." They also sought "to shape a people and landscape" that would "fit their techniques of observation."[50] Along the Yodo River, the Home Ministry's effort "to shape a people and landscape" began by reducing the Yodo from one formed by myriad riparian relations to one that was principally defined by hydraulic processes that could be studied, predicted, and controlled.[51]

Historians have typically relegated the Yodo to a separate, secondary, and passive role in their analysis of these Home Ministry reports and the subsequent work to reengineer the Yodo. Politicians, administrators, entrepreneurs, or engineers are given credit for controlling or improving a river or conversely blamed for failing to accurately measure floodwaters or anticipate a breached levee. Writing in 1970, the renowned geologist Koide Haku used a cinematic metaphor to express this common perspective: "Rivers have both natural and social histories ... Flooding is a frame (*koma*) of their natural history, and flood

---

49   The historian of science Theodore Porter argues that, despite their reputation for flaunting their mathematical acumen, graduates of the École Polytechnique and other engineers in nineteenth-century France rarely relied on numbers alone in their decision making by also consistently accounting for personal and political factors when making budgets and crafting public policy. Theodore Porter, "French State Engineers and the Ambiguities of Technocracy," in *Trust in Numbers: The Pursuit of Objectivity in Science and Public Life* (Princeton: Princeton University Press, 1995), 114–47.

50   Scott, *Seeing Like a State*, 82.

51   Scott explains that there are "five characteristics" to these kinds of "state simplifications": 1) They are "*interested*, utilitarian facts"; 2) they are typically "*documentary* facts" (both words and numbers); 3) they are often "*static* facts"; 4) they are usually "*aggregate* facts" (grouped so as to lessen each fact's particularities); and 5) they are "*standardized* facts." He cautions not to assume that these "simplifications" mean "simple-minded," rather they should be seen as necessary and sophisticated tools of statecraft that provide officials with a "synoptic view of the ensemble" by "collapsing or ignoring distinctions that might otherwise be relevant." Emphases in the original. Scott, *Seeing Like a State*, 80–81.

damage is a frame of their social history."[52] Okino articulated a similar view in 1917, when he addressed the Civil Engineering Society of Japan as its newly elected president.[53] In his prepared speech, Okino uncharitably blamed the disastrous flooding along the Kiso and Yodo Rivers in the 1880s on the Dutch engineers' insistence on promoting a "low-water" policy for water transport and their failure to understand the geography of Japan.[54] He went on to congratulate the "engineers of our nation" (*wagakuni no gijutsusha*)—namely, himself and his subordinates—for having developed the "high-water" approach appropriate for Japan's short, fast-flowing rivers.[55] Perhaps Okino had merely forgotten, but De Rijke's 1890 plan had included the term "high water" in its title and the Dutch engineer had clearly expounded why this new approach was being adopted over the previous "low-water" policy that had been advanced by the Home Ministry.[56] Nevertheless, the point here is that Okino, the doyen of Japanese engineers and newly elected president of the Civil Engineering Society, attributed the flooding of 1885 and 1889 to human error and not to the river. He believed that a better understanding of the river would achieve the broader goal of reducing flood damage. His worldview, and one likely shared by most in the audience that day, was one in which the scientifically trained specialist either grasped or failed to grasp the physical laws of nature that brought summertime monsoons and typhoons to Japan and caused this mountainous country's short, swift rivers to overflow their banks and levees. In this telling, the river is a passive object to be studied and transformed, or even be conquered, through human initiative, calculative ability, and modern technology. Yet, as this study demonstrates, the active role the Yodo River played in people's livelihoods reminds us of how this and other rivers were

---

52   Koide Haku, *Nihon no kasen: shizen shi to shakai shi* (Tokyo: Tōkyō Daigaku Shuppankai, 1973), vi. Koide's expression is similar to the geographer Gilbert White's well-known maxim from 1945: "Floods are 'acts of God,' but flood losses are largely acts of man." Gilbert Fowler White, "The Human Adjustment to Floods: A Geographical Approach to the Flood Problem in the United States," PhD diss., University of Chicago, 1945, 2.

53   Okino's classmate in Paris and later supervisor at the Home Ministry, Furuichi Kōi had been the first president and Okino's immediate predecessor.

54   Okino Tadao, "Doboku Gakkai dai sankai sōkai kaichō kōen," *Doboku Gakkai zasshi* 3, no. 1 (February 1917): 7.

55   Focused on detailing the advances Japan had made in road, port, and river construction, Okino concluded his speech by emphasizing that the future management of the country's civil engineering projects was their "responsibility" (*sekinin*). Both by critiquing the Dutch engineers and by underscoring the responsibility his fellow Japanese engineers had for safeguarding the country's future, Okino was providing a clear expression of what Hiromi Mizuno calls "scientific nationalism." Mizuno, *Science for the Empire*, 180–84, and Okino, "Doboku Gakkai dai sankai sōkai kaichō kōen," 8–10.

56   De Rijke, "With Reports Concerning the Yodogawa and Yamatogawa," 314–16.

vital participants in the reframing of the complex riparian relations that they co-constituted. Similarly, the people living along the Yodo also held a key place in the reframing of these relations in terms of flood control.

3   Local Communities

Farmers, fishers, and boat operators in the late nineteenth century continued to negotiate their occasionally conflicting relations and rights to the region's rivers as had been the case for generations. People had long and through hard labor transformed the low-lying alluvial plains, rolling hills, and steep mountains into productive paddies, fields, and forests from the outskirts of Osaka, Kyoto, and Fushimi to the distant headwaters of the Yodo's many tributaries. A 1903 report, for example, noted that nearly 90 percent of the land in Nishinari County along the Yodo River north of Osaka was devoted to agriculture.[57] It also listed seventy different kinds of marketable crops ranging from many types of beans and grains to all manner of fruits and vegetables grown within Osaka Prefecture.[58] According to this same report, the fertility of the region benefited from the "crisscross of countless large and small rivers" and "abundance of irrigation canals."[59] This plentitude of fresh water enabled farmers to grow rice, which was recorded as the most cultivated crop in Osaka and Kyoto Prefectures in the early twentieth century.[60] There were several types of rice, however, and from the 1880s along much of the low-lying area of the Yodo and its main tributaries, farmers had shifted from growing the *senbon* variety to the late-harvesting *jinriki*. This change apparently owed to the better performance of *jinriki* in the region's water-retaining soil.[61] To irrigate these rice paddies, irrigation associations (typically *kumi* or *gō*) annually repaired or built anew weirs (*iseki*) of wood, stone, and compacted dirt that jutted out into the region's rivers to draw water into their irrigation sluices. Where the bank of a river was too high, farmers installed hefty waterwheels to scoop water up and into a chute or pipe that poured into nearby paddies. A survey carried out by Kyoto Prefecture around 1900 reported that, of the more than two hundred waterwheels operating along the lower Uji River, most were positioned to

---

57   "Nōgyō shi," in *Ōsaka-fu shi*, ed. Ōsaka-fu (Osaka: Ōsaka-fu, 1903), 3:3.

58   "Nōgyō shi," in *Ōsaka-fu shi*, 3:25–29.

59   "Nōgyō shi," in *Ōsaka-fu shi*, 3:2.

60   "Nōgyō shi," in *Ōsaka-fu shi*, 3:2; *Kyōto-fu shi*, 2:546–51.

61   *Kumiyama-chō shi*, 2:285.

irrigate adjacent paddies.[62] By obstructing the flow of water in this way, these weirs and waterwheels inevitably became points of conflict with boat pilots, fishers, and downstream farmers.[63]

Just as farmers had acquired exclusive usufruct rights to portions of the river and its banks for irrigation and other activities, fishers also had long held rights to catch specific kinds of fish at different times of year in designated areas. In the upper reaches of the Yodo River system, such as those explored by the biologist Imanishi Kinji during his research on mayfly larvae in 1935 (introductory chapter), fishing was a seasonal by-employment centered on catches of trout, char (*iwana*), sweetfish, and salmon. Downstream, however, fishing was the primary livelihood of many communities. Around Ogura Lake, which lay at the confluence of the Uji, Kizu, and Katsura Rivers before they flowed into the Yodo, three "fishing" villages won an 1882 court ruling that affirmed their centuries-old right to enter private property (*shiyūchi*) when fishing in the lake.[64] Four years later, these same villages formed the Ōike Fishing Association (Ōike Gyogyō Kumiai) and in 1888 reported using 167 registered boats, hundreds of nets, baited and unbaited traps, 11,000 baited lines, and even 172 harpoons to catch over 20,000 kg of fish.[65] By far their largest landing was carp (nearly half of the total catch by weight), but they also caught significant amounts of eel, catfish, chub (*moroko*), freshwater goby (*gori*), "three lips" (*hasu*), freshwater shrimp, and other fish.[66] And from 1886, they received permission to start a hatchery and stock the lake with upwards of 100,000 carp annually. The Ogura could support this amount and variety of fish because of its size and the fact that it was replenished with fresh water from the Uji River and smaller streams.[67] Further downstream near the city of Osaka, fishers most commonly used four-armed scoop nets (*yotsude mochiami*)—different

---

62   A smaller number of waterwheels were also used to power rice and sawmills and in the manufacture of various metal goods. *Uji-shi shi*, 4:96–98.

63   The historian Watanabe Takashi identifies seven types of irrigation-related conflict amongst farmers during the Tokugawa period. Watanabe Takashi, *Hyakushōtachi no suishigen sensō: Edo jidai no mizuarasoi o ou* (Tokyo: Sōshisha, 2014), 55–59.

64   *Kumiyama-chō shi*, 2:280–81.

65   "Otodokegaki," reprinted in *Kumiyama-chō shi*, 2:284–85.

66   The total reported catch in 1888 was 5,490 *kan* of fish with different kinds of carp making up 2,620 *kan* (i.e., *funa, koi* and *kamatsuka* carp) of that total and various small fish (*zako*) making up another 2,000 *kan*. One *kan* equals 3.75 kg. *Kumiyama-chō shi*, 2:283.

67   As noted in the introductory chapter, the official history of the reclamation of the Ogura Lake includes a section on the flora and fauna written by well-known scientists that documented the shear variety of plants, shellfish, fish, and birds that lived in and around the lake before it was drained and transformed into rice paddies in the late 1930s. Ogura-ike Tochi Kairyō-ku, ed., *Ogura-ike kantaku shi* (Uji: Ogura-ike Tochi Kairyō-ku, 1962), 254–95.

from the kinds of nets found on the Ogura—to catch an even greater range of fish owing to their proximity to the estuary and bay.[68] Nonetheless, among the reported river fish caught in Osaka in 1888, the most common were carp, catfish, eel, and freshwater shrimp.[69]

Whereas farmers and fishers earned their livelihood at fixed locations along the Yodo and other rivers, boat pilots and their boats connected these communities to each other and to the region's urban centers of Osaka, Fushimi, and Kyoto. In the 1870s and 1880s, the bustle of traffic on the Yodo was quite unlike the quiet, contemplative river the philosopher Watsuji Tetsurō and his companions journeyed down in 1926 (introductory chapter). In fact, until the early twentieth century, there were thirty-one active riverports (*hama*) on the Yodo River between Osaka and Fushimi, and dozens more ports along the Kizu, Uji, and Katsura Rivers.[70] From at least the sixteenth century, versatile shallow-draft riverboats collectively called *yodobune* ("Yodo boats") plied the waters of the Yodo and its tributaries, shipping salt, oils, charcoal, fruits and vegetables, and other goods from the region's towns and villages to the cities of Fushimi, Kyoto, and Osaka. Tea was another important upstream product with a considerable downstream market.[71] The areas facing the Uji and Kizu Rivers were particularly renowned for their fragrant Uji tea, which was popular throughout the country and, following the signing of a commercial treaty with the United States in 1858, became a significant export commodity to America where the "green tea" was consumed with milk and sugar.[72] On their way upstream, these riverboats shipped a variety of products and finished goods to these rural

---

68   According to an 1894 national survey of freshwater and marine fisheries, most freshwater fishers in Osaka Prefecture lived in the rural counties surrounding the city and typically sold their catch to wholesale merchants within Osaka city. Nōshōmushō Nōmukyoku, ed., *Suisan jikō tokubetsu chōsa* (Tokyo: Nōshōmushō, 1894), 2:245–47. On the three-century-old freshwater fish markets in Osaka, see Yagi Shigeru, "Kinsei Ōsaka no kawazakana ichiba," in *Mibunteki shūen no hikaku shi*, ed. Tsukada Takashi (Osaka: Seibundō Shuppan, 2010), 61–106; Sakai Ryōsuke, *Zakoba uoichiba shi* (Osaka: Seizandō Shoten, 2008), 14–41, 312–13.

69   An 1888 report compiled by Osaka Prefecture recorded the number of fishing associations (*gyogyō kumiai*), members, types of boats, kinds of gear, and varieties of fish caught. "Meiji 21-nen naisuimen gyoka kokō oyobi shuyō gyokaku buppinmoku shuyō gyosen," Osaka-fu (1888), reprinted in Ōsaka-fu Gyogyōshi Hensan Kyōkai, ed., *Ōsaka-fu gyogyōshi* (Osaka: Ōsaka-fu Gyogyōshi Hensan Kyōkai, 1997), 352.

70   *Kumiyama-chō shi*, 2:236.

71   *Uji-shi shi*, ed. Hayashi Tatsusaburō and Fujioka Kenjirō, vol. 3, *Kinsei no rekishi to keikan* (Uji: Uji Shiyakusho, 1976), 378–403.

72   Uji-based tea merchants (*cha-donya*) began exporting tea first through Yokohama in 1859 and later through Hyōgo (Kobe) when it opened to foreign trade in 1867. After silk, tea was the most valuable export commodity for Japan in the late nineteenth century. Iishi Kanji,

communities. On the Kizu River near the port of Hamadai, for instance, there were pens to store the night soil shipped from downstream cities until it has sufficiently aged for use as fertilize on the region's prized tea.[73] As discussed in the introductory chapter, some of the larger *yodobune* riverboats were known as *sanjikkokubune* and outfitted to carry as many as twenty-eight passengers on regularly scheduled overnight routes between the cities of Kyoto, Fushimi, and Osaka. By no later than 1871, steamboats also began carrying passengers and later towing barges up and down the Yodo River alongside the wind, pole, and towline-propelled *yodobune*.[74] In 1888, Kyoto Prefecture recorded that steamboats and other riverboats together transported over 200,000 passengers on the Yodo.[75] In addition, there were as many as twenty-nine ferry crossings within Osaka in 1903 and several more further upstream, such as the Yamazaki Ferry in present-day Ōyamazaki Town and the Heita Ferry in present-day Higashiyodogawa Ward of Osaka, where people and goods crossed the otherwise impassable Yodo and its tributaries.[76] Even in 1907, a government survey counted 7,463 riverboats departing Osaka for Fushimi and 3,864 departures from Fushimi for Osaka. Furthermore, the survey reported 570 boats arriving in Fushimi from ports on the Kizu River, forty-seven boats from places along the Uji River, and 9,610 arrivals from the Takase Canal (Kyoto).[77] Until the widespread opening of regional railways and the completion of engineering work to the Yodo and other rivers in the second decade of the twentieth century, much of the Kinai region's commercial geography continued to be centered on these riparian corridors where goods and people moved up and downstream.[78]

"Bakumatsu-ishin-ki no Yamashiro chagyō: raisangyō to Nihon kindaika," *Ritsumeikan keizaigaku* 39, no. 5 (1990): 493–521; *Uji-shi shi*, 3:597–606.

73   *Kumiyama-chō shi*, 2:237; Hino Shōshō, *Kinai kasen kōtsū shi kenkyū* (Tokyo: Yoshikawa Kōbunkan, 1986), 97–98.

74   Hino, *Kinai kasen kōtsū shi kenkyū*, 120–21.

75   Kyōto-fu Shomuka, *Kyōto fuchi gairan* (Kyoto: Kyōto-fu, 1888), table 146, unpaginated, National Diet Library, Tokyo.

76   Miki Masafumi, *Mizu no miyako to toshi kōtsū: Ōsaka no nijū-seiki* (Osaka: Seizandō, 2003), 82. To restrict and regulate the movement of people, the Tokugawa government had limited the number of ferries across most large rivers. There were only four official ferries on the Yodo until the Tenpō Reforms (1841–43) when the regime allowed the opening of several more ferries. Hino, *Kinai kasen kōtsū shi kenkyū*, 258–59.

77   A different survey reported that riverboats carried 60,000 passengers between Fushimi and Osaka in 1906. Fushimi-chō, ed., *Gotairei kinen Kyōto-fu Fushimi-chō shi* (Fushimi: Fushimi-chō Yakuba, 1929, reprinted 1972), 400–1.

78   For example, in 1877, Japan's second railway to begin service ran between Kyoto and Kobe via Osaka. This line eventually became part of the Tōkaidō line, which from 1895 began service to Tokyo. In 1892, the Osaka Railway (Ōsaka Tetsudō) began service between central Osaka and Nara. Four years later in 1896, the Nara Railway (Nara Tetsudō) began

Some of the upstream and downstream communities connected by riverboat traffic and commerce disagreed about other issues regarding the use and management of the Yodo and its tributaries. One of the oldest areas of disagreement stemmed from the twofold effects of logging. The first was the use of rivers to run logs to downstream lumberyards. Within the Yodo River basin, one of the best-known places for log running was Kyoto Prefecture's Ōi River, a mountainous tributary of the Katsura.[79] Along the Ōi, raftsmen lashed logs of specified lengths together, attached a rudder, and piloted their load to downstream lumberyards. From at least the seventeenth century, downstream fishers and irrigation associations demanded that these raftsmen only run their logs during designated periods of the year, typically early or late summer, to avoid damaging irrigation sluices and the large wooden weirs fishers operated to catch returning sweetfish. Even when run during the specified times, these log rafts would occasionally come apart, allowing loose logs to hurl into and damage these sluices and weirs or get caught on rocks where they could create dangerous logjams.

The second issue of upstream deforestation and downstream riverbed sedimentation was more intractable and problematic. Although the new government had established a system of government-owned and Home Ministry-administered forests in 1872, the Home Ministry lacked the financial and technical resources to manage those lands.[80] Consequently, impoverished villages often had to regulate as best they could the access and use of the adjacent forest lands to which they had historical rights. Needless to say, during the 1870s and 1880s, many villagers and lumber operators abandoned previous forest management practices, which had sought to limit logging and promote

running between Nara and Kyoto via Fushimi. And, in 1904, the Kyoto Railway (Kyōto Tetsudō) began service between Kyoto and Maizuru on the Japan Sea. Shinshū Ōsaka-shi Shi Hensan Iinkai, *Shinshū Ōsaka-shi shi*, 5:460–70; Asao Naohiro et al., eds., *Kyōto-fu no rekishi* (Tokyo: Yamakawa Shuppansha, 1999), 291–92.

79   Kitakuwata-gun, ed., *Kyōto-fu Kitakuwata-gun shi* (Kyoto: Kitakuwata-gun, 1923), 193–99, and *Kyōto-fu shi*, ed. Kyōto-fu (Kyoto: Kyōto-fu, 1915), 1:685–88. For a similar discussion of log rafting on the Shō and other rivers in Toyama Prefecture, see Michael Lewis, *Becoming Apart: National Power and Local Politics in Toyama, 1868–1945* (Cambridge: Harvard University Asia Center, 2000), 148–50.

80   In an effort to both increase its control over forest resources and strengthen its tax base, in 1872 the government began to survey and categorize the country's vast forest lands as imperial forests (*goryōrin*), state forests (*kanrin* and later *kanyūrin*), and privately held forests (*min'yūrin*) with the final category of privately held woodlots and forests being taxed for the first time in accord with the country's new land tax system. Conrad D. Totman, *Japan's Imperial Forest, Goryōrin, 1889–1945*. (Folkestone: Global Oriental, 2007), 106–21.

the planting of seedlings.[81] Instead, in a number of areas, they clear-cut entire mountainsides for lumber and charcoal.[82] A 1915 survey of the forestry industry in Kyoto Prefecture chronicles that the period of the 1870s and 1880s was marked by "indiscriminate logging (*ranbatsu*) with no accompanying planting of seedlings." This led to the "transformation of beautiful forests (*birin*) into bald mountains (*hageyama*)."[83] This report emphasizes how some semblance of forestry management and erosion prevention was initiated by the national and prefectural governments in the 1880s; nonetheless, these efforts were piecemeal at best and limited to the Kiso and Yodo River basins.[84] In his 1897 treatise on flood and erosion control, the engineer Ichikawa Yoshitaka explained that, when reaching the "summit of a crumbling mountain" nearly 15 km behind Tanakura Village along the Kizu River, one "gazes in all directions upon the whiteness of crumbling bald mountains (*kuzure hage no yamayama*) that can be said to resemble fallen snow or as if under a mantle of white cloth."[85] The whiteness Ichikawa described was from the mountain's exposed granite; without a layer of protective topsoil and vegetation the rock easily crumbled and eroded through constant exposure to temperature fluctuations,

---

81   Using case studies from different regions, both Conrad D. Totman and Mizumoto Kunihiko describe the policies and practices entailed in what Totman sees for the Tokugawa period as the emergence of "regenerative forestry." Conrad D. Totman, *The Green Archipelago: Forestry in Preindustrial Japan* (Berkeley: University of California Press, 1989), 149–69, and Mizumoto Kunihiko, "Dosha-dome yakunin to nōmin," in *Kinsei no mura shakai to kokka* (Tokyo: Tōkyō Shuppankai, 1987), 221–73.

82   The historian Matsuzawa Yūsaku explains that both government forestry policies and village forestry practices were in disarray (*muchitsujō jōtai*) during first decades of the Meiji period. With uncharacteristic hyperbole, Totman goes even further to argue that, "To put the matter boldly, the Meiji government's 1870s–1880s program of woodland reorganization created the greatest conflict between government and people in the entire history of Japan. It was in essence a contest for control of the realm." By the 1880s, Totman emphasizes that the changing regulatory regime and overall rural hardship had "produced a surge of reckless logging, woodcutting, and arson." Matsuzawa Yūsaku, "Shinrin to sonraku no Meiji ishin," in *"Meiji hyakugojū-nen" de kangaeru: kindai ikōki no shakai to kūkan* (Tokyo: Yamakawa Shuppansha, 2018), 31–42; Totman, *Japan's Imperial Forest*, 101, 130.

83   *Kyōto-fu shi*, 1:659. A 1903 report for Osaka Prefecture makes similar observations about the "indiscriminate logging" and "clearing of land" (*kaikon*) following the Meiji Restoration. "Doboku, kōtsū kikan narabi tochi suimen," in *Ōsaka-fu shi*, ed. Ōsaka-fu (Osaka: Ōsaka-fu, 1903), 4:73.

84   *Kyōto-fu shi*, 1:662–66; Ōsumikai Naimushō Shi Henshū Iinkai, ed., *Naimushō shi* (Tokyo: Chihō Zaimu Kyōkai, 1971), 3:71–72.

85   As noted in chapter 3, the engineer Ichikawa Yoshikata describes in his book the design of various flood-control structures and the chronic problem of topsoil erosion in the headwaters of the Kizu River and elsewhere in Kyoto Prefecture. Ichikawa, "Kuzure hageyama no jikkyō zusetsu," *Suiri shinpō*, 2, unpaginated.

wind, and rain.[86] Washing into mountain streams, this granular sediment settled downstream on the riverbeds of the Kizu, Uji, Katsura, and Yodo. During
the final decades of the nineteenth century, these riverbeds rose by an average of 40 cm, clogging irrigation sluices, and creating ever-shifting sandbars
and shoals that made navigation both difficult and dangerous.[87] While seemingly distant and unrelated, the riparian relations of the Yodo River inextricably bound downstream fishing, farming, and shipping communities to these
upstream logging communities.

In the 1880s and into the 1890s, some disputes between upstream and downstream communities along the Yodo took on an overtly political tone through
the influence of the Movement for Freedom and Popular Rights and the continuing efforts of the prefectural and central governments to establish a stable
system of national governance. Two projects highlight the contested character
of infrastructure and the role of local politicians in channeling and shaping
the debate over the future of the Yodo River. The first of these was the planning
and construction of the Lake Biwa Canal (Biwa-ko Sosui).[88]

As one of Japan's first multipurpose water projects, the planned canal would
draw water from Lake Biwa to enable small boats to sail between the lake and
the Yodo River, supply homes and industry in Kyoto with water, and generate hydroelectricity to power among other things the country's first electric
streetcars.[89] This proposed canal stoked fears among downstream communities, especially following the flood of 1885, for its potential to exacerbate

---

86   For description and illustrative map of these "bald mountains" to the east of Osaka and
      Kyoto, see Chiba Tokuji, *Hageyama no bunka* (Tokyo: Gakuseisha, 1970), 83.
87   Furushima Toshio, *Kisei jinushisei no seisei to tenkai* (Tokyo: Iwanami Shoten, 1952), 3;
      Uji-shi shi, 4:213.
88   For a detailed discussion of the conflicting politics and views of the residents and journal-
      ists *within* Kyoto about this ambitious project, see Takaku Reinosuke, "Biwa-ko sosui kōji
      no jidai," in *Kindai Nihon to chiiki shinkō: Kyōto-fu no kindai* (Kyoto: Shibungaku Shuppan,
      2007), 118–93.
89   The Lake Biwa Canal was designed and supervised by Tanabe Sakurō (1861–1944). Based
      on his senior thesis at the Imperial College of Technology (Kōbu Daigakkō), the original
      plan did not include hydroelectric power generation. In order to overcome a 36 m differ-
      ence in elevation in the original plan, Tanabe proposed adding hydroelectric powered
      motors to pull boats atop submersible flatcars up and down slopes on both sides of the
      Nagara and Hinooka Hills. Tanabe and Takagi Bunpei (1843–1910), the first chair of the
      Kyoto Chamber of Business and Industry, came up with this plan after visiting and con-
      sulting with the mining engineer who built a similar hydroelectric facility for the mines in
      Aspen, Colorado. Kyōto Shinbunsha, ed., *Biwa-ko sosui no hyaku-nen: jujutsu hen* (Kyoto:
      Kyoto-shi Suidōkyoku, 1990), 54–83. For a contemporary summary in English of the tech-
      nical aspects of the Lake Biwa Canal, see Sakuro Tanabe, "The Lake Biwa-Kioto Canal,
      Japan," *Scientific American* 75, no. 19 (7 November 1894): 341, 345, 346.

flooding along the Yodo. The Osaka Prefectural Assembly repeatedly petitioned the Home Ministry from the summer of 1885 to halt construction on
the Lake Biwa Canal, arguing that if money was to be spent it should be on the
repair of existing levees and bridges and in preparing for the next big flood.[90]
Representatives from villages and counties neighboring the Yodo River continued to push the Osaka Prefectural Assembly and Osaka Governor Tateno Gōzō
(1842–1908) to seek a delay in the construction of the canal and to demand
that Kyoto Prefecture provide funds for the construction of floodworks for the
Yodo River where it flows through Osaka Prefecture. On 27 December 1888,
and after several efforts to stop or suspend the Lake Biwa Canal project, the
Osaka Prefectural Assembly expressed resigned acceptance of the canal in a
petition to Home Minister Matsukata Masayoshi (1835–1924). In this petition
and in a similar one sent to the governor of Osaka Prefecture that same day,
the assembly requested the national government to pay for preventative work
to the levees and sluices along the Yodo River within its prefecture in order
to address anticipated changes in water level due to the canal.[91] Eventually,
arguments over the canal appear to have been resolved when Kyoto Prefecture
declared the completion of the canal portion of this multipurpose project
in 1890.[92]

The second project that pitted upstream and downstream prefectures and
politicians against one another was the dredging of the Seta River. This river
drained Lake Biwa into the Uji, and from there into the Yodo. From as early as
the seventeenth century, village leaders on the shores of Lake Biwa had repeatedly petitioned for the clearing of boulders and dredging of shoals along the
entire river system between the lake and Osaka. In doing so, they hoped to
lower the level of the lake and the risk of flooding, reclaim additional land on
its shore, and more easily ship their products to the country's largest commercial center. Many Osaka merchants and shipping concerns eventually came
to ally with these lakeside villages because they believed improved navigation
between the city and lake would also enhance their trade with the northern

---

90   See, for example, "Biwako sosui kōji ni kansuru kengi" (11 July 1885), in *Ōsaka-fukai shi*, ed.
     Ōsaka-fu (Osaka: Ōsaka-fu, 1911), chapter 6, section 2, 74–77.

91   "Kengi" (27 December 1888), in Ōsaka-fu, *Ōsaka-fukai shi*, chapter 6, section 2, 170–75, and
     "Biwa-ko sosui kōji ni tai suru yobō kōji no jicchi o nozomu kengi" (27 December 1888), in
     Ōsaka-fu, *Ōsaka-fukai shi*, chapter 6, section 2, 175–79.

92   The project was fully completed in 1895 with the addition of a new canal, to replace the
     older and shallower Takase Canal, running southward and parallel to the Kamo River to
     its terminus in Fushimi. Between 1908 and 1912, a second canal was built with the pri-
     mary purpose of supplying Kyoto with drinking water from the lake. Kyōto Shinbunsha,
     Biwa-ko sosui no hyaku-nen, 144–96.

reaches of the archipelago through the port of Tsuruga on the Japan Sea. The downstream villages on these rivers vehemently opposed any widening or deepening of the river for fear that the increased flow of water would heighten the risk of flooding in their communities.[93]

A half century earlier during the early years of the Tenpō era (1830–44) and following several decades of petitions and counter petitions, the Tokugawa government oversaw the dredging of the entire length of the Seta-Uji-Yodo River system. In addition to using the dredged dirt and rock for patching and strengthening levees, the authorities in Osaka even built a small mountain, Tenpōzan, in the port from sediment that had washed downstream during what was dubbed the "Big Dig of the Tenpō era" (*Tenpō no ōsarae*).[94] The results of this "big dig" did not last long. Over the next few decades, successive floods and unchecked deforestation led to the riverbed becoming choked with sediment and rock.[95] Accompanying these rising riverbeds during the 1870s and 1880s were calls for renewed dredging from areas along Lake Biwa in what had become part of Shiga Prefecture. From the summer of 1890, the new governor of Shiga Prefecture, Iwasaki Shōjirō (1846–95), and the Shiga Prefectural Assembly initiated a two-year-long dispute with the downstream prefectures of Kyoto and Osaka by requesting the Home Ministry to fund their plans to straighten and dredge the upper Seta River.[96] In response to the efforts of Shiga Prefecture, downstream villages and towns, as well as the prefectural assemblies in Osaka and Kyoto, quickly protested by reiterating arguments their forebearers would have recognized about how changing the river channel and deepening it would encourage the silting of riverbeds and the amount of water that could flow into the Yodo during floods.[97] Many in Osaka were also

---

93   Fukuyama Akira, *Kinsei Nihon no suiri to chiiki: Yodogawa chiiki o chūshin ni* (Tokyo: Yūkakusan, 2003), 227–30.

94   Hattori Takeshi, *Kindai chihō seiji to suiri doboku* (Kyoto: Shibunkaku Shuppan, 1995), 182–90.

95   As with the Fudō River (chapter 3), riverbeds that rose above the surrounding land and were only kept in place by levees are called in Japanese "ceiling rivers" (*tenjōgawa*). For a description of these rivers in the Kinai region, see Chiba, *Hageyama no bunka*, 79–83.

96   In its comprehensive history of flooding and flood control for Lake Biwa, the Lake Biwa Flood Control Association reprinted many documents related to flood events, engineering projects, and Shiga prefectural petitions and protests. For petitions, surveys, and reports from Shiga Prefecture requesting the Home Ministry to survey and dredge the Seta River, see Biwa-ko Chisuikai, ed., *Biwa-ko chisui enkaku-shi* (Ōtsu: Biwa-ko Chisuikai, 1925), 336–490, 806–34.

97   "Shiga-ken Setagawa kōji ni kansuru kengi" (5 December 1890), in Ōsaka-fu, *Ōsaka-fukai shi*, chapter 6, section 2, 197–98; Biwa-ko Chisuikai, *Biwa-ko chisui enkaku-shi*, 348–53; and Hattori, *Kindai chihō seiji*, 202–7.

opposed to further dredging and widening of the Seta River because they did not want to exacerbate the silting of the city's already shallow port.[98]

Within the riparian assemblages formed along the Yodo River, the prefectural politics surrounding the Lake Biwa Canal and Seta River projects cut into and across existing regional riparian relations. In retrospect, the flooding of the Yodo in 1885 proved to be the watershed event that disrupted those riparian relations and stimulated the formation of new ones around the singular issue of flood control. Although not as severe, the 1889 flooding occurred just as the Lake Biwa Canal was nearing completion, thereby bringing together advocates for flood control in Osaka and Kyoto Prefectures. Even in 1890, when the Lake Biwa Canal was almost finished, local activists residing in riverside communities in southern Kyoto Prefecture had already begun aligning their interests with those located on or near the Yodo River in Osaka Prefecture.[99] Many in Kyoto and Osaka were also in agreement about their shared interest in compelling the Home Ministry to provide the funding and technical expertise to repair and improve their levees. One gathering of interest occurred on 11 September 1891 when a number of activists and politicians met at a restaurant in Osaka's Amishima-chō. This meeting appears to have been scheduled to coincide with a visit from Yumoto Yoshinori (1849–1918), a representative from Saitama Prefecture in the lower house of the Imperial Diet and a member of the centrist Great Achievement Party (Taiseikai). Yumoto met with local activists, politicians, and fellow Diet members from several prefectures, personally inspecting the floodworks along many of the country's large rivers in preparation for submitting new legislation during the 2nd Diet to begin in December of that year.[100] At the meeting, he was also joined by six other Diet

---

98   Shinshū Ōsaka-shi Shi Hensan Iinkai, *Shinshū Ōsaka-shi shi*, 5:425–26.

99   Within Kyoto Prefecture, for example, residents in Kii, Kuse, and Uji Counties protested the building of the Lake Biwa Canal without efforts to reduce the threat of flooding along the Yamashina and Yodo Rivers. "Katsuragawa sujirosen no tsukekae," *Yomiuri shinbun*, 23 October 1889, 1; and "Uji Kii gunmin no gekidō," *Yomiuri shinbun*, 1 May 1890, 2. The historian Hattori Takashi discusses similar regional divisions within Osaka Prefecture where representatives from the area around southern Sakai refused to support flood control along the Yodo, which flowed through the northern part of the prefecture. Hattori, *Kindai chihō seiji*, 219–23.

100   In August and September 1891, newspapers like the *Yomiuri shinbun* carried reports about Yumoto's visits to significant rivers in Gifu, Aichi, Toyama, Ishikawa, Fukui, Nagano, and Niigata Prefectures. "Kisogawa kaishū kōji shisatsu no Yumoto daigishi," *Yomiuri shinbun*, 17 August 1891, 1; "Hokuriku sanken junkai," *Yomiuri shinbun*, 20 August 1891, 2; "Chisui ni nesshin na Yumoto Yoshinori daigishi, kyō Shinanogawa," *Yomiuri shinbun*, 23 August 1891, 1; "Yumoto daigishira ga ensetsukai: Echigo," *Yomiuri shinbun*, 30 August 1891, 2; "Yumoto Yoshinori daigishi ga Toyama, Ishikawa no kasen o chōsa," *Yomiuri shinbun*, 11 September 1891, 2.

members, who belonged to the Liberal Party (Jiyūtō) and represented districts
in Osaka and Kyoto Prefectures, as well as sixteen activists and politicians who
were engaged in flood control and related activities in Kyoto and Osaka.[101] An
important outcome of the meeting was an agreement between the representatives of these two prefectures to cooperate on the problem of the Yodo River by
petitioning their respective governors, the Home Ministry, and by supporting
Yumoto's broader effort to pass legislation through the Imperial Diet. The Home
Ministry acquiesced to the growing pressure to address the issue of flood control and ordered Okino Tadao to conduct a comprehensive survey of the Yodo
between April and September of 1892.[102] Okino's survey coincided with the
first meeting of Kyoto, Osaka, and Shiga prefectural representatives in Kyoto
on 23 August 1892 to discuss Shiga Prefecture's plans for the Seta River.[103] These
negotiations quickly broke down, but Shiga Prefecture persisted in gathering
signatures and petitioning the national government until the Home Ministry
finally agreed the following month to carry out part of Shiga Prefecture's calls
for the dredging and channel improvement of the Seta River.[104] After setting
several conditions, including a promise from the Home Ministry to pursue the
issue of flood control along the Yodo River. In December 1892, Osaka and Kyoto
Prefectures agreed to allow the work on the Seta to proceed.[105]

The issue of flood control went beyond local interests to become a shared
concern for communities as different and distant from each other as farming villages on the shores of Lake Biwa and the industrial districts of Osaka.

---

101   The other named Diet members in this newspaper article were Matsuno Shinkurō of
      Kyoto and the following representatives from Osaka Prefecture: Kikuchi Kanji, Matano
      Kagetaka, Awaya Shinazō, Higashio Heitarō, and Toyoda Bunzaburō. "Yodogawa kaishū
      ni tsuki Ōsaka Kyōto no daigishi oyobi suiri iin no kaigō," *Yomiuri shinbun*, 14 September
      1891, 1.
102   An example of the pressure being applied to the Home Ministry is the following peti-
      tion wherein the Osaka Prefectural Assembly directly requested Home Minister
      Shinagawa Yajirō (1843–1900) to begin extensive improvement work on the Yodo in 1893
      and that the entire cost should be drawn from national treasury (*kokko shiben*). "Kengi"
      (12 December 1891), in Ōsaka-fu, *Ōsaka-fukai shi*, chapter 6, section 2, 204–8.
103   From Osaka and Kyoto, a number of the attendees were long-term activists and politi-
      cians in the movement to gain greater support and funding for flood control. From Osaka,
      these included Ōhashi Fusatarō, Nakatani Tokuyasu, Maeda Kinjirō, Ueda Shigetarō, and
      Ueba Hakaru. Attendees from Kyoto comprised Imamura Jinbei, Okada Sakichi, Fujita
      Kensuke, Tanaka Sukeshirō, Irie Tōzō, and Tsukiyama Saburōhei. Biwa-ko Chisuikai,
      Biwa-ko chisui enkaku-shi, 811; Hattori, *Kindai chihō seiji*, 205–6.
104   Biwa-ko Chisuikai, *Biwa-ko chisui enkaku-shi*, 812–27.
105   Between 18 January and 26 February 1893, the Home Ministry cleared, dredged, and
      embanked a short stretch of the Seta River between Mount Dainichi and the area where
      the Ōto River flows into it. Biwa-ko Chisuikai, *Biwa-ko chisui enkaku-shi*, 827–30.

To overcome prefectural, urban, and rural discrepancies, these local activists undertook the lengthy process of forming coalitions to lobby their prefectural governors and assemblies as well as the national government to contribute more resources toward flood control. At the same time, activists and politicians in the three prefectures formed local and regional flood-control organizations, such as the Shiga-based Lake Biwa Flood Control Association (Biwa-ko Chisuikai) in 1889 and the Prefectural Flood Association League (Dōmei Fuken Chisuikai) in 1893, which brought together groups from all three prefectures, to better coordinate their fundraising and lobbying efforts.[106] Occurring during the fluid political period just before and after the 1889 promulgation of the Constitution of the Empire of Japan and the 1890 opening of the Imperial Diet, the behind-the-scenes political machinations leading to these local and regional alliances remain murky. What is known is that particularly active figures like the politicians Ōhashi Fusatarō (1860–1935) of Osaka and Tanaka Sukeshirō (1868–1941) of Kyoto met repeatedly with their counterparts in other counties and prefectures to build regionwide support around the issue of flood control for the Yodo River. By and large, these men were not accidental activists who found their cause in the alleviation of suffering from the Yodo's flooding, rather most belonged to rural landowning families who, for whatever altruistic motives they expressed, were also acting on behalf of their own landed-class interests. Ōhashi, for example, was the scion of generations of headmen for Hanaten Village. He went on to serve as village mayor in 1887 before being elected to the Osaka Prefectural Assembly where he served for twenty-six years between 1891 and 1917.[107] Tanaka was one of Ōhashi's key counterparts in Kyoto Prefecture. He served as mayor of his home village, was subsequently elected to the Kyoto Prefectural Assembly, and from 1902 had four consecutive terms as the representative for Kyoto's second electoral district in the Imperial Diet.[108] In contemporary accounts of these meetings in county and prefectural assembly halls, there is little or no mention of the fishers, loggers, boat pilots, and tenant farmers whose lives were so intimately bound to the Yodo and its tributaries. Instead, in petition after petition, it was the rural elite who spoke on behalf of the suffering "people" (*jinmin*) and the "villagers in each village" (*kakumura sonmin*).[109] While there is little doubt that the fishers and tenant

---

106   Biwa-ko Chisuikai, *Biwa-ko chisui enkaku-shi*, 785–86, 839–40.

107   Ogawa Kiyoshi, *Yodogawa no chisui ou: Ōhashi Fusatarō* (Osaka: Tōhō Shuppan, 2010).

108   *Shinsen daigishi retsuden* (Tokyo: Kinkōdō Shoseki, 1902), 20; Nichigai Asoshiētsu, ed., *Seijika jinmei jiten: Meiji-Shōwa* (Tokyo: Nichigai Asoshiētsu, 2003), 376.

109   See, for example, "Kengi" (12 December 1891), in Ōsaka-fu, *Ōsaka-fukai shi*, chapter 6, section 2, 204–8, and "Yodogawa kairyō kōji shikō ni tsuite no kengi" (25 December 1896), in Ōsaka-fu, *Ōsaka-fukai shi*, chapter 6, section 2, 259–62.

farmers also experienced hardship due to the flooding, they lacked the same status and venues by which to raise their concerns in the regionwide deliberations that shaped the future of the Yodo River and the human lives linked to it.

4   Conclusion

A turbulent stream of events and historical actors coalesced to create the conditions that would begin the radical transformation of the region's riparian relations. In 1885, and again in 1889, the Yodo River's flooding foiled the efforts of the Home Ministry and its engineers at maintaining existing routes of navigation and a complex arrangement of levees and floodplains. This double deluge also destroyed lives and livelihoods in riverside communities all along the Yodo River and compelled their wealthier members to become politically active at the local, regional, and for the first time, at the national level.[110] This particular confluence of a flooding Yodo River, technocratic knowledge, and political activism contributed to the construction of flooding as an existential problem for those communities and the region as a whole. To understand and control the Yodo's increasing tendency to exceed its river channel, these engineers surveyed and measured the Yodo at specified locations within its broader river basin. In this way, they began the process of abstracting the river from its encompassing riparian relations and reducing it to a problem of hydraulics. At the same time, local activists and politicians drew on these surveys and reports when calling upon the national government to take over the responsibility of reengineering the river and funding that enormous project. Addressing the technical and political aspects of the Yodo's flooding, the plans by De Rijke in 1890 and especially Okino's in 1894 to "improve" the Yodo provided a new and comprehensive vision of river engineering and management. This techno-political solution for the Yodo River, however, far surpassed the capacity of the Osaka, Kyoto, and Shiga prefectural governments and therefore became a central part of a nationwide effort to develop a national system of river management. As is discussed in the next chapter, this bold new approach to the Yodo and other large rivers is what came to be Japan's modern river regime.

---

110   After hearing reports about the 1885 flood, Ōhashi Fusatarō left his legal studies in Tokyo and his position as the personal clerk for the politician Hatoyama Ichirō to return to his home village on the outskirts of Osaka. Upon seeing the damage caused by the flooding, he is said to have vowed to devote his life to preventing the Yodo from ever causing such destruction again. Ogawa, *Yodogawa no chisui ou*, 79–85.

CHAPTER 5

Constructing the Modern River Regime in Japan

In speaking of it [the River Law] as a whole, it must be thought of as
having taken the form of not seeing the people for the river.

一概ニ言ヘバ川ヲ見テ人見ズト云フヤウナ姿ニ出来テ居ルト考ヘ
ル成キ筈デアリマス。

MITSUKURI RINSHŌ[1]
箕作麟祥

∵

On 24 March 1896, near the end of the ninth session of the Imperial Diet, the
lower and upper houses passed Japan's first River Law (Kasenhō). The law's
sixty-six articles provided the state with the authority to plan, fund, and execute
river projects that were deemed to have a "significant connection to the public
interest" (*kōkyō no rigai ni jūdai no kankei ari*). As such, the River Law was also
the first of its kind to explicitly regulate "public" property (*kōbutsu*) and would
be the only such law until the 1919 passage of the Road Law (Dōrohō). While
broad in scope, the new law was also vague about the limits of government
authority. The renowned legal scholar and member of the House of Peers,
Mitsukuri Rinshō (1846–97), voiced his concerns about the proposed law on
the floor of the Diet, commenting that the law was taking the "form of not seeing the people for the river." Mitsukuri emphasized the lack of provisions and
protections in the law for individuals and communities who had long-standing
rights and relations with their local and regional rivers. Despite Mitsukuri's
own misgivings and those of others, the law passed both houses unanimously.
In the years after 1896, the River Law, along with the technocratic expertise of
the Home Ministry and funding approved by the Imperial Diet, established
the techno-political framework that shaped the construction of Japan's modern river regime. This law and Mitsukuri's unease could be interpreted as an

---

1 The debates and commentaries on the proposed River Law in the Imperial Diet were published in each house's respective public record: "Kasen hōan," in Naikaku Kanpōkyoku, ed.,
   Kanpō: Kizokugiin giji sokkiroku 41 (daily ed. 25 March 1896), 563.

example of the increasing power and authority of the state. But given the turbulent and uncertain political changes of the three decades before the founding of the Diet and the law's passage, this law and others like it were less an expression of the preexisting power of the state and more of an example of a powerful state itself coming into being. That is, the state did not create this law so much as the modern state was itself an *effect* of the River Law and the kinds of political practice and activity that manifested it.

1   Making Modern River Regimes

From the late nineteenth century onward, government engineers and officials throughout the world began reengineering the main rivers flowing through their countries and colonies in increasingly similar ways. Although the implementation of these individual projects was still necessarily local and regional in scope, they were influenced by the transnational flow of techno-political ideas and ethos that gave them shape. Moreover, with the spread of industrial capitalism, these technocrats could tap into unprecedented technical and financial resources to carry out their plans. In Japan and elsewhere, it was the industrial, imperial, and global character of these riparian projects that most differentiates them from earlier approaches to river management.[2]

While adapting their projects to the varying needs of dry and wet, flat, and mountainous regions, national and colonial governments around the globe at the time often had shared aims and used common means to reengineer rivers and their co-constituting riparian relations. The collapse of the Qing Empire in 1912, for example, meant that the Yellow and other rivers received the attention of that country's engineers and technicians as well as from advisors from Germany, the Netherlands, and the United States.[3] From the final decades of the nineteenth century, Dutch engineers also played a central role in tapping the main rivers of Java and Madura to build unprecedentedly large irrigation

---

2   Although emphasizing the continuity between "early modern" and "modern" river projects carried out on the Echigo Plain of present-day Niigata Prefecture, the historian Philip C. Brown explains that these modern projects were different from earlier projects because: "Modern economic development supplied new resources for civil engineering projects both directly and indirectly. Funds from Japan's imperial expansion exemplify the latter." Philip C. Brown, "Constructing Nature," in *Japan at Nature's Edge: The Environmental Context of a Global Power*, ed. Ian Jared Miller, Julia Adeney Thomas, and Brett L. Walker (Honolulu: University of Hawai'i Press, 2013), 90–91.
3   David Pietz, *The Yellow River: The Problem of Water in Modern China* (Cambridge: Harvard University Press, 2015), 79–86.

systems in the colonial East Indies.[4] From the 1870s in colonial India, British engineers began a "new era" of designing massive, perennial irrigation systems that enabled the widespread settlement of the arid "wastelands" of the Indus River valley.[5] Based on lessons from British projects in India and elsewhere at the turn of the century, engineers in the arid western United States promoted an "Indian system" of water management and focused on the Mississippi and Sacramento Rivers where the Army Corps of Engineers developed what eventually became its "levees only" approach to reclamation and flood control.[6] This same period along the Rhône and other rivers of France signaled, according to the historian Sara B. Pritchard, "the beginning of a distinct shift in the scale and scope of river development."[7] And this equally applies to the Rhine, Oder, Danube, and other large rivers of Europe.[8] Each in their own way and, as suggested here, frequently with colonial antecedents, these governments and the engineers in their employ contributed to the formation and spread of this modern river regime.

---

4   Wim Ravesteijn, "Between Globalization and Localization: The Case of Dutch Civil Engineering in Indonesia, 1800–1950," *Comparative Technology Transfer and Society* 5, no. 1 (2007): 32–64; Wim Ravesteijn, "Controlling Water, Controlling People: Irrigation Engineering and State Formation in the Dutch East Indies," *Itinerario* 31, no. 1 (2007): 89–118.

5   The historian David Gilmartin argues that it was with the Triple Canal project, built between 1905 and 1915 to enable water transfers between tributaries of the Indus that this "new era" of water management really came into fruition. David Gilmartin, *Blood and Water: The Indus River Basin in Modern History* (Oakland: University of California Press, 2015), 145, 155.

6   Hunter Rouse and Simon Ince, *History of Hydraulics* (New York: Dover Publications, 1963), 226; Martin Reuss, "Andrew A. Humphreys and the Development of Hydraulic Engineering: Politics and Technology in the Army Corps of Engineers, 1850–1950," *Technology and Culture* 26, no. 1 (1985): 1–33; Donald Worster, *Rivers of Empire: Water, Aridity, and the Growth of the American West* (Oxford: Oxford University, 1992), 143–56; Jessica B. Teisch, *Engineering Nature: Water, Development, and the Global Spread of American Environmental Expertise* (Chapel Hill: University of the North Carolina Press, 2011), 28–37.

7   Sara B. Pritchard, *Confluence: The Nature of Technology and the Remaking of the Rhône* (Cambridge.: Harvard University Press, 2011), 36.

8   Commenting on the origins of nineteenth century efforts to straighten the Rhine, the historian David Blackbourn argues that, while the Johann Gottfried Tulla's 1825 vision to "rectify" or straighten the Rhine focused on flood control, the engineer from Baden should not be blamed for the resultant increase in downstream flooding, but instead for "changing mental horizons, making certain things thinkable that had not been thinkable before." He goes on to show how these horizons were vastly expanded in the late nineteenth and early twentieth century as German engineers sought the "conquest of nature" by thoroughly reengineering the country's rivers. David Blackbourn, *The Conquest of Nature: Water, Landscape, and the Making of Modern Germany* (New York: W. W. Norton 2006), 117, 189–228; Severin Hohensinner, et al., "Changes in Water and Land: The Reconstructed Viennese Riverscape from 1500 to the Present," *Water History* 5, no. 2 (2013): 145–72.

Changing over time and from place to place, this modern river regime was as much a process as it was a product. After all, it was not as if the engineers and administrators in each of these countries had by virtue of their education and training gained a special ability to *perceive* the universal laws of nature and build more rational and efficient river works. Rather, they were all participants, in one way or another, in the development of the profession of modern engineering that increasingly reflected each other's endeavors and emboldened each to *produce* similar kinds of river works. As discussed in chapters 3 and 4, that process often involved studying and teaching at each other's universities, touring each other's worksites, visiting international expositions, publishing and reading each other's articles in trade journals, buying or building the same kinds of equipment, and applying like logistics to the management of resources and labor. For the rivers within their purview, the results of these activities demonstrated their frequently shared desire to "control" flooding and "improve" water flow for the promotion of agriculture, industry, and navigation. The near simultaneous emergence of this modern river regime along different waterways around the world should not be interpreted as "Westernization" with its assumptions about European origins, the "diffusion" of European science, technology, and culture, and the "adaptation" by societies around the world to these "Western" methods and ideas.[9] Instead, the contemporaneous quality of these efforts to reengineer rivers around the globe during this period should be seen as an example of what Carol Gluck calls "synchronic modernity" or as Zvi Ben-Dor Benite describes as "global modernity."[10] The preexisting riparian relations along all of these rivers also gave a diachronic cast to these modern engineering projects in the way that *both* the human and nonhuman past shaped, but did not determine, the channel of these rivers, the kinds of fish and waterfowl inhabiting these waters, and people's placement of levees, weirs, and irrigation sluices.[11] In emphasizing these prehistories of the modern river regime here and in the earlier chapters, I do not intend to

---

9   Gurminder K. Bhambra, "Talking among Themselves? Weberian and Marxist Historical Sociologies as Dialogues without 'Others,'" *Millennium* 39, no. 3 (2011): 679.

10   Both historians Gluck and Benite offered these terms in their contributions to an *American Historical Review* forum about the concept of "modernity." Carol Gluck, "The End of Elsewhere: Writing Modernity Now," *American Historical Review* 116, no. 3 (2011): 681; Zvi Ben-Dor Benite, "Modernity: The Sphinx and the Historian," *American Historical Review* 116, no. 3 (2011): 650–51.

11   In his observation about how the rapids and falls of the Columbia River formed "critical sites in a geography of energy" that attracted Native American fishers long before the US Corps of Engineers built its hydroelectric dams, the historian Richard White writes, "As we now understand rivers, they seek the most efficient and uniform expenditure of energy possible. Rivers constantly adjust; they compensate for events that affect them. They are,

resurrect a form of modernization theory with its assumptions about the progressive flow of history and teleologic universalism as was famously suggested by the historian of Chinese science Joseph Needham (1900–95) when he frequently described different societies' approaches toward science and technology as separate "cultural rivers" flowing "into the sea of modern science."[12] While the meaning and use of the concept of modernity and its distinction from modernization theory have generated much discussion over the years, most studies continue to overlook the manner in which landscapes and riverscapes, objects and artifacts, and nonhuman creatures have both been transformed and contributed to the transformation of these localized processes of global historical change.[13] The archaeologists Andrew Bauer and Steve Kosiba's fluvial concept of "entrainment" is helpful here for explaining how fish, rivers, and levees can exhibit "social roles ... that emerge in historically and contextually specific flows of action" contributed to the formation of this modern river regime along the Yodo River and was subsequently applied to many of Japan's other large rivers.[14]

In Japan and elsewhere around the world in the late nineteenth and early twentieth centuries, national and colonial governments were crucial in promoting and building this modern river regime. Historians, sociologists, economists, and political scientists in Japan have shown for several decades how the modern state was instrumental in the development of the country's rivers and other "natural resources."[15] Similarly, the English-language scholarship

---

in this sense, historical: products of their own past history." Richard White, *The Organic Machine: The Remaking of the Columbia River* (New York: Hill and Wang, 1995), 12.

12   Joseph Needham, "Science and Society in East and West," *Science and Society* 28, no. 4 (1964): 386.

13   In observing the way the meaning of modernization itself has also changed, the historian Ian Miller points out how the mid-twentieth century markers of modernization in Japan, such as "rates of consumption and the use of inanimate energy sources, for example—are now read as registers of environmental costs." Ian Jared Miller, "Writing Japan at Nature's Edge: The Promises and Perils of Environmental History," in *Japan at Nature's Edge: The Environmental Context of a Global Power*, ed. Miller, Thomas, and Walker, 3.

14   Andrew M. Bauer and Steve Kosiba, "How Things Act: An Archaeology of Materials in Political Life," *Journal of Social Archaeology* 16, no. 2 (2016): 123.

15   In English, both Eric Dinmore and Michael Lewis have examined how regional and national governments in Japan have come to view rivers as natural resources: Eric Dinmore, "High-Growth Hydrosphere: Sakuma Dam and the Socio-Natural Dimensions of 'Comprehensive Development' Planning in Post-1945 Japan," in *Environment and Society in the Japanese Islands: From Pre-History to the Present*, ed. Bruce L. Batten and Philip C. Brown (Corvallis: Oregon State University Press, 2015), 114–35; Michael Lewis, *Becoming Apart: National Power and Local Politics in Toyama, 1868–1945* (Cambridge: Harvard University Asia Center, 2000). In Japanese, there is a wide-ranging literature on

on Japan has examined the many ways in which the modern state came into being following the 1868 Meiji Restoration and extended its power through education, taxation, conscription, the monarchy and oligarchs, national ministries and political parties, mid-level bureaucrats and local elites, intellectuals, religious organizations, labor unions, and women's groups.[16] These studies have valuably replaced earlier views of the modern Japanese state as a monolith dominated by a few elites and institutions. In its place, they have provided a more complex perspective that accounts for the roles played by a variety of social groups and organizations that shaped the body politic and, in some cases, question the assumption of the state as an *a priori* entity. Whether applying liberal, pluralist, Marxian, Weberian, or Foucauldian approaches, most studies of the modern state in Japan use a "statist" approach, wherein the state is seen as a clear set of decision-making and policy-forming institutions, largely autonomous from Japanese society, and exercising sovereign authority over the population within the boundaries of the Japanese nation-state.[17]

---

so-called natural resources, but the following are suggestive of the developmental mindset that has shaped state policies towards regions, rivers, and the surrounding seas: Ariizumi Sadao, *Meiji seijishi no kiso katei: chikō seiji jōkai shiron* (Tokyo: Yoshikawa Kōbunkan, 1980); Mikuriya Takashi, *Seisaku no sōgō to kenryoku: Nihon seiji no senzen to sengo* (Tokyo: Tōkyō Daigaku Shuppankai, 1996); Satō Jin, *"Motazaru kuni" no shigenron: jizoku kanō na kokudo o meguru mō hitotsu no chi* (Tokyo: Tōkyō Daigaku Shuppankai, 2011); Takahashi Yoshitaka, *"Shigen hanshoku no jidai" to Nihon no gyogyō* (Tokyo: Yamakawa Shuppansha, 2007).

16 Brian Platt, *Burning and Building: Schooling and State Formation in Japan, 1750–1890* (Cambridge: Harvard University Press, 2004); Okuda Haruki, *Meiji kokka to kindaiteki tochi shoyu* (Tokyo: Dōseisha, 2007); Takashi Fujitani, *Splendid Monarchy: Power and Pageantry in Modern Japan* (Berkeley: University of California Press, 1996); Michio Umegaki, *After the Restoration: The Beginning of Japan's Modern State* (New York: New York University Press, 1988); Carol Gluck, *Japan's Modern Myths: Ideology in the Late Meiji Period* (Princeton: Princeton University Press, 1985); Edward E. Pratt, *Japan's Protoindustrial Elite: The Economic Foundations of the Gōnō* (Cambridge: Harvard University Press, 1999); Germaine A. Hoston, *Marxism and the Crisis of Development in Prewar Japan* (Princeton: Princeton University Press, 1986); Trent E. Maxey, *The "Greatest Problem": Religion and State Formation in Meiji Japan* (Cambridge: Harvard University Press, 2014); Andrew Gordon, *Labor and Imperial Democracy in Prewar Japan* (Berkeley: University of California Press, 1991); Sheldon Garon, *Molding Japanese Minds* (Princeton: Princeton University Press, 1997).

17 Following political scientist Timothy Mitchell, the anthropologists Aradahana Sharma and Akhil Gupta broadly divide postwar American political science approaches into "statist approaches" and an earlier "systems approaches," which they explain emerged in the 1950s and 1960s in response to the "difficulties in delineating the boundaries of 'the state' and argued for abandoning the study of states in favor of the broader idea of a 'political system.'" Aradhana Sharma and Akhil Gupta, eds., *The Anthropology of the State: A Reader* (Malden: Blackwell, 2006), 8; Timothy Mitchell, "The Limits of the State: Beyond

The result is that most studies about the modern state in Japan tend to focus on what are typically described as state-society relations. And, as argued throughout this study, divergent approaches to state-society relations often assume a series of shared modern binaries where the social and natural, cultural and material, human and nonhuman are seen to exist in separate ontological realms.[18] In recent years, however, scholars from a number of fields who describe themselves as "new materialists" or "post-humanists" have critiqued the underpinning of this modern state-society binary for: 1) how it assumes the modern categories of state, society, and nature prior to those categories existence; 2) how it overlooks the historically contingent and frequently contested manner in which those modern categories emerged; 3) how it ignores plants and animals as well as objects and artifacts, along with their biological processes and material properties, by foregrounding the political activities of human actors and their institutions; and 4) how, when these nonhumans are included in these analyses, they are regularly reduced to passive natural resources to be owned or managed by individuals, communities, and states.[19] This recent research suggests that states have been a critical actor in the formation of the modern river regime in Japan and elsewhere, but local communities and the rivers themselves also played important roles.

As is discussed in chapter 4, it was this confluence of actors across the Yodo River basin in the 1880s and early 1890s that led to the formation of Japan's

---

Statist Approaches and Their Critics," *The American Political Science Review* 85, no. 1 (1991): 77–96; Timothy Mitchell, "Society, Economy, and the State Effect," in *State/Culture: State-Formation after the Cultural Turn*, ed. George Steinmetz (Ithaca: Cornell University Press, 1999), 76–97. See also Michael Mann, *The Sources of Social Power: The Rise of Classes and Nation States, 1760–1914* (Cambridge: Cambridge University Press, 1993), 44–54.

18   Bruno Latour, *We Have Never Been Modern* (Cambridge: Harvard University Press, 1993). See also Ian Jared Miller, *The Nature of the Beasts: Empire and Exhibition at the Tokyo Imperial Zoo* (Berkeley: University of California Press, 2012); Robert Stolz, *Bad Water: Nature, Pollution, and Politics in Japan, 1870–1950* (Durham: Duke University Press, 2014); Brett L. Walker, *Toxic Archipelago: A History of Industrial Disease in Japan* (Seattle: University of Washington Press, 2010).

19   See, for example, Karen Barad, *Meeting the Universe Halfway: Quantum Physics and the Entanglement of Matter and Meaning* (Durham: Duke University Press, 2008); Andrew M. Bauer and Mona Bhan, *Climate without Nature: A Critical Anthropology of the Anthropocene* (New York: Cambridge University Press, 2018); Jane Bennett, *Vibrant Matter: A Political Ecology of Things* (Durham: Duke University Press, 2010); Diana Coole and Samantha Frost, eds., *New Materialisms: Ontology, Agency, and Politics* (Durham: Duke University Press, 2010); Philippe Descola, *Beyond Nature and Culture* (Chicago: University of Chicago Press, 2013); Tim Ingold, *Being Alive: Essays on Movement, Knowledge and Description* (New York: Routledge, 2011); Timothy Morton, *Hyperobjects: Philosophy and Ecology after the End of the World* (Minnesota: University of Minnesota Press, 2013).

modern river regime. The Home Ministry's work on the Yodo has long been understood to be an early and important example of a new approach to river management in Japan. Yet, I would argue that it became the template for similar engineering projects that were carried out along the country's rivers in the following decades. The Yodo River's frequent flooding was central to changes in riparian relations between the river and downstream communities, but it was the surveys and reports of the Yodo submitted by Johannis de Rijke and Okino Tadao that proved instrumental in proposing a scientific and technical method to managing Japan's rivers. Their successive plans required support from local elites and funding that only the national government could provide. Therefore, politics were an integral part of this reframing of preexisting riparian relations. This chapter discusses how local politicians from different regions, together with Home Ministry engineers, played a decisive role in the drafting and passing of both the River Law and a budget for what was officially entitled the Yodo River Improvement Works (Yodogawa Kairyō Kōji). In 1897, a year after the promulgation of the River Law, the Imperial Diet also passed the Erosion Prevention Law (Sabōhō) and Forestry Law (Shinrinhō) and shortly after had provided funding for the Home Ministry to begin work on the Tone, Kiso, and eventually seven other large rivers.[20] These projects were beset with budget shortfalls and delays. Furthermore, the completion of construction on the Yodo River in 1910 coincided with the disastrous flooding across the Kantō region and inundation of Tokyo. As is shown below, 1910 proved to be a critical year after which the Imperial Diet quickly approved a two-phase plan that called for the reengineering of upwards of sixty-five rivers across the country. The techno-political process that had converged on the Yodo River in the early and mid-1890s produced a prototype to river management that over the next few decades led to the reengineering of regional riparian relations across the country and the construction of Japan's modern river regime.

Like the segmented and regionally specific river regimes it replaced, this new national river regime was more than a sum of the levees, weirs, and sluice gates that were built along rivers throughout the country. Together with the recently promulgated constitution, the 1896 River Law created a techno-political *framework* that distinguished between natural and human phenomena and spelled out the rights and obligations of individuals and the differing levels of government regarding the country's rivers. Through a series of Home Ministry planned and managed projects, this seemingly abstract framing via rules and

---

20 The ten rivers that were "improved" through the application of the River Law between 1896 and 1910 were the Tone, Chikugo, Yodo, Yoshino, Takahashi, Onga, Kuzuryū, Kiso, Shō, and Shinano Rivers.

regulations took on material, and in some cases concrete, form as first the Yodo and then the Tone and other large rivers were "improved."[21] In effect, this framework embedded into the curvilinear channels of these rivers the interests and concerns of powerful rural landowners and the emerging industrial elite and their allies in the Home Ministry and Imperial Diet. In the process, the less powerful—the tenant farmers harvesting riverside reeds and other vegetation, fishers and the fish they pursued, as well as birds and the wetlands themselves—were excluded from the calculations used to reengineer rivers. The result effectively *enframed* those riparian relations deemed of importance within value-laden boundaries and excluded those that there were deemed unnecessary or irrelevant to the building of a wealthy and strong nation. Given the central role these rivers had in agriculture and industry at the time, this reframing of the country's rivers was crucial in the Local Improvement Movement (Chihō Kairyō Undō), the widespread tenant-landlord disputes, and the production of an agro-industrial landscape centered increasingly on the needs and dictates of Osaka, Tokyo, and other regional metropolises.

This reframing of riparian relations also contributed to the broader process of delineating what constituted natural, political, and social spheres of activity in modern Japan. In addition to the industrial, imperial, and global qualities that made these river projects particularly modern, the effort to "improve" these rivers also exemplified how the meaning and boundaries of the modern categories of *shizen* (nature), *kokka* (state), and *shakai* (society) in Japan were themselves being surveyed, negotiated, and constructed along with the river's new levees, weirs, and irrigation canals.[22] In reengineering these rivers, Home Ministry engineers reduced complex riparian relations by reframing them as a natural phenomenon governed by the narrower principles of the natural sciences. At the same time, the Home Ministry interacted in novel

21   I borrow the notion of "framing" from Michel Callon who in describing an "anthropology of markets" developed the idea to explain how calculative agents such as businesses or engineers entangle and disentangle particular relations from their calculative frameworks. See, for example, Michel Callon, "Introduction: The Embeddedness of Economic Markets in Economics," in *The Laws of the Markets* (Oxford: Blackwell, 1998), 1–54.

22   Rather than assume the existence of the categories of nature, state, and society (and their equivalent Japanese neologisms) and use them ahistorically in analyses of the past, this chapter argues that it is necessary to recognize how the binaries between society and nature as well as state and society were, in the political scientist Timothy Mitchell's words, the "effect" of complex and often contested processes, such as can be seen with the reengineering of these rivers. Timothy Mitchell, "Society, Economy, and the State Effect," 76–97. See also Timothy Lemke, "A Genealogy of the Modern State," in *Foucault, Governmentality, and Critique* (New York: Routledge, 2016), 25–40.

ways with individuals, households, and communities by appropriating land from riverside residents, directing its professional technicians and engineers to redesign channels, hiring wage labor to build levees, policing levees and river-beds, and other routinized activities. Through these often mundane activities and relations, long-standing riparian relations were being reengineered and new boundaries were being produced that demarcated what constituted state and society. While Mitsukuri may have demurred about exactly where these boundaries were being drawn, he tellingly voted for the River Law and did not question the distinction between rivers and people or the proposed law's focus on the former over the later. As a middle-aged scholar and legislator who had spent his career studying and translating European laws and legal institutions into Japanese, he had already come to distinguish between the categories of nature, society, and the state. But for most other people in Japan at the time, these boundaries and distinctions would be learned and built through their shifting relations with entities like local rivers, each other, and their governing institutions.

2   Techno-politics of Flood Control

The 1889 promulgation of the Constitution of the Empire of Japan and 1890 establishment of the Imperial Diet created new institutions for governing the country. These changes to national governance coincided with increasing concerns about the costs of dredging waterways, maintaining and building levees, and paying for flood relief. It should not be surprising then that the Diet quickly became the main venue in which to renegotiate the administrative division of riparian labor and costs that had been agreed upon at the 1875 Assembly of Prefectural Governors. Prominent in these legislative debates of the early 1890s were representatives from prefectures with large rivers flowing through them and Home Ministry engineers and officials who had experienced the difficulties of carrying out earlier riparian projects. After several years of lobbying and debate, what resulted was the formation of a techno-political framework through which to govern the country's primary waterways and eventually the formation of Japan's modern river regime.

Although the constitution inaugurated a nationwide system of representative government, the political franchise was severely curtailed in a manner that directly shaped the political practice of governing the country's rivers. The right to vote and hold office was limited to roughly 470,000 men who paid 15 yen or more annually in national taxes (about 1 percent of the population), so the three hundred members of the lower house of the Diet overwhelmingly voiced the interests of wealthy rural landowners and to a lesser extent their well-heeled urban allies.[23] Many Diet members were themselves owners of properties planted with commercial crops and typically tilled by tenant farmers, and they therefore had a vested interest in preventing the flooding of their land.[24] Seeking to relieve their prefectures (and themselves) of the costs of river work assigned to them under the 1875 Levee Measure, some Diet representatives argued that the national government should fund all but the smaller river projects. In this way, these measures echoed the concerns of those who had attended the Assembly of Prefectural Governors nearly two decades earlier in 1875. The formation of political parties in the 1880s and the establishment of the Imperial Diet in 1890, however, transformed the political landscape within which river policy was being debated at both the regional and national levels. One of the immediate results of this changing political climate was the Home Ministry's ordering engineers like De Rijke and later Okino to draw up plans to deal with flood control for the Tone, Kiso, and especially the Yodo Rivers.

During its first session, the lower house of the Diet debated a few dozen different proposals and bills ranging from lowering the property tax to the establishment of a prefectural assembly in Hokkaidō.[25] Although much of the Diet's three-month session was preoccupied with the passage of its first national budget, Yumoto Yoshinori, the representative for the fourth electoral district in Saitama Prefecture, managed to submit a short six-point proposition concerning the administration of the country's rivers.[26] In it, he argued that the national government should assume all of the costs and responsibilities

---

23   Following the end of the First Sino-Japanese War in 1895, rural wealthy elites often found themselves at odds with the growing influence and political clout of urban commercial and industrial interests and their calls for electoral reforms that favored urban areas and increases to land taxes to pay for expanding military and infrastructural expenditures. Mitani Taichirō, "The Establishment of Party Cabinets, 1898–1932," in *The Cambridge History of Japan: The Twentieth Century*, ed. Peter Duus (Cambridge: Cambridge University Press, 1988), 6:68–72.

24   Ogawa Makoto speculated that the mounting demands better flood controls were due in part to landowners reclaiming flood-prone common areas (*iriai*), such as marshlands and floodplains, from which they then earned income by renting it to tenant farmers. Ogawa Makoto, "Chisui, risui, tochi kairyō no taikeiteki seibi," in *Nihon nōgyō hattatsu-shi: Meiji ikō ni okeru*, ed. Nōgyō Hattsu-shi Chōsakai (Tokyo: Chūō Kōronsha, 1954), 150.

25   See, for example, the list of proposals (*kengian*) and bills (*hōan*) on the schedule for 2 March 1891. Naikaku Kanpōkyoku, ed., *Kanpō: Shūgiin giji sokkiroku* 60 (daily ed. 3 March 1891), 975–82.

26   Although Yumoto presented his proposal entitled "Chisui ni kansuru kengian" during the Diet's first session, the deliberations over the national budget left little time to discuss this or many other proposals and bills until the second session began in December 1891.

for managing, improving, and repairing those rivers deemed to fall under its jurisdiction, including the lakes, marshes, and other wetlands connected to those rivers. Moreover, he believed that prefectures should bear the ordinary costs of maintaining the smaller rivers under their jurisdiction and that irrigation associations should bear the cost of preparing for flood prevention (*kōsui yobō nado no junbi*). Nonetheless, Yumoto stressed that regardless of whether it was erosion prevention in the mountains or "low-water" and "high-water" policies on the plains, the administration of the country's largest rivers should be the responsibility of the national government and costs for their upkeep and repair should be borne by the national treasury. Given that this was only a proposal, not an actual bill, and that most Diet members understood well the costs of river management, Yumoto's recommendations passed with little dissent and was placed on the schedule for the Diet's third session in 1893.

Yumoto's proposal was part of a broader effort by this Saitama legislator and his allies to transform the governance of the country's main rivers. Under the strict deflationary policies of Finance Minister Matsukata Masayoshi in the 1880s, government leaders in Tokyo had expressed little interest in increasing funding or reforming the government's riparian policies to better account for the costs of river work and flood damage. As explained earlier, national government leaders deemed many of these costs to be "defensive work" (*bōgyo no kō*) and therefore the responsibility of the relevant prefectures in terms of implementation and funding. Facing this dithering response by the national government, Yumoto and some of his fellow politicians and activists sought to rise above competing regional and ministerial interests to forge a broad consensus surrounding the reformation of national riparian policy. In December 1890, Yumoto, Yamada Shōzaburō (1843–1916) of Gifu, Ōhashi Fusatarō of Osaka, and others met in Tokyo to form the Flood Control Association (Chisui Kyōkai), which had its office in the downtown Kitasaya district along the Nihonbashi Canal.

Ōhashi, Yamada, and Yumoto all hailed from areas that historically had suffered from flooding and whose prefectures were unable or unwilling to carry out the kinds of costly engineering projects that they and their landowning constituents demanded. The flooding of the Yodo River in 1885 had led Ōhashi, the son of a village headman on the outskirts of Osaka, to give up his legal studies in Tokyo so that he could commit himself to preventing a recurrence of such flooding. Yamada had grown up in the polder lands between the Kiso and Nagara Rivers, and while still a teenager he succeeded his late father as village

---

Naikaku Kanpōkyoku, *Kanpō: Shūgiin giji sokkiroku* 16 (daily ed. 18 December 1891), 244–47.

head and levee supervisor (*teibō torishimariyaku*) for Kanō domain in Mino Province. Following the Meiji Restoration, he served in the Gifu Prefectural Assembly where he advocated for river work along the Kiso River. In 1880 and 1881, he helped to establish two regional associations that advocated the building of irrigation and floodworks.[27] For his part, Yumoto was the eleventh child to the notable Tajima family of Kobari Village (present-day Gyōda City), which lay halfway between the Tone and Ara Rivers and along the Minumadai Canal.[28] After the Restoration, he was elected to the Saitama Prefectural Assembly and became deeply involved in the prefecture's promotion of education as well as new ideas regarding medicine and sanitation, irrigation, and flood control.[29] Despite their hailing from different regions, these leaders of the Flood Control Association generally shared a similar family pedigree as rural elites and the common objective of relieving their rural communities of the costs of river work and devastation caused by flooding.

The formation of the Flood Control Association built upon the efforts of regional river and irrigation groups that had emerged in the 1880s. As examined in chapter 4, the activists and politicians in these often local or prefectural groups, together with Home Ministry engineers and the Yodo River itself, had played a key role in bridging differences between upstream and downstream communities and building support for river work between counties along and away from the Yodo and its main tributaries. Similarly, the Flood Control Association aimed to bridge divergent regional and political party interests to form a nationwide coalition advocating for the national government to shoulder the administrative responsibilities and costs of maintaining the country's largest rivers. One way the association did this was by having Yumoto and other members visit areas affected by floods to survey the damage and meet with local river groups and politicians. In August 1891, for example, Yumoto

---

27   Kiso Sansen Ryūiki Shi Henshū Iinkai, ed., *Kiso sansen ryūiki shi* (Nagoya: Kensetsushō Chūbu Chihō Kentsukyoku, 1992), 386–87; Patricia G. Sippel, "*Chisui*: Creating a Sacred Domain in Early Modern and Modern Japan," in *Public Spheres, Private Lives in Modern Japan, 1600–1950: Essays in Honor of Albert M. Craig*, ed. Andrew Gordon, Gail Lee Bernstein, and Kate Wildman Nakai (Harvard University Asia Center, 2005), 172–81.

28   As a child, Yumoto's name was Tajima Masutarō, and because he had apparently shown promise from a young age, he was sent to Edo in 1862 to be adopted into the family of Magome Kageyu, who were hereditary district heads (*chō nanushi*) of Ōdenma district in Nihonbashi and operated a prosperous packhorse business that had served the Tokugawa since the early seventeenth century. The Tajima and Magome families had conjugial relations dating back generations. For a biography of Yumoto's early years, see Oya Geni, *Yumoto Yoshinori-kun shōden* (Kōnosu-chō: Yamamoto Chōjirō, 1892); Nichigai Asoshiētsu, ed., *Seijika jinmei jiten: Meiji-Shōwa* (Tokyo: Nichigai Asoshiētsu, 2003), 665.

29   Prime Minister Hara Takashi, *Yumoto Yoshinori tokushi joi no ken* (1918), unpaginated.

and Inoue Kakugorō (1860–1938), the representative for the ninth electoral district in Hiroshima Prefecture, made a highly publicized tour of rivers in Toyama, Ichikawa, and Fukui Prefectures. Even before their departure, the *Yomiuri shinbun* announced their upcoming trip.[30] During their stopover in the city of Takaoka in Toyama Prefecture, the two Diet members are reported have had an audience of over three thousand.[31] As already noted in chapter 4 it was on this same junket that Yumoto went to the Yodo River basin to meet with likeminded activists and politicians from Osaka and Kyoto Prefectures.

In addition to these tours, meetings, and speeches, the association also began printing and distributing its own publication, *Chisui zasshi* (*Flood Control Journal*), to facilitate communication between the national organization headquartered in downtown Tokyo and its members in prefectures as distant as Saga in the south and Niigata in the north. In its inaugural issue, the editors explained the purpose of the association was not to endorse particular river projects, rather to promote the study of flood control (*chisui*) by sharing and disseminating information about past and present projects and technologies used inside and outside Japan.[32] The contents of the first and later issues bore out this promise. Published in December 1890, the first issue included an extract of Cornelis Johannes van Doorn's influential 1873 essay on river engineering, an article about the history of efforts to block off the Kiso River at Aburajima, another on current improvement work being carried out along the Fuji River, a report on Shiga Prefecture's plans to dredge the Seta River (i.e., one of the Yodo River's main tributaries), charts listing the costs of flooding along the Kiso River in Gifu Prefecture (dating all the way back to 1830), and the reported costs related to flooding by prefecture between 1880 and 1889. In total, twelve issues of the journal were released before publication ceased in 1894. Throughout these issues, the journal included articles about past and recent river projects, reports on current undertakings, and updates on the association and its activities. In this way, the publication created a seemingly apolitical conduit that drew together many wealthy and powerful people concerned with the problem of river management.

From the second issue, the *Chisui zasshi* also began to publish a list of the association's membership, thereby making the commitment by association members and their common cause more public. This list eventually reached close to five hundred published names and ran for several pages. The list of members was divided by prefecture beginning with Tokyo and its most

---

30 "Hokuriku sanken junkai," *Yomiuri shinbun*, 20 August 1891, 2.
31 "Yumoto daigishira ga enetsukai," *Yomiuri shinbun*, 30 August 1891, 2.
32 "Chisui Kyōkai yōshi," *Chisui zasshi* 1 (17 December 1890): 1–6.

prominent residents, such as Prime Minister Yamagata Aritomo, the Finance and Home ministers, and other members of the Imperial Diet and national government. After highlighting these members of national prominence, the list went on to name numerous governors, dozens of legislators from both the upper and lower houses of the Diet, and village, town, and city mayors.[33] This membership list was regularly updated and among the newly added names were a number of Home Ministry engineers. Furuichi Kōi and Okino Tadao, for instance, joined the association in time to have their names released in the third issue.[34] In short, the Flood Control Association represented a national coalition of powerful techno-political interests. It also gave voice to the common concern about reforming riparian governance that was shared by many central government ministers and engineers as well as propertied local and prefectural politicians.

Between 1890 and 1896, the Flood Control Association actively cultivated relations with irrigation and river-related organizations that cut across regional and political allegiances. Within the Imperial Diet as well, Yumoto and his colleagues, including Katō Kiemon (1857–1923) and Matano Keikō (1853–1911) from Aichi and Osaka Prefectures, respectively, worked to forge a bloc of likeminded legislators who pushed for fundamental changes in the way the central government approached river management. Instrumental to this effort was the 1892 founding of the Flood Control Group (Chisuikai). At their initial meetings, members belonging to so-called "government" parties like the National Association (Kokumin Kyōkai), "peoples" parties like the Liberal Party (Jiyūtō) and Progressive Party (Kaishintō), and independents met to discuss the structure and aims of their new organization.[35] The Flood Control Group held its first general meeting on 15 January 1893 at the Isejin restaurant in central Tokyo, with at least 150 Diet members representing prefectures from around the country. Yumoto spoke to his colleagues about endorsing a bill in the Diet for the national government to assume responsibility for work on eleven large rivers.[36] At general meetings like this one in 1893, the group sponsored speeches about river- and flood-related issues from its members,

---

33   "Honkai kiji," *Chisui zasshi* 2 (January 1891): 34–47.
34   For the listing of Furuichi and Okino, see "Nigatsuchū nyūkai shokun hidari no gotoshi," *Chisui zasshi* 3 (February 1891): 49, 51.
35   "Chisuikai," *Yomiuri shinbun*, 22 November 1892, 1; "Chisuikai no kengian," *Yomiuri shinbun*, 27 November 1892, 2; "Chisuikai sōritsu iinkai," *Yomiuri shinbun*, 3 December 1892, 1; "Chisuikai konshinkai," *Yomiuri shinbun*, 13 December 1892, 1.
36   "Chisuikai taikai," *Yomiuri shinbun*, 17 January 1893, 1; "Teisei: Chisuikai taikai," *Yomiuri shinbun*, 19 January 1893, 1.

received guests from allied associations, and discussed and voted on proposi-
tions to be submitted on the floor of the Diet itself.[37]

The Flood Control Group brought Diet members together in common cause
and conversation about what river policies to pursue at the national level,
but there were disagreements within the organization about which rivers
to prioritize and how ambitious their agenda should be. For example, there
were two divergent proposals presented to the lower house by Flood Control
Group members during the 4th Diet session. On 13 January 1893, Asaka Kokukō
(1856–1914), a representative from Tokyo and founding member of the Flood
Control Group, put forward a request for the funding of dredging and levee
construction along fourteen rivers. After a lengthy discussion his request was
narrowly voted down with fifty-nine in favor and sixty-one against.[38] During
that same session, Yumoto had already submitted a more modest proposal for
the national government to begin new river work on four major rivers—the
Kiso, Yodo, Tone, and Shinano.[39] The lower house quickly voted to assign
a committee to research Yumoto's recommendations and voted for him to
serve as its chair. After delivering and debating the committee's report, on
17 February the lower house passed the proposal with 104 votes against and
127 votes in favor.[40] In this way, inside and outside the Diet, Yumoto and his
fellow lawmakers succeeded in forging a broad coalition that reached across
party and regional differences to draft legislation on river administration that
transformed the central government's funding of flood-control projects.

As the institutions of representative government developed at the national
level throughout the 1890s, political parties and special-interest groups like
these two flood-control organizations were increasingly able to draft and ultimately shape government policy on a variety of issues. The opportunity to
pass major flood-control legislation came toward the end of the second pre-
miership of Itō Hirobumi (1841–1909) from 1892 to 1896 when he broke with
his fellow oligarch Yamagata over the issue of keeping political parties out of
the ruling cabinet to ally with the Liberal Party.[41] With formal support from

---

37   At their 5 June 1894 general meeting, for example, there were reported to be about
      one hundred people in attendance, including members of another organization—the
      Alliance for Flood Control Implementation (Chisui Kisei Dōmeikai). "Chisuikai taikai no
      giketsu," Yomiuri shinbun, 6 June 1894, 2.
38   "Jūyon taisen chisui-hi kokko shishutsu no seigan," in Naikaku Kanpōkyoku, Kanpō:
      Shūgiin giji sokkiroku 26 (daily ed. 13 January 1893), 647–52.
39   "Kiso, Yodo, Tone, Shinano yondaisen no chisui ni kansuru kengian," in Naikaku
      Kanpōkyoku, Kanpō: Shūgiin giji sokkiroku 9 (daily ed. 10 December 1892), 192–96.
40   "Kiso, Yodo, Tone, Shinano yondaisen no chisui ni kansuru kengian," in Naikaku
      Kanpōkyoku, Kanpō: Shūgiin giji sokkiroku 37 (daily ed. 17 February 1893), 834–46.
41   Mitani, "The Establishment of Party Cabinets," 65.

Itō and the end of the financial and political exigencies resulting from the
First Sino-Japanese War (1894–95) with the Qing Empire, on 10 March 1896
Yumoto formally submitted the bill for the River Law, which passed the lower
house and was forwarded to the upper house on 14 March.[42] In the upper
house, Furuichi Kōi was called upon to represent the government and respond
to legislators' questions ranging from the proposed law's differences with
Tokugawa-period flood-control policies to its general scope and intent.[43]
While the upper house was deliberating the bill for the River Law, the lower
house approved funding for Okino's revised improvement plan for the Yodo
River.[44] Finally, on 26 and 27 March—just days before the closing of the 9th
Imperial Diet—the upper house approved both the River Law and the funding to improve the Yodo River.[45] In the following year, the Diet also speedily
passed the related Forestry Law and Erosion Prevention Law, which along with
the River Law were referred to at the time as the "three flood-control laws"
(chisui sanpō). The historian Michael Lewis has pointed out that the type of
"river politics" leading to the passage of these laws also created a "pattern of
interaction between local and national politicians [that] endured" to shape
subsequent public works projects throughout the twentieth century.[46]

Where the River Law reflected a broad techno-political confluence at the
national level, it also marked the ascendancy of a new approach to river management that had a long-term influence on the reframing of relations between
rivers, local communities, and governmental authority. The River Law replaced
the administrative system that had evolved to govern the country's rivers by
providing the relevant government minister, in most cases the Home Minister,
with the legal authority to plan, fund, and execute projects that were deemed
to have a "significant connection to the public interest" (kōkyō no rigai ni
jūdai no kankei ari).[47] For example, although the law continued to delegate

---

42   "Kasen hōan," in Naikaku Kanpōkyoku, Kanpō: Shūgiin giji sokkiroku 38 (daily ed.
      15 March 1896), 613–16.

43   "Kasen hōan," in Naikaku Kanpōkyoku, Kanpō: Kizokugiin giji sokkiroku 37 (daily ed.
      17 March 1896), 427–29.

44   Kensetsushō Kinki Chihōkyoku, ed., Yodogawa hyaku-nen shi (Osaka: Kensetsushō Kinki
      Chihōkyoku, 1974), 339–40.

45   "Kasen hōan," in Naikaku Kanpōkyoku, Kanpō: Kizokugiin giji sokkiroku 41 (daily ed.
      25 March 1896), 603–8.

46   Michael Lewis examines the 1896 River Law in the context of Toyama Prefecture and
      argues that the River Law became a primary means by which local politicians in Toyama
      could gain national funding for local riparian projects, albeit at the expense of weakened
      local autonomy. Michael Lewis, Becoming Apart, 73–117.

47   "Kasenhō," in Hōrei zensho, ed. Naikaku Kanpōkyoku (Tokyo: Naikaku Kanpōkyoku,
      1896), 120–31.

responsibility for smaller rivers to the prefectures, Article 8 stipulated that the national government had the authority to execute "improvement work" (*kairyō kōji*) on river projects that were defined as extending beyond a single prefecture or those that were deemed particularly difficult, very costly, or part of a larger river project.[48] The River Law also forbade the private ownership of riverbeds and water flow, both of which were affirmed to be the property of the state.[49] In this regard, the law sustained the older Tokugawa principle that granted the government suzerain rights over the country's waters and expressed the influence of French and German legal ideas on Japan's new constitution and codices of laws.

In addition to prohibiting the private ownership of the country's rivers and their flowage, the law included four articles that addressed usufruct rights regarding rivers, their waters, banks and beds, regardless of existing customary practice or historical precedent. Specifically, the law granted the national government, or delegated to an appropriate prefectural entity, the authority to regulate the movement of boats, rafts, and logs on a river (Article 16); the building, rebuilding, or moving of structures that impede, draw from, or pour into a river (Article 17); the utilization of the bed and water flow of a river (Article 18); and any construction or other act that altered the direction, cleanliness, amount, width, and depth of the water flow or bed of a river (Article 19).[50] In the event of dangerous high-waters (*kōsui no kiken*), the law granted the prefectural authorities the extraordinary right to seize property, to appropriate wood, bamboo, soil and other materials, to requisition horses, wagons, and other means of transport, and to remove houses and other structures (Article 23).[51] In order to prevent or lessen washouts, landslides, and other problems related to flooding, the law also authorized the ordering of adjacent landowners to pay for the upkeep of part or all of the planting of that land with trees, bamboo, brush, or grass and even the expropriation of that land through the Land Expropriation Law (Tochi Shūyōhō) (Article 46).[52] Moreover, "to increase the public benefit of a river and remove or reduce public harm" (*kasen no kōri o zōshin shi mata wa kōgai o jokyaku moshiku wa keigen suru*), the law authorized restrictions on adjacent land and houses along with areas to be used for the construction of new river channels (Articles 47 and 48).[53] Finally, for those individuals who failed to follow these regulations and decisions pertaining to them, the law also

---

48   "Kasenhō," 121–22.
49   "Kasenhō," 122.
50   "Kasenhō," 123.
51   "Kasenhō," 124.
52   "Kasenhō," 128.
53   "Kasenhō," 128.

granted the proper authorities the right to fine them upward of 200 yen and to order the police, who were part of the Home Ministry, to enforce these regulation and decisions (Articles 57 and 58).[54]

The River Law exemplified the emerging techno-political framework that helped form Japan's modern river regime and govern the nation as a whole. It was the first and only law, until the passage of the Road Law in 1919, to clearly regulate "public property" (kōbutsu). The vagueness of the law's definition of "public interest" (kōkyō no rigai) also allowed for considerable leeway in interpretation, extending the central government's authority into the affairs of communities as well as prefectural and local governments. Accordingly, the law played an important role in reshaping long-standing riparian relations between rivers, the communities along them, and the governmental entities authorized to regulate and reengineer them. In terms of politics, the law was ambiguous in defining who should determine what the "public interest" was and what the limits should be when the state claimed to act in the interests of the public and nation. This ambiguity is perhaps not surprising considering the rising influence at the time of the state bureaucracy and the concept of bureaucratic transcendentalism. In fact, Tsuzuki Keiroku (1861–1923), the person most likely to have drafted the final version of the River Law, had in 1892 written essays about this very concept and entitled them "Bureaucratism" (Kanri ron) and "Transcendentalism" (Chōzen shugi).[55] He argued that government ministers through their very roles within the constitutional system, were entrusted to serve the interests of the nation by making decisions based on rigorous research and not on the uninformed opinions of the people, the self-interests of political parties, or the mercurial will of the Diet.[56] Following the sometimes violent protests associated with the Home Ministry's efforts to expropriate land for its work along the Kiso River during the 1880s, the River Law expressed Tsuzuki's and other Home Ministry officials' views about the need for the state to have the ultimate authority to develop wise and well-informed plans and to implement them with limited interference from local

---

54   "Kasenhō," 130.

55   Tsuzuki Keiroku studied politics and finance in both Germany and France, was the son-in-law of oligarch Inoue Kaoru (Home Minister from 1892 to 1894), secretary and confidant of Prime Minister Yamagata Aritomo, and during most of the drafting and passage of the River Law, served as the head of the Civil Engineering Bureau (Dobokukyoku) within the Home Ministry. Junji Banno, The Establishment of the Japanese Constitutional System, trans. J. A. A. Stockwin (London: Routledge, 1992), 31–38; Keikōkai, ed., Tsuzuki Keiroku-den (Tokyo: Yumani Shobō, 2002).

56   Tsuzuki Keiroku, "Kanri ron" and "Chōzen shugi," in Kanryōsei keisatsu: Nihon kindai shisō taikei, ed. Yui Masaomi and Obinata Sumio (Tokyo: Iwanami Shoten, 1990), 157–63, 163–76.

communities and political parties. The enhanced state power granted by the River Law was not overlooked. As emphasized at the beginning of this chapter, it was during deliberation in the upper house about the bill for the River Law that Mitsukuri Rinshō faulted several provisions of the law for their ambiguity and the unprecedented authority they appeared to grant the Home Ministry.[57] Where the law did touch on usufruct and property rights, the focus was overwhelmingly on clarifying the authority of the Home Ministry, for example, to tax potential users, requisition building materials from adjacent lands, and appropriate land to accomplish "river improvement work" (*kasen no kairyō kōji*). By making the country's rivers the sole object of this new legal instrument, the law provided Home Ministry officials and engineers with the authority to reduce long-standing riparian relations to those that they deemed to be of the greatest "public interest." Perhaps not surprisingly, the public that seems to have most mattered was the voting public of rural elites whose representatives in the Diet controlled the budgets for the Home Ministry and other government ministries.

The River Law not only clarified the authority of the Home Ministry to decide and undertake projects that it deemed to be important, but it also simplified the funding model that would henceforth be used to pay for new river projects. As discussed in chapter 3, the national government under the old administrative system negotiated in 1875 oversaw and paid for the straightening, dredging, diverting of rivers, and control of erosion in what it called "preventative work" (*yobō no kō*), leaving the prefectures to attend to the more localized "defensive work" (*bōgyo no kō*) of levee building and repair. This arrangement proved unworkable for two reasons. On the one hand, from the 1880s onward, local elites and prefectural authorities argued that they could no longer assume the burden of this costly "defensive work." On the other hand, Home Ministry officials and engineers, such as De Rijke and Okino, found the administrative division of labor and engineering projects confounding because it expected them to leave integral levee work to the prefectures while attending to larger "preventative work" along portions of the country's main rivers. Under the River Law, this administrative and budgetary distinction was eliminated. In its place, the national government could essentially administer and cover the costs of

---

57   After having studied law in Germany and France, Mitsukuri returned to Japan to play a significant role in the translation and interpretation of European law into Japan. In translating among other things, the Napoleonic Code (Code civil des Français), for instance, he is credited with providing the Japanese translations for essential legal terms like "right" (*kenri*), "obligation" (*gimu*), and "constitution" (*kenpō*). Tazaki Tetsurō, "Mitsukuri Rinshō," in *Kokushi daijiten*, ed. Kokushi Daijiten Henshū Iinkai (Tokyo: Yoshikawa Kōbunkan, 1992), 13:368.

any river project that the Home Ministry determined to have a "significant connection to the public interest." Since the early 1890s, politicians, including Yumoto Yoshinori, Yamada Shōzaburō, and Ōhashi Fusatarō, had been raising these issues inside and outside the Imperial Diet. Their clamoring for more river funding had been abruptly suspended in 1894 when Japan entered the costly but ultimately successful war with the Qing Empire over which of the two powers would exercise supreme influence on the Korean peninsula.

Following the war and the conclusion of treaty negotiations in November 1895, Japan won a sizable indemnity from the Qing government that directly influenced debates in the 9th Diet about funding for public works, such as the River Law and two bills to fund new engineering projects along the Yodo River and the Chikugo River in southern Kyushu. Unwilling to raise land taxes on themselves to pay for the greater scale and scope of the Yodo and other proposed river projects, the predominantly landowning membership of the Diet finally approved the use of a sliver of the more than 360 million yen indemnity from the Qing Empire for these river projects.[58] However, owing to ongoing budget shortfalls and a subsequent war with the Russian Empire in 1904–05, the Home Ministry was only able to apply its enhanced authority to ten river projects throughout the country between 1896 and 1910.[59]

During this fifteen-year period, two of the most important projects were undertaken along the Yodo and Tone Rivers.[60] Mostly following Okino's 1894 plan, the Yodo River Improvement Works succeeded in transforming three lengthy areas within the Yodo River basin by dredging and building a barrage at the headwaters of the Seta River; shifting channels and extending levees to separate the Katsura, Uji, and Kizu Rivers from each other and Ogura Lake as

58 The Qing Empire paid this indemnity to Japan over a seven-year period beginning in 1897. Equivalent to roughly two-and-half years of the Japanese government's revenue at the time. While most of this money was channeled to the military, some of it provided a vital funding source for the reengineering of the Yodo, Chikugo, and other flood-prone rivers. Takeuchi Minoru, ed., *Nicchū kokkō kihonbunken shū* (Tokyo: Sōsōsha, 1993), 1:48.

59 After passage of the River Law and before the financial exigencies of the 1904–5 Russo-Japanese War, the Home Ministry began improvement projects along the following six rivers: Yodo, Kiso, Tone, Chikugo, Shō, and Kuzuryū. It was not until 1906, however, that the River Law was applied to new work along the Onga, Shinano, Yoshino, and Takahashi Rivers. Matsuura Shigeki, *Kokudo no kaihatsu to kasen: jōri-sei kara damu kaihatsu made* (Tokyo: Kashima Shuppankai, 1989), 115.

60 While the River Law was also applied to the Kiso River for dredging and construction carried out between 1898 and 1912, this work largely extended and completed dredging and levee building already begun under what was subsequently called the Lower Kiso River Improvement Works (Kisogawa Karyū Kaishū Kōji), which had been implemented on a year-by-year basis between 1887 and 1900 along the lower Kiso, Nagara, and Ibi Rivers. Gifu-ken, ed., *Gifu-ken chisuishi* (Gifu: Gifu-ken, 1953), 2:485–544.

they flowed into the Yodo; and excavating an entirely new downstream channel to the bay with a high-water capacity of 5,560 m³/s that was kept separate from the city of Osaka by a barrage-equipped series of levees. This Yodo River Improvement Project was completed over fifteen years (1896–1910), cost over thirteen million yen, expropriated 1,137 ha of land, moved 4,329 people and their homes, dredged and excavated over 10 million m³ of soil, built or widened more than seventy levees with a total length of some 40 km, and eliminated numerous meanders to straighten the overall river channel.[61]

For the larger and longer Tone River, the Home Ministry applied the River Law to construction beginning in 1900. At that time, the ministry only had the resources to reengineer a portion of the Tone so it divided its work on the river into three stages with the first being the 42 km stretch from Sawara to the mouth of the river at Chōshi.[62] It was through this flat area, where it was often difficult to distinguish the Tone River from its interconnected lakes and marshes, that the ministry built new levees and water-gates to separate the river from the Yoda and Nasaka Lakes as well as a 20 km long levee along the right bank from Sawara to Sasagawa. In carrying out this work, Ministry engineers focused on creating an unobstructed and relatively straight channel. They oversaw the elimination of distributaries and meanders to make a single riverbed that it dredged to a uniform depth and gradually widened from 600 to 1,300 m so that it could handle up to 3,750 m³/s of water during floods. Within this wide channel designed to high-water specifications, the ministry also dredged a narrower 180–330 m wide "low-water channel" (*teisuiro*) that would preserve an average depth of 4.5 to 5.5 m for riverboat traffic. Altogether, this dredging and construction of levees on the lower Tone River required nine years, nearly six million yen, the expropriation of 632 ha of mostly farm land, the dredging and excavation of over 20 million m³ of soil, and the building of about 40 km of levees.[63] Meanwhile, in 1902, Furuichi Kōi is believed to have played an instrumental role in drafting a plan that would relocate the village of Yanaka in order to allow floodwaters from the Watarase with its poisonous affluent from the upstream Ashio Copper Mine to overflow into the Akama

---

61   Kensetsushō Kinki Chihōkyoku, *Yodogawa hyaku-nen shi*, 383–435.
62   Further upstream on the Tone River during this period, the Home Ministry also oversaw limited repair work on the channel and levees below the Kawamata sluice to the Kasai Canal (Kasai Yōsui), work on the levees and embankments where the Edo River diverges from the Tone River, and erosion control work around Mount Haruna in Gunma prefecture. Tonegawa Hyaku-nen Shi Henshū Iinkai, ed., *Tonegawa hyaku-nen shi* (Tokyo: Kokudo Kaihatsu Gijutsu Kenkyū Sentā, 1987), 605.
63   Ōkuma Takashi, *Tonegawa chisui no hensen to suigai* (Tokyo: Tōkyō Shuppankai, 1981), 137–52; Tonegawa Hyaku-nen Shi Hensan Iinkai, *Tonegawa hyaku-nen shi*, 603–22.

Marsh rather than into the Tone River.[64] To execute the work along the Yodo, Tone, and the other eight rivers for which the River Law had been enacted during this time, the Home Ministry also imported and manufactured some of its own steam-powered dredgers and tugboats, locomotives and mining carts, and other kinds of industrial construction equipment so that it could undertake the sheer scale of these river reengineering projects. Although the technical specifications of Okino's and other engineers' plans and the use of novel construction equipment certainly heralded a new era in river engineering and management, the politics behind the drafting and passage of the River Law were also instrumental in the formation of Japan's modern river regime.

The River Law clarified the authority and budgetary responsibilities of national and prefectural governments; it also established the legal framework through which the Home Ministry and its engineers could reengineer the country's rivers and thereby the riparian relations they helped constitute. The national government's approach was neither unique to Japan nor entirely new. Rather, the Home Ministry and its engineers were participants in a "global modernity" wherein colonial and national governments the world over explained that they were "improving" rivers by preventing their destructive floods and by tapping a vast "natural resource" for the benefit of a nation's or colony's agriculture and industry. Moreover, the blueprint for the Home Ministry's efforts to "improve" the country's rivers was none other than Okino's 1894 plan that targeted flood control with few allowances for navigability, fishing, or other uses. To accomplish this goal along the Yodo, Okino called for the excavation of a new straighter channel through the delta; the dredging of sandbars and shoals to create a primary channel of uniform depth; the building of taller and stronger levees; and the construction of two large barrages to allow for greater and more centralized control of the flow and level of the river's water. The specifications of these various design features were all based on the highest floodwaters the Yodo was predicted to exhibit, which itself was a calculation based on the historic flooding of the river in 1885. Thus, while

---

64   Ōkuma Takashi, *Kōzui to chisui no kasen shi: suigai seiatsu kara juyō e* (Tokyo: Heibonsha, 1988), 163–65. Much has rightly been written in Japanese and English about the Ashio Copper Mine pollution incident itself and the government's reluctant response. For a survey of this history in Japanese and the most relevant work in English, see the following: Shōji Kichirō and Sugai Masurō, *Tsūshi: Ashio kōdoku jiken, 1877–1984* (Yokohama: Seoroshi Shobō, 2014); Alan Atwood Stone, "The Vanishing Village: The Ashio Copper Mine Pollution Case, 1890–1907," PhD diss., University of Washington, 1974; Fred Notehelfer, "Japan's First Pollution Incident," *Journal of Japanese Studies* 1, no. 2 (1975): 351–83; Kenneth Strong, *Ox against the Storm: A Biography of Tanaka Shozo, Japan's Conservationist Pioneer* (Vancouver: University of Columbia Press, 1977); Walker, *Toxic Archipelago*, 71–107; Stolz, *Bad Water*, 19–116.

required to work with the Diet and its politicians who controlled the ministry's budget, Home Ministry officials and engineers gained the enhanced authority to begin reengineering the country's biggest rivers in accordance with what it determined to be in the best interest of the public. In this way, the River Law enabled the Home Ministry to begin building Japan's modern river regime. Ministry officials and engineers externalized from their plans and projects a myriad of riparian relations that it chose to ignore or simply did not fully understand at the time in order to redesign the nation's rivers with the primary aim of protecting against the flooding of the nation's farmlands and factories. Correspondingly, from 1896 onward, the River Law also played a vital role in reframing riparian relations along the Yodo, Tone, and other important rivers around the country by contributing to the ongoing elaboration of new boundaries and meanings for state, society, and nature.

3   The 1910 Flooding of Tokyo and Paris

What had begun as a modest effort to reengineer portions of ten rivers became, after 1910, an orchestrated endeavor to reengineer all of the country's main rivers. The result of these measures was the building of Japan's modern river regime. Although fourteen years had passed since the promulgation of the 1896 River Law, the Home Ministry had to date only been able to initiate a handful of engineering projects along select portions of major rivers. In the meantime, the population of the country had grown by almost 20 percent, arable and often irrigated land had continued to increase, factories had begun to replace farmland around the expanding edges of cities, railways were extending deeper into the country's steep river valleys, and the nation had defeated the Russian Empire in a costly war, and through that victory acquired new leaseholds and colonial territories on the continent. Together with its European and North American peers, Japan was rapidly becoming a modern, industrial, and imperial power. In 1910, however, a disastrous flood on the scale of the earlier 1742 and 1786 floods (chapter 2) inundated the capital city of Tokyo and much of the Kantō Plain. In that same year, Paris and the surrounding French countryside had also suffered an enormously destructive flood. A comparison of the experience and response to these two floods is illustrative of the Japanese state's drive to build a modern river regime that permanently transformed riparian relations along its primary rivers.

     The flood in Japan began on 1 August 1910 as a series of summer storms. After a week of nearly continuous rain, the saturated soil of the Kantō region's mountains and highlands could hold no more water. Countless underground springs bubbled into streams, which in turn gushed from steep mountain valleys and into already swollen rivers as they began to pour forth into the bottom-lands of the Kantō Plain. These streams and rivers inexorably flowed downhill along the path of least resistance into one another and together into the Tone, Ara, and Tama Rivers. Bound for the Pacific Ocean and Tokyo Bay, these larger rivers began bursting levees as they sought out their historic routes to the sea, which remained etched in the region's geologic memory. Once free of their levee-bound riverbeds, the racing rivers slowed as they spread over shallow valleys, inundating fields and farms in five prefectures across the Kantō region. All the while, the rain kept falling.

By 10 August, the floodwaters had surged across the whole of the Kantō Plain and were pouring into Tokyo proper. Already well above the level of the devastating flood of 1907, the Ara River posed the greatest threat to the capital. Running west to east across the north of the city, the Ara became the Sumida River where it abruptly turned southward toward Tokyo Bay. For its part, the Sumida marked the western end of a broad delta that extended eastward for nearly 20 km to the Edo River, which flowed along the base of the Shimōsa Highlands in Chiba Prefecture. During the previous two decades, much of Tokyo's industrial and urban growth had occurred on this delta. Where the waters of the 1702, 1742, and 1786 flooding of the Ara and the Sumida Rivers had mostly inundated fields and farms, they now increasingly coursed through city streets and across factory floors.

Amidst that week's reportage on the rising water, the national daily *Yomiuri shinbun* ran a full-page article on 12 August entitled the "Water Torture of Tokyo." In the article, the reporter wrote of the difficulty of traveling the day before to various parts of the city where the flooding of local streams had inundated neighborhoods and begun to cut off street and rail traffic. In the flood-prone area of Mukōjima on the eastern bank of the Sumida, the water had risen to more than a meter "above the flood boards" at Suijin Shrine, Kanegafuchi Filature, Hashimoto Paper Processing Factory, and the villas of Count Gotō Shinpei (1857–1929) and the Sumo Elder of Kasugano Stable.[65] In Tokyo and elsewhere in Japan, flooding below the floorboards was a common if irksome event during the summer; it rarely warranted comment in a major newspaper like the *Yomiuri*. That the water had risen so high above the floorboards without the bursting of a major levee was reason for concern, comment, and speculation as to when and where one of the levees protecting Tokyo would fail.

The first breach occurred later that day. When making his way along the levee at Mukōjima, the *Yomiuri* reporter explained that he suddenly heard the loud, discordant beating of a drum. Hurrying to the nearby Shirahige Shrine,

65   "Mizuzeme no Tōkyō," *Yomiuri shinbun*, 12 August 1910, 6.

where people were furiously sandbagging, he was told the drumming was a signal relayed from further to the north about the collapse of a levee on the Ayase River. In past breaches of the Ayase, floodwaters poured southward on the inside of the levee through Mukōjima's districts like Ko'ume and into the populous Honjo Ward.[66] And this time was no different. Despite the additional soil and clay that had been added to the levees at Ayase and Mukōjima following the flooding of 1907, the levee at Mukōjima failed after the one at Ayase had given way. Elsewhere, other levees were also breaking along the Ara, Tama, Tone, and several smaller canals and rivers. The worst, however, was yet to come.

During the next two days, the rivers continued their relentless rise. As an elderly resident of the area near Shirahige Shrine explained to the *Yomiuri* reporter, the waters flowing before them on 11 August were from the heavy rains that had fallen two days earlier. The Sumida River, he stressed, would not crest until the water from the previous day's heavy rains reached the city.[67] The old man's prediction proved correct. Over the next two days, another storm blew over the region, and the rising waters of the Ara pushed their way southward through broken levees to turn both sides of the river from Kawaguchi to the bay into what was often described as a "sea of mud" (*doroumi*).

By the time the clouds finally cleared on 16 August, the weather station at Naguri Village west of Tokyo had measured a record 1,219 mm of rain in just over two weeks.[68] In Tokyo, the floodwaters were more than 3 m in some areas. Where possible, people moved their families and possessions into second-story attics or onto rooftops. Others camped atop levees, found shelter in railroad boxcars, or slogged their way to makeshift refugee centers set up at local schools, shrines, and temples.[69] As relief and recovery operations began, the Home Ministry released a report estimating that across nineteen prefectures over 340,000 ha had been flooded, nearly half a million homes had been damaged, another four thousand homes had been swept away, and some 1,434 people were either missing or dead.[70] In the city of Tokyo alone, the flooding caused well over one hundred million yen in damage, left nearly 200,000 thousand homes and buildings severely damaged or destroyed, swept away or damaged nearly nine hundred bridges, and killed fifty-two people.[71]

66   "Mizuzeme no Tōkyō," 6.
67   "Mizuzeme no Tōkyō," 6.
68   Saitama-ken, ed., *Arakawa* (Urawa: Saitama-ken, 1988), 3:88.
69   "Mizuzeme no Tōkyō," 6.
70   "Higai chōsa tōkei," *Yomiuri shinbun*, 20 August 1910, 2.
71   Tōkyō-fu Naimubu Shomuka, *Meiji yonjūsan-nen Tōkyō-fu suigai tōkei* (Tokyo: Tōkyō-fu Naimubu Shōmuka, 1911), 2–6.

Earlier that same year, a record-breaking flood also inundated Paris for several weeks. Although wintertime flooding was not unusual, exceptionally warm weather in early January 1910 melted the mountain snowpack and brought heavy rains to the region, causing the Seine to swell some 6 m over its normal level as it flowed through Paris. The effect on the City of Light was devastating. As the city's extensive underground infrastructure filled with water, basement power generators and pumps stopped working, the recently electrified city grew dark, the Métro came to a halt, and sewers and cesspools belched forth their putrid contents onto the streets. Afterward, the government recorded that over 24,000 homes had been flooded, almost 14,000 people evacuated, about 55,000 people had required hospitalization, and put the damage at roughly 400 million francs.[72]

During the flooding in Tokyo that summer, some found it remarkable that both national capitals had suffered such destructive flooding in the very same year. As if in response to such talk, one observer dismissed these idle comparisons by pointing out a number of differences, such as the slow-rising character of the Seine, Japan's steeply sloped rivers, Paris' higher and sturdier buildings, and the varying infrastructure of the two cities.[73] A senior secretary in the French embassy in Tokyo offered the even more pointed comment that the flooding in Tokyo was a "minor tragedy" (shōsanji) not to be compared to the horrendous damage wrought by the flooding in Paris. He went on to assert that the French government had been more humane in issuing immediate orders to control the price of bread and later offered monetary relief to the afflicted.[74] In his history of the 1910 Paris Flood, the historian Jeffery Jackson confirms the secretary's observation, but also clarifies that the authorities in Paris sought to control bread prices because they feared a "breakdown of law and order" and were frequently accused of being overly stingy when doling out relief funds and loans.[75] Just beneath the surface in both of these commentaries lay a common criticism of Japan as being less technologically developed, less humane, and less civilized than France. Nonetheless, people who had read reports and seen photos of Paris under water must have been amazed at the similar power of the Seine and Sumida to wreak havoc on these metropolitan capitals. What these contemporary observers did not comment on were the common ways in which engineers, politicians, and ministerial officials in the two countries attempted to prevent such flooding before and after 1910.

---

72   Jeffrey H. Jackson, *Paris under Water: How the City of Light Survived the Great Flood of 1910* (New York: Palgrave-Macmillan, 2010), 205.

73   Tanaka Jirō, "Kōsui zatsuwa," *Yomiuri shinbun*, 18 August 1910, 5.

74   "Pari no kōsui to Tōkyō," *Yomiuri shinbun*, 20 August 1910, 4.

75   Jackson, *Paris under Water*, 89, 195–202.

In the aftermath of the 1910 floods, both national governments embraced the modern river regime. Despite obvious geographic and cultural differences, the technocratic overseers of rivers in France and Japan revived existing plans and pursued a panoply of similarly inspired projects along the Seine and Sumida that in subsequent years would be used to reengineer rivers throughout both nations and empires and would presage the later pursuit of multipurpose development plans centered on massive hydroelectric dams. In France and Japan, these once region-shaping rivers drew the attention of nation-building officials and their respective ministries who appointed special commissions to channel legal, financial, and technical expertise toward the goal of "improving" their rivers.[76] As discussed in chapters 3 and 4, state engineers in the two metropoles drew on lessons learned from widely circulated books and reports and from university lecture halls. They toured completed projects in metropoles and colonies to produce plans based on a scientific view of the river as belonging to an entire basin (*ryūiki* and *bassin*) and their role within the even larger hydrological cycle.[77] Sharing this broad hydraulic vision, engineers in both countries began their work by dispatching well-funded survey teams equipped with gauges, theodolites, plumb lines, and other instruments to measure the seasonal variation of channels and water flow at key points along the rivers and their tributaries. Ultimately, they sought, as James C. Scott has argued, to make these rivers even more "legible."[78] And afterward they drafted plans to redesign the Seine and Sumida to protect the surrounding countryside and to mobilize what had come to be seen as a natural resource for

---

76   In October 1910, the Imperial Diet in Japan approved the formation of a forty-five-member Special Flood Control Survey Committee: "Chin Rinji Chisui Chōsakai kansei," in Ōkurashō Insatsukyoku, *Kanpō*, No. 8198, (daily ed. 18 October 1910), 445. "Floods in France: Precautionary Measures by the Government," *The Times*, 9 July 1910, 7; "The Paris Floods Commission," *The Times*, 24 August 1910, 13. For a broad overview of changes to river management in France with a focus on the Rhône, see Pritchard, *Confluence*, esp. chapter 1.

77   In France, for example, Thomé De Gamond (1807–76), who was an engineer and well-known advocate of a channel tunnel below the Straits of Dover, argued for the "transformation of the wild stream into a civilized river" and to subject rivers to "the absolute discipline of a totally stable regime." Thomé de Gamond Louis Joseph Aimé, *Mémoire sur le régime général des eaux courantes. Plan d'ensemble pour la transformation de l'appareil hydraulique de la France* (Paris: Dunod, 1871). Quoted in Francois Molle, "River-Basin Planning and Management: Social Life of a Concept," *Geoforum* 40, no. 3 (2009): 486; Jamie Linton, "Is the Hydrologic Cycle Sustainable? A Historical-Geographical Critique of a Modern Concept," *Annals of the Association of American Geographers* 98, no. 3 (2008): 630–49.

78   James C. Scott, *Seeing Like a State: How Certain Schemes to Improve the Human Condition Have Failed* (New Haven: Yale University Press, 1998), 2–3.

the development of national economies.[79] These engineering designs, identified in Japan as a "high-water" approach to river engineering, included dredging entire stretches of rivers to uniform depths, raising the height of floodwalls
and levees, rebuilding bridges with narrower pilings and higher clearances,
using diversionary canals to channel floodwaters around urban areas, and proposing ways to improve the navigability and port facilities in each of the capital cities. The French government soon suspended all plans and construction
during the First World War of 1914–18. The Japanese government, on the other
hand, deployed over the next two decades an array of dredgers, excavators,
pumps, and other industrial equipment as well as battalions of wage-earning
laborers along the Tone River and the middle and lower sections of the Ara
River. In the end, the Sumida was essentially replaced by the massive concrete-
lined Ara River Drainage Canal (Arakawa Hōsuiro).

The two great floods that struck Tokyo and Paris in 1910 were a historical coin-
cidence, but the similarity of plans and engineering work carried out along the
Sumida and the Seine after the flooding suggest a shared history that belongs
to an era of global modernity.[80] This shared history also included these two
rivers as historical actors. As emphasized in the earlier chapters, these rivers
were actors that caused these events and invited responses from other actors.
In the case of Japan, this involved Tokyo's residents, Diet politicians, and Home
Ministry engineers. Although the circumstances that led to the flooding of the
Sumida and the Seine differed, in the early twentieth century government officials and engineers in both countries worked from a common script that suggested how each should fashion their own techno-political response. Rather
than looking upon Paris or other European metropoles as a fixed fount of
scientific knowledge during this period, modern engineering knowledge and
technology used in Japan and France at this time were in constant circulation

79   In 1888, the Tokyo Municipal Planning Committee met repeatedly over several months
      to discuss hundreds of projects, including the improvement of the Sumida River. *Tōkyō
      shiku kaisei iinkai gijiroku*, 18 October 1888, reprinted in Fujimori Terunobu, ed., *Tōkyō
      toshi keikaku shiryō shūsei* (Tokyo: Honnoyūsha, 1987), 1:184–88. "Paris a Seaport: History
      of the Project," *The Times*, 21 December 1910, 15; "Flood Dangers in Paris: Protective
      Measures," *The Times*, 13 January 1928, 14. The historian Sabine Barles provides a brief
      overview of some of the projects that were carried out along the Seine in the decades
      after the flood of 1910 in "The Seine as a Parisian River: Its Imprint, Its Ascendancy, and Its
      Mutual Dependencies in the Eighteenth through the Twentieth Century," in *Rivers Lost,
      Rivers Regained: Rethinking City-River Relations*, ed. Uwe Lübken, Martin Knoll, and Dieter
      Schott (Pittsburgh: University of Pittsburgh Press, 2017), 57–58.
80   Benite, "Modernity: The Sphinx and the Historian"; Sheldon Garon, "Transnational
      History and Japan's 'Comparative Advantage'," *Journal of Japan Studies* 43, no. 1 (2017):
      65–92; Prasenjit Duara, *The Crisis of Global Modernity: Asian Traditions and a Sustainable
      Future* (Cambridge: Cambridge University Press, 2015), 53–91.

and an essential part of the transnational relations that increasingly bound Paris, Delft, and Berlin to Tokyo, Osaka, and other cities and places around the globe. The uneven distribution of wealth and political power ensured that the balance of those transnational relations was highly unequal and mediated by the developing international system centered on the empires and states of Europe, Japan, and the United States. Thus, when engineers and government authorities in Tokyo and Paris transformed local riparian relations along the Sumida and the Seine, they did so within these interconnected national, imperial, and global contexts.

4   The Effects of Building Japan's Modern River Regime

Few of the main rivers in central Japan escaped the effects of the 1910 flooding. Even fewer escaped the Home Ministry's efforts to reengineer rivers in the following decades. In 1911, the Imperial Diet approved a plan and budget that authorized the Home Ministry to apply the River Law in two phases to sixty-five rivers over the next decades. Because the ministry's subsequent reengineering of these rivers often changed their channel, depth, and slope, prefectural governments were obliged to carry out similar projects on the smaller rivers and irrigation canals that either flowed into or drew water from these larger rivers. In the aftermath of the 1910, existing riparian relations along major and minor waterways around the country were gradually reassembled to form Japan's modern river regime. Budget cutting and the Great Kantō Earthquake of September 1923 forced a shrinkage of the first phase of river work, and Japan's invasion of Manchuria and then the rest of China in the 1930s led to the permanent postponement of the second phase of river projects. The ministry, nonetheless, oversaw work on about forty rivers during these three decades in accordance with the "high-water" principles that had been first institutionalized in the earlier Yodo River Improvement Works. This entailed the narrowing of floodplains, the straightening of channels, and the building of bigger and stronger levees with the primary aim of preventing flooding, and secondarily to improve the supply of water to rural and urban communities. Although the devastating effects of flooding were reduced, the consequences for other riparian relations along the Tone and Yodo Rivers were irreversible. The ministry replaced looping meanders, broad floodplains, and the sandbars and islands that were common to most rivers with straight and narrow channels in an effort to make them more efficient at shedding summertime floodwaters. At the same time, they built weirs, barrages, and eventually upstream dams across these rivers to better control seasonal fluctuations in waterflow. Moreover, many of the marshes and lakes through which these rivers once flowed were severed from their life-preserving rivers and subsequently drained or buried. As a result, the relations that held various riparian assemblages together frayed and often completely unraveled.

Following the flooding of August 1910, Diet members and government officials moved quickly to reassess the nation's priorities. The inundation of Tokyo and the surrounding Kantō region temporarily cut all railway and telegraph lines between Prime Minister Katsura Tarō, at that time summering at the base of Mount Asama in the resort town of Karuizawa, and his government in Tokyo as they entered into the final negotiations of the treaty that led to Japan's annexation of Korea on 22 August.[81] Once the floodwaters receded and the prime minister returned to the capital, the national government formed a forty-five-member Special Flood Control Survey Committee (Rinji Chisui Chōsakai) to review the country's existing efforts to prevent flooding and how to utilize the country's rivers to promote agricultural and industrial development.[82] The committee was composed top officials in various government ministries, several Diet members, and seven engineers, including Furuichi Kōi and Okino Tadao.[83] The committee also included the retired Yumoto Yoshinori, who as noted earlier had been a Diet member from Saitama Prefecture and was instrumental in the drafting and passage of the 1896 River Law.

Meeting for the first time on 25 October 1910 the committee deliberated over how best to respond to the immediate damage to levees, roads, and bridges.[84] They also sought to draft a nationwide plan to prevent this kind of flooding and destruction in the future. For the sake of expediency and perhaps to limit criticism of political favoritism, the criteria used by the committee to determine the number of river projects and their priority boiled down to the following: the area of flat land (*heichi menseki*) within a river basin and the amount of flood damage recorded between 1896 and 1907.[85] Citing the authority granted to the government in Article 8 of the River Law, the committee agreed on a list

---

81   "Denshin denwa futsū," *Yomiuri shinbun*, 6 August 1910, 2; "Tetsudō fuku mata futsū," *Yomiuri shinbun*, 6 August 1910, 2; "Tetsudō fukkyū kasho," *Yomiuri shinbun*, 7 August 1910, 2; "Shachū no Katura-kō," *Yomiuri shinbun*, 7 August 1910, 2.

82   "Chin Rinji Chisui Chōsakai kansei," 445; "Chokurei kōfu: Rinji Chisui Chōsakai kansei," *Yomiuri shinbun*, 19 October 1910, 2; Osumikai Naimushō Shi Henshū Iinkai, ed., *Naimushō shi* (Tokyo: Chihō Zaimu Kyōkai, 1971), 3:24–27.

83   An additional four Home Ministry engineers were appointed to serve on the committee in a provisional or organizing capacity. "Chisuikai iin ninmei," *Tōkyō asahi shinbun*, 20 October 1910, 2.

84   "Rinji Chisui Chōsakai," *Yomiuri shinbun*, 26 October 1910, 2.

85   "Chisui chōsa sho-mondai," *Tōkyō asahi shinbun*, 14 November 1910, 2. The meeting minutes for the Special Flood Control Survey Committee's deliberation of proposed river work are archived at the Shisei Senmon Toshokan, Tokyo, as Rinji Chisui Chōsakai, *Rinji Chisui Chōsakai giji sokukiroku* (1910); Matsuura, *Kokudo no kaihatsu to kasen*, 116–18.

of fifty rivers that it divided into two phases of engineering work. During the first phase, they proposed that work on a total of twenty rivers should commence in the next year and be carried out within an eighteen-year period. During this phase, they also advised that surveys be conducted on the other thirty rivers that could then be used for the second phase of river work.[86] In the end, the committee added an additional fifteen smaller rivers to the proposal's second phase of river projects. This included, for instance, the Sakawa River in Kanagawa Prefecture that had given the Tokugawa government such difficulty following the 1707 eruption of Mount Fuji.

In January 1911, the committee formally submitted its proposal to the 27th Imperial Diet.[87] Although the proposal promised to renew efforts in forest conservation and erosion prevention, it clearly emphasized the expansion of the modern river regime of straightening and containing downstream waterways behind bigger and stronger levees. During one of seven question and answer sessions with the Diet's Budget Committee in February 1911, Okino cited the projects he had overseen along the Yodo River as an example of how the Home Ministry's emphasis on straightening downstream drainage systems without the same attention to upstream tributaries could be applied to other rivers. "Generally, if the main channel (*honryū*) of a river can be improved (*kaishū*) to enhance drainage (*sotsū*)," the senior engineer explained, "many tributaries can be controlled by improving or heightening portions of their levees. Because this is so, it has been decided that prefectural funds will first be used to improve tributaries."[88] In other words, to prevent a repeat of the widespread flooding of 1910, he argued for another division of rivers and resources in which the attention of the Home Ministry should be directed toward reengineering the country's main river channels and the prefectures should attend to those river's tributaries. With this focus on "improving" the "main channel" of Japan's largest rivers, the plan placed the Tone, Shinano, and Yodo Rivers at the top of its total list of sixty-five rivers to be worked on over the following decades (Table 2).

With the 1910 flood having directly affected the Tone River, the Home Ministry's lead engineers spent several weeks and months studying the scale and effects of the flooding before thoroughly revising and expanding the existing plans for the river. Unquestioning in their commitment to the high-water approach of engineering and administering rivers, these engineers instead

86 Osumikai Naimushō Shi Henshū Iinkai, *Naimushō shi*, 3:24–25.
87 Naikaku Kanpōkyoku, ed., *Kanpō: Shūgiin giji sokkiroku* 3 (daily ed. 22 January 1911), 23; "Jūyō hōan naiyō," *Tōkyō asahi shinbun*, 21 January 1911, 4; "Chisuihi no tsuika," *Yomiuri shinbun*, 22 January 1911, 2.
88 Naikaku Kanpōkyoku, ed., *Dai nijūnana kai teikoku gikai: shūgiin yosan iin dai ni bunka kaigiroku* 5 (daily ed. 3 February 1911), 56.

questioned just how high the water was in August 1910 with some estimates
suggesting that it had exceeded 11,000 m³/s (400,000 *shaku* per second) below
where the upstream Tori River flows into the Tone.[89] For his part, Okino issued
a plan for the Tone River that nearly doubled the high-water capacity of the
previous improvement plan's second stage of construction from 3,750 m³/s
(135,000 cubic *shaku* per second) to 6,960 m³/s (250,000 cubic *shaku* per second). This channel capacity, he argued, would be enough to drain the floods
that strike the Tone River basin once every five to ten years.[90] Although not as
ambitious as Okino's recommended high-water channel, the Home Ministry
ultimately revised its earlier three-stage plan for the Tone River by heightening the levees on the already completed stage below the town of Sawara and
expanding its plans for the middle and upper sections of the Tone.

During these next two stages of construction along the Tone River, the
ministry spent most of the subsequent two decades until 1930 straightening,
dredging, and containing 162 km of the river between downstream Sawara
and upstream Shibane Village in Gunma Prefecture. The ministry also reengineered how the Kinu and Kokai Rivers flowed into the Tone and implemented
extensive levee, revetment, and dredge work to the whole of the Edo River from
Sekiyado to Tokyo Bay. In addition, the Home Ministry also carried out the plan
described above for the lower Watarse River where it infamously removed
Yanaka Village and its protective levees in order turn the nearby Akama Marsh
into a retention reservoir for poisonous slag from the upstream Ashio Copper
Mine.[91] While much of the dredged material from these projects was used to
build the Tone's massive levees, the remaining material was also dumped on
both sides of the river to reclaim new land by burying the countless small lakes,
marshes, and wetlands that until that time had been an integral part of the
river itself. Between 1910 and 1930, the ministry spent over 68 million yen on the
Tone that included the dredging of nearly 100 million m³ of soil and purchase
and expropriation of 6,240 ha of riverside land where locals had their homes,
farmed, moored boats, dried fishing nets, and venerated their dead in temple
cemeteries. The funds were also spent on strengthening and building 318 km
of levees to produce a smooth curvilinear channel that could carry up to 5,570
m³/s of high water to the diversion at the Edo River and 4,130 m³/s from there

---

89   Ōkuma, *Tonegawa chisui no hensen to suigai*, 154–55; Tonegawa Hyaku-nen Shi Hensan
      Iinkai, *Tonegawa hyaku-nen shi*, 546–47.

90   His revised estimate was for the section between where the Tori River enters the Tone
      River at the border of Gunma and Saitama Prefectures and Edo River leaves it at the
      border of Saitama and Chiba Prefectures. Ōkuma, *Tonegawa chisui no hensen to suigai*,
      153–54; Tonegawa Hyaku-nen Shi Hensan Iinkai, *Tonegawa hyaku-nen shi*, 543–45.

91   Tonegawa Hyaku-nen Shi Hensan Iinkai, *Tonegawa hyaku-nen shi*, 662–76.

TABLE 2   Approved by the Imperial Diet in 1911, this is a list of sixty-five river projects to be directly funded by the national government and administered by the Home Ministry. They were ranked according to the amount of flat area within their river basins, recorded flood damage between the years 1896 and 1907, and divided into Phase I (1911–1928), Phase II (1929–), and later projects. Based on Matsuura Shigeki, *Kokudo no kaihatsu to kasen: jōri-sei kara damu kaihatsu made* (Tokyo: Kajima Shuppankai, 1989), 116

River	Area of river basin		Average annual flood damage (1896–1907)		
	Rank	Area (km^2)	Rank	Yen	Phase I and II
Tone	1	2365	1	5,619,664	I
Shinano	2	1014	2	3,588,650	I
Yodo	3	718	4	2,343,855	I
Kiso	4	529	3	2,695,486	I
Naka (Ibaraki)	5	473	30	172,298	II
Kitagami	6	459	8	1,013,986	I
Ara	7	398	9	987,456	I
Agano	8	386	11	838,517	I
Omono	9	369	7	1,212,697	I
Abukuma	10	303	15	511,080	II
Tenryū	11	286	13	596,511	II
Ōyodo	12	231	47	17,732	II
Chikugo	13	190	22	278,932	II
Mabechi	14	175	41	40,680	II
Iwaki	15	165	33	126,438	I
Mogami	16	160	16	448,143	I
Fuji	17	155	5	1,930,207	I
Yoshii	18	153	36	93,100	II
Naka (Tokyo)	19	145	26	200,575	II
Yoshino	20	121	10	898,608	I
Yahagi	21	121	31	170,900	II
Kuzuryū	22	120	6	1,232,965	I
Hai	23	119	42	37,581	I
Yoneshiro	24	115	38	76,056	II
Jinzū	25	113	19	355,753	II
Shōnai	26	109	18	356,690	II
Gō	27	105	45	24,245	II
Midori	28	105	34	104,157	I
Yamato	29	99	23	278,667	II

TABLE 2   (*cont.*)

River	Area of river basin		Average annual flood damage (1896–1907)		
	Rank	Area (km²)	Rank	Yen	Phase I and II
Tedori	30	98	20	344,572	II
Kuji	31	95	37	80,492	II
Kikuchi	32	91	40	42,174	II
Takahashi	33	91	29	179,545	I
Tama	34	88	27	192,679	II
Naruse	35	88	28	190,622	II
Seki	36	87	25	201,491	II
Aisaka	37	87	49	11,875	II
Kako	38	86	21	322,652	I
Kino	39	86	17	417,984	II
Sendai (Tottori)	40	86	50	4,832	II
Shō	41	85	12	718,454	I
Sendai (Kagoshima)	42	85	43	33,662	II
Asahi	43	80	32	158,433	II
Onga	44	76	24	243,954	I
Ashida	45	63	39	51,212	II
Yura	46	62	14	592,324	II
Watari	47	61	35	98,216	II
Kuma	48	61	48	14,286	II
Tsurumi	49	59	44	33,485	II
Ōno (Ōita)	50	58	46	19,914	II
Sagami	51	57			
Hiji	52	55			
Yabe	53	52			
Kano	54	49			
Maruyama	55	47			
Kimotsuki	56	46			
Ōta (Shizuoka)	57	45			
Toyo	58	45			
Shira	59	45			
Ōita	60	44			
Sakawa	61	44			

TABLE 2 (*cont.*)

River	Area of river basin		Average annual flood damage (1896–1907)		
	Rank	Area (km²)	Rank	Yen	Phase I and II
Suzuka	62	43			
Ōta (Kōchi)	63	41			
Natori	64	40			
Niyodo	65	40			

downstream to Chōshi and the Pacific Ocean.[92] Similarly, for the building of the new Ara River Drainage Canal through the more populous area around eastern Tokyo between 1913 and 1930, the Home Ministry expropriated 1,088 ha of land, removed several temples and shrines and nearly 1,300 households to create a 22 km long channel with a high-water capacity of 4,170 m³/s that was 583 m wide where it flowed into Tokyo Bay.[93] During all three stages of what came to be collectively called the Tone River Improvement Works (Tonegawa Kaishū Kōji) between 1900 and 1930, laborers and machines excavated a total of 214 million m³ of soil, which exceeded the roughly 200 million m³ of soil excavated by the French and Americans in the construction of the Panama Canal. With this combination of centralized management, financing from the national government, industrial equipment, and tens of thousands of workers,

---

92 For example, a stone memorial on the grounds of the temple Enmeiji, in present-day Abiko City, commissioned by Hashimoto Masao and dated May 1914, testifies to the relocation of the about eighty gravestones from their original location near the river to a new location on higher ground. Abiko-shi Shi Kyōiku Iinkai, ed., *Abiko-shi shi: kingendai hen* (Abiko: Abiko-shi Shi Kyōiku Iinkai, 2004), 205; Naimushō Tōkyō Doboku Shucchōjo, *Tonegawa kaishū kōji gaiyō* (Tokyo: Naimushō Tōkyō Doboku Shucchōjo, 1930), 21–40; Ōkuma, *Tonegawa chisui no hensen to suigai*, 142; Tonegawa Hyaku-nen Shi Hensan Iinkai, *Tonegawa hyaku-nen shi*, 598–99, 623–61.

93 The local historian Kinuta Yukie conducted oral interviews with longtime residents about their experiences before, during, and after the building of the Ara River Drainage Canal between 1911 and 1930. She describes how many residents had been reluctant to sell their land to the Home Ministry for fear that they would not receive a fair market price and others outright refused until they were forcibly removed. Kinuta Yukie, *Arakawa hōsuiro* (Tokyo: Shinsō Shuppan, 1990), 64–119; Naimushō Tōkyō Doboku Shucchōjo, *Arakawa karyū kaishū kōji gaiyō* (Tokyo: Naimushō Tōkyō Doboku Shucchōjo, 1924), 9–24; Arakawa Karyū Kōji Jimusho Nanajūgo-nen Shi Henshū Iinkai, ed., *Toshi o yuku Arakawa: Arakawa karyū kōji jimusho nanajūgo-nen shi* (Tokyo: Kensetsuhō Kantō Chihō Kensetsukyoku Arakawa Karyū Kōji Jimusho, 1990), 69–124.

these river projects also succeeded in removing the higher riverbeds that had resulted from the 1783 eruption of Mount Asama.[94]

In 1916 in the Kinai region, the Home Ministry began preparations for another round of high-water construction on the Yodo River. Before the Imperial Diet voted in 1911 to approve funding for this work on the Yodo and nineteen other rivers, the ministry had begun in 1907 to dredge a narrow "low-water flow" (*teisui ryūryō*) channel within the existing river bed with a minimum depth at low tide of 70 to 150 cm from just below the narrows between Mount Otoko and Mount Tennō to the estuary in order to maintain the busy shipping route between Osaka and Fushimi (the riverport for Kyoto).[95] A typhoon in October 1917 that caused the Yodo to breach some of its levees led to local organizations and politicians again clamoring for better flood protection. In response, the Home Ministry began what it called a "supplementary improvement" (*kaishū zōho*) plan for the Yodo River and scheduled construction to be carried out between 1918 and 1923.[96] The inflationary woes due to the First World War and flagging government budgets thereafter meant that this supplementary project was delayed until 1920 and dragged on until its completion in 1931. As with the Tone River, the engineers supervising the work along the Yodo River during the 1920s did not question the principles of the modern river regime. Instead, they followed them by strengthening, extending, and heightening existing levees; expropriating all remaining private property within the river channel and further removing all sandbars and obstacles to the flow of water; and again redesigned the critical confluence of the Katsura, Uji, and Kizu Rivers near the soon to be drained and reclaimed Ogura Lake.[97] Although maintaining the same high-water capacity of 5,560 m³/s for the main channel, the Home Ministry spent in excess of 14 million yen to dredge the river channel deeper by an average of 30 cm and used more than 8.8 million m³ of excavated soil to strengthen or build a total of 109 km of levees.[98]

Over the nearly two decades during which the Home Ministry reengineered the downstream portion of the Yodo, Tone, and many other large rivers, it was the key actor in the reassembly of various riparian relations along these rivers. With the greater legal, technical, and financial resources of the national government, the ministry also helped prefectural governments and

94   Ōkuma Takashi estimates that during these projects an average of 1.5 to 2 m of riverbed was removed from the Tone and Edo rivers. Ōkuma, *Kōsui to chisui no kasenshi*, 167–68.

95   Naimushō Ōsaka Doboku Shucchōjo, ed., *Yodogawa kaishū zōho kōji gaiyō* (Osaka: Naimushō Ōsaka Doboku Shucchōjo, 1930), 13–16.

96   *Yodogawa kaishū zōho kōji gaiyō*, 16–20; Shinshū Ōsaka-shi Shi Hensan Iinkai, ed. *Shinshū Ōsaka-shi shi* (Osaka: Ōsaka-shi, 1994), 6:492–95.

97   *Yodogawa kaishū zōho kōji gaiyō*, 21–53; *Shinshū Ōsaka-shi shi*, 6:495–97.

98   *Yodogawa kaishū zōho kōji gaiyō*, 20, 33–34, 37–38.

irrigation associations to rebuild and pay for larger levees, stronger embankments, and reinforced sluices at these rivers' confluences with smaller tributaries and canals. In this way, these massive riparian projects contributed to the changing riverscapes of urban and rural areas alike. In cities like Osaka and Tokyo, riverside land was valued for its ready access to water for industrial production and waste disposal as well as for the transport of coal and other raw materials from freight terminals and oceangoing ships. Across the rural areas of the Kinai and Kantō regions, these projects employed tens of thousands of mostly rural residents who, when not planting or harvesting their fields, found employment digging and hauling soil, carrying construction materials, and building levees.[99] Working alongside teams of horses and new dredgers, excavators, and locomotives, these men and women excavated and deepened river channels and hauled rock and soil to build the immense levees required to keep these rivers in place.[100] All along the lower Tone River, for example, the new levees ranged from 5 to 7 m in height and grew to be as much as 65 m wide.[101] In a region where the slightest elevation difference caused homes and fields to flood more frequently, these levees dominated the resulting riverscape and obscured all view and access to the river from the surrounding countryside. Having himself been raised in the riverside village of Fukawa, the folklorist Yanagita Kunio (1875–1962) lamented the reengineering of the Tone River in his preface to the 1938 republication of the well-known 1855 gazetteer *Tonegawa zushi* by Fukawa native Akamatsu Sōtan:

The levees have become unduly tall. In place of the wanning flow of water transport, trains run across numerous bridges. The white sails that formed a moving forest of pine trees has also disappeared. So many

---

99   At its peak in the second stage of construction from Sawara upstream to Toride in 1914–16, for example, the Home Ministry employed between 543,740 and 659,265 people annually. Tonegawa Hyaku-nen Shi Hensan Iinkai, *Tonegawa hyaku-nen shi*, 629. In his history of rural life in twentieth-century Toyama Prefecture, Simon Partner briefly describes the work and accompanying reclamation along the Agano River, which was listed eighth on the Special Flood Control Survey Committee's 1911 list of sixty-five river projects. Simon Partner, *Toshié: A Story of Village Life in Twentieth Century Japan* (Berkeley: University of California Press, 2004), 71–72.

100   Due to labor shortages during the planting and harvest season as well as the surge in factory jobs during the First World War, the Home Ministry relied heavily on horses to pull bucket cars (*toro*) of soil along temporary railways. In 1914, the ministry employed a total of 65,900 horses on the stage two area of construction on the Tone River. In 1915, that number rose to a high of 80,675 horses and thereafter steadily declined until in 1919 when it reached 14,692 horses. Tonegawa Hyaku-nen Shi Hensan Iinkai, *Tonegawa hyaku-nen shi*, 632.

101   Tonegawa Hyaku-nen Shi Hensan Iinkai, *Tonegawa hyaku-nen shi*, 626.

takasebune came with the wind to the various riverports (*kawaminato*), but everywhere the river and its banks have been completely carved up. The houses, from whose upper floors one could sit and see the river and the lantern lights reflected in the water, have also vanished.[102]

While Yanagita himself had long given up living in the countryside to write from Tokyo about the demise of rural Japan and its folkways, his observations about how these river projects were irrevocably changing the country's riverscapes suggests the extent of the transformation that had occurred to these waterways and the lifeways with which they were so intimately intertwined.

Perhaps the most frequently cited and misunderstood example of the vicissitudes to river life in the late nineteenth and early twentieth centuries was that of the demise of riverboat traffic.[103] As explained in chapter 4, the spread of Kinai regional and eventually a national network of railways required decades to build and therefore did not signal an immediate death knell for water transport.[104] Even as existing railways were extended and new lines built, riverboats complemented rather than competed with the more expensive railways by delivering bulky rural products like grains, tea, lumber, sake, and soy sauce from villages and towns to the nearest train station.[105] From these rural train stations, railways typically shipped these goods to freight stations in the city from where they were often again loaded onto riverboats and delivered to specific merchants, marketplaces, and factories within the city. In fact, the growing economies and populations of Osaka and Tokyo from the late nineteenth century led to an increase in the number of boats operating within these cities. During this time, however, what constituted a riverboat itself began to change as shallow-draft steamboats began to ply the waters of the Yodo, Tone, and other large rivers. These steamboat companies used the prevailing infrastructure of riverports and wharf merchants, and with their more reliable travel schedule,

102   Yanagita Kunio, "Kaidai," in Akamatsu Sōtan, *Tonegawa zushi* (Tokyo: Iwanami Shoten, 1938), 3.
103   Suzuki Kunizō (1904–?), a boatwright originally from the riverport of Ōhori on the Tone River (chapter 2), recounted in an interview with the doctor and author Junichi Saga about the difficulties of sailing *takasebune* along the river and in Lake Kasumigaura during the early twentieth century. Junichi Saga, *Memories of Wind and Waves: A Self-Portrait of Lakeside Japan*, trans. Juliet Winters Carpenter (Tokyo: Kodansha International, 2002), 48–66.
104   Iizuka Takafusa, "Meiji-ki ni okeru kasen shū'un no chiikiteki henka: Yodogawa ryūiki, Kisogawa ryūiki, Tonegawa ryūiki o chūshin ni," *Chiiki seisakugaku jānaru* 6, no 2. (2017): 27–47.
105   Oikawa Yoshinobu, "Sangyō kakumei-ki no riku'un to suiun," in *Sōron suijō kōtsū shi: suijō kōtsū shi kenkyū no kadai to tenbō*, ed. Yuzuki Manabu (Tokyo: Bunken Shuppan, 1996), 339–59.

they began to carry an increasing amount of the passengers and perishable goods between cities and the surrounding countryside.[106] The continued importance of inland navigation in the first decades of the twentieth century is also suggested by the Home Ministry's inclusion of narrow "low-water" shipping channels in their early twentieth-century engineering plans for the Yodo and Tone Rivers.[107] While steamboats could navigate the faster waters in these straighter and narrower shipping channels, human- and wind-propelled riverboats found the task ever more arduous. Many of these wooden riverboats in the Kinai and Kantō were repurposed as ferries, workboats for river construction projects, and as barges pulled by steamboats. The Home Ministry also began policing these rivers at great expense and with much effort to ensure the levees, revetments, and other structures were not damaged through unapproved usage. From 1911 the ministry established three police branch offices on the Yodo River system between the Seta River and Osaka.[108] And along the Tone River from 1911 to 1934, for instance, the police recorded 2,552 incidences involving the inappropriate use of anchors and towropes, 2,776 incidences of people disregarding the prohibition on allowing animals to graze on levees and embankments, and 4,621 incidents of people dumping rocks, soil, and garbage on the levees.[109] It was not until the 1920s and the cumulative effect of the Home Ministry's and prefecture's declining commitment to dredge rivers of sandbars, continued railway building, and finally the introduction of petrol-powered trucks that brought a gradual end to rural riverboat traffic.[110]

---

106   The following 1910 guidebook for steamboat travel in the Kantō region provides information about 121 river and lakeside ports, nearly all of which had served as ports since the seventeenth century. The guidebook describes, for instance, Sawara as the preeminent commercial center in Chiba Prefecture with both a riverport and railway station, 3,500 buildings, and a population of 25,000 people. It then goes on to list the number of boats leaving daily for different destinations, distances to other important ports, local products (*meisan*), and places of interest ranging from a local bank and government offices to local shrines, temples, restaurants, and hotels (*ryokan*). Kisen Nikyaku Toriatsukainin Rengōkai, ed., *Tonegawa kisen kōro annai* (Tokyo: Kisen Nikyaku Toriatsukainin Rengōkai, 1910), 133–36.

107   These government policies and projects promoting inland navigation were neither uniformly implemented nor felt. For example, the Home Ministry's 1905 completion of the barrage where Lake Biwa drained into the Seta River dramatically lowered the water level in the downstream Uji River, effectively ending riverboat traffic along that critical tributary of the Yodo River. *Uji-shi shi*, ed. Hayashi Tatsusaburō and Fujioka Kenjirō, vol. 4, *Kinsei no rekishi to keikan* (Uji: Uji Shiyakusho, 1978), 250.

108   *Uji-shi shi*, 4:227.

109   Tonegawa Hyaku-nen Shi Hensan Iinkai, *Tonegawa hyaku-nen shi*, 603.

110   The historian William Steele describes the rapid building of modern bridges and paved roads throughout Japan from the 1920s onward. M. William Steele, "Across the Tama: Bridges and Roads, Rivers, and Rocks," in *Local Realities and Environmental Changes in the History of East Asia*, ed. Liu Ts'ui-jung (New York: Routledge, 2016), 181–204.

The Home Ministry's reengineering and regulation of rivers also had a dramatic influence on river and other freshwater fishing in the Yodo and Tone. As described in the introductory chapter, the initial Yodo River Improvement Works succeeded in reducing the risk of flooding, but also reduced the water level of Ogura Lake by as much as 1 to 2 m and thereby worsened its already declining water quality.[111] Over the next two to three decades, the complex riparian relations that had long sustained one of the largest wetlands in the country slowly unraveled as the lake shrunk, fish died, malaria set in, and local communities petitioned the government for relief.[112] That relief came in the form of the national government's compensation to the lake's fishing community and in 1933 the administration of the eight-year project that completely drained and reclaimed the lake.[113] In the Kantō region, the Home Ministry's work on the Tone River did not immediately affect the region's important carp, catfish, eel, and loach fisheries because it did not dramatically change the water levels or water quality in sizable marshes like the Tega and Inba or the downstream Lake Kasumigaura.[114] The salmon and trout fisheries, however, never recovered. As seen with the 1844 agreement between Fusa, Fukawa, and nearby villages discussed in chapter 1, these long-established fishing communities along the Tone River were already grappling with increased competition and declining catches of the river's renowned salmon and trout. In 1888 and 1890, the state issued regulations prohibiting the use of dragnets and anchored nets (see fig. 13) in order to help conserve these fish runs and more specifically to prevent them from creating problems for flood control and impeding riverboat traffic.[115] Nonetheless, until the 1910s, fishing communities on the Tone River continued to catch salmon in great numbers: in 1913, for example, the fishers from the town of Fusa alone hauled in 3,750 kg (1,000 *kan*) of this highly coveted fish.[116] But just a few years later in 1919 and following the completion of most of the channel excavation along the Tone River, an annual report on

---

111   *Uji-shi shi*, 4:226.

112   Uji-shi Rekishi Shiryōkan, ed., *Ogura-ike: soshite, kantaku wa okonawareta* (Uji: Uji-shi Rekishi Shiryōkan, 2011), 16–19.

113   Ogura-ike Tochi Kairyō-ku, ed., *Ogura-ike kantaku shi* (Uji: Ogura-ike Tochi Kairyō-ku, 1962).

114   Chiba-ken Katori-gun Yakusho, ed., *Chiba-ken Katori-gun shi* (Chiba: Chiba-ken Katori-gun Yakusho, 1921), 48–50.

115   *Chiba-ken no rekishi: tsūshi hen, kin-gendai*, ed. Chiba-ken Shiryō Kenkyū Zaidan (Chiba: Chiba-ken, 2002), 1:515–16.

116   Abiko-shi Shi Kyōiku Iinkai, *Abiko-shi shi: kingendai hen*, 216–22.

Chiba Prefecture's fisheries explained that the catch for both salmon and trout had become "exceedingly small" (*kiwamete sukunashi*).[117]

The Home Ministry's massive projects on the Tone, Yodo, and elsewhere also caused a wave of related construction along smaller rivers and canals. When straightening and dredging the country's main rivers, the ministry also typically changed the location and water level relative to their many tributaries, distributaries, and irrigation and drainage canals. Although the ministry covered the cost and supervised the building of new embankments, revetments, levees, sluices, and gates where these smaller waterways entered and left the larger rivers, it required prefectures and localities to pay for and manage most of the remaining work on these smaller rivers and canals. In 1917 in Saitama Prefecture, for instance, the prefectural government established a new Water Use Section (Suirika) to coordinate with local governments and irrigation associations to draw up plans to "improve" (*kairyō*) the Kasai and Minumadai Canals, together with other minor rivers that irrigated and drained much of the prefecture's fields and paddies.[118] Between 1917 and 1935, with surveys conducted and plans agreed upon, the prefecture oversaw river work along thirteen major waterways and seven minor ones that had the Tone and Ara Rivers as their headwaters.[119] The prefecture straightened the Kasai Canal of meanders, dredged it to a greater and consistent depth, and removed barriers that obstructed the flow of water.[120] At the same time, irrigation associations began installing new steam and later electric-powered pumps that replaced the once common use of waterwheels to lift water from rivers and canals and into paddy fields.[121] Similar modifications were made to the irrigation canals and smaller rivers in the Kinai region. After the completion of the Home Ministry's Yodo River Improvement Works, Osaka Prefecture oversaw work between 1909 and 1913 on the irrigation canals and the Ai River into which these canals drained. The ministry's aim was to regularize the width, depth, and slope of the waterways in order to "improve" water flow through the entire river system.[122] The

---

117   Chiba-ken Naimubu, ed., *Chiba-ken suisan ippan* (Chiba: Chiba-ken Naimubu, 1919), 11.

118   *Shinpen Saitama-ken shi: tsūshi hen, kingendai*, ed. Saitama-ken (Urawa: Saitama-ken, 1989), 2:506–8.

119   "Saitama-ken yōhaisui kairyō jigyō gaiyō," in *Shinpen Saitama-ken shi: shiryō hen, kingendai*, ed. Saitama-ken (Urawa: Saitama-ken, 1996), 4:192–99.

120   Kasai Yōsuiro Tochi Kairyōku, ed., *Kasai Yōsui shi: tsūshi hen* (Kasukabe: Kasai Yōsuiro Tochi Kairyōku, 1988), 486–87.

121   *Chiba-ken no rekishi: bekkan minzoku*, ed. Chiba-ken Shiryō Kenkyū Zaidan (Chiba: Chiba-ken, 1999), 1:89–93; *Uji-shi shi*, 4:98, 103.

122   Hattori Takeshi, *Kindai chihō seiji to suiri doboku* (Kyoto: Shibunkaku Shuppan, 1995), 348–53.

historian Hattori Takashi and others have shown these alterations to the riparian relations along these smaller waterways impacted farming methods, land reform efforts, and landlord-tenant relations. These changes also clearly demonstrate how the Home Ministry's building of a modern river regime ramified from the country's biggest rivers down to local streams and canals.

After 1910, the Home Ministry continued its reengineering of the Yodo, Tone, and numerous other important rivers, thereby dramatically modifying riparian relations and the riverscapes they constituted throughout the country. Although the ministry never achieved the Special Flood Control Survey Committee's ambitious goal of reengineering fifty, let alone sixty-five, rivers, it applied the unprecedent resources of the nation and empire as well as tapped into a transnational flow of science and technology to transform many of the country's largest and most important rivers. Moreover, as individual prefectures simultaneously carried out similar work on smaller upstream and downstream waterways, the ministry's projects proved themselves to be scalable to a degree unimagined previously.

5   Conclusion

Japan's modern river regime came into being between 1896 and 1930. The reengineered downstream portions of the country's main rivers were the materialization of a techno-political framework that had originally been resolved in the 1890s by politicians and their most influential constituents, Home Ministry officials and engineers, and the rivers themselves. This framework and subsequently the channels of many of country's major rivers reflected the realignment away from a diversity of riparian relations to converge primarily on the problem of flood control. This convergence was institutionalized in the 1896 River Law and the subsequent 1897 Erosion Prevention and Forestry Laws. With their promulgation, the Home Ministry used these laws and its own enhanced authority to favor some riparian relations over others in its reengineering of river channels to protect and promote specific kinds of agricultural and industrial development. A comparison of the techno-political responses to the 1910 flooding in Tokyo and Paris has emphasized the global modernity of which Japan and its rivers increasingly belonged. In the aftermath of the 1910 flooding of Tokyo and the Kantō region, the Imperial Diet supported the Home Ministry's efforts to build out this modern river regime along the Tone, Yodo, and several other sizable rivers in the name of serving a broadly defined public interest. But this reengineering also necessitated the reassembly of existing riparian relations with new ones that included steamboats, pumps for irrigation, massive levees, and the near absence of salmon and their fishers.

Japan's modern river regime also divided and framed complex riparian relations in terms of political, social, and natural processes and phenomena.[123] State, society, and nature were not preexisting, independent entities, rather they were the "effects" of building techno-political frameworks like the modern river regime that served to reassemble existing environmental relations according to these new boundaries. This is not to say that society was alienated from nature or from the state, but that the modern river regime and similar projects helped create these seemingly real and distinct entities.[124] Like boulders in a river, shaping and being shaped by the current, the emergent entities of state, society, and nature were influenced by and in turn themselves influenced riparian relations through the discursive, juridical, and technological practices associated with them. In defining rivers strictly in terms of hydraulic processes and reengineering them to become efficient drainage channels, the Home Ministry and its engineers also contributed to the broader redefinition of these waters as natural objects. The ministry also reified an emerging boundary between nature and society by exercising the authority granted to it under the River Law and Land Expropriation Law to clear people's homes, fields, wharves, and even cemeteries from areas on and along rivers and subsequently policed the use of these reengineered channels. In their agreeing or refusal to sell their lands, move or be removed from these river channels, and follow or shirk new laws and regulations by continuing to graze their animals, grow crops within river channels, and moor their boats in prohibited places,

---

123   Alongside the modern monarchy, prisons, public health measures, zoological gardens, and social management efforts, and a variety of other campaigns and reforms from the late nineteenth century, these efforts to "improve" Japan's rivers played a role in the reification of these modern categories by physically separating rivers from the communities that lived along them and redefining relations between these communities and the emerging modern state. Daniel Botsman, *Punishment and Power in the Making of Modern Japan* (Princeton: Princeton University Press, 2005); Susan L. Burns, "Constructing the National Body: Public Health and the Nation in Nineteenth-Century Japan," in *Nation Work: Asian Elites and National Identities*, ed. Timothy Brook and Andre Schmid (Ann Arbor: The University of Michigan Press, 2000), 17–49; Takashi Fujitani, *Splendid Monarchy: Power and Pageantry in Modern Japan* (Berkeley: University of California Press, 1996); Sheldon Garon, *Molding Japanese Minds* (Princeton: Princeton University Press, 1997); Miller, *The Nature of the Beasts*.

124   This phenomenon was not limited to Japan; it has been global in effect. The political scientist Timothy Mitchell writes similarly about how "techno-power" rearranged relations along the Nile River in Egypt and more broadly throughout the twentieth-century world: "Overlooking the mixed way things happen, indeed, producing the effect of neatly separate realms of reason and the real world, ideas and their objects, the human and the nonhuman, was how power was coming to work in Egypt, and in the twentieth century in general." Timothy Mitchell, *Rule of Experts: Egypt, Techno-Politics, and Modernity* (Berkeley: University of California Press, 2002), 52. See also Mitchell, *Society, Economy, and the State Effect*, 95.

residents of riverside communities also participated in the formation of an evolving boundary between society and state in modern Japan. And rivers also shaped the boundaries between themselves and the communities through which they flowed by breaching levees, changing their course, and clogging irrigation sluices with tons of sediment. These waterways equally influenced the development of the modern state and society by affecting decisions about who would be responsible for the maintenance and repair of levees, sluices, and canals. In a word, this history of the formation of Japan's modern river regime is a turbulent one. And as the following epilogue suggests, this history has continued into the twenty-first century.

Epilogue

This book has shown how the rivers of Japan are both hydrologically and historically dynamic. By focusing on the Yodo River in the Kinai region and the Tone River in the Kantō region from the seventeenth to the early twentieth centuries, this book has followed the changes to environmental relations that emerged between these rivers, the mostly rural communities who lived along them, and the governing institutions, officials, and engineers they employed. In doing so, I have avoided using the dominant progressive, declensionist, and contextualist narratives with their reliance on the modernist worldview wherein society, state, and nature are used as preexisting and ontologically distinct entities. This study instead provides a history about riparian relations and the assemblages they constituted. The two chapters of Part 1 demonstrate how from the seventeenth century the combined fluvial work of the Tone and other rivers, hundreds of villages located near and far from these rivers, and the Tokugawa government and its officials reassembled existing riparian assemblages to help produce the Kantō region and its riverscapes. The result was the formation of fishing, shipping, and irrigation networks that bound villages to towns and cities and were critical to the Tokugawa's capacity to govern. While the 1868 Meiji Restoration set forth revolutionary transformations throughout the country, the three chapters of Part 2 together demonstrate how it was only from the 1890s that long existing riparian relations sustaining fishing, water transport, and irrigated farming along the Tone, Yodo, and other large rivers truly began to unravel. These chapters also emphasize the confluence of local villages and their political representatives, the Home Ministry and its engineers, and the rivers themselves in the formation of a new techno-political framework enshrined in the 1896 River Law that was used to build the country's modern river regime.

This regime, which began in the late nineteenth century, has continued to shape riparian relations into the twenty-first century. Based on a single-minded focus of preventing flooding by efficiently draining water from the land, this approach to riparian administration and engineering has spread along every major and most minor rivers throughout the country during the twentieth century. Starting from the more populous downstream portions of these rivers and working its way up to their headwaters in the distant mountain ranges, first the Home Ministry and later its aptly named successor the Construction Ministry (Kensetsushō) built over several decades a seemingly unbroken series of revetments, levees, weirs, erosion-control structures, and massive multipurpose dams on the country's rivers. Today, the downstream extent of the Yodo and

Tone Rivers are completely lined by levees that can reach 10 m high and tens of meters wide to carry at their widest point a maximum high-water capacity of 12,000 m³/s for the Yodo and 17,500 m³/s for the Tone. Further upstream, the main tributaries of these two rivers are crossed by dams that have transformed steep mountain valleys into deep snaking reservoirs. More than twice the capacity deemed necessary by Home Ministry engineers following the flooding of 1910, these still wider and taller river channels reflect the calculations of later generations of engineers who studied the widespread flooding in the Kantō region caused by the 1947 Typhoon Kathleen and a 1953 typhoon that swept over the Kinai region. This twentieth-century transformation of these rivers and the riparian relations they helped constitute have contributed to the production of dramatically new riverscapes throughout the country.

While the enclosure of rivers in hulking earthen levees and the fading of the white sails of riverboats and fishing boats are frequently cited as signs of wider changes to rural life and the riparian relations with which they were often bound, the disappearance of most of these region's wetlands has been routinely ignored. This may have to do with the fact that there was nothing particularly new or modern about the drainage and reclamation of wetlands. As discussed in Part 1 of this book, well before the modern period, villages, wealthy merchants, and governing officials had individually and at times together already reclaimed most of the low-lying areas of the Kantō and Kinai regions. For areas along rivers and river-fed lakes and marshes like the Ogura and Biwa in the Kinai region and the Inba, Tega, and Kasumigaura in the Kantō region, however, these reclaimed fields and paddies were generally wetter, were the first to flood, and therefore were typically less fertile. Despite the pressure to reclaim neighboring wetlands, rural villages had also depended upon, managed, and protected these surviving wetlands as village commons.[1] Until the mid-twentieth century, these wetlands in the Kantō and Kinai regions played an important role in rural communities by providing them with valuable green manure, nutrient-rich sediment, feed for farm animals, materials for weaving and thatching, and scrub brush for firewood and other uses. Although marginally productive as waterside fields and paddies, these wetlands and the broad floodplains of rivers continued to play a vital role in flood control through their absorption and retention of the floodwaters that remained an undesired and yet regular occurrence in both regions.

---

1   For Lake Biwa, see Sano Shizuyo, "Traditional Use of Resources and Management of Littoral Environments of Lake Biwa," in *Environment and Society in the Japanese Islands: From Pre-History to the Present*, ed. Bruce L. Batten and Philip C. Brown (Corvallis: Oregon State University Press, 2015), 75–95.

With the building of the modern river regime in the twentieth century, the role of these wetlands changed and their value to rural communities declined. Larger and stronger levees meant floods were less frequent. When these rivers did flood, however, they tended to be more destructive and deadly. Behind these levees, the introduction of steam and later electric pumps also made it easier for villages and irrigation associations to move and drain water. In addition, the increasing production and use of chemical fertilizers, manufactured goods, and electricity and natural gas for heating and cooking meant there was little demand for these wetland's once valued sedges, reeds, and scrub brush.[2] Moreover, in response to the 1919 Rice Riots and the broader problem of rural poverty and tenant-landlord struggles, the Imperial Diet passed the Reclamation Promotion Law (Kaikon Joseihō) to provide national funding for the clearing of woodlands and draining of wetlands in order to boost food production.[3] Through the widespread reengineering of the country's rivers, new laws, and the national government's financial and administrative support, local municipalities and prefectures alike intensified their reclamation of small and large wetlands throughout the country. Beyond promoting and facilitating local reclamation schemes, the national government also played a more direct role by funding and overseeing several national reclamation projects (*kokuei kaikon jigyō*) that drained vast wetlands throughout the country and converted them into productive acreage. As already explained in the introductory chapter, the first of these national reclamation projects was Ogura Lake, which between 1933 and 1941 was completely drained to create 2,294 ha of rice paddies. These intertwined efforts to discipline rivers, extend irrigation, encourage reclamation, and carry out land reform spread throughout the Japanese empire as can be seen through notable examples like the Zengwen River in Taiwan and the Man'gyŏng River in Korea.[4] In the postwar period, these sizable nationally funded and administered reclamation projects continued

---

2 Katayama Naoki, Yuki Baba, Yoshinobu Kusumoto, and Koichi Tanaka, "A Review of Post-War Changes in Rice Farming and Biodiversity in Japan," *Agricultural Systems* 132 (2015): 73–84; Hiromi Mizuno, "Rasa Island: What Industrialization to Remember and Forget," *The Asia-Pacific Journal: Japan Focus* 15, no. 1 (2017), https://apjjf.org/2017/01/Mizuno.html, accessed 1 March 2018.
3 In 1923, the Reclamation Promotion Law was amended to specifically enable funding for irrigation and drainage projects.
4 Ya-wen Ku, "Taming the Blind Snake: Flooding Disasters and River Regulation of the Zengwen River in Colonial Taiwan," in *Landscape Change and Resource Utilization in East Asia: Perspectives from Environmental History*, ed. Ts'ui-jung Liu, Andrea Janku, and David Pietz (New York: Routledge, 2018), 58–75; Takenori Matsumoto and Seung-jin Chung, "Water Management Projects and Floods/Droughts in Colonial Korea: The Case of the Man'gyŏng River in Honam Plain," *Acta Koreana* 20, no. 1 (2017): 173–93.

unabated with the signature project of the Kantō region being the reclamation of much of the Inba Marsh between 1946 and 1968. All told, over the course of the twentieth century, nearly 90 percent of the country's wetlands (excluding Hokkaidō) were reclaimed for farming and other uses.[5] Transcending the militarism and imperialism of the Asia-Pacific War and the postwar occupation of the country, these national reclamation projects externalized these wetlands from the common techno-political framework employed to build and administer the country's modern river regime for much of the twentieth century. Instead of seeking ways to improve the flood control capacity of these many smaller wetlands, engineers and officials in the Home Ministry and later the Construction Ministry envisioned a grander techno-political solution to the persistent problem of flooding—high-wall ferroconcrete dams.

Along with its efforts to reengineer the lower portions of the country's main rivers for flood control, the Home Ministry also began approving the building of large dams on the upstream tributaries of these same rivers. By 1925, there were eighteen such dams with a height of over 30 m, such as the Ōmine Dam on the Uji River in the Kinai region and the Kurobe and Nakaiwa dams on the Kinu River in the Kantō region.[6] Until that time most of these dams had been designed with a primary use in mind, such as the supply of water or electricity to nearby urban area.[7] From the 1920s, however, Home Ministry officials and engineers began discussing the potential of dams to serve multiple purposes, including flood control, under what would become a policy of "river water control" (*kasui tōsei*). In a lengthy 1925 article that influenced the adoption of this "control" policy, Monobe Nagaho (1888–1941), an engineering professor at Tokyo Imperial University and later head of the Home Ministry's engineering

---

5 In a report released in 2000, the Geospatial Information Authority of Japan (Kokudo Chiriin) calculated that the amount of wetlands in the late nineteenth and early twentieth centuries totaled 938.63 sq km (2110.62 sq km with the inclusion of Hokkaidō). In their national survey between 1996 and 1999, these wetlands only totaled 112.32 km² (820.99 km² with Hokkaidō). Kokudo Chiriin, "Nihon zenkoku no shicchi menseki henka no chōsa kekka (2000)," https://www.gsi.go.jp/kankyochiri/shicchimenseki2.html, accessed 13 July 2019.

6 In the 1964 revision of the River Law, Article 44 defines a "dam" (*damu*) as a structure that blocks a river and measures 15 m or more from its foundation to its crest and is built for the purpose of storing water. In Japanese, structures that are shorter than 15 m are generally called *seki*. Denshi Seifu no Sōgō Madoguchi, "Kasenhō," https://elaws.e-gov.go.jp/search/elawsSearch/elaws_search/lsg0500/detail?lawId=339ACo000000167#G, accessed 1 September 2019.

7 The first concrete dam in Japan was the Nunobiki Dam, which was built between 1897 and 1900 on the Ikuta River in Hyōgo Prefecture to create a water supply reservoir for the city of Kobe. Isohata Hiroshi, "Kobe Nunobiki damu, oyobi kanren shisetsu no kensetsu: kensetsu kiroku shashin no bunseki," *Dobokushi kenkyū* 19 (1999): 281–92.

experiment center, wrote: "In times of torrential rainfall, ten-something or rather tens of hours of precipitation can be stored at their source. During droughts if the necessary amount of this water can be released for electric power generation, irrigation, and water transport, the area (*shikichi*) of the river can be greatly reduced (*yohodo shukushō ga deki*).... This area, that is the area outside the levees, can be used as farmland."[8] His emphasis on using dams to catch and retain rainwater and reducing the area required for riverbeds in order to further reclaim these wetlands and expand farmland expressed the sincere hope of many of his fellow technocrats at the time to control the country's rivers through the use of modern science and technology. This optimism was needed along the country's biggest rivers during the 1930s because even after two decades of "improvement" work they continued to flood. For example, while the reengineering of the upper and middle portions of the Tone River had mostly succeeded in preventing major levee breaches along those portions of the river throughout the 1930s, this upstream success sent greater volumes of floodwaters downstream into the lower Tone River. The levees and wetlands of the lower Tone, however, were ill equipped to contain this amount of water and consequently suffered successive floods in 1935, 1938, and 1941. The new "control" policy promised to prevent these floods by retaining the sudden and heavy rainfall released by storms and typhoons behind upstream multipurpose dams. Then, under the careful eye of government officials, the stored water would be released at a measured rate to generate electricity and supply water to rural and urban areas alike.[9] The appeal of being able to control these rivers mirrored efforts elsewhere in Japan to mobilize and discipline society for continued imperial expansion and war. In the two decades between 1925 and 1945, the government approved the building of an additional sixty-nine large dams throughout the country. And as the Japanese empire expanded from Taiwan and Korea to include Manchuria (Manchukuo), its engineers participated by designing and supervising the construction of massive multipurpose dam projects like those centered on the enormous Fengman and Sup'ung dams.[10]

---

8   Monobe Nagaho, "Chosuiyō jūryoku sekitei no tokusei narabi ni sono gōriteki sekkei hōhō," *Doboku Gakkaishi* 11, no. 5 (1925): 11; Kokudo Seisaku Kikō, ed., *Kokudo o tsukutta doboku gijutsushatachi* (Tokyo: Kashima Shuppankai, 2000), 250–55.

9   One of the difficulties of using the same reservoirs to catch rainwater and retain that water for droughts and drier seasons is that the reservoirs need to be both empty and full at the right times of the year. Given that 70 percent of annual precipitation in Japan falls during the four months of the year, these reservoirs are often unable to drain quickly enough between large rain events.

10   An-chi Tung, "Hydroelectricity and Industrialization: The Economic, Social, and Environmental Impacts of the Sun Moon Lake Power Plants," in *Sediments of Time: Environment and Society in Chinese History*, ed. Mark Elvin (Cambridge: Cambridge

In the postwar period, government officials looked upon rivers as playing a critical role in their reconstruction plans for Japan's war-ravaged economy and society. With the initial financial and technical support of the United States-led occupation, the postwar government undertook an unprecedented dam-building boom that resulted in the building of over 1,500 new dams by the end of the century.[11] Generally in line with the high modernist aspirations of government planners around the globe during this time, Construction Ministry officials and engineers and their political allies saw in the building of massive multipurpose dams a solution to the overriding aim of making Japan self-sufficient through the reorganization of the electric industry (*denki jigyō saihensei*) and use of comprehensive national planning (*kokudo sōgō kaihatsu*).[12] Acting in line with these policies and in direct response to the flooding of the Uji and Yodo Rivers in 1953, the Construction Ministry issued its Basic Plan for the Improvement of the Yodo River System (Yodogawa Suikei Kashū Kihon Keikaku) with its center piece being the Amagase Dam on the Uji River. When completed in 1964, this concrete arch dam drowned a significant portion of the Uji River valley (including the older Ōmine Dam) with its reservoir of 26 million m³ of water.[13] Following the 1947 flooding in the Kantō region, the Construction Ministry oversaw the building of several multipurpose dams like the much-heralded Yagisawa Dam at the headwaters of the Tone River. Erected between 1959 and 1967, the Yagisawa Dam impounds over 200 million m³ of water, making it the largest reservoir in the Kantō region and one of the largest in the country.[14] While the advent of these massive multipurpose dams led to a thorough revision of the original River Law in 1964, these dams did not cause a significant shift in the mentality that had built Japan's modern river regime.[15] Rather, these modern monoliths fit within the

University Press, 1998), 728–55; Aaron Moore, *Constructing East Asia: Technology, Ideology, and Empire in Japan's Wartime Era, 1931–1945* (Stanford: Stanford University Press, 2013), 150–87.

11   Eric Dinmore, "Concrete Results? The TVA and the Appeal of Large Dams in Occupation-Era Japan," *Journal of Japanese Studies* 39, no. 1 (2013): 1–38.

12   Mikuriya Takashi, *Seisaku no sōgō to kenryoku: Nihon seiji no senzen to sengo* (Tokyo: Tōkyō Daigaku Shuppankai, 1996), 159. Sara Pritchard describes similar aims and concerns amongst French technocrats in their efforts to develop France's rivers in the postwar period. Sara B. Pritchard, *Confluence: The Nature of Technology and the Remaking of the Rhône* (Cambridge: Harvard University Press, 2011).

13   The Amagase Dam is 73 m high, has a crest length of 254 m, and produces 92,000 kW.

14   The Yagisawa Dam is 131 m high, has a crest length of 352 m, and produces 240,000 kW.

15   An English-language translation of the revised 1964 River Law is included in the four-volume set of documents edited by the Construction Ministry. Kensetsushō Kasenkyoku, ed., *Kasenhō shiryō shū* (Tokyo: Nihon Kansen Kyōkai, 1966), 1:316–42.

modernist framework that sought to control the country's rivers for the "public good" by preventing flooding as well as providing electricity and drinking water for the rapidly growing urban population.[16]

From the 1890s until today, local politicians and central government officials have used the shibboleth of "*chisui*" (flood control) to secure both public support and national funding for the building of Japan's modern river regime. By straightening and narrowing riverbeds, dredging sandbars to prevent the growth of vegetation and speed the flow of water, removing gravel for construction, building of numerous barrages and weirs across the lower portions of rivers, and erecting upstream dams, the Construction Ministry's officials and engineers abstracted the hydraulic processes of the country's rivers from their broader riparian relations. This kind of narrow understanding of rivers and the building of a national riparian infrastructure around it came at a well-documented cost to local communities, political institutions, and of course the rivers themselves. In addition to the surrounding loss of wetlands and the various creatures who lived in them, the reengineering of rivers removed sand and gravel that filtered pollutants, altered water temperatures and sped up currents, reduced the nutrients for invertebrates and other organisms, fragmented habitats, became impassible for migrating fish, and decreased stopover sites and food sources for migrating birds. By failing to account for these and other ecological dimensions of riparian relations, the Construction Ministry contributed to the formation of riverscapes that also rendered rivers less hospitable to people whose livelihood and recreation depended on healthy riparian habitats. Moreover, just as with the Home Ministry in the prewar period, the Construction Ministry for most of the postwar period relied on coercive means like land expropriations and the withdrawal of funding for other projects to gain control of sites to build its dams and other kinds of river works.[17] For the most part, these sites were in rural areas and the dams and other river works mostly benefited distant urban areas. By externalizing local participation from the deliberative framework employed to determine where large projects were to be located, national interests superseded local interests and urban concerns were prioritized over those of rural communities.[18] The historian Michael

---

16   Eric Dinmore, "High-Growth Hydrosphere: Sakuma Dam and the Socio-Natural Dimensions of "Comprehensive Development" Planning in Post-1945 Japan," in *Environment and Society in the Japanese Islands: From Pre-History to the Present*, ed. Bruce L. Batten and Philip C. Brown (Corvallis: Oregon State University Press, 2015), 114–35.

17   Daniel P. Aldrich, *Site Fights: Divisive Facilities and Civil Society in Japan and the West* (Ithaca: Cornell University Press, 2010), 95–118.

18   In his study of the postwar student movement, Kenji Hasegawa examines the strained relations between locals and student activists during the early 1950s as they tried to forge

Lewis also argues that the "river politics" of the early twentieth century were the prototype of all later pork-barrel infrastructural projects that have dramatically shaped the landscapes and riverscapes of the archipelago.[19] The engineer Miyamura Tadashi observes that one of the side effects of excluding local participation in river-related decisions has been to lull people into complacency, allowing these communities to believe the massive levees and central government have everything under control, and thereby lower local preparedness when the inevitable flood occurs.[20] Yet, despite the rising criticism from within Japanese society, various restrictions on people's and other creature's access and use of river channels, and the tremendous outlay already paid during the past century to construct levees and dams, in the twenty-first century the Ministry of Land, Infrastructure, Transport, and Tourism has shown little hesitancy in its pursuit of bigger levees and more dams.[21] And almost as in response to these persistent efforts to control them, the rivers of Japan have continued to inundate the cities and towns that have crowded all along their downstream extents. The residents of the Kinai region learned this all too well when in July 2018 monsoon rains and a typhoon left in their wake widespread flooding, destruction, and the death of over 250 people. And in October of the following year the people of the Kantō region suffered a similar fate when one of the biggest typhoons ever recorded blew northward across the Kantō region dropping an unprecedented amount of rain, breaching levees in seven

---

an alliance against the central government's ultimately successful effort to build the Ogōchi Dam on the headwaters of the Tama River. Kenji Hasegawa, *Student Radicalism and the Formation of Postwar Japan* (Singapore: Palgrave Macmillan, 2019), 89–124. See also M. William Steele, "The History of the Tama River: Social Reconstructions," in *A History of Water: Water Control and River Biographies*, ed. T. Tvedt and E. Jakobsson (London: I. B. Tauris, 2006), 231–32.

19   Michael Lewis, *Becoming Apart: National Power and Local Politics in Toyama, 1868–1945* (Cambridge: Harvard University Asia Center, 2000), 75, 113–14.

20   Miyamura Tadashi, *Suigai: chisui to suibō no chie* (Tokyo: Chūō Kōron, 1985), 213–24.

21   In 2001, administration of the country's rivers changed when the Construction Ministry merged with the Ministry of Transport (Un'yushō), National Land Agency (Kokudochō), and the Hokkaidō Development Agency (Hokkaidō Kaihatsuchō) to form the new Ministry of Land, Infrastructure, and Transport (Kokudo Kōtsūshō), whose official name in English changed in 2008 to the Ministry of Land, Infrastructure, Transport, and Tourism (MLIT) with the addition of the Japan Tourism Agency (Kankōchō) to the ministry's portfolio of agencies. Within MLIT, the Water and Disaster Management Bureau (Mizukanri Kokudo Hozenkyoku) currently administers most issues concerning the nation's first-class rivers, such as the planning and construction of river works, flood and erosion prevention measures, and the protection of riparian environments. Kokudo kōtsūshō, "Mizukanri Kokudo Hozenkyoku," http://www.mlit.go.jp/mizukokudo/index .html, accessed 17 May 2019.

prefectures, causing more than a trillion yen in damage, and taking the lives of nearly ninety people. While there were no catastrophic levee breaches along the Yodo and Tone Rivers during these most recent floods, this flooding is a reminder that even today when channeled, diverted, and dammed by a myriad of levees, weirs, multiton concrete tetrapods, and massive multipurpose dams, the rivers of Japan continue to flow, albeit sometimes into undesired places and at frightening volumes, and contribute to the environmental relations that are an integral part of people's lives.

These floods and the damage they cause also suggest that in this time of quickening climate change a more capacious understanding of rivers that includes their broader riparian relations would be a good place to begin anew. This understanding should start with a greater recognition of how vital rivers remain to the lives and livelihoods of people in both rural and urban Japan. In fact, one of this book's aims has been to show that rivers are not just a part of nature, out there in the Japanese countryside, but that rivers have long been and will continue to be an essential part of people's daily lives. While these rivers can certainly destroy levees and the homes, businesses, and lives those massive walls were meant to protect, this modern river regime has also ensured that these waterways have persisted, even if in their diminished form, to play an essential role by providing water, food, and energy to communities throughout the country. Today, Japan is an extraordinarily urbanized society with about 90 percent of the population living in one of the country's many cities, but it is still agriculture, and hence the food people eat, that makes up just over 70 percent of the country's river water consumption.[22] Moreover, in both rural and urban areas, it is treated river water that most people drink and industries use for cooling and manufacturing. The conurbation that includes Kyoto, Osaka, and Kobe, for example, draws on the Yodo River to meet nearly all the water needs of its residents and industries.[23] In the Kantō region, the Tokyo metropolitan area draws much of its water from the Tone River system. Overlapping with this rural supply of water to urban areas is the supply of hydroelectricity from all those dams at the headwaters of the country's rivers. In 2012, these dams transformed the energy flow of the country's rivers into 836 billion kWh (7.6 percent of all energy generated that year in Japan).[24] And,

---

22 Based on 2015 data, agriculture makes up 72 percent of all river water usage and 33 percent of all groundwater usage. Kokudo Kōtsūshō, ed., *Nihon no suishigen no genkyō* (Tokyo: Kokudo Kōtsūshō, 2018), 4.

23 Kokudo Kōtsūshō, ed., *Nihon no suishigen* (Tokyo: Kokudo Kōtsūshō, 2014), 64–73.

24 This figure includes all hydroelectric dams making more than 1,000 kW of electricity. Although hydroelectric dams continued to generate about the same amount of electricity in Japan between 1970 and 2014, the share of electricity produced by these dams

following the 2011 Fukushima disaster's demonstration of the real dangers and costs of nuclear energy production, the value of the country's rivers to produce hydroelectricity has again been affirmed.[25]

In highlighting the ways in which rivers and riparian relations are critical to the political economy of Japan, it is also necessary to recognize those environmental relations that lack a clear commodity value and whose temporal and spatial scales may escape the standard metrices used to evaluate such relations. The more than century-long building and working within the modern river regime, however, has produced a powerful path of dependency that preempted a broader appreciation of rivers and alternative approaches to river management. In fact, it was only after decades of local protests against water pollution and excessive dam building, a rising demand for recreational places in and outside of cities, and the deindustrialization and bursting of the economic bubble in the early 1990s that the National Diet again revised the River Law in 1997 to incorporate for the first time environmental concerns and the views of local communities in planning future river projects.[26] In other words, the techno-political framework that had for so long externalized many kinds of riparian relations was being reassembled to require their inclusion. While the inclusion of local views in the planning of river projects has progressed at a ponderous pace, officials at the municipal, prefectural, and national level have carried out thousands of small and large projects to improve water quality, help fish migrate, reintroduce both gravel and vegetation, and create riffles and pools that support the variety of organisms needed for complex riparian ecosystems to thrive.[27] The vast majority of these "restoration" projects, however, are limited in scope and scale, predominantly working within the confines of the levees, floodwalls, sluices, revetments, and dams that have been inherited from the twentieth century. There has been no "comprehensive national plan" or even river-basin plans, to "restore" the country's rivers.

---

decreased from about 20 percent in 1970 to 7.6 percent in 2014 with the increasing reliance on fossil fuels and nuclear power. Kokudo Kōtsūshō, *Nihon no suishigen*, 76–77.

25 The difficulties of the Fukushima clean-up are also a reminder that there are still no permanent storage sites for the waste generated by the nuclear power industry in Japan and there are no communities willing to accept the risk or stigma of storing these highly toxic materials.

26 River Bureau, Ministry of Construction, *The River Law* (Tokyo: Infrastructure Development Institute-Japan, 1997).

27 Keigo Nakamura, Klement Tockner, and Kunihiko Amano, "River and Wetland Restoration: Lessons from Japan," *Bioscience* 56, no. 5 (2006): 419–29; Paul Waley, "Ruining and Restoring Rivers: State and Civil Society in Japan," *Pacific Affairs* 78, no. 2 (2005): 195–215; Chino Tsunehide, "Kasenhō kaisei no seisaku katei to kasen gijutsu kanryō no kadai ishiki," *Kankyō shakaigaku kenkyū* 17 (2011): 126–40.

Nor could there truly be one because just as the medieval essayist Kamo no Chōmei observed: "the current of the river does not cease ... the water is never the same." That is, while the rivers of Japan remain, past riparian relations can never truly be restored. But in these smaller local projects, there are glimmers of hope reflecting people's greater appreciation and awareness of the rivers and riparian relations within which we are all entangled.

Bibliography

Websites

Denshi Seifu no Sōgō Madoguchi. "Kasenhō." https://elaws.e-gov.go.jp/search/elaws Search/elaws_search/lsg0500/detail?lawId=339AC0000000167#G.

Kokudo Chiriin. "Nihon zenkoku no shicchi menseki henka no chōsa kekka (2000)." https://www.gsi.go.jp/kankyochiri/shicchimenseki2.html.

Kokudo Kōtsūshō. "Mizukanri Kokudo Hozenkyoku." http://www.mlit.go.jp/mizukokudo/index.html.

Kokudo Kōtsūshō. "Nihon no kawa: zenkoku no ikkyū kasen o shōkai." http://www.mlit.go.jp/river/toukei_chousa/kasen/jiten/nihon_kawa/index.html.

Mizukanri Kokudo Hozenkyoku. "2019 Kasen dētabukku." https://www.mlit.go.jp/river/toukei_chousa/kasen_db/pdf/2019/0-1allv3.pdf.

Local Histories

Abiko-shi Kyōiku Iinkai, ed. *Abiko-shi shi: kingendai hen*. Abiko, Chiba: Abiko-shi Kyōiku Iinkai, 2004.

Abiko-shi Kyōiku Iinkai, ed. *Abiko-shi shi: kinsei hen*. Abiko, Chiba: Abiko-shi Kyōiku Iinkai, 2005.

Abiko-shi Kyōiku Iinkai, ed. *Abiko-shi shi: shiryō hen*. Vols. 1–9. Abiko, Chiba: Abiko-shi Kyōiku Iinkai, 1979–2002.

Asao Naohiro, Yoshikawa Shinji, Ishikawa Toshio, Mizumoto Kunihiko, eds. *Kyōto-fu no rekishi*. Tokyo: Yamakawa Shuppansha, 1999.

Chiba-ken Katori-gun Yakusho, ed. *Chiba-ken Katori-gun shi*. Chiba: Chiba-ken Katori-gun Yakusho, 1921.

Chiba-ken Shiryō Kenkyū Zaidan, ed. *Chiba-ken no rekishi*. Vols. 1–25. Chiba: Chiba-ken, 1998–2008.

Chiba-shi Shi Hensan Iinkai, ed. *Tenpō-ki no Inba-numa horiwari fushin*. Chiba: Chiba-shi, 1998.

Chōshi-shi Shi Hensan Iinkai, ed. *Chōshi-shi shi*. Chōshi, Chiba: Chōshi-shi Shi Hensan Iinkai, 1956.

Edogawa-ku Kyōiku Iinkai, ed. *Subara monjo*. Vols. 1–10. Tokyo: Edogawa-ku Kyōiku Iinkai, 1983–91.

Fushimi-chō, ed. *Gotairei kinen Kyōto-fu Fushimi-chō shi*. Fushimi: Fushimi-chō Yakuba, 1929.

Gifu-ken, ed. *Gifu-ken chisuishi*. Vols. 1–2. Gifu: Gifu-ken, 1953.

Gifu-ken, ed. *Gifu-ken shi: shiryō hen.* Vols. 1–22. Gifu: Gifu-ken, 1965–2003.

Gifu-ken, ed. *Gifu-ken shi: tsūshi hen.* Vols. 1–10. Gifu: Gifu-ken, 1965–2003.

Hanyū-shi Shi Henshū Iinkai, ed. *Hanyū-shi shi.* Vols. 1–2. Hanyū: Hannyū Shiyakusho, 1971.

Hayashi Tatsusaburō and Fujioka Kenjirō, eds. *Uji-shi shi.* Vols. 1–7. Uji, Kyoto: Uji-shi, 1974–83.

Ishii Susumu and Uno Shun'ichi, eds. *Chiba-ken no rekishi.* Tokyo: Yamakawa Shuppansha, 2000.

Kashiwa-shi Hensan Iinkai, ed. *Kashiwa-shi: kindai hen.* Kashiwa: Kashiwa-shi Kyōiku Iinkai, 2000.

Kashiwa-shi Hensan Iinkai, ed. *Kashiwa-shi: kinsei hen.* Kashiwa: Kashiwa-shi Kyōiku Iinkai, 1995.

Kashiwa-shi Hensan Iinkai, ed. *Kashiwa-shi: shiryō hen.* Vols. 1–11. Kashiwa: Kashiwa Shiyakusho, 1969–74.

Kitakuwata-gun, ed. *Kyōto-fu Kitakuwata-gun shi.* Kyoto: Kitakuwata-gun, 1923.

Kōnosu-shi Shishi Hensan Chōsakai, ed. *Kōnosu-shi shi: shiryō hen.* Vols. 1–3. Kōnosu, Saitama: Kōnosu-shi Shishi Hensan Chōsakai, 2000–6.

Kōnosu-shi Shishi Hensan Chōsakai, ed. *Kōnosu-shi shi: tsūshi hen.* Vols. 1–7. Kōnosu, Saitama: Kōnosu-shi Shishi Hensan Chōsakai, 1989–98.

Koshigaya-shi Shishi Hensanshitsu, ed. *Koshigaya-shi shi: shiryō hen.* Vols. 1–4. Koshigawa, Saitama: Koshigaya-shi Shishi Hensanshitsu, 1972–75.

Koshigaya-shi Shishi Hensanshitsu, ed. *Koshigaya-shi shi: tsūshi hen.* Vols. 1–2. Koshigawa, Saitama: Koshigaya-shi Shishi Hensanshitsu, 1975–77.

Koshigaya-shi Shishi Hensanshitsu, ed. *Koshigaya-shi shi: zoku shiryō hen.* Vols. 1–3. Koshigawa, Saitama: Koshigaya-shi Shishi Hensanshitsu, 1981–82.

Kumiyama-chō Shi Hensan Iinkai, ed. *Kumiyama-chō shi.* Vols. 1–2. Kumiyama, Kyoto: Kumiyama-chō, 1986–89.

Kumiyama-chō Shi Hensan Iinkai, ed. *Kumiyama-chō shi: shiryō hen.* Kumiyama, Kyoto: Kumiyama-chō, 1992.

Kyōto-fu, ed. *Kyōto-fu shi.* Vols. 1–2. Kyoto: Kyōto-fu, 1915.

Kyōto-shi, ed. *Shiryō Kyōto no rekishi.* Vols. 1–16. Tokyo: Heibonsha, 1979–94.

Mito-shi Shi Hensan Iinkai, ed. *Mito-shi shi.* Vols. 1–9. Mito, Ibraki: Mito-shi, 1963–98.

Nagareyama Hakubutsukan, ed. *Nagareyama-shi shi: bekkan—Tonegawa unga shiryō shū.* Nagareyama, Chiba: Nagareyama-shi, 1985.

Ōsaka-fu, ed. *Ōsaka-fukai shi.* Vols. 1–5. Osaka: Ōsaka-fu, 1911–33.

Ōsaka-fu, ed. *Ōsaka-fu shi.* Vols. 1–5. Osaka: Ōsaka-fu, 1903.

Saitama-ken, ed. *Arakawa.* Vols. 1–5. Urawa: Saitama-ken, 1987–88.

Saitama-ken, ed. *Shinpen Saitama-ken shi: shiryō hen.* Vols. 1–26. Urawa, Saitama: Saitama-ken, 1981–91.

Saitama-ken, ed. *Shinpen Saitama-ken shi: tsūshi hen.* Vols. 1–7. Urawa, Saitama: Saitama-ken, 1981–91.

Sawara-shi Hensan Iinkai, ed. *Sawara-shi shi: shiryō hen.* Vols. 1–3. Sawara, Chiba: Sawara Shiyakusho, 1996–98.

Sawara Shiyakusho, ed. *Sawara-shi shi.* Sawara, Chiba: Sawara Shiyakusho, 1966.

Shinshū Ōsaka-shi Shi Hensan Iinkai, ed. *Shinshū Ōsaka-shi shi.* Vols. 1–10. Osaka: Ōsaka-shi, 1988–96.

Tōkyō Shiyakusho, ed. *Tōkyō-shi shikō: hensai hen.* Vols. 1–5. Tokyo: Tōkyō-shi, 1914–17.

Tōkyō-to Minato-ku Kyōiku Iinkai, ed. *Daiba: naikai odaiba no kōzō to chikuzō.* Tokyo: Minato-ku Kyōdo Shiryōkan, 2000.

Tōkyō-to Shiyakusho, ed. *Tōkyō-shi shikō: shigai hen.* Vols. 1–87. Tokyo: Tōkyō-to, 1914–96.

Tone-machi Shi Hensan Iinkai, ed. *Tone-machi shi: shiryō shū.* Vols. 1–3. Tone: Tone-machi, 1983.

Yamashiro-chō, ed. *Yamashiro-chō shi: honbun.* Yamashiro, Kyoto: Yamashiro Machi-yakuba, 1987.

Primary and Secondary Sources

Abele, Mike. "Peasants, Skinners, and Dead Cattle: The Transformation of Rural Society in Western Japan, 1600–1890." PhD diss., University of Illinois at Urbana-Champaign, 2018.

Adas, Michael. *Machines as the Measure of Men: Science, Technology, and Ideologies of Western Dominance.* Ithaca: Cornell University Press, 1989.

Aihara Masayoshi. "Meiji-ki no Kamedagawa tenchū Tone unga kaisaku ni miru chiiki to hito no haikei." *Hōsei chiri* 33 (2002): 1–15.

Akamatsu Sōtan. *Tonegawa zushi.* Tokyo: Iwanami Shoten, 1938.

Akiyama, Tomohide. *A Forest Again: Lessons from the Ashio Copper Mine and Reforestation Operations.* Translated by Shiro Okabe and Sadao Hatta. Tokyo: Food and Agriculture Policy Research Center, 1992.

Aldrich, Daniel P. *Site Fights: Divisive Facilities and Civil Society in Japan and the West.* Ithaca: Cornell University Press, 2010.

Allaby, Michael, ed. *A Dictionary of Ecology.* New York: Oxford University Press, 1998.

Aoki Toshiyuki. "Kagakuteki shikō no hattatsu to rangaku." In *Jugaku kokugaku yōgaku,* ed. Rai Ki'ichi, 295–332. Tokyo: Chūō Kōronsha, 1993.

Arakawa Karyū Kōji Jimusho Nanajūgo-nen shi Henshū Iinkai, ed. *Toshi o yuku Arakawa: Arakawa karyū kōji jimusho nanajūgo-nen shi.* Tokyo: Kensetsushō Kantō Chihō Kensetsukyoku Arakawa Karyū Kōji Jimusho, 1990.

Ariizumi Sadao. *Meiji seijishi no kiso katei: chikō seiji jōkyō shiron*. Tokyo: Yoshikawa Kōbunkan, 1980.

Ashida Koreto, Mamiya Kotonobu, Nemoto Seiji, eds. *Shinpen Musashi fudokikō*. Vols. 1–12. Tokyo: Yūsankaku, 1996.

Ashihara Shūji. *Kawazakana zushi*. Nagareyama, Chiba: Ronshobō, 1984.

Asquith, Pamela J. "Sources for Imanishi Kinji's Views of Sociality and Evolutionary Outcomes." *Journal of Biosciences* 32, no. 4 (2007): 635–41.

Asquith, Pamela J., and Arne Kalland, eds. *Japanese Images of Nature: Cultural Perspectives*. Richmond: Curzon Press, 1997.

Auslin, Michael R. *Negotiating with Imperialism: The Unequal Treaties and the Culture of Japanese Diplomacy*. Cambridge: Harvard University Press, 2004.

Bandō Tadashi, Tanigawa Yukie, and Mayumi Sakurai. "Ogura-ike kantakuchi (Kyōto) no shokubutsu-sō." *Kyōto Kyōiku Daigaku kankyō kyōiku kenkyū nenpō* 9 (2001): 85–99.

Banno, Junji. *The Establishment of the Japanese Constitutional System*. Translation of *Meiji kenpō taisei no kakuritsu*. Translated by J. A. A. Stockwin. London: Routledge, 1992.

Barad, Karen. *Meeting the Universe Halfway: Quantum Physics and the Entanglement of Matter and Meaning*. Durham: Duke University Press, 2008.

Barles, Sabine. "The Seine as a Parisian River: Its Imprint, Its Ascendancy, and Its Mutual Dependencies in the Eighteenth through the Twentieth Century." In *Rivers Lost, Rivers Regained: Rethinking City-River Relations*, edited by Uwe Lübken, Martin Knoll, and Dieter Schott, 47–62. Pittsburgh: University of Pittsburgh Press, 2017.

Bartholomew, James R. "Modern Science in Japan: Comparative Perspectives." *Journal of World History* 4, no. 1 (1993): 101–16.

Batten, Bruce L., and Philip C. Brown, eds. *Environment and Society in the Japanese Islands: From Pre-History to the Present*. Corvallis: Oregon State University Press, 2015.

Bauer, Andrew M., and Mona Bhan. *Climate without Nature: A Critical Anthropology of the Anthropocene*. New York: Cambridge University Press, 2018.

Bauer, Andrew M., and Steve Kosiba. "How Things Act: An Archaeology of Materials in Political Life." *Journal of Social Archaeology* 16, no. 2 (2016): 115–41.

Beasley, W. G. "Meiji Political Institutions." In *The Cambridge History of Japan: The Nineteenth Century*, edited by Marius B. Jansen, 618–73. Cambridge: Cambridge University Press, 1989.

Befu, Harumi. "Village Autonomy and Articulation with the State." *The Journal of Asian Studies* 25, no. 1 (1965): 19–32.

Belhoste, Bruno, and Konstantinos Chatzis. "From Technical Corps to Technocratic Power: French State Engineers and Their Professional and Cultural Universe in the First Half of the 19th Century." *History and Technology* 23, no. 3 (2007): 209–25.

Bello, David. "An Intermittent Order Contrived on Sand: Managing Water, Siltage, Locusts, and Cultivators on the Lower Yangzi in the Early 1800s." In "Grassroots History: Global Environmental Histories from Below." Edited by Robert Michael Morrissey and Roderick I. Wilson, eds., special issue, *Resilience: A Journal of the Environmental Humanities* 3 (2016): 14–33.

Benite, Zvi Ben-Dor. "Modernity: The Sphinx and the Historian." *American Historical Review* 116, no. 3 (2011): 638–52.

Bennett, Jane. *Vibrant Matter: A Political Ecology of Things.* Durham: Duke University Press, 2010.

Berry, Mary Elizabeth. *Japan in Print: Information and Nation in the Early Modern Period.* Berkeley: University of California Press, 2006.

Bhambra, Gurminder K. "Talking among Themselves? Weberian and Marxist Historical Sociologies as Dialogues without 'Others'." *Millennium* 39, no. 3 (2011): 667–81.

Biernacki, Richard. "Method and Metaphor after the New Cultural History." In *Beyond the Cultural Turn: New Directions in the Study of Society and Culture,* edited by Victoria Bonnell and Lynn Hunt, 62–92. Berkeley: University of California Press, 1999.

Biwa-ko Chisuikai, ed. *Biwa-ko chisui enkaku shi.* Ōtsu: Biwa-ko Chisuikai, 1925.

Blackbourn, David. *The Conquest of Nature: Water, Landscape, and the Making of Modern Germany.* New York: W. W. Norton, 2006.

Blackbourn, David. "'Time Is a Violent Torrent:' Constructing and Reconstructing the Rhine in Modern German History." In *Rivers in History: Perspectives on Waterways in Europe and North America,* edited by Christof Mauch and Thomas Zeller, 11–25. Pittsburgh: University of Pittsburgh Press, 2008.

Bokuryū Katsumi. "Kinsei kuniyaku-bushin taisei no seiritsu to tenkai." *Hōsei Daigaku Daigakuin kiyō* 10 (1983): 11–26.

Botsman, Daniel. *Punishment and Power in the Making of Modern Japan.* Princeton: Princeton University Press, 2005.

Bowden, Sean. "Human and Nonhuman Agency in Deleuze." In *Deleuze and the Non/Human,* edited by Jon Roffe and Hannah Stark, 60–80. New York: Palgrave Macmillan, 2015.

Brown, Philip C. "Call It a 'Wash'? Historical Perspectives on Conundrums of Technological Modernization, Flood Amelioration, and Disasters in Modern Japan." *The Asia-Pacific Journal: Japan Focus* 12, no. 7 (2014). https://apjjf.org/2014/12/7/Philip-C.-Brown/4074/article.html.

Brown, Philip C. *Central Authority and Local Autonomy in the Formation of Early Modern Japan: The Case of Kaga Domain.* Stanford: Stanford University Press, 1993.

Brown, Philip C. *Cultivating Commons: Joint Ownership of Arable Land in Early Modern Japan.* Honolulu: University of Hawai'i Press, 2011.

Brown, Philip C. "The Mismeasure of Land: Land Surveying in the Tokugawa Period." *Monumenta Nipponica* 42, no. 2 (1987): 115–55.

Brunton, R. Henry. *Schoolmaster to an Empire: Richard Henry Brunton in Meiji Japan, 1868–1876*. New York: Greenwood Press, 1991.

Buchanan, R. A. "The Diaspora of British Engineering." *Technology and Culture* 27, no. 3 (1986): 501–24.

Buchanan, R. A. "Institutional Proliferation in the British Engineering Profession, 1847–1914." *Economic History Review* 38, no. 2 (1985): 42–60.

Buchanan, R. A. "Science and Engineering: A Case Study in British Experience in the Mid-Nineteenth Century." *Notes and Records of the Royal Society of London* 32, no. 2 (1978): 215–23.

Burns, Susan L. "Constructing the National Body: Public Health and the Nation in Nineteenth-Century Japan." In *Nation Work: Asian Elites and National Identities*, edited by Timothy Brook and Andre Schmid, 17–49. Ann Arbor: The University of Michigan Press, 2000.

Buysing, D. J. Storm. *Handleiding tot de Kennis der Waterbouwkunde voor de kadetten van der waterstaat en der genie*. Breda: Koninklijke Militaire Akademie, 1864.

Callon, Michel. "Introduction: The Embeddedness of Economic Markets in Economics." In *The Laws of the Markets*, 1–54. Oxford: Blackwell, 1998.

Carter, Robert E. *The Kyoto School: An Introduction*. Albany: State University of New York Press, 2013.

Casey, Edward S. *Getting Back into Place: Toward a Renewed Understanding of the Place-World*. Bloomington: Indiana University Press, 2009.

Chambers, David Wade, and Richard Gillespie. "Locality in the History of Science: Colonial Science, Technoscience, and Indigenous Knowledge." *Osiris* 15 (2000): 221–40.

Chiba-ken Naimubu, ed. *Chiba-ken suisan ippan*. Chiba: Chiba-ken Naimubu, 1919.

Chiba Tokuji. *Hageyama no bunka*. Tokyo: Gakuseisha, 1970.

Chino Tsunehide. "Kasenhō kaisei no seisaku katei to kasen gijutsu kanryō no kadai ishiki." *Kankyō shakaigaku kenkyū* 17 (2011): 126–40.

Cioc, Mark. *The Rhine: An Eco-Biography, 1815–2000*. Seattle: University of Washington Press, 2002.

Clancey, Gregory K. *Earthquake Nation: The Cultural Politics of Japanese Seismicity, 1868–1930*. Berkeley: University of California Press, 2006.

Coole, Diana, and Samantha Frost, eds. *New Materialisms: Ontology, Agency, and Politics*. Durham: Duke University Press, 2010.

Cronon, William. *Nature's Metropolis: Chicago and the Great West*. New York: W. W. Norton, 1991.

De Gamond, Aimé Thomé. *Mémoire sur le régime général des eaux courantes. Plan d'ensemble pour la transformation de l'appareil hydraulique de la France*. Paris: Dunod, 1871.

DeLanda, Manuel. *Assemblage Theory*. Edinburgh: Edinburgh University Press, 2016.

Deleuze, Gilles. *Difference and Repetition*. Translated by Paul Patton. New York: Columbia University Press, 1995.

Deleuze, Gilles, and Claire Parnet. *Dialogues II*. Translated by Hugh Tomlinson and Barbara Habberjam. New York: Columbia University Press, 2002.

Deleuze, Gilles, and Felix Guattari. *A Thousand Plateaus: Capitalism and Schizophrenia*. Minneapolis: University of Minnesota Press, 1987.

Descola, Philippe. *Beyond Nature and Culture*. Chicago: University of Chicago Press, 2013.

Dinmore, Eric. "Concrete Results? The TVA and the Appeal of Large Dams in Occupation-Era Japan." *Journal of Japanese Studies* 39, no. 1 (2013): 1–38.

Dinmore, Eric. "'Mountain Dream' or the 'Submergence of Fine Scenery'? Japanese Contestations over the Kurobe Number Four Dam, 1920–1970." *Water History* 6, no. 4 (2014): 315–40.

Diogo, Maria Paula, and Dirk van Laak, eds. *Europeans Globalizing: Mapping, Exploiting, Exchanging*. London: Palgrave Macmillan, 2016.

Divall, Colin. "A Measure of Agreement: Employers and Engineering Studies in the Universities of England and Wales, 1897–1939." *Social Studies of Science* 20, no. 1 (1990): 65–122.

Doboku Gakkai, ed. *Meiji igo: honpō doboku to gaijin*. Tokyo: Doboku Gakkai, 1942.

Doboku Gakkai, ed. *Nihon doboku shi: Meiji izen*. Tokyo: Iwanami Shoten, 1936.

Doboku Gakkai Dobokushi Kenkyu Iinkai, ed. *Furuichi Kōi to sono jidai*. Tokyo: Doboku Gakkai, 2004.

"Dobokuryō kengi suisei kōsei no gi utagai." May 1874. National Archives of Japan, Tokyo.

Duara, Prasenjit. *The Crisis of Global Modernity: Asian Traditions and a Sustainable Future*. Cambridge: Cambridge University Press, 2015.

Duara, Prasenjit. *Rescuing History from the Nation: Questioning Narratives of Modern China*. Chicago: University of Chicago Press, 1995.

Dupré, John. *Processes of Life: Essays in the Philosophy of Biology*. Oxford: Oxford University Press, 2012.

Dyer, Henry. "Engineering in Japan." *The Times*. Engineering Supplement. 18 March 1908.

Dyer, Henry. *The Education of Civil and Mechanical Engineers*. London: E. & F. N. Spon, 1880.

Elshakry, Marwa. "When Science Became Western: Historiographical Reflections." *Isis* 101, no. 1 (2010): 98–109.

Evenden, Matthew D. "Locating Science, Locating Salmon: Institutions, Linkages, and Spatial Practices in Early British Columbia Fisheries Science." *Environment and Planning D: Society and Space* 22, no. 3 (2004): 355–72.

Fausch, Kurt D. *For the Love of Rivers*. Corvallis: Oregon State University Press, 2015.

Fausch, Kurt D., Christian E. Torgersen, Colden V. Baxter, and Hiram W. Li. "Landscapes to Riverscapes: Bridging the Gap between Research and Conservation of Stream Fishes." *Bioscience* 52, no. 6 (2002): 483–98.

Foster, Michael D. "The Metamorphosis of the Kappa: Transformation of Folklore to Folklorism in Japan." *Asian Folklore Studies* 57, no. 1 (1998): 1–24.

Frumer, Yulia. *Making Time: Astronomical Time Measurement in Tokugawa Japan.* Chicago: University of Chicago Press, 2018.

Frumer, Yulia. "Translating Words, Building Worlds: Meteorology in Japanese, Dutch, and Chinese." *Isis* 109, no. 2 (2014): 785–820.

Fujii Hatsuo. *Doboku jinbutsu jiten.* Tokyo: Atene, 2004.

Fujii Tetsuhiro. *Ono Tomogorō no shōgai.* Tokyo: Chūō Kōronsha, 1985.

Fujimori Terunobu. *Meiji no Tōkyō keikaku.* Tokyo: Iwanami Shoten, 1990.

Fujimori Terunobu, ed. *Tōkyō toshi keikaku shiryō shūsei.* Vols. 1–34. Tokyo: Honnoyūsha, 1987–88.

Fujita Satoru. *Bakuhansei kokka no seiji shiteki kenkyū: Tenpō-ki no chitsujo gunji gaikō.* Tokyo: Azekura Shobō, 1989.

Fujita Satoru. *Kinsei no sandai kakumei.* Tokyo: Yamakawa Shuppan, 2002.

Fujitani, Takashi. *Splendid Monarchy: Power and Pageantry in Modern Japan.* Berkeley: University of California Press, 1996.

Fukagawa, Hidetoshi, and Tony Rothman. *Sacred Mathematics: Japanese Temple Geometry.* Princeton: Princeton University Press, 2008.

Fukaya Katsumi. "Tanaka Kyūgu: Jikata kōsha no minsei gijutsu." In *Kōza Nihon gijutsu no shakai shi: jinbutsu hen kinsei,* edited by Nagahara Keiji, Yamaguchi Tetsuji, and Fukaya Katsumi, 155–79. Tokyo: Nihon Hyōronsha, 1986.

Fukuda Tōru. *Kinsei shinden to sono genryū.* Tokyo: Kokon Shoin, 1986.

Fukuyama Akira. *Kinsei Nihon no suiri to chiiki: Yodogawa chiiki o chūshin ni.* Tokyo: Yūkakusan, 2003.

Funakagami. Author and publisher unknown. 1802. National Diet Library, Tokyo.

Fukuzawa, Yukichi. *The Autobiography of Fukuzawa Yukichi.* Translated by Eiichi Kiyooka. New York: Columbia University Press, 1966.

Fukuzawa Yukichi. *Fukuō jiden.* Tokyo: Jiji Shinpōsha, 1899.

Furuichi Kōi. "Doboku Gakkai dai ikkai sōkai kaichō kōen." *Doboku Gakkai zasshi* 1, no. 1 (1915): 1–4.

Furuichi Kōi. *Motes des mes voyages d'étude.* 1879. Unpublished manuscript. Furuichi Bunko, Civil Engineering Library, Tokyo University.

Furushima Toshio. *Kisei jinushisei no seisei to tenkai.* Tokyo: Iwanami Shoten, 1952.

Gabe Masao, Hirose Yoshihiro, and Nishikawa Makoto, eds. *Meiji zenki chihōkan kaigi shiryō shūsei.* Series 1, Vols. 1–8. Tokyo: Kashiwa Shobō, 1996.

Gabe Masao, Hirose Yoshihiro, and Nishikawa Makoto, eds. *Meiji zenki chihōkan kaigi shiryō shūsei.* Series 2, Vols. 1–6. Tokyo: Kashiwa Shobō, 1997.

Gandy, Matthew. "The Paris Sewers and the Rationalization of Urban Space." *Transactions of the Institute of British Geographers* 24, no. 1 (1999): 23–44.

Garon, Sheldon. *Molding Japanese Minds.* Princeton: Princeton University Press, 1997.

Garon, Sheldon. "Transnational History and Japan's 'Comparative Advantage'." *Journal of Japan Studies* 43, no. 1 (2017): 65–92.

Gilmartin, David. *Blood and Water: The Indus River Basin in Modern History.* Oakland: University of California Press, 2015.

Gluck, Carol. "The End of Elsewhere: Writing Modernity Now." *American Historical Review* 116, no. 3 (2011): 676–87.

Gluck, Carol. *Japan's Modern Myths: Ideology in the Late Meiji Period.* Princeton: Princeton University Press, 1985.

Gluck, Carol, and Anna L. Tsing, eds. *Words in Motion: Toward a Global Lexicon.* Durham: Duke University Press, 2009.

Gooday, Graeme J. N., and Morris F. Low. "Technology Transfer and Cultural Exchange: Western Scientists and Engineers Encounter Late Tokugawa and Meiji Japan." In "Beyond Joseph Needham: Science, Technology, and Medicine in East and Southeast Asia." Edited by Morris F. Low. Special issue. *Osiris*, 2nd ser., 13 (1998): 99–128.

Gordon, Andrew. *Labor and Imperial Democracy in Prewar Japan.* Berkeley: University of California Press, 1991.

Gorō Terao. *"Shizen" gainen no keisei shi: Chūgoku, Nihon, Yoroppa.* Tokyo: Nōsan Gyoson Bunka Kyōkai, 2002.

Gotō Masatoshi. *Kinsei gyogyō shakai kōzō no kenkyū.* Tokyo: Yamakawa Shuppansha, 2001.

Gotō Masatoshi. "Shōtoku-Kyōhō-ki ni okeru shimo-Tonegawa chū-ryūiki no gyogyō to muramura." In *Kokuritsu rekishi minzoku hakubutsukan kenkyū hōkoku*, no. 115 (2004): 161–76.

Gotō Yōichi and Tomoeda Ryūtarō, eds. *Kumazawa Banzan.* Vol. 30, *Nihon shisō taikei.* Tokyo: Iwanami Shoten, 1971.

Grove, Richard. *Green Imperialism: Colonial Expansion, Tropical Island Edens, and the Origins of Environmentalism, 1600–1860.* Cambridge: Cambridge University Press, 1995.

Hacking, Ian. *The Social Construction of What?* Cambridge: Harvard University Press, 1999.

Hager, Willi H., and Corrado Gisonni. "Henry Bazin—Civil Engineer." *Journal of Hydraulic Engineering* 129, no. 3 (2003): 171–75.

Hager, Willi H., and Corrado Gisonni. "Henry Bazin—Hydraulician." *American Society of Civil Engineers Conference Proceedings* (2003): 90–115.

Hagiwara Susumu, ed. *Asamayama Tenmei funka shiryō shūsei.* Vol. 1–5. Maebashi: Gunma-ken Bunka Jigyō Shinkōkai, 1985–95.

Hanes, Jeffrey E. "Contesting Centralization? Space, Time, and Hegemony in Meiji Japan." In *New Directions in the Study of Meiji Japan*, edited by Helen Hardacre, 485–95. Leiden: Brill, 1997.

Hanley, Susan B. "Urban Sanitation in Preindustrial Japan." *Journal of Interdisciplinary History* 18, no. 1 (1987): 1–26.

Hara Hidesaburō, Minegishi Sumio, Sasaki Junnosuke, and Nakamura Masanori, eds. *Taikei Nihon kokka shi: kinsei*. Tokyo: Tōkyō Shuppankai, 1975.

Hara Junji. "Kinsei zenki Tonegawa ryūiki no gyogyō." *Umikami-chō shi kenkyū*, no. 31 (1990): 1–25.

Hara Takashi. *Yumoto Yoshinori tokushi joi no ken*. 1918. National Archives, Tokyo.

Harada Kan, ed. *Miyako meisho zue*. Tokyo: Jinbutsu Ōraisha, 1967.

Hardin, Garrett. "The Tragedy of the Commons." *Science* 162, no. 3859 (1968): 1243–48.

Hare, Thomas Blenman. "Reading Kamo no Chōmei." *Harvard Journal of Asiatic Studies* 49, no. 1 (1989): 173–228.

Harootunian, Harry D. *Overcome by Modernity: History, Culture, and Community in Interwar Japan*. Princeton: Princeton University Press, 2000.

Harvey, David. *Paris, Capital of Modernity*. New York: Routledge, 2003.

Hasegawa, Kenji. *Student Radicalism and the Formation of Postwar Japan*. Singapore: Palgrave Macmillan, 2019.

Hashimoto Naoko. *Kōchi kaihatsu to keikan no shizen kankyōgaku Tonegawa ryūiki no kinsei kankyō o chūshin ni*. Tokyo: Kokin Shoin, 2010.

Hatoyama Haruko. *Hatoyama no isshō*. Tokyo: Ōsorasha, 1997.

Hattori Takeshi. *Kindai chihō seiji to suiri doboku*. Kyoto: Shibunkaku Shuppan, 1995.

Hawks, Francis L. *Narrative of the Expedition of an American Squadron to the China Seas and Japan: Performed in the Years 1852, 1853, and 1854, under the Command of Commodore M. C. Perry, United States Navy, by Order of the Government of the United States*. Washington, DC: A. O. P. Nicholson, 1856.

Hayami Akira and Miyamata Matarō, eds. *Keizai shakai no seiritsu: 17–18 seiki*. Vol. 1, *Nihon keizai shi*. Edited by Umemura Mataji, Shinbo Hiroshi, Nakamura Takafusa, Nishikawa Shunsaku, Hayami Akira, Yasuba Yasukichi, and Abe Takeshi. Tokyo: Iwanami Shoten, 1988.

Hayek, Matthias, and Annick Horiuchi, eds. *Listen, Copy, Read: Popular Learning in Early Modern Japan*. Brill's Japanese Studies Library 46. Leiden: Brill, 2014.

Heidegger, Martin. *Being and Time*. Translated by J. Macquarrie and E. Robinson. Oxford: Basil Blackwell, 1962.

Heisig, James. *Philosophers of Nothingness: An Essay on the Kyoto School*. Honolulu: University of Hawai'i Press, 2001.

Helin, Jenny, Tor Hernes, and Daniel Hjorth, eds. *The Oxford Handbook of Process Philosophy and Organizational Studies*. Oxford: Oxford University Press, 2014.

Hino Shōshō. *Kinai kasen kōtsū shi kenkyū*. Tokyo: Yoshikawa Kōbunkan, 1986.

Hino Shōshō. *Kinsei Yodogawa suiun shiryō shū*. Kyoto: Dōhōsha Shuppan, 1982.

H. I. H. Crown Prince Naruhito [Emperor Reiwa]. "Edo and Water." In *Asia and the History of the International Economy: Essays in Memory of Peter Mathias*, edited by A. J. H. Latham and Heita Kawakatsu, 40–48. New York: Routledge, 2018.

Hodges, Matt. "Rethinking Time's Arrow: Bergson, Deleuze and the Anthropology of Time." *Anthropological Theory* 8, no. 4 (2008): 399–429.

Hohensinner, Severin, Bernhard Lager, Christoph Sonnlechner, Gertrud Haidvogl, Sylvia Gierlinger, Martin Schmid, Fridolin Krausmann, and Verena Winiwarter. "Changes in Water and Land: The Reconstructed Viennese Riverscape from 1500 to the Present." *Water History* 5, no. 2 (2013): 145–72.

Honda Kanosuke. *Kawa-jō fūu tomari nikki*. Transcribed and edited by Watanabe Hideo. In *Kinsei kōtsū no shiteki kenkyū*, edited by Maruyama Yasunari, 391–411. Tokyo: Bunken Shuppan, 1998.

Hoston, Germaine A. *Marxism and the Crisis of Development in Prewar Japan*. Princeton: Princeton University Press, 1986.

Howell, David L. *Geographies of Identity in Nineteenth-Century Japan*. Berkeley: University of California Press, 2005.

Howell, David L. "Hard Times in the Kantō: Economic Change and Village Life in Late Tokugawa Japan." *Modern Asian Studies* 23, no. 2 (1989): 349–71.

Hoy, David Couzens. *The Time of Our Lives: A Critical History of Temporality*. Cambridge: MIT Press, 2009.

Ichikawa Yoshikata. *Suiri shinpō*. Tokyo: Hakubunkan, 1897. National Diet Library, Tokyo.

Ienaga Saburō, Inoue Mitsutada, Ōno Susumu, and Sakamoto Tarō, eds. *Nihon shoki*. In *Nihon koten bungaku taikei*. Vols. 67–68. Tokyo: Iwanami Shoten, 1965–67.

Iguchi Shōhei. "Furuichi Kōi no kengaku ryokōki." Pts. 1–3. *Nihon no kawa* 30 (October 1984): 54–74; 31 (April 1985): 33–62; 33 (March 1986): 35–65.

Iijima Chiaki. "Tenmei-Kansei-ki no 'Kinō tedai' fushin: kasen fushin no baai." *Shinano* 54, no. 4 (2002): 233–60.

Iishi Kanji. "Bakumatsu-ishin-ki no Yamashiro chagyō: raisangyō to Nihon kindaika." *Ritsumeikan keizaigaku* 39, no. 5 (1990): 493–521.

Iizuka Takafusa. "Meiji-ki ni okeru kasen shū'un no chiikiteki henka: Yodogawa ryūiki, Kisogawa ryūiki, Tonegawa ryūiki o chūshin ni." *Chiiki seisakugaku jānaru* 6, no 2. (2017): 27–47.

Imanishi Kinji. *A Japanese View of Nature: The World of Living Things*. Translated by Pamela J. Asquith, Heita Kawakatsu, Shusuke Yagi, and Hiroyuki Takasaki. London: RoutledgeCurzon, 2002.

Imanishi Kinji. *Seibutsu no sekai*. Vol. 1, *Imanishi Kinji zenshū*, edited by Itani Junichirō and Saitō Kiyoaki, 1–164. Tokyo: Kōdansha, 1993–94.

Imoto Nōichi, Hori Nobuo, and Muramatsu Tomotsugu, eds. *Matsuo Bashō shū*. Vol. 41, *Nihon koten bungaku zenshū*. Tokyo: Shōgakukan, 1972.

Ingold, Tim. *Being Alive: Essays on Movement, Knowledge and Description*. New York: Routledge, 2011.

Ingold, Tim. "Footprints through the Weather-World: Walking, Breathing, Knowing." In "Making Knowledge." Supplement, *Journal of the Royal Anthropological Institute* 16, No. S1 (2010): S121–39.

Ingold, Tim. *Perception of the Environment: Essays in Livelihood, Dwelling, and Skill*. New York: Routledge, 2011.

Inō Tadataka Kenkyūkai, ed. *Tadataka to Inō-zu*. Tokyo: Awa Puran'ningu, 1998.

Inobe Shigeo, Maruyama Jirō, Kuroita Katsumi, Umasugi Tarō, eds. *Tokugawa jikki*. In *Shintei zōho kokushi taikei*. Vols. 38–47. Tokyo: Yoshikawa Kōbunkan, 1964–66.

Inoue Seitarō. *Sabō-kō dai'i*. Osaka: Naimushō Ōsaka Doboku Shucchōjo, 1891. National Diet Library, Tokyo.

Ishida Hidemi, ed. *Saishū nikki: Kamogawa, 1935*. Kyoto: Kyōto Daigaku Gakujutsu Shuppankai, 2002.

Ishii Kenji. *Zusetsu wabune shiwa*. Tokyo: Shiseidō, 1983.

Ishikawa Eisuke. *Ōedo ekorojī jijō*. Tokyo: Kōdansha, 2000.

Ishikawa Eisuke. *Ōedo risaikuru jijō*. Tokyo: Kōdansha, 1997.

Ishiyama Hidekazu. "Toshi Edo ni okeru suigai shi kenkyū no genjō to kadai." *Tōkyō-to Edo Tōkyō hakubutsukan kenkyū hōkoku*, no. 16 (2010): 5–18.

Ishizuki Minoru. *Kindai Nihon no kaigai ryūgaku shi*. Tokyo: Chūō Kōron, 1992.

Ishizuki Minoru. "Overseas Study by Japanese in the Early Meiji Period." Translated by Andrew Fraser. In *The Modernizers: Overseas Students, Foreign Employees, and Meiji Japan*, edited by Ardath W. Burks, 161–83. Boulder: Westview Press, 1985.

Isohata Hiroshi. "Kobe Nunobiki damu, oyobi kanren shisetsu no kensetsu: kensetsu kiroku shashin no bunseki." *Dobokushi kenkyū* 19 (1999): 281–92.

Itō Yasuo. *Kōzui to ningen: sono sōkoku no rekishi*. Tokyo: Kokin Shoin, 2010.

Itō Yasuo, ed. *Ranjin kōshi Esseru Nihon kaisō-roku* [English title provided: Memoirs of G. A. Escher: Japan 1873–1878]. Mikuni: Mikuni-chō, 1990.

Itō Yasuo. "Ranjin yatoi kōshi to sono chisui shisō." *Kyōto rekishi saigai kenkyū* 2 (2002): 1–5.

Itō, Yoshiaki. "Development of Ecology in Japan, with Special Reference to the Role of Kinji Imanishi." *Ecological Research* 6, no. 2 (1991): 139–55.

Itō Yoshiichi. *Edo jimawari keizai no tenkai*. Tokyo: Kashiwa Shobō, 1966.

Itō Yoshiichi. *Edo jōsuidō no rekishi*. Tokyo: Yoshikawa Kōbunkan, 1996.

Izumi Seiji. *Bakufu no chiiki shihai to daikan*. Tokyo: Dōseisha, 2001.

Izumi Seiji. "Kinsei shoki ikkoku gōchō no kenkyū: Shōhō gōchō o chūshin ni." *Chiiki seisaku kenkyū* 8, no. 2 (2005): 1–19.

Jackson, Jeffrey H. *Paris under Water: How the City of Light Survived the Great Flood of 1910*. London: Palgrave Macmillan, 2010.

Jackson, Terrence. *Network of Knowledge: Western Science and the Tokugawa Information Revolution*. Honolulu: University of Hawai'i Press, 2016.

James Leffel & Co. *Construction of Mill Dams, Comprising also the Building of Race and Reservoir Embankments and Head Gates, the Measurement of Streams, Gauging of Water Supply, &c*. Springfield, Ohio: O. J. Leffel & Co., 1874.

Jannetta, Ann Bowman. *The Vaccinators: Smallpox, Medical Knowledge, and the Opening of Japan*. Stanford: Stanford University Press, 2007.

Japan Commission on Large Dams. *Dams in Japan: Past, Present and Future*. London: CRC Press, 2009.

Jinnai, Hidenobu. *Tokyo: A Spatial Anthropology*. Translated by Kimiko Nishimura. Berkeley: University of California Press, 1995.

Johnson, Walter. "On Agency." *Journal of Social History* 37, no. 1 (2003): 113–24.

Jones, Hazel J. *Live Machines: Hired Foreigners and Meiji Japan*. Vancouver: University of British Columbia Press, 1980.

Jordan, David P. *Transforming Paris: The Life and Labors of Baron Haussmann*. New York: Simon and Schuster, 1995.

Joyce, Patrick, ed. *The Social in the Question: New Bearings in History and the Social Sciences*. London: Routledge, 2002.

Judd, Richard W. *Second Nature: An Environmental History of New England*. Amherst: University of Massachusetts, 2014.

Kamibayashi Yoshiyuki. *Nihon no kawa o yomigaeraseta gishi de Reike*. Tokyo: Sōshisha, 1999.

Kamo no Chōmei. "An Account of a Ten-Foot Hut (*Hōjōki*, 1212)." Translated by Anthony H. Chambers. In *Traditional Japanese Literature: An Anthology, Beginnings to 1600*, edited by Haruo Shirane, 624–35. New York: Columbia University Press, 2007.

Kamo no Chōmei. *Hōjōki*. In vol. 30, *Nihon koten bungaku taikei*, edited by Nishio Minoru, 23–45. Tokyo: Iwanami Shoten, 1957.

Karlin, Jason G. *Gender and Nation in Meiji Japan: Modernity, Loss, and the Doing of History*. Honolulu: University of Hawai'i Press, 2014.

Kasai Yōsuiro Tochi Kairyōku, ed. *Kasai Yōsui shi: shiryō hen*. Kasukabe: Kasai Yōsuiro Toshi Kairyō-ku, 1989.

Kasai Yōsuiro Tochi Kairyōku, ed. *Kasai Yōsui shi: tsūshi hen*. Kasukabe: Kasai Yōsuiro Tochi Kairyōku, 1988.

Kasulis, Thomas. *Engaging Japanese Philosophy: A Short History*. Honolulu: University of Hawai'i Press, 2018.

Katayama, Naoki, Yuki Baba, Yoshinobu Kusumoto, and Koichi Tanaka. "A Review of Post-War Changes in Rice Farming and Biodiversity in Japan." *Agricultural Systems* 132 (2015): 73–84.

Katō Takashi. "Nakagawa bansho no kinō to sono tokushitsu." *Kōtsūshi kenkyū*, no. 12 (1984): 27–46.

Kawana Noboru. "Kantō ni okeru kasen unyu kikō no seiritsu." *Rekishi chiri* 89, no. 4 (1960): 54–64.

Kawana Noboru. *Kashi ni ikiru hitobito: Tonegawa suiun no shakai shi.* Tokyo: Heibonsha, 1982.

Kawana Noboru. *Kinsei Nihon no kawabune kenkyū.* Vols. 1–2. Tokyo: Nihon Keizai Hyōronsha, 2003–5.

Kawana Noboru. *Kinsei Nihon suiun shi no kenkyū.* Tokyo: Yūzankaku Shuppan, 1984.

Kawanabe, Hiroya, Machiko Nishino, and Masayoshi Maehata, eds. *Lake Biwa: Interactions between Nature and People.* Dordrecht: Springer, 2014.

Keikōkai, ed. *Tsuzuki Keiroku-den.* Tokyo: Yumani Shobō, 2002.

Kelly, William W. *Irrigation Management in Japan: A Critical Review of Japanese Social Science Literature.* Ithaca: Cornell University China-Japan Program, 1982.

Kelly, William W. *Water Control in Tokugawa Japan: Irrigation Organization in a Japanese River Basin, 1600–1870.* Ithaca: Cornell University, 1982.

Kensetsushō Kantō Chihō Kensetsukyoku Arakawa Jōryū Kōji Jimusho, ed. *Arakawa jōryū kaishū rokujū-nen shi.* Kawagoe: Kensetsushō Kantō Chihō Kensetsukyoku Arakawa Jōryū Kōji Jimusho, 1979.

Kensetsushō Kasenhō Kenkyūkai, ed. *Kasenhō chikujō kaisetsu.* Tokyo: Zenkoku Kajo Hōrei Shuppan, 1980.

Kensetsushō Kasenkyoku, ed. *Kasenhō shiryō shū.* Vols. 1–4. Tokyo: Nihon Kasen Kyōkai, 1966–69.

Kensetsushō Kinki Chihōkyoku, ed. *Yodogawa hyaku-nen shi.* Osaka: Kensetsushō Kinki Chihōkyoku, 1974.

Kikuchi Toshio. *Shinden kaihatsu.* Tokyo: Kokin Shoin, 1959.

Kikuchi Toshio. *Zoku shinden kaihatsu: jirei hen.* Tokyo: Kokon Shoin, 1986.

Kim, Kyu Hyun. *The Age of Visions and Arguments: Parliamentarianism and the National Public Sphere in Early Meiji Japan.* Cambridge: Harvard University Press, 2008.

Kimizuka Yoshihiko. "Bakufu goyō sumi-yaku no tenkai to sonraku." *Shikai* 33 (1986): 29–48.

Kimura Motoi. *Mura no kataru Nihon no rekishi.* Vols. 1–2. Tokyo: Soshiete, 1983.

Kimura Naoe. "'Shakai' ga umare, 'sosaechii' ga kieru: Meiji-ki ni okeru 'shakai' gainen hensei to kōkyōken no kōzō." *Gakushūin Joshi Daigaku kiyō* 19 (2017): 53–78.

Kinsei Shiryō Kenkyūkai, ed. *Edo machibure shūsei.* Vols. 1–22. Tokyo: Hanawa Shobō, 1994–2012.

Kinuta Yukie. *Arakawa hōsuiro.* Tokyo: Shinsō Shuppan, 1990.

Kisen Nikyaku Toriatsukainin Rengōkai, ed. *Tonegawa kisen kōro annai.* Tokyo: Kisen Nikyaku Toriatsukainin Rengōkai, 1910.

Kiso Sansen Rekishi Bunka Shiryō Henshū Kentōkai. *Meiji kaishū kansei hyaku-shūnen tokubetsu-gō: Kiso sansen rekishi bunka no chōsa kenkyū shiryō.* Kuwana: Kokudo Kōtsūshō Chūbu Chihō Seibikyoku Kisogawa Karyū Kasen Jimusho Chūsaka, 2013.

Kiso Sansen Ryūiki Shi Henshū Iinkai, ed. *Kiso sansen ryūiki shi.* Nagoya: Kensetsu Chūbu Chihō Kensetsukyoku, 1992.

Kitahara Itoko. *Edo-jō sotobori monogatari.* Tokyo: Chikuma Shobō, 1999.

Kitō Hiroshi. *Bunmei to shite no Edo shisutemu.* Tokyo: Kōdansha, 2002.

Knight, Catherine. "Conservation Movement in Post-War Japan." *Environment and History* 16 (2010): 349–70.

Koide Haku. *Nihon no kasen kenkyū: chiikisei to kobetsusei.* Tokyo: Tōkyō Daigaku Shuppankai, 1972.

Koide Haku. *Nihon no kasen: shizen shi to shakai shi.* Tokyo: Tōkyō Daigaku Shuppankai, 1973.

Kokudo Kōtsūshō, ed. *Nihon no suishigen.* Tokyo: Kokudo Kōtsūshō, 2014.

Kokudo Kōtsūshō, ed. *Nihon no suishigen no genkyō.* Tokyo: Kokudo Kōtsūshō, 2018.

Kokudo Seisaku Kikō, ed. *Kokudo o tsukutta doboku gijutsushatachi.* Tokyo: Kashima Shuppankai, 2000.

Kokushi Daijiten Henshū Iinkai, ed. *Kokushi daijiten.* Vols. 1–17. Tokyo: Yoshikawa Kōbunkan, 1979–97.

Kondō Toragorō. "Ranryō Indo Jyawa-tō doboku jigyō shisatsu fukumeisho." 1897. Yodogawa Shiryōkan, Hirakata City, Osaka Prefecture.

Kranakis, Eda. "Social Determinants of Engineering Practice: A Comparative View of France and America in the Nineteenth Century." *Social Studies of Science* 19, no. 1 (1989): 5–70.

Ku, Ya-wen. "Taming the Blind Snake: Flooding Disasters and River Regulation of the Zengwen River in Colonial Taiwan." In *Landscape Change and Resource Utilization in East Asia: Perspectives from Environmental History*, edited by Ts'ui-jung Liu, Andrea Janku, and David Pietz, 58–75. New York: Routledge, 2018.

Kudo Yuichiro. "Absolute Chronology of Archaeological and Paleoenvironmental Records from the Japanese Islands, 40–15 ka BP." In *Environmental Changes and Human Occupation in East Asia During OIS3 and OIS2*, edited by Ono Akira and Masami Izuho, 13–32. Oxford: Archaeopress, 2012.

Kume, Kunitake. *The Iwakura Embassy, 1871–73: A True Account of the Ambassador Extraordinary & Plenipotentiary's Journeys of Observation through the United States and Europe.* Vols. 1–5. Richmond: Curzon, 2002.

Kurasawa Gō. *Shohan no kyōiku seisaku.* Tokyo: Yoshikawa Kōbunkan, 1986.

Kyōto-fu Shomuka. *Kyōto fuchi gairan.* Kyoto: Kyōto-fu, 1888. National Diet Library, Tokyo.

Kyōto Shinbunsha, ed. *Biwa-ko sosui no hyaku-nen: jujutsu hen*. Kyoto: Kyoto-shi Suidōkyoku, 1990.

Kyū-Kōbu Daigakkō Shiryō Hensankai, ed. *Kyū-Kōbu Daigakkō shiryō dō furoku*. Tokyo: Seishisha, 1977.

LaFleur, William R. "A Turning in Taishō: Asia and Europe in the Early Writings of Watsuji Tetsurō." In *Culture and Identity: Japanese Intellectuals During the Interwar Years*, edited by J. Thomas Rimer, 234–56. Durham: Duke University Press, 1990.

Latour, Bruno. *Pandora's Hope: Essays on the Reality of Science Studies*. Cambridge: Harvard University Press, 1999.

Latour, Bruno. *Reassembling the Social: An Introduction to Actor-Network-Theory*. Oxford: Oxford University Press, 2005.

Latour, Bruno. *We Have Never Been Modern*. Cambridge: Harvard University Press, 1993.

Lefebvre, Henri. *The Production of Space*. Translated by Donald Nicholson-Smith. Cambridge: Blackwell, 1991.

Lemke, Thomas. *Foucault, Governmentality, and Critique*. New York: Routledge, 2016.

Leopold, Luna B. *A View of the River*. Cambridge: Harvard University Press, 1994.

Lewis, Michael. *Becoming Apart: National Power and Local Politics in Toyama, 1868–1945*. Cambridge: Harvard University Asia Center, 2000.

Linton, Jamie. "Is the Hydrologic Cycle Sustainable? A Historical-Geographical Critique of a Modern Concept." *Annals of the Association of American Geographers* 98, no. 3 (2008): 630–49.

Liu, Lydia H. *Translingual Practice: Literature, National Culture, and Translated Modernity—China, 1900–1937*. Stanford: Stanford University Press, 1995.

Liu, Ts'ui-jung, ed. *Local Realities and Environmental Changes in the History of East Asia*. London: Routledge, 2016.

Machida Takahisa. "Kanpō ni-nen saigai o motorashita taifū no shinro to tenkō no fukugen." *Chigaku zasshi* 123, no. 3 (2014): 363–77.

Maffioli, Cesare S. "Italian Hydraulics and Experimental Physics in Eighteenth-Century Holland: From Poleni to Volta." In *Italian Scientists in the Low Countries of the XVIIth and XVIIIth Centuries*, edited by C. S. Maffioli and L. C. Palm, 243–75. Amsterdam: Rodopi, 1989.

Malpas, Jeff. *Heidegger's Topology: Being, Place, and World*. Cambridge: MIT Press, 2006.

Mann, Michael. *The Sources of Social Power: The Rise of Classes and Nation States, 1760–1914*. Cambridge: Cambridge University Press, 1993.

Marcon, Federico. *The Knowledge of Nature and the Nature of Knowledge in Early Modern Japan*. Chicago: University of Chicago Press, 2015.

Massey, Doreen B. *For Space*. London: Sage Publications, 2005.

Masuda Hiromi. "Shokusan kōgyō seisaku to kasen shū'un." *Shakai keizai shigaku* 48, no. 6 (1982): 6–22.

Matsumoto, Takenori, and Seung-jin Chung. "Water Management Projects and Floods/ Droughts in Colonial Korea: The Case of the Man'gŏyng River in Honam Plain." *Acta Koreana* 20, no. 1 (2017): 173–93.

Matsuura Shigeki. *Kokudo no kaihatsu to kasen: jōrisei kara damu kaihatsu made.* Tokyo: Kashima Shuppankai, 1989.

Matsuura Shigeki. *Kokudo-zukuri no ishizue: kawa ga kataru Nihon no rekishi.* Tokyo: Kashima Shuppankai, 1997.

Matsuura Shigeki. *Meiji no kokudo kaihatsushi: kindai doboku gijutsu no ishizue.* Tokyo: Kashima Shuppankai, 1992.

Matsuura Shigeki. "Okino Tadao to Meiji kaishū." *Suiri kagaku* 40, no. 6 (1997): 90–119.

Matsuura Shigeki. *Tonegawa kingendai shi.* Tokyo: Kokon Shoin, 2016.

Matsuura Shigeki. "Wasurerareta gijutsusha—Yamada Torakichi." *Suiri kagaku* 43, no. 5 (1999): 96–113.

Matsuzawa Yūsaku. "Shinrin to sonraku no Meiji ishin." In *"Meiji hyakugojū-nen" de kangaeru: kindai ikōki no shakai to kūkan,* edited by Danieru V. Botsuman, Tsukata Takashi, and Yoshida Nobuyuki, 31–42. Tokyo: Yamakawa Shuppansha, 2018.

Mauch, Christof, and Thomas Zeller, eds. *Rivers in History: Perspectives on Waterways in Europe and North America.* Pittsburgh: University of Pittsburgh Press, 2008.

Maxey, Trent E. *The "Greatest Problem": Religion and State Formation in Meiji Japan.* Cambridge: Harvard University Press, 2014.

Mayeda, Graham. *Time, Space, and Ethics in the Thought of Watsuji Tetsurō, Kuki Shūzō, and Martin Heidegger.* New York: Routledge, 2006.

McClain, James L., John M. Merriman, and Ugawa Kaoru, eds. *Edo and Paris: Urban Life and the State in the Early Modern Era.* Ithaca: Cornell University Press, 1994.

McClain, James L., and Osamu Wakita, eds. *Osaka: The Merchant's Capital of Early Modern Japan.* Ithaca: Cornell University Press, 1999.

McCormack, Gavin. *Japan at Century's End: Emptiness of Affluence.* Armonk: M. E. Sharpe, 1996.

McCormack, Gavin. "Modernity, Water, and the Environment in Japan." In *Companion to Japanese History,* edited by William M. Tsutsui, 443–59. Malden: Wiley-Blackwell, 2007.

Megill, Allan. *Historical Knowledge, Historical Error: A Contemporary Guide to Practice.* Chicago: University of Chicago Press, 2007.

Merleau-Ponty, Maurice. *Nature: Course Notes from the Collège de France.* Translated by Robert Vallier. Evanston: Northwestern University, 2003.

Miki Masafumi. *Mizu no miyako to toshi kōtsū: Ōsaka no nijū-seiki.* Osaka: Seizandō, 2003.

Mikuriya Takashi. *Seisaku no sōgō to kenryoku: Nihon seiji no senzen to sengo.* Tokyo: Tōkyō Daigaku Shuppankai, 1996.

Miller, Ian Jared. *The Nature of the Beasts: Empire and Exhibition at the Tokyo Imperial Zoo.* Berkeley: University of California Press, 2012.

Miller, Ian Jared, Julia Adeney Thomas, and Brett L. Walker, eds. *Japan at Nature's Edge: The Environmental Context of a Global Power*. Honolulu: University of Hawai'i Press, 2013.

Milne, John. "Seismometry and Engineering in Relation to the Recent Earthquake in Japan." *Nature* 45, no. 1154 (1891): 127.

Milne, John. *Seismology*. London: Kegan Paul, Trench, Trübner & Co., 1898.

Mitani, Taichirō. "The Establishment of Party Cabinets, 1898–1932." In *The Cambridge History of Japan: The Twentieth Century*, edited by Peter Duus, 55–96. Cambridge: Cambridge University Press, 1988.

Mitchell, Timothy. "The Limits of the State: Beyond Statist Approaches and Their Critics." *The American Political Science Review* 85, no. 1 (1991): 77–96.

Mitchell, Timothy. *Rule of Experts: Egypt, Techno-Politics, and Modernity*. Berkeley: University of California Press, 2002.

Mitchell, Timothy. "Society, Economy, and the State Effect." In *State/Culture: State-Formation after the Cultural Turn*, edited by George Steinmetz, 76–97. Ithaca: Cornell University Press, 1999.

Miyamura Tadashi. *Suigai: chisui to suibō no chie*. Tokyo: Chūō Kōron, 1985.

Miyoshi, Masao. *As We Saw Them: The First Japanese Embassy to the United States*. Berkeley: University of California Press, 1979.

Mizoguchi, Koji. *The Archaeology of Japan: From the Earliest Rice Farming Villages to the Rise of the State*. Cambridge: Cambridge University Press, 2013.

Mizumoto Kunihiko. *Kinsei no mura shakai to kokka*. Tokyo: Tokyo Daigaku Shuppankai, 1987.

Mizumoto Kunihiko. "Kinsei no shizen to shakai." In *Nihon rekishi kōza: kinsei shakai ron*, edited by Rekishigaku Kenkyūkai and Nihonshi Kenkyūkai, 161–92. Tokyo: Tōkyō Daigaku Shuppankai, 2005.

Mizumoto Kunihiko. *Mura: hyakushōtachi no kinsei*. Tokyo: Iwanami Shoten, 2015.

Mizuno, Hiromi. "Rasa Island: What Industrialization to Remember and Forget." *The Asia-Pacific Journal: Japan Focus* 15, no. 1 (2017). https://apjjf.org/2017/01/Mizuno.html.

Mizuno, Hiromi. *Science for the Empire: Scientific Nationalism in Modern Japan*. Stanford: Stanford University Press, 2009.

Molle, Francois. "River-Basin Planning and Management: Social Life of a Concept." *Geoforum* 40, no. 3 (2009): 484–94.

Monobe Nagaho. "Chosuiyō jūryoku sekitei no tokusei narabi ni sono gōriteki sekkei hōhō." *Doboku Gakkaishi* 11, no. 5 (1925): 995–1157.

Moore, Aaron. *Constructing East Asia: Technology, Ideology, and Empire in Japan's Wartime Era, 1931–1945*. Stanford: Stanford University Press, 2013.

Moore, Aaron. "'The Yalu River Era of Developing Asia': Japanese Expertise, Colonial Power, and the Construction of the Sup'ung Dam." *Journal of Asian Studies* 72, no. 1 (2013): 115–39.

Mōri Toshihiko. *Meiji ishin seiji shi josetsu.* Tokyo: Miraisha, 1967.

Moriyama, Takeshi. *Crossing Boundaries in Tokugawa Society: Suzuki Bokushi, a Rural Elite Commoner.* Brill's Japanese Studies Library 41. Leiden: Brill, 2013.

Morse, Edward Sylvester. *First Book of Zoölogy.* New York: D. Appleton and Co., 1879.

Morse, Edward Sylvester. "Traces of Early Man in Japan." *Nature* 17, no. 89 (1877): 89.

Morton, Timothy. *Hyperobjects: Philosophy and Ecology after the End of the World.* Minneapolis: University of Minnesota Press, 2013.

Mulder, Rouwenhorst Anthonie Thomas Lubertus. "Het Nederlandsche Handelsestablissement te Port-Said." *Tijdschrift van het Koninklijk Instituut van Ingenieurs,* no. 287 (1877): 288–92.

Mulder, Rouwenhorst Anthonie Thomas Lubertus. "Korte Mededeelingen Overjapan En Meen Bepaald over De Voornaamste Havens Die in Dat Rijk Gevonden Worden." *Tijdschrift van het Koninklijk Instituut van Ingenieurs,* no. 91 (1887): 92–102.

Mulder, Rouwenhorst Anthonie Thomas Lubertus. "Over een drietar zeestraten in den Japanschen archipel." *Tijdschrift van het Koninklijk Instituut van Ingenieurs,* no. 205 (1892–1893), 205–28.

Murakami Tadashi. *Edo bakufu no daikan gunzō.* Tokyo: Dōseisha, 1997.

Murakami Tadashi. "Kantō gundai no seiritsu ni kansuru ichikōsatsu." In *Bakuhansei kokka seiritsu katei no kenkyū: Kanei-ki o chūshin ni,* edited by Kitajima Masamoto, 108–18. Tokyo: Yoshikawa Kōbunkan, 1977.

Murakami Tadashi. "Kinsei Kantō no chiikiteki tokushitsu to kadai." In *Bakuhan shakai no tenkai to Kantō,* edited by Murakami Tadashi, 1–18. Tokyo: Yoshikawa Kōbunkan, 1986.

Murakami Tadashi, Izumi Seiji, Satō Takayuki, and Nishizawa Atsuo, eds. *Tokugawa bakufu zen-daikan jinmei jiten.* Tokyo: Tōkyōdō Shuppan, 2015.

Muramatsu Teijirō. "Oyatoi gaikokujin to Nihon no doboku gijutsu." *Doboku Gakkaishi,* no. 61 (1976): 9–16.

Murata Michibito. "Hōei gannen Yamatogawa tsukekae tetsudai-bushin ni tsuite." *Ōsaka Daigaku Daigakuin Kenkyūka* 20 (1986): 21–44.

Murata Michibito. *Kinsei no Yodogawa chisui.* Tokyo: Yamakawa Shuppan, 2009.

Naikaku Kanpōkyoku, ed. *Dai nijūnana kai teikoku gikai: shūgiin yosan iin dai ni bunka kaigiroku.* Vol. 5. 3 February 1911. National Diet Library, Tokyo.

Naikaku Kanpōkyoku, ed. *Hōrei zensho.* Tokyo: Naikaku Kanpōkyoku, 1896.

Naikaku Kanpōkyoku, ed. *Kanpō: Kizokugiin giji sokkiroku.* 1890–1945. National Diet Library, Tokyo.

Naikaku Kanpōkyoku, ed. *Kanpō: Shūgiin giji sokkiroku.* 1890–1945. National Diet Library, Tokyo.

Naimushō Dobokukyoku, ed. *Chisui jigyō ni kansuru tōkaisho.* Tokyo: Naimushō Dobokukyoku, 1917. National Diet Library, Tokyo.

Naimushō Dobokukyoku, ed. *Doboku kōyōroku.* Tokyo: Yūrindō, 1881.

Naimushō Dobokukyoku Kasenka, ed. *Dobokukyoku daisanjūkai tōkei nenpyō: zenhen.* Tokyo: Naimushō Dobokukyoku Kasenka, 1937. National Diet Library, Tokyo.

Naimushō Eiseikyoku Hozen Eisei Chōsa Shitsu, ed. *Kakuchi ni okeru "mararia" ni kan-suru gaikyō.* Tokyo: Naimushō Eiseikyoku, 1919. National Diet Library, Tokyo.

Naimushō Ōsaka Doboku Shucchōjo, ed. *Yodogawa kaishū zōho kōji gaiyō.* Osaka: Naimushō Ōsaka Doboku Shucchōjo, 1930.

Naimushō Tōkyō Doboku Shucchōjo, *Arakawa karyū kaishū kōji gaiyō.* Tokyo: Naimushō Tōkyō Doboku Shucchōjo, 1924.

Naimushō Tōkyō Doboku Shucchōjo. "Reiganjima ryōsui-hyō reii to Tōkyō wanjū nado chōi narabi ni Horie ryōsui-hyō reii to no kankei." 1927. National Diet Library, Tokyo.

Naimushō Tōkyō Doboku Shucchōjo. *Tonegawa kaishū kōji gaiyō.* Tokyo: Naimushō Tōkyō Doboku Shucchōjo, 1930. National Diet Library, Tokyo.

Naitō Akira. *Edo to Edo-jō.* Tokyo: Kashima Shuppankai, 1966.

Nakamura, Keigo, Klement Tockner, and Kunihiko Amano. "River and Wetland Restoration: Lessons from Japan." *Bioscience* 56, no. 5 (2006): 419–29.

Nakamura Tsuko. "Inō Tadataka ga Seto naikai sokuryō de shiyō shita tenmon sokki to 'yachū sokuryō no zu' no kansokuchi." *Kagakushi kenkyū,* no. 273 (2015): 3–15.

Nakanishi Tatsuharu. *Hōreki chisui to Hirata Yukie: Shijitsu to kenshō no ayumi.* Nagoya: Arumu, 2015.

Nakayama Masatami. "Chūsei kinsei no Tonegawa chūryū chiiki ni okeru chikei kankyō to shakai shi: Asamayama no daifunka to Tonegawa no sekae." *Rekishi chirigaku* 39, no. 3 (1997): 1–24.

Needham, Joseph. "Science and Society in East and West." *Science and Society* 28, no. 4 (1964): 385–408.

Negishi Shigeo, Ōtomo Kazuo, and Satō Takayuki, eds. *Kinsei no kankyō to kaihatsu.* Tokyo: Shibunkaku, 2010.

Nenzi, Laura. *Excursions in Identity: Travel and the Intersection of Place, Gender, and Status in Edo Japan.* Honolulu: University of Hawai'i Press, 2008.

Nichigai Asoshiētsu, ed. *Seijika jinmei jiten: Meiji-Shōwa.* Tokyo: Nichigai Asoshiētsu, 2003.

Nihon Kokuyū Tetsudō, ed. *Nihon kokuyū tetsudō hyaku-nen shi.* Tokyo: Nihon Kokuyū Tetsudō, 1969.

Nihon Shiseki Kyōkai, ed. *Ōkubo Toshimichi monjo.* Vols. 1–10. Tokyo: Tōkyō Daigaku Shuppankai, 1967–69.

Nishida Masaki. "Kawayoke to kuniyaku-bushin." In *Kōza Nihon gijutsu no shakai shi: doboku,* edited by Nagahara Keiji and Yamaguchi Tetsuji, 227–60. Tokyo: Nihon Hyōronsha, 1984.

Nishikawa Takeomi. *Edo naiwan no minato to ryūtsū.* Tokyo: Iwata Shoin, 1993.

Niwa Kunio. "Kinsei ni okeru san'ya kakai no shoyū-shihai to Meiji no henkaku." In *Nihon no shakai shi: kyōkai ryōiki to kōtsū*, edited by Asao Naohiro, 173–213. Tokyo: Iwanami Shoten, 1987.

Nixon, Rob. *Slow Violence and the Environmentalism of the Poor*. Cambridge: Harvard University Press, 2011.

Nōshōmushō Nōmukyoku, ed. *Suisan jikō tokubetsu chōsa*. Tokyo: Nōshōmushō, 1894. National Diet Library, Tokyo.

Notehelfer, Fred G. "Japan's First Pollution Incident." *Journal of Japanese Studies* 1, no. 2 (1975): 351–83.

Ogawa Kiyoshi. *Yodogawa no chisui ou: Ōhashi Fusatarō*. Osaka: Tōhō Shuppan, 2010.

Ogawa Makoto. "Chisui, risui, tochi kairyō no taiketeki seibi." In vol. 4, *Nihon nōgyō hattatsu shi: Meiji ikō ni okeru*, edited by Nihon Nōgyō Hattatsushi Chōsakai, 117–232. Tokyo: Chūō Kōronsha, 1954.

Ogawa, Tsukane, Mitsuo Morimoto, and Seki Kowa. *Mathematics of Takebe Katahiro and History of Mathematics in East Asia*. Tokyo: Mathematical Society of Japan, 2018.

Oguma, Eiji. *The Boundaries of "the Japanese": Korea, Taiwan and the Ainu, 1868–1945*. Translated by Leonie R. Stickland. Melborne: Trans Pacific Press, 2017.

Ogura-ike Tochi Kairyō-ku, ed. *Ogura-ike kantaku shi*. Uji: Ogura-ike Tochi Kairyō-ku, 1962.

Oikawa Yoshinobu. "Sangyō kakumei-ki no riku'un to suiun." In *Sōron suijō kōtsū shi: suijō kōtsū shi kenkyū no kadai to tenbō*, edited by Yuzuki Manabu, 339–59. Tokyo: Bunken Shuppan, 1996.

Ōishi Manabu. *Kyōhō kaikaku no chiiki seisaku*. Tokyo: Yoshikawa Kōbunkan, 1996.

Ōishi Manabu, ed. *Kyōhō kaikaku to shakai henyō*. Tokyo: Yoshikawa Kōbunkan, 2003.

Ōishi Shinzaburō. *Tenmei san-nen Asama daifunka*. Tokyo: Kadokawa Shoten, 1986.

Okada Yoshirō. *Kyūreki tokuhon: Nihon no kurashi o tanoshimu 'koyomi' no chie*. Osaka: Sōgensha, 2015.

Okino Tadao. "Doboku Gakkai dai sankai sōkai kaichō kōen." In *Doboku Gakkai zasshi* 3, no. 1 (February 1917): 1–10.

Okino Tadao Kenkyū Shiryō Chōsa Iinkai, ed. *Okino Tadao to Meiji kaishū*. Tokyo: Doboku Gakkai, 2010.

Okuda Haruki. *Meiji kokka to kindaiteki tochi shoyu*. Tokyo: Dōseisha, 2007.

Ōkuma Takashi, ed. *Kawa o seishita kindai gijutsu*. Tokyo: Heibonsha, 1994.

Ōkuma Takashi. *Kōzui to chisui no kasen shi: suigai seiatsu kara juyō e*. Tokyo: Heibonsha, 1988.

Ōkuma Takashi. *Tonegawa chisui no hensen to suigai*. Tokyo: Tōkyō Daigaku Shuppankai, 1981.

Ōkurashō, ed. *Nihon zaisei keizai shiryō*. Vols. 1–11. Tokyo: Zaisei Keizai Gakkai, 1922–25.

Ōkurashō Insatsukyoku. "Chin Rinji Chisui Chōsakai kansei." In *Kanpō*, No. 8198 (daily ed. 18 October 1910): 455.

Okuya Kōichi. "Tanaka Shōzō no kasen to chisui no shisō (2)." *Sapporo Gakuin Daigaku Jinbun Gakkai kiyō*, no. 101 (2017): 1–30.

Olson, Richard G. *Science and Scientism in Nineteenth-Century Europe*. Urbana: University of Illinois Press, 2008.

O'Neill, Karen M. *Rivers by Design: State Power and the Origins of Flood Control*. Durham: Duke University Press, 2006.

Ōsaka-fu Gyogyōshi Hensan Kyōkai, ed. *Ōsaka-fu gyogyōshi*. Osaka: Ōsaka-fu Gyogyōshi Hensan Kyōkai, 1997.

Ōsumikai Naimushō-shi Henshū Iinkai, ed. *Naimushō shi*. Vols. 1–4. Tokyo: Chihō Zaimu Kyōkai, 1970–71.

Ōta Nanpo, ed. *Chikkyō yohitsu*. Tokyo: Kokusho Kankōkai, 1917.

Ōta Naohiro. *Bakufu daikan Ina-shi to Edo shūhen chiiki*. Tokyo: Iwata Shoin, 2010.

Ōtani Sadao. *Edo bakufu chisui seisaku no kenkyū*. Tokyo: Yūsankaku Shuppan, 1996.

Ōtani Sadao. "Kinsei ni okeru Sekiyado-atari no chisui jijō." *Chiba-ken shi kenkyū* 19 (2002): 9–15.

Ōtsu Hide, Sakurai Eiji, Fujii Jōji, Yoshida Yutaka, and Li Sonshi, eds. *Iwanami kōza Nihon rekishi*. Vols. 1–22. Tokyo: Iwanami Shoten, 2013–15.

Ōtsuki Fumihiko, ed. *Genkai: Nihon jisho*. Tokyo: Self-published, 1889–91. National Diet Library, Tokyo.

Oya Geni. *Yumoto Yoshinori-kun shōden*. Kōnosu-chō, Saitama: Yamamoto Chōjirō, 1892. National Diet Library, Tokyo.

Ōyodo Shōichi. *Gijutsu kanryō no seiji sangaku: Nihon no kagaku gijutsu no makuaki*. Tokyo: Chūō Kōronsha, 1997.

Partner, Simon. *Toshié: A Story of Village Life in Twentieth Century Japan*. Berkeley: University of California Press, 2004.

Picon, Antoine. "French Engineers and Social Thought, 18th–20th Centuries: An Archeology of Technocratic Ideals." *History and Technology* 23, no. 3 (2007): 197–208.

Pietz, David A. *The Yellow River: The Problem of Water in Modern China*. Cambridge: Harvard University Press, 2015.

Platt, Brian. *Burning and Building: Schooling and State Formation in Japan, 1750–1890*. Cambridge: Harvard University Press, 2004.

Poovey, Mary. *Making a Social Body: British Cultural Formation, 1830–1864*. Chicago: University of Chicago Press, 1995.

Porter, Theodore M. *Trust in Numbers: The Pursuit of Objectivity in Science and Public Life*. Princeton: Princeton University Press, 1995.

Pratt, Edward E. *Japan's Protoindustrial Elite: The Economic Foundations of the Gōnō*. Cambridge: Harvard University Press, 1999.

Pritchard, Sara B. *Confluence: The Nature of Technology and the Remaking of the Rhône*. Cambridge: Harvard University Press, 2011.

Raj, Kapil. "Beyond Postcolonialism ... and Postpositivism: Circulation and the Global History of Science." *Isis* 104, no. 2 (2013): 337–47.

Rankine, William J. M. *Manual of Civil Engineering*. London: Charles Griffin, 1861.

Rasmussen, Mattias B. "Seasons, Timings, and the Rhythms of Life." In *Living with Environmental Change: Waterworlds*, edited by Kirsten Hastrup and Cecilie Rubow, 232–36. London: Routledge, 2014.

Ravesteijn, Wim. "Between Globalization and Localization: The Case of Dutch Civil Engineering in Indonesia, 1800–1950." *Comparative Technology Transfer and Society* 5, no. 1 (2007): 32–64.

Ravesteijn, Wim. "Controlling Water, Controlling People: Irrigation Engineering and State Formation in the Dutch East Indies." *Itinerario* 31, no. 1 (2007): 89–118.

Ravesteijn, Wim. "Dutch Engineering Overseas: The Creation of a Modern Irrigation System in Colonial Java." *Knowledge, Technology and Policy* 14, no. 4 (2002): 126–44.

Ravina, Mark. *Land and Lordship in Early Modern Japan*. Stanford: Stanford University Press, 1999.

Ravina, Mark. "Wasan and the Physics That Wasn't: Mathematics in the Tokugawa Period." *Monumenta Nipponica* 48, no. 2 (1993): 205–24.

Reuss, Martin. "Andrew A. Humphreys and the Development of Hydraulic Engineering: Politics and Technology in the Army Corps of Engineers, 1850–1950." *Technology and Culture* 26, no. 1 (1985): 1–33.

Reuss, Martin, and Stephen H. Cutcliffe, eds. *The Illusory Boundary: Environment and Technology in History*. Charlottesville: University of Virginia Press, 2010.

Rinji Chisui Chōsakai. *Rinji Chisui Chōsakai giji sokukiroku*. 1910. Shisei Senmon Toshokan, Tokyo.

Riskin, Jessica. *The Restless Clock: A History of the Centuries-Long Argument over What Makes Living Things Tick*. Chicago: University of Chicago Press, 2016.

River Bureau, Ministry of Construction. *The River Law*. Tokyo: Infrastructure Development Institute-Japan, 1997.

Roberts, Luke S. *Mercantilism in a Japanese Domain: The Merchant Origins of Economic Nationalism in 18th-Century Tosa*. Cambridge: Cambridge University Press, 1998.

Rouse, Hunter, and Simon Ince. *History of Hydraulics*. New York: Dover Publications, 1963.

Rubinger, Richard. *Popular Literacy in Early Modern Japan*. Honolulu: University of Hawai'i Press, 2007.

Saga, Junichi. *Memories of Wind and Waves: A Self-Portrait of Lakeside Japan*. Translated by Juliet Winters Carpenter. Tokyo: Kodansha International, 2002.

Saitō Gesshin. *Bukō nenpyō*. Edited by Imai Kingo. Vols. 1–2. Tokyo: Chikuma Shobō, 2003.

Saitō Gesshin. *Edo meisho zue*. Vols. 1–7. Edo: Subaraya Mohei, 1834–36. National Diet Library, Tokyo.

Saitō Yoshiyuki, ed. *Mibunteki shūen to kinsei shakai 2: umi to kawa ni ikiru.* Tokyo: Yoshikawa Kōbunkan, 2007.

Sakai Ryōsuke. *Zakoba uoichiba shi.* Osaka: Seizandō Shoten, 2008.

Sakai Yūji. "Kinsei zenki Shimōsa ni okeru kumiai mura to kenchi." *Rekishi chirigaku*, no. 121 (1983): 1–16.

Saldanha, Arun. *Space after Deleuze.* New York: Bloomsbury, 2017.

Sanada Hidekichi. *Nihon suiseikō ron.* Tokyo: Iwanami Shoten, 1932.

Satō Jin. *"Motazaru kuni" no shigenron: jizoku kanō na kokudo o meguru mō hitotsu no chi.* Tokyo: Tōkyō Daigaku Shuppankai, 2011.

Schatzki, Theodore R. *The Timespace of Human Activity: On Performance, Society, and History as Indeterminate Teleological Events.* Lanham: Lexington Books, 2010.

Scott, James C. *Seeing Like a State: How Certain Schemes to Improve the Human Condition Have Failed.* New Haven: Yale University Press, 1998.

Segal, Ethan Isaac. *Coins, Trade, and the State.* Cambridge: Harvard University Press, 2011.

Sharma, Aradhana, and Akhil Gupta. "Introduction: Rethinking Theories of the State in an Age of Globalization." In *The Anthropology of the State: A Reader*, edited by Aradhana Sharma and Akhil Gupta, 1–41. Malden: Blackwell, 2006.

Shihōshō Hōseishi Gakkai, ed. *Tokugawa kinrei kō.* Vols. 1–11. Tokyo: Sōbunsha, 1959–61.

Shinn, Terry. "The Industry, Research, and Education Nexus." In *The Modern Physical and Mathematical Sciences*, edited by Mary Jo Nye, 133–53. The Cambridge History of Science 5. Cambridge: Cambridge University Press, 2002.

Shinsen daigishi retsuden. Tokyo: Kinkōdō Shoseki, 1902. National Diet Library, Tokyo.

Shirane, Haruo. *Japan and the Culture of the Four Seasons: Nature, Literature, and the Arts.* New York: Columbia University Press, 2012.

Shōji Kichirō and Sugai Masurō. *Tsūshi: Ashio kōdoku jiken, 1877–1984.* Yokohama: Seoroshi Shobō, 2014.

Sippel, Patricia G. "*Chisui*: Creating a Sacred Domain in Early Modern and Modern Japan." In *Public Spheres, Private Lives in Modern Japan, 1600–1950: Essays in Honor of Albert M. Craig*, edited by Andrew Gordon, Gail Lee Bernstein, and Kate Wildman Nakai, 154–84. Cambridge: Harvard University Asia Center, 2005.

Sivasundaram, Sujit. "Sciences and the Global: On Methods, Questions, and Theory." *Isis* 101 (2010): 146–58.

Smith, Cecil O. "The Longest Run: Public Engineers and Planning in France." *American Historical Review* 95, no. 3 (1990): 657–92.

Smith, Thomas C. *Agrarian Origins of Modern Japan.* Stanford: Stanford University Press, 1959.

Soeda Yoshiya. *Naimushō no shakai shi.* Tokyo: Tōkyō Daigaku Shuppankai, 2007.

Spafford, David. *A Sense of Place: The Political Landscape in Late Medieval Japan.* Cambridge: Harvard University Asia Center, 2013.

Steele, M. William. "Goemon's New World View." In *Alternative Narratives in Modern Japanese History*, 4–18. New York: Routledge Curzon, 2003.

Steele, M. William. "The History of the Tama River: Social Reconstructions." In *A History of Water: Water Control and River Biographies*, edited by T. Tvedt and E. Jakobsson, 217–36. London: I. B. Tauris, 2006.

Stolz, Robert. *Bad Water: Nature, Pollution, & Politics in Japan, 1870–1950*. Durham: Duke University Press, 2014.

Stone, Alan Atwood. "The Vanishing Village: The Ashio Copper Mine Pollution Case, 1890–1907." PhD diss., University of Washington, 1974.

Strong, Kenneth. *Ox against the Storm: A Biography of Tanaka Shozo, Japan's Conservationist Pioneer*. Vancouver, B.C.: University of Columbia Press, 1977.

Sugimoto, Fumiko, Kären Wigen, and Cary Karacas, eds. *Cartographic Japan: A History in Maps*. Chicago: University of Chicago Press, 2016.

Sugiyama Shūkichi. "Ōsaka shinki kasetsu kyōryō oyobi kōhi yosan kettei." *Kōgakkaishi* 5, no. 53 (1886): 1058–60.

Suzuki Bokushi. *Hokuetsu seppu*. Edited by Okada Takematsu. Tokyo: Iwanami Shoten, 2001.

Takagi Shōsaku. "'Shōgun no umi' to iu ronri: kujira unjō o tegakari to shite." In *Suisan no shakai shi*, edited by Gotō Masatoshi and Yoshida Nobuyuki, 171–93. Tokyo: Yamakawa Shuppansha, 2002.

Takahashi Yoshitaka. *"Shigen hanshoku no jidai" to Nihon no gyogyō*. Tokyo: Yamakawa Shuppansha, 2007.

Takahashi Yutaka. *Gendai Nihon doboku shi*. Tokyo: Shōkokusha, 1990.

Takahashi Yutaka. *Kawa kara mita kokudo ron*. Tokyo: Kashima Shuppankai, 2011.

Takahashi Yutaka. *Kawa to kokudo no kinki: suigai to shakai*. Tokyo: Iwanami Shinsho, 2012.

Takaku Reinosuke. *Kindai Nihon to chiiki shinkō: Kyōto-fu no kindai*. Kyoto: Shibungaku Shuppan, 2007.

Takasaki Tetsurō. *Ten issai o nagasu: Edo-ki saidai no kanpō suigai saikoku daimyō ni yoru tetsudai-bushin*. Tokyo: Kashima Shuppan, 2001.

Takeoka Mitsutada. *Yodogawa chisuishi*. Osaka: Yodogawa Chisuishi Kankōkai, 1931.

Takeuchi Minoru, ed., *Nicchū kokkō kihonbunken shū*. Vols. 1–2. Tokyo: Sōsōsha, 1993.

Takiguchi Masaya. "Edo no gōshō no tabi: Kaei yon-nen no dōchū nikki." *Kōtsūshi kenkyū* 61 (2006): 25–50.

Tanabe, Sakuro. "The Lake Biwa-Kioto Canal, Japan." *Scientific American* 75, no. 19 (1894): 341, 345, 346.

Tanji Kenzō. *Kantō kasen suiun shi no kenkyū*. Tokyo: Hōsei Daigaku Shuppankyoku, 1984.

Tanji Kenzō. *Kinsei kōtsū unyu shi no kenkyū*. Tokyo: Yamakawa Kōbunkan, 1996.

Tazi, Nadia, ed. *Keywords: Nature*. Vol. 5, *Keywords: For a Different Kind of Globalization*. New York: Other Press, 2005.

Teisch, Jessica B. *Engineering Nature: Water, Development, and the Global Spread of American Environmental Expertise*. Chapel Hill: University of the North Carolina Press, 2011.

Thomas, Julia Adeney. *Reconfiguring Modernity: Concepts of Nature in Japanese Political Ideology*. Berkeley: University of California Press, 2001.

Titsingh, Isaac. *Illustrations of Japan*. Translated from French by Frederic Shoberd. London: Printed for R. Ackermann, 1822.

Toby, Ronald P. *Engaging the Other: 'Japan' and Its Alter-Egos, 1550–1850*. Brill's Japanese Studies Library 65. Leiden: Brill, 2019.

Toby, Ronald P. "Rescuing the Nation from History: The State of the State in Early Modern Japan." *Monumenta Nipponica* 56, no. 2 (2001): 197–237.

Toby, Ronald P. *State and Diplomacy in Early Modern Japan: Asia in the Development of the Tokugawa Bakufu*. Princeton: Princeton University Press, 1984.

Tokugawa, Tsunenari. *The Edo Inheritance*. Tokyo: International House of Japan, 2009.

Tōkyō Daigaku Shuppankai, ed. *Tōkyō Daigaku: sono hyaku-nen*. Tokyo: Tōkyō Daigaku Shuppankai, 1977.

Tōkyō-fu naimubu shomuka. *Meiji yonjūsan-nen Tōkyō-fu suigai tōkei*. Tokyo: Tōkyō-fu Naimubu Shōmuka, 1911. National Diet Library, Tokyo.

Tonegawa Hyaku-nen Shi Hensan Iinkai, ed. *Tonegawa hyaku-nen shi*. Tokyo: Kokudo Kaihatsu Gijutsu Kenkyū Sentā, 1987.

Totman, Conrad D. *The Green Archipelago: Forestry in Preindustrial Japan*. Berkeley: University of California Press, 1989.

Totman, Conrad D. *Japan's Imperial Forest, Goryōrin, 1889–1945*. Folkestone, UK: Global Oriental, 2007.

Totman, Conrad D. "Preindustrial River Conservancy: Causes and Consequences." *Monumenta Nipponica* 47, no. 1 (1992): 59–76.

Tsing, Anna L. *The Mushroom at the End of the World: On the Possibility of Life in Capitalist Ruins*. Princeton: Princeton University Press, 2015.

Tsing, Anna L. "On Nonscalability: The Living World Is Not Amenable to Precision-Nested Scales." *Common Knowledge* 18, no. 3 (2012): 505–24.

Tsujimura Yōkichi. "Soda-kō." *Kōgakkaishi* 5, no. 57 (1886): 1357–1405.

Tsukada Takashi. *Mibunron kara rekishigaku o kangaeru*. Osaka: Azekura Shobō, 2000.

Tsukamoto Manabu. *Ikiru koto no kinseishi: jinmei kankyō no rekishi kara*. Tokyo: Heibonsha, 2001.

Tung, An-chi. "Hydroelectricity and Industrialization: The Economic, Social, and Environmental Impacts of the Sun Moon Lake Power Plants." In *Sediments of Time: Environment and Society in Chinese History*, edited by Mark Elvin, 728–55. Studies in Environment and History. Cambridge: Cambridge University Press, 1998.

Ui, Jun, ed. *Industrial Pollution in Japan*. Tokyo: United Nations University, 1992.

Uji-shi Rekishi Shiryōkan, ed. *Ogura-ike: soshite, kantaku wa okonawareta*. Uji: Uji-shi Rekishi Shiryōkan, 2011.

Umegaki, Michio. *After the Restoration: The Beginning of Japan's Modern State*. New York: New York University Press, 1988.

UNESCO Higashi Ajia Bunka Kenkyū Sentā, ed. *Shiryō: oyatoi gaikokujin*. Tokyo: Shōgakukan, 1975.

Unno Fukuju. *Seiō gijutsu no inyū to Meiji shakai*. Tokyo: Yuhikaku, 1982.

Van der Weele, Pieter Izaak. *De geschiedenis van het N.A.P.* [I.E. Normaal Amsterdams Peil]. Delft: Rijkscommissie voor Geodesie, 1971.

Van de Ven, Gerard P., ed. *Man-Made Lowlands: History of Water Management and Land Reclamation in the Netherlands*. Utrecht: Matrijs, 1993.

Van Doorn, Cornelis Johannes. "Chisui sōron." 5 February 1873. Japan Society of Civil Engineers, Tokyo.

Van Doorn, Cornelis Johannes. "Kasui kaishū no kōan." 4 February 1873. Japan Society of Civil Engineers, Tokyo.

Van Gasteren, L. A., ed. *In een Japanse stroomversnelling: Berichten van nederlandse watermannen—rijswerkers, ingenieurs, werkbazen—1872–1903*. Amsterdam: Euro Books, 2000.

Vaporis, Constantine N. *Tour of Duty: Samurai, Military Service in Edo and the Culture of Early Modern Japan*. Honolulu: University of Hawai'i Press, 2008.

Wakita, Osamu. "The Emergence of the State in Sixteenth-Century Japan: From Oda to Tokugawa." *Journal of Japanese Studies* 8, no. 2 (1982): 343–67.

Waley, Paul. "Ruining and Restoring Rivers: State and Civil Society in Japan." *Pacific Affairs* 78, no. 2 (2005): 195–215.

Walker, Brett L. *Toxic Archipelago: A History of Industrial Disease in Japan*. Seattle: University of Washington Press, 2010.

Ward, J. V. "Riverine Landscapes: Biodiversity Patterns, Disturbance Regimes, and Aquatic Conservation." *Biological Conservation* 83, no. 3 (1998): 269–78.

Watanabe Hideo. *Kinsei Tonegawa suiun shi no kenkyū*. Tokyo: Yoshikawa Kōbunkan, 2002.

Watanabe Kōji. *Tonegawa takasebune*. Nagareyama, Chiba: Ronshobō, 1990.

Watanabe Takashi. *Asamayama daifunka*. Tokyo: Yoshikawa Kōbunkan, 2003.

Watanabe Takashi. *Hyakushōtachi no suishigen sensō: Edo jidai no mizuarasoi o ou*. Tokyo: Sōshisha, 2014.

Watson, Thomas Colclough. "On the Use of Fascines in the Public Works of Holland." *Minutes of Proceedings of the Institution of Civil Engineering* 41 (1875): 158–70.

Watsuji, Tetsurō. *A Climate: A Philosophical Study*. Translated by Geoffrey Bownas. Tokyo: Government Publishing Bureau, 1961.

Watsuji, Tetsurō. *Watsuji Tetsurō's Rinrigaku: Ethics in Japan*. Translated by Yamamoto Seisaku and Robert E. Carter. Albany: State University of New York, 1996.

Watsuji Tetsurō. *Watsuji Tetsurō zenshū*. Edited by Abe Yoshishige. Vols. 1–20. Tokyo: Iwanami Shoten, 1961–63.

White, Gilbert Fowler. "The Human Adjustment to Floods: A Geographical Approach to the Flood Problem in the United States." PhD diss., University of Chicago, 1945.

White, Richard. *The Organic Machine: The Remaking of the Columbia River*. New York: Hill and Wang, 1995.

Wigen, Kären. "Culture, Power, and Place: The New Landscapes of East Asian Regionalism." *American Historical Review* 104, no. 4 (1999): 1183–2001.

Wigen, Kären. *The Making of a Japanese Periphery, 1750–1920*. Berkeley: University of California Press, 1995.

Wigen, Kären. *A Malleable Map: Geographies of Restoration in Central Japan, 1600–1912*. Berkeley: University of California Press, 2010.

Willcocks, William, Sir, and James Ireland Craig. *Egyptian Irrigation*. London: E. & F. N. Spon, 1913.

Williams, Raymond. *Keywords: A Vocabulary of Culture and Society*. New York: Oxford University Press, 1983.

Wilson, Roderick I. "Placing Edomae: The Changing Environmental Relations of Tokyo's Early Modern Fishery." In "Grassroots History: Global Environmental Histories from Below." Edited by Robert Michael Morrissey and Roderick I. Wilson, eds., special issue, *Resilience: A Journal of the Environmental Humanities* 3 (2016): 242–89.

Worster, Donald. *Rivers of Empire: Water, Aridity, and the Growth of the American West*. Oxford: Oxford University, 1992.

Yagi Shigeru. "Kinsei Ōsaka no kawazakana ichiba." In *Mibunteki shūen no hikaku shi*, edited by Tsukada Takashi, 61–106. Osaka: Seibundō Shuppan, 2010.

Yamazaki Yūkō. "Naimushō no kasen seisaku." In *Michi to kawa no kindai*, edited by Takamura Naosuke, 69–108. Tokyo: Yamakawa Shuppansha, 1996.

Yanabu Akira. *Honyakugo seiritsu jijō*. Tokyo: Iwanami Shinsho, 1982.

Yanabu Akira. *Honyaku no shisō: shizen to Nature*. Tokyo: Chikuma Shobō, 1995.

Yodogawa Kindai Kaishū no Akebono Kenkyūkai, ed. *Yodogawa Oranda gishi monjo: Oubun kanren hen*. Hirakata: Kensetsushō Kinki Chihō Kensetsukyoku Yodogawa Kōji Jimusho, 1997.

"Yodogawa kōzui no sai ryūshitsu kyōryō." *Kōgakkaishi* 5, no. 53 (1886): 1056–58.

Yokoyama Akio. *Kinsei kasen suiun shi no kenkyū: Mogamigawa suiun no rekishiteki tenkai o chūshin to shite*. Tokyo: Yoshikawa Kōbunkan, 1980.

Yoshida Hatsusaburō. *Nara denki ensen meisho zue*. Nara: Nara Denki Tetsudō Kabushiki Kaisha, 1928.

Yoshida Nobuyuki. "Edo no tsumi tonya to hashike yado." *Kokuritsu rekishi minzoku hakubutsukan kenkyū hōkoku*, no. 103 (2003): 447–54.

Yoshida Nobuyuki. *Kyodai jōkamachi Edo no bunsetsu kōzō*. Tokyo: Yamakawa Shuppansha, 1999.

Yoshida Nobuyuki. "Shūun to takigi: Edo no butsuryū infura to nenryō." In Yoshida Nobuyuki, *Toshi: Edo ni ikiru*, 197–244. Tokyo: Iwanami Shoten, 2015.

Yoshida Nobuyuki. "Soshiabirite to bunsetsu kōzō." In *Dentō toshi: bunsetsu kōzō*, edited by Yoshida Nobuyuki and Itō Takeshi, v–x. Tokyo: Tōkyō Daigaku Shuppankai, 2010.

Yoshizumi Mieko. "Tetsudai-bushin ichiran-hyō." *Gakushūin Daigaku Bungakubu kenkyū nenpō* 15 (1968): 87–119.

Young, Michael Dunlop. *The Metronomic Society: Natural Rhythms and Human Timetables*. Cambridge: Harvard University Press, 1988.

Yui Masaomi and Obinata Sumio, eds. *Kanryōsei keisatsu: Nihon kindai shisō taikei*. Tokyo: Iwanami Shoten, 1990.

Index